WATCHING
WILDLIFE
SOUTHERN AFRICA

Luke Hunter
Susan Rhind
David Andrew

Lonely Planet Publications
Melbourne Oakland London Paris

☆ LUANDA

Malanje ●

Saurimo ●

ANGOLA

**DEMOCRATIC
REPUBLIC
OF THE
CONGO
(ZAÏRE)**

Parc Natio
de l'Upen

Kolwezi ●

Lubumba

Parque
Nacional da
Quiçama

Mwinilunga ●

West Lunga
NP

Solwezi ●

Ching

LOBITO ●

Kuito ●

Parque Nacional
da Cameia

Liuwa
Plain
NP

Zambezi ●

Kuvango ●

Menongue ●

Mongu ●

Kafue
NP

Mumbwa ●

Namwal

Lubango ●

Parque Nacional
do Bicuari

Senanga ●

*Lake
Itezhi-
Tezhi*

Lochinvar
NP

Namibe ●

Parque Nacional
da Mupa

Sioma
Ngwezi
NP

Zambezi

Katima
Mulilo ●

Zambezi

Victoria
Falls

*L
Kai*

Ondjiva ●

Kunene River

Okavango River

Bwabwata
NP

Caprivi Strip

Kasane ●

Livingstone

Ruacana ●

Oshikango ●

Rundu ●

Mamili
NP

*Okavango
Delta*

Chobe
NP

Victoria
Hwange

Oshakati ●

Kaudom
GR

Tsodilo
Hills

Moremi
WR

Hwange
NP

Skeleton
Coast NP

Etosha
NP

Tsumeb ●

Nxai Pan NP

Otavi ●

Grootfontein ●

Maun ●

Makgadikgadi
Pans NP

Terrace Bay ●
Torra Bay ●

Huab River

Outjo ●

Waterberg
Plateau Park

Otjiwarongo ●

Franciste

Ugab River

Brandberg
National (2573m) ▲
West Coast
RA

NAMIBIA

Ghanzi ●

Orapa ●

Selebi-

Central
Kalahari
GR

Serowe ●

Cape Cross SR

Gobabis ●

Henties Bay ●
Swakopmund ●

☆ **WINDHOEK**

Mahalapye ●

Walvis Bay ●

Rehoboth ●

BOTSWANA

Khutse
GR

Molepolole ●

Pilans

Tropic of Capricorn

Namib-
Naukluft
Park

Naukluft
(1973m) ▲

Maltahöhe ●

Mariental ●

Mabuasehube
GR

GABORONE ●

Kanye ●

Lobatse ●

City

Kgalagadi
Transfrontier
Park

Mmabatho ●
Mafikeng ●

Brukkaros
(1586m) ▲

Tshabong ●

Molopo River

**ATLANTIC

OCEAN**

Keetmanshoop ●

Vryburg ●

Potchefstroom ●

Lüderitz ●
Kolmanskop ●

Aus ●

Kuruman ●

Kroonstad ●

Fish River
Canyon Park

Augrabies
Falls NP

Tswalu Private
Desert Reserve

Kimberley ●

BLOEMFONTEIN ●

Ai-Ais ●

Upington ●

Vaalbos NP

MASE

Orange River

LESO

Richtersveld
NP

Orange River

Springbok ●

SOUTH AFRICA

De Aar ●

Aliwal North ●

Middelburg ●

Queenstown ●

Cederberg
Wilderness
Area

Karoo NP

Graaff-Reinet ●

Beaufort West ●

Mountain
Zebra NP

Grahamstown ●

Saldanha ●

Tsitsikamma
NP

Addo
Elephant NP

Eas
Lo

CAPE TOWN ☆
Stellenbosch ●

Paarl ●
Worcester ●

George ●

Knysna ●

Mossel Bay ●

Jeffrey's
Bay

**Port
Elizabeth**

Cape Peninsula NP

Cape of
Good Hope

Hermanus ●

De Hoop NR

ELEVATION

▨	2000m
	1000m
	500m
	250m
	0

Lake Mweru
Lake Tanganyika
Mbala
Sumbu NP
Kawambwa
Nakonde
Chitipa
Kasama
Shiwa
Ngandu
Nyika NP
Livingstonia
Mansa
Mpika
Mzuzu
Nkhata Bay
Lake
Malawi
Likoma Island
Rovuma River
Palma
Moçimboa da Praia
Ndola
Kasanka
South
Luangwa
NP
North
Luangwa
NP
Cóbuè
Metangula
Niassa
Reserve
Kanona
Mfuwe
MALAWI
Kapin Mposhi
Chipata
Kasungu
NP
Lichinga
Montepuez
Pemba
Metoro
Lake Malawi
NP
LILONGWE
Mandimba
ZAMBIA
LUSAKA
Cassacatiza
Cape Maclear
Cuamba
MOZAMBIQUE
Lake Cahora
Bassa
Liwonde
NP
Lake Chilwa
Namialo
Namapula
Nacala
Chirundu
Mana
Pools NP
Kariba
Tete
Zomba
Blantyre
Mt Mulanje
(3001m)
Mozambique
Island
Chinhoyi
Nyamapanda
Lengwe
NP
Angoche
HARARE
Nyanga
NP
Quelimane
Marondera
ZIMBABWE
Kwe Kwe
Gweru
Mutare
Vumba BR
Chimanimani
NP
Chimoio
Gorongosa
NP
Bulawayo
Masvingo
Mt Binga
(2436m)
Beira
Matobo
NP
Gwanda
Save Valley
Conservancy
Gonarezhou
NP
Zinave NP
Save River
Bazaruto
NP
Messina
Banhine
NP
Inhassoro
Vilankulo
Louis
Trichardt
Polokwane
Kruger
NP
Limpopo River
Inhambane
Tropic of Capricorn
Blyde
River
Canyon
NR
Nelspruit
PRETORIA
Johannesburg
MBABANE
MAPUTO
Bilene
Xai-Xai
Namaacha
Praia de
Závora
Inhaca Island
Bethal
Piet Retief
SWAZILAND
Ndumo GR
Tembe Elephant
Reserve
Itala GR
Mkuzi GR
Phinda RR
Ladysmith
Hluhluwe-
Umfolozi
Park
Greater St Lucia
Wetland Park
Richards Bay
Pietermaritzburg
Durban
Drakensberg
Park
Port
St Johns

TANZANIA

SEYCHELLES

COMOROS

MAYOTTE
(France)

Analalava
Mahajanga

ANTANANARIVO

Mozambique Channel

MADAGASCAR

Fianarantsoa

Toliara

INDIAN OCEAN

0   250   500km
0   150   300mi

Watching Wildlife Southern Africa
1st edition – January 2002

Published by
Lonely Planet Publications Pty Ltd ABN 36 005 607 983
90 Maribyrnong St, Footscray, Victoria 3011, Australia

Lonely Planet offices
Australia Locked Bag 1, Footscray, Victoria 3011
USA 150 Linden St, Oakland, CA 94607
UK 10a Spring Place, London NW5 3BH
France 1 rue du Dahomey, 75011 Paris

Photographs
Many of the images in this guide are available for licensing from
Lonely Planet Images.
email: lpi@lonelyplanet.com.au
Web site: www.lonelyplanetimages.com

Front cover photograph
Giraffe (John Hay)

Back cover photographs (from left to right)
Hippopotamus (Andrew van Smeerdijk)
Comet moth (Dennis Jones)
White-faced owl (Andrew MacColl)

ISBN 1 86450 035 2

Printed by The Bookmaker International Ltd
Printed in China

CONTENTS

AUTHORS

Luke Hunter
Melbourne-born Luke decided at the age of three to work with big cats in Africa. Twenty years later he embarked on his PhD at the University of Pretoria, working out methods to reintroduce cheetahs and lions into areas where they had been wiped out. A hiatus from academia led him to write and photograph a book on cheetahs, followed by a film-making sojourn at the Australian Broadcasting Corporation's Natural History Unit. He is now continuing his work on wild cats in South Africa, based from Monash University. He is convinced that a combination of paying tourists and conservation-oriented research represents the greatest hope for protecting Africa's wildlife.

Susan Rhind
Susan was raised on a farm in Western Australia and has always been besotted by animals. After working as a nurse and science teacher, she followed her real passion and became a wildlife biologist. She ventured to Africa for a break following the completion of her PhD, and spent nearly two years working and travelling around seven of Africa's countries. Susan has scientifically studied dolphins, monkeys and Australian marsupials, and is coauthor of *Watching Wildlife East Africa*. She currently lectures in ecology at the Australian National University.

David Andrew
After his father was mauled by a gorilla at Howletts Zoo, David's family fled the wilds of England to live somewhere safer – Australia! There David created *Wingspan* and *Australian Birding* magazines; edited *Wildlife Australia* magazine; and among other jobs has been a research assistant in Kakadu NP, a birding guide for English comedian Bill Oddie and an editor of Lonely Planet guides. He was coordinating author for LP's *Watching Wildlife East Africa*, contributed to *Watching Wildlife Australia* and is now the Series Publishing Manager for the Watching Wildlife guides.

FROM THE AUTHORS

Luke Hunter
Thanks to the staff of South African National Parks, particularly Adel Smit and to Lee Vincent and Jeff Gaisford of KZN Wildlife. Many researchers and specialists provided valuable information, especially Adrian Bailey, Joel Berger, Vic Cockcroft, John Dini, Andrew Hockly, Mike Hoffman, Robyn Keene-Young, Andrew Mortimer, Stephen Mulholland, Simon Murray, Karl Rosenberg, Dion Sadie, Rob Slotow, Gus van Dyk and Martin Whiting. I'm grateful to Ansie Dippenaar for the map of Karoo NP and to Harvey Croze for the rhodopsin idea. Afroventures provided exceptional support in Botswana; thanks to Phillip Lategan and especially to Seagal Tembwe and Moffat Nsiwa of Afroventures, two of the finest guides I've met. Thanks also to Des Pretorius and his staff at Camp Moremi, Darren and Michelle McKissock at Nxabega, Sonja and Brendan Ferrar at Savute Camp, the lovely Mbina Ntshwabi at Chobe Game Lodge, and thanks again to Adriaan and Jo Erasmus for the bed at Tswalu.
Thanks a stack to the LP team for a great series, especially to David Andrew and Sean Pywell for launching it, to Miranda Wills for her speedy editing and to Andy van Smeerdijk for some excellent

suggestions about Botswana. My family, as always, provided unfailing support, particularly Russ and Nol for the astonishing gift of a new lens when my gear was stolen, Dan for his equally generous laptop largesse and Tim for tireless proofreading. I am extremely grateful to Jonathan Scott for his terrific Preface; his many beautiful books nurtured my love for Africa. And finally, thanks to Sophie Wise; a lovelier traveling companion and expert game-spotter I have yet to meet.

Susan Rhind

I owe considerable thanks to many for smoothing the travel path and providing information. In Zimbabwe I am particularly grateful to Flo Nyongoro and Alison Hewitt (African Adventures), Steve Pope (Chipembere Safaris), Craig MacRae (Sengwa Safaris), Beat Accorsi (Shamwari Safaris), John Stevens (John Stevens Safaris) and Peter Ginn (Peter Ginn Birding Safaris). Thanks also to the staff of River Lodges of Africa, Hwange Safari Lodge, Mbizi Game Park, Kazuma Trails, Toddhall Tours, Shearwater and Elephant Sands Safari Lodge. In Malawi, Central African Wilderness Safaris, Ulendo Travel, Mike and staff at Mvuu (Liwonde), and David Foot and team (Nyika Safaris) gave me considerable assistance. Jens Haugaard provided invaluable detail on Malawi's birds, and Will and Valerie Darwall introduced me to the intricacies of cichlids. Thanks also to Chinteche Lodge and Kayak Africa. In Zambia, Penny Mae and Doris Glasspool of Kachelo Travel were fantastic and made it all happen. Thanks to Tagd Wixsted and Edmund of Kasanka Trust, and the staff and guides of Chinzombo Safaris, Kafunta River Lodge, Wildlife Camp, Basanga Trails, Royal Zambezi Lodge and Chiawa Camp.

THIS BOOK

LUKE Hunter researched and wrote the Nature in Southern Africa, Wildlife-Watching and Habitats chapters; the South Africa, Namibia and Botswana sections of the Parks and Places chapter (including the introduction); the Mammals section of the Wildlife Gallery chapter; and the Introduction to the book. Susan Rhind researched and wrote the Zimbabwe, Malawi and Zambia sections. David Andrew researched and wrote the Birds section with assistance from Luke Hunter; and Andrew van Smeerdijk contributed supplementary information to several sections.

FROM THE PUBLISHER

THE idea for this series came from David Andrew and was supported by Chris Klep, Nick Tapp and Sue Galley. The concept was developed further by Sean Pywell and Jane Bennett; Sean became the first series editor and Mathew Burfoot designed the layout for the series. Maps for *Watching Wildlife Southern Africa* were drawn by Ray Thomson and Simon Tillema. Editing and proofing were done by Miranda Wills, Sean Pywell, Andrew van Smeerdijk, Thalia Kalkipsakis and David Andrew (with assistance from Janet Brunckhorst, Jennifer Garrett and Andrew Bain). Layout was by Vicki Beale with assistance from Wendy Wright. Most of the photos were sourced and supplied by LPI – special thanks to all at LPI who put in much extra effort for this title. Jamieson Gross designed the cover. Mapping was checked by Michael Blore and Chris Klep; layout was checked by David Andrew, Michael Blore and Glenn van der Knijff.

PREFACE

WHEN I left my home in England 25 years ago to travel overland through Africa, it was the realization of a dream. Finally I was going to make a safari for myself, camp out under star-filled skies, listen to the sounds of elephants and hyenas, and see my first big cats in the wild. In those days guide books were for identifying what you saw – giving it a name. But I was looking for something more. I wanted to know how the animals and birds lived, how the web of life fitted together. What I didn't want was to have to wade through an exhaustive list of every animal and bird I might see – if only *Watching Wildlife Southern Africa* had been available then.

In those days South Africa still lived under the cloud of apartheid, so after a quick visit to Kruger National Park I headed for Botswana (where I spent a year working) before returning to East Africa which remains my home to this day. But I had already glimpsed such gems as Botswana's Okavango Delta, Hwange National Park in Zimbabwe, and the Luangwa Valley and Kafue National Park in Zambia. What treasures await the traveller to these destinations! But don't make the mistake of trying to see everything. Cast off your workaday persona and savour the essence of Africa. Take time to watch, look and listen.

I have always felt that Lonely Planet was an evocative title for a series of books. There is a poignancy that speaks to me of our responsibility to cherish and help protect the staggering diversity of life that our planet still sustains. But time is running out. I have seen huge changes since I first set foot in Africa. Tens of thousands of rhinos and hundreds of thousands of elephants have been slaughtered, and the bushmeat trade has reached staggering proportions.

Africa is blessed with wonderful friendly people, but many of them live in abject poverty and view wildlife as either a threat to life and property or as competition for scarce resources. Only by helping to reduce poverty and by including local communities in efforts to conserve wilderness areas can we hope to provide a meaningful future for people and wildlife. I hope that by learning more about Southern Africa and its spectacular wildlife you will return home with a renewed commitment to protect our planet.

Jonathan Scott

Jonathan Scott is an award-winning wildlife photographer and author of more than a dozen books on Africa's wildlife. He is the co-presenter of the popular BBC/Animal Planet television series *Big Cat Diary* filmed in Kenya's Masai Mara National Reserve. Jonathan is married to wildlife photographer Angie Scott, and they live within five minutes' drive of Nairobi National Park.

INTRODUCTION

MORE than any other continent, Africa is synonymous with wildlife and there are two truly exceptional regions here for viewing it. For many, East Africa has traditionally been 'classic' safari country but Southern Africa now outranks it in terms of numbers of foreign visitors (and, of course, most of them come for the wildlife). While the diversity and density of species here is exceeded in some forests of Central Africa and South America, there is nowhere else on earth where such a variety of wildlife is so visible. Even a week's tour of the parks here guarantees sightings of dozens of mammal species and hundreds of birds, as well as sundry reptiles and smaller fry. For the wildlife devotee, Southern Africa will probably deliver the safari of a lifetime.

This book aims to assist and enhance the process. For the first-timer, we cover the basic 'how-to' information for planning a visit, specifying the best times, the various safari options, suitable equipment and clothing, the best places to see particular species and so on. Then, for everyone from the complete novice to the wildlife specialist, we detail how to extract the most once you're here. The most productive reserves of Southern Africa are reviewed in detail, providing information on the specific wildlife attractions of each destination and the finer points of finding them. We cover a range of different parks and reserves, including everything from the largest national parks to lesser-known attractions noted for a particular species that's hard to find elsewhere. Additionally, we've gone for diversity over duplication, so that coastal, desert, fynbos and wetland reserves appear alongside the typical savanna-grassland ones for which Africa is so well known. The book does not aim to cover every reserve – there are over 500 of them in Southern Africa – but you will find the very best of them here.

To help with identification, our Wildlife Gallery illustrates over 270 species most likely to be seen, all of them in colour photographs. But more than that, the Gallery also provides a little interpretation of animal behaviour and ecology. Beyond simply ticking species off a list, Southern Africa offers exceptional opportunities to truly observe animals, whether it's interpreting the vocalisations of vervet monkeys, unravelling the chain of command among different vulture species or perhaps even anticipating where and when a kill might happen. We hope you'll find this book provides the clues for that extra insight.

Above all, we hope it inspires you to keep on watching wildlife. Whether it encourages and aids your first trip, a return visit or even just an armchair safari, we want the book to increase your enjoyment of wildlife. Money from wildlife-watching tourism is very much the main form of revenue for conservation in Africa. However you decide to go on safari, keep on doing it! And if your stories enthuse a friend, encourage them to do likewise; if this book has helped you at all, pass it on to someone else who is thinking of going.

HOW TO USE THIS BOOK

YOU'RE here to see the animals and we're here to help you: *Watching Wildlife Southern Africa* shows you how to recognise the major players and advises you on where to find them. This book is also packed with background information on wildlife habitats, advice on getting started, when to go and how to prepare. There are also detailed watching tips (eg, which trail or pan to go to), and clues on the best time to look. Read on to help plan your wildlife-watching adventure and get the best out of this treasure-trove.

Nature

Wildlife-Watching

Habitats

Parks and Places

Wildlife Gallery

Each chapter is colour coded to help you navigate through the book – look for the thumb tabs.

Getting Started There are two main ways to go about watching wildlife: pick your animals and then find out where to go; or choose where you want to go and then find out what's there. In Southern Africa you'll see a lot of the same wildlife in a lot of places (eg, wildebeests and zebras); but for other animals you'll need to go to certain places (eg, Lengwe NP for Woodwards' batises). The key chapters cover both approaches: Parks and Places describes where to go and what's there; and the Wildlife Gallery tells you about the animals. Flipping between these chapters will tell you almost everything you need to know.

Index The quickest way to find out about an animal or reserve is to look it up in the Index. Animals are arranged into groups according to their common names (Burchell's zebra comes under zebras) – page numbers in bold indicate a photo of that animal. Reserves are listed alphabetically by name.

Table of Contents This gives you a quick overview of the book. We've colour-coded each chapter to help you find your way around until you're more familiar with the layout.

Highlight page   *Animal's range*   *Group page*

Wildlife Gallery This is a run-down of all the key species and groups: what they look like (and how to tell them apart) and the kinds of things you can see them doing. This chapter is divided into three sections: Mammals, Birds, and More Creatures Great and Small (eg, reptiles).

Key animals are presented as feature pages, which describe unusual and interesting aspects of their ecology. A side-bar next to the main text summarises some of their main characteristics (eg, behaviour, breeding and preferred habitat); and a Hotspots box lists some places where they might be

Summary information   *Hotspots: where to find animals*

found (use this as a link to the Parks and Places chapter). A small map indicates each species' range.

Other animals appear in family (or closely related) groups – these pages are packed with photos to help you work out what's what.

Parks and Places Organised country by country and starting with an introduction to the overall region, this chapter describes the best national parks, reserves and other places in which to see wildlife. Each country section begins with an overview (including itineraries). Specific destinations, eg, national parks and other reserves, are ordered alphabetically according to their importance for wildlife-watching. Thus major attractions, such as Kruger NP, are given more-detailed treatment and less-frequented reserves may be covered in only one page. Facts for travellers (like location, contacts, accommodation and wildlife rhythms), watching tips and wildlife highlights are summarised for each; and a colour map points out major features and good wildlife-viewing areas.

Wildlife-Watching Essential background reading. This chapter tells you when to go and how to look, and explains the ins and outs of safaris, guides, equipment and field guides. Special features cover diving and snorkelling, birdwatching, photography and some safari alternatives, such as walking or canoe trips.

General park information

Wildlife highlights **Parks and Places** *Park map*

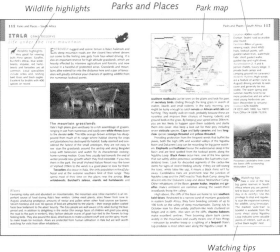

Watching tips

Wildlife-Watching

Nature in Southern Africa We explain the reasons behind Southern Africa's great biodiversity and introduce some of the conservation issues.

Habitats Describes Southern African ecosystems in simple terms.

Resource Guide This lists recommended field guides and other books, reliable tour operators and wildlife-related web sites.

Glossary Explains any confusing words in the text.

NATURE IN SOUTHERN AFRICA

An introduction to Southern Africa's natural history

IF you wanted to see what the world and its wildlife was like a million years ago, there's nowhere on earth like Africa to do it. For reasons that are still far from clear, Africa is a refuge for the great Pleistocene fauna that perished elsewhere around the world. While Australia, North America and South America lost an average of 79% of their mammalian megafauna in the last 100,000 years, Africa's deficit was only around 14%.

One theory suggests that African wildlife – on the continent with the longest human history by far – was better adapted to avoiding human predation. There is, perhaps, some evidence for this idea, but the role of climatic change is widely considered far less speculative. Worldwide, the alternating periods of cooling known as glacials ('ice ages') and warm spells called interglacials, fueled changes in the world's fauna, killing off those that couldn't cope with the rapid cycling of extremes. In the midst of the extinctions and replacements, Africa never knew the great ice blankets that cloaked other continents and its climatic constancy is thought to be part of the reason so many species persisted.

Indeed, the climatic fluctuations in Africa were mild enough to promote diversity rather than diminish it. They transformed the Southern African landscape largely into what it is today, shrinking tropical forests and permitting the spread of the *Acacia* savannas that still dominate. As habitats opened up, the herbivores radiated out in an explosion of new species and their predators followed suit.

Today, there is no place comparable for its diversity and density of large mammals. And they are merely the most conspicuous members of one of the richest wildlife communities on the planet. Be it large mammals, small ones, birds, reptiles, fish or invertebrates, Southern Africa is a sanctuary for an astonishing diversity of life. We can never know exactly what our forebears saw when they gazed out over African landscapes a million years ago – but for a pretty good idea, this place is superb.

ENVIRONMENT

The lie of the land

While it may not be immediately apparent, most of Southern Africa actually sits on a high plateau. Lying between 1000 and 2000m above sea level, the southern uplands cover most of Namibia, South Africa, Zimbabwe, Zambia and Malawi, and then stretch northwards into East Africa where they peter out in the highlands of Ethiopia and Somalia. Except for a few scattered massifs in the middle of the Sahara Desert and the Atlas Mountains of North Africa, the rest of the African continent lies under 1000m.

In Southern Africa, the plateau has sheer escarpments on the southern and eastern edges – the Drakensberg and Lebombos – and in the west, the Naukluft. In its centre, the plateau dips like a massive, flat-bottomed bowl with Botswana sitting in the middle of it; indeed the most apparent feature when travelling across Botswana is its uniform flatness. Encircling the escarpment on three sides is a coastal plain that runs all around Southern Africa and on which sits many major settlements.

Highs and lows

Although the southern plateau is fairly uniform, it's broken up by high points (the mountains) and low ones (the valleys and their rivers). The highest part of the plateau is the Drakensberg Range. Many peaks here rise above 3000m, the highest being Lesotho's Thabana-Ntlenyana at 3482m. The nest highest point, southern Malawi's Mulanje Plateau just tops 3000m, followed by the Nyika Plateau straddling northern Malawi and northeastern Zambia, which has a number of mountains around 2500m. Zimbabwe's Eastern Highlands, which spill over into Mozambique, are slightly lower but no less impressive. Other notable highpoints in the region include the Western Cape's distinctive fold mountains, Namibia's Naukluft Massif and isolated inselbergs scattered throughout Namibia and the Karoo.

Originating in the highlands and carving their way across the plateau to the oceans are many major rivers and their tributaries. In a continent of aridity, watercourses are a focal point for life and many parks and reserves are bisected or bounded by rivers. Greatest of them all is the Zambezi. At 2740km long, it forms Zambia's southern border with Namibia, Botswana and Zimbabwe and is the centrepiece of dozens of reserves including four national parks: Victoria Falls, Matusadona (on Lake Kariba's shores), Mana Pools and Lower Zambezi. Traditionally, the Zambezi is considered the dividing line for the Southern African region but this omits Zambia and Malawi which are included in this book. Other key rivers include the Okavango, which drains into Botswana's flat basin to form the Okavango Delta; the Limpopo which forms the northern boundaries of Kruger and Dongola National Parks (NPs) and South Africa's border with Zimbabwe; and the 2250km-long Orange which drains from the Drakensberg Range and passes through Augrabies Falls, Fish River Canyon, and Richtersveld NPs before draining into the Atlantic.

Climate

Despite Africa's relatively unscathed emergence from the ice ages (see the introduction to this chapter), going back further in time reveals a pattern of repeated fluctuations from wet to dry and from warm to cool. For much of the last 15 million years, hot and dry has dominated African conditions. We could

Perturbations

Described by ecologists as 'perturbations', Southern Africa experiences regular ecological disturbances which create both opportunity and adversity for wildlife. For many species, drought, flood and fire usually create little hardship – the animals simply move away. Those unable to do so, furnish predators with an easy meal, at least until the supply runs out. Lions, hyenas and jackals feast on drought-weakened grazers, crocodiles gorge on carcasses washed down by floods; and storks, kites and kestrels patrol the leading edge of fires for fleeing reptiles and rodents. For plants, perturbations may be equally life-giving. Fresh grasslands burst to life after fires clear away old growth and many protea species only disgorge their seeds after a scorching; both provide herbivores of all sizes with a glut of new food. Similarly, the silt deposited by floods creates fertile beds for new growth and trees destroyed by fire or flood waters provide nutrients for seedlings and thousands of invertebrate species.

say that's still the case today but in fact, the earth is in the middle of a warm, moist period and conditions in the past were even more arid, and wetter episodes even fewer.

Even so, for most western visitors Southern Africa is hot and, most of the time, dry. Seasonal labels don't translate very well here; essentially, the seasons fall into a cool, dry period between May and October and a hot, wet one from November to April. You'll still hear familiar names of seasons but they're fairly loosely applied; winter is the cool, dry period and summer the hot, wet one. Sometimes, 'spring' gets a brief look-in at the juncture between them (September to October) but the term 'autumn' is hardly ever used.

Temperatures across the region are consistently warm; the winters are mild and the summers, hot. Most summer days hit maximums around 30°C and top 40°C fairly often in low-lying areas. This is the rainy season but a rainfall gradient running from east (where falls are heaviest) to west creates the wettest summers in southern Mozambique and KwaZulu-Natal and, relatively, the driest ones along the Namibian coast. Combined with warm, moist air from the Indian Ocean, summer rainfall creates stifling humidity in the east, whereas the cold Atlantic doesn't shed nearly as much moisture, so humidity is less in the west.

Winter days are pleasant, peaking around 20°C and are usually dry. On the low areas, winter nights are fairly mild whereas the Drakenberg peaks will be snow covered. In desert areas such as the Kalahari and the Namib, warm winter days are followed by subzero nights.

The main aberration in the overall pattern is restricted to the southwestern Cape. While temperature ranges for winter and summer are much the same as elsewhere, rainfall occurs during the cool, windy winters and summers are dry. The interaction between geography and climate dictates patterns in vegetation (see the Habitats chapter).

WILDLIFE

Origins

For a continent so rich in wildlife, relatively little of it has African origins, at least at the group level. Among the mammals, only a few groups actually arose in Africa; the rest poured in about 30 million years ago when Africa suddenly emerged from millions of years of isolation by colliding with Europe. The resulting land bridge enabled animals to both emigrate and immigrate. Truly African mammalian groups include the primates, elephants and hyraxes (known as dassies in Southern Africa), bats, insectivores, elephant shrews and the aardvark. Some of them, such as the monkeys and elephants, flooded out of Africa to colonise other parts of the globe. Groups which travelled the other way and populated Africa from outside include most of the carnivores, ungulates, hares, squirrels and many rodents.

Even so, that's not to say most African mammals are not African. Land bridges seeded Africa with new groups of mammals but most contemporary species arose from that founding stock for the first time here. Gazelles, giraffes, zebras, lions, leopards and cheetahs are among the suite of modern species that evolved in Africa from immigrant ancestors. At the other extreme, species like the common otter, red fox and red deer (see the boxed text 'Where the antelope and the antelope play' in the Savanna section of the Habitats chapter) are very recent arrivals from Europe and haven't spread south of the Sahara.

Birds, reptiles and amphibians are far more ancient inhabitants of Africa. The fossil record for birds is meagre but by 35 million years ago, most African groups were already established or, like today's Palaearctic migrants, commuting regularly from other continents. Similarly, most reptiles and amphibians have an African ancestry that has run unbroken for tens of millions of years (hundreds of millions in the case of crocodiles). Regardless of their provenance and antiquity, Africa's diverse wildlife of today is the result of a profound climactic unpredictability, tapering off into the relative constancy of recent times. The species which could demonstrate adaptability and versatility proliferated – those which could not died out or survived in isolated pockets.

The adaptable colonists

The variability of Africa's climate has created a fauna dominated by adaptable generalists. These are the species tolerant of regular environmental change and able to exploit the niches created by changing habitats. The alcephaline antelopes (wildebeests and their relatives) are a good example. As tropical forests contracted during the hot, dry periods, open savanna and grasslands replaced them. The alcephalines were able to expand into the shifting habitat and at least 30 new species arose in the last five million years. Disregarding the impact of our own species, wildebeests, hartebeests and their kin have extremely wide distributions reflecting their tolerance for a wide range of habitats.

There are many other examples such as the mega-herbivores (elephants, rhinos and buffaloes), many carnivores, rodents and a few primates. Indeed, viewed collectively, the versatility of African wildlife is perhaps its most apparent feature. A great many of the species you are likely to see have (or had) natural distributions which span much of sub-Saharan Africa and surprisingly few species are restricted to one habitat type. Those forms that are, comprise a special collection of relicts, endemics and ancients.

Hotspots of endemicity

In the midst of constant climatic variation over the last 15 million years, a few places in Southern Africa remained far more stable. Where quirks of local geography maintained a boundary between competing waves of climatic change, enclaves of locally adapted species could persist for millions of years while the habitat shifted and changed around them.

Some of these areas can be viewed as the nucleus of a certain habitat type; the extent of that habitat may expand and shrink as the climate varies, but the hub remains stable. The Namibian coastal plain is one such nucleus. A consistently arid interior teamed with a cold ocean offshore has maintained a cool, dry habitat for millions of years. Its aridity has sometimes advanced in great surges to link with the Sahara and the arid Horn of Africa and then contracted again during wet periods. But a narrow band along Namibia's coast has always been cool and dry. It's a harsh environment to our way of thinking but its constancy has given rise to a haven for endemic species, among them bustards, beetles, reptiles and over 2000 species of plant.

A similar refuge occurs along the Cape coast. However, although cold like the Namibian coast, air from the warm Indian Ocean sheds moisture as it encounters the Cape fold mountains, creating a more productive habitat. Those mountains and the surrounding Karoo desert have isolated the Cape from the advances of tropical Africa during wet periods for at least 60 million years. It's a seclusion reflected in the unique flora and fauna including endemic sugarbirds, canaries and antelopes.

HUMANS & WILDLIFE

The cradle of humankind

As the birthplace of our species, Africa has hosted humans and their precursors longer than any other continent. For much of hominid evolution, our progenitors were probably forager-scavengers rather than outright predators, but for at least two million years there has been evidence to suggest we actively hunted. Intelligent, organised and omnivorous, these early humans would have been given a wide berth by most species and our hunting ancestry is probably the reason most wild animals still flee when they see modern people on foot.

Even so, it's very unlikely hominids had widespread effects on wild animal populations for millions of years. Until very recently in our evolution, we were vulnerable to the same population checks and ecological constraints that have prevented global dominance by a single species. Early humans may have depleted populations of some species and perhaps even contributed to the occasional extinction, but hominids were just as susceptible to the same forces. Indeed, we modern humans are the sole surviving line of at least 12 different hominid species, some of them coexisting at the same time. We may never know what destroyed these other attempts at humanity; environmental catastrophe, predation, disease or perhaps

Wildlife's guardian angel: the tsetse fly

Sometimes called Africa's greatest conservationist, the tsetse fly is one of the primary reasons why such considerable areas in Africa are still given over to wildlife. The fly is the vector for sleeping sickness or 'nagana' as it's known in Southern Africa (from the Zulu uNakane meaning 'the pest'). Nagana is actually caused by a trypanosome (a microscopic blood parasite), but it's the fly's blood-sucking habits that infect people and animals. Africa's indigenous wildlife is immune to the disease, but livestock and people are not. Infected humans and cattle develop malaria-like symptoms which can ultimately be fatal. For African peoples and colonizing Europeans alike, that was reason enough to keep out of tsetse-infested areas, allowing wildlife to persist by default. This century, spraying with insecticides like DDT cleared many areas of the parasite by the 1960s. Even so, nagana is still widespread, especially in conservation areas, and old habits die hard. The Botswanan government is presently considering a revival of the spraying schemes for the Okavango despite very real potential for enormous ecological damage.

competition with a more successful species – very possibly our ancestors.

Regardless, it's important to remember that extinction is a natural process that has been going on since life began. But only very recently has the activity of one species, modern *Homo sapiens*, caused extinction on a scale estimated to be between 100 to 1000 times the natural rate. And although the most devastating effects came with the arrival of the Europeans, the process had already begun with the indigenous people of Southern Africa.

The utopia myth

It's tempting to think that, prior to the Western invasion, Africa's human population lived in complete harmony with its wildlife. Compared with the destruction wrought by Europeans it may seem reasonable, but it ignores the fact that Southern Africa's indigenous people had advanced, organised societies in which wildlife was utilised. Hunting was a daily fact of life and there is considerable evidence to suggest that where human numbers were high, wildlife populations either moved away or were depleted. In addition to subsistence hunting, powerful feudal cultures like the Zulus conducted ceremonial hunts in which thousands of animals were killed to display the king's power and benevolence. Some modern game reserves like Huhluwe-Umfolozi and Swaziland's Hlane were once royal hunting grounds for this explicit purpose.

Our 'ecological footprint' was further exacerbated by livestock. The popular notion of pastoralism in Africa sometimes assumes indigenous Africans endured as hunter-gatherers until contact with Europeans. But herding in sub-Saharan Africa is at least 3500 years old, probably originating in northeast Africa and spreading gradually southwards. By the first millennium AD, livestock ownership was widespread in Southern Africa with significant effects on wildlife. Livestock competed with indigenous ungulates for grazing and modified habitats to the extent that naturally rare species may have been edged towards extinction. The first historically recorded African mammal to disappear, the blue antelope, was already in decline as a result of this competition long before Europeans shot the last of them. Similarly, predators have long been killed in defence of our herds and even today, pastoralists using traditional weapons make short work of large carnivores.

The considerable impact notwithstanding, there were two important differences between Africans and Europeans in their exploitation of wildlife. Firstly, African religious beliefs lacked the three-tiered hierarchy of monotheistic religions – God, Man, Nature – which held that the natural world existed solely for people to exploit. Most African religions are grounded in the belief that humans exist as part of an indivisible entity that includes the gods and all aspects of the natural world. It's a system which, traditionally, accorded far greater tolerance and respect for wildlife than the European view. The other fundamental difference lay in technology. Southern Africa's people simply did not have the technological means to further exploit the natural world. Had gunpowder and firearms been an African innovation, it's certain at least some of the ecological damage we associate with European colonisation would have occurred centuries earlier.

The taming of Africa

Speculation aside, the last 400 years has seen successive waves of Europeans exert unrivaled dominion over Southern Africa's wildlife resources. Even before the Portuguese, Dutch, British and Germans formally divvied up the region as their own, European hunters were carving out personal fortunes based on ivory. The same routes that transported slaves and gold from inland Africa to trading settlements, ports and ultimately, Europe and 'The Americas', also carried the tusks of hundreds of thousands of elephants. Other wildlife was shot for skins and meat or simply because it could be.

With permanent European settlement, the persecution spread and intensified as people cleared wildlife to make way for livestock. Settlers also transported the European notion of sport hunting to Africa so that even where wildlife was too abundant to utilise, it was shot for amusement. Surprisingly, very few species were exterminated; the blue antelope was lost by 1800 and the quagga, a uniquely marked zebra subspecies, by 1878. But extinctions are merely the most dramatic symptom of a relentless process of attrition at the hands of Europeans which now sees wildlife restricted largely to protected areas. With the same degree of dedication that once annihilated wildlife, conservationists are now scrambling to preserve it.

CONSERVATION

From inception to contraception

The modern era of African conservation began in 1897 with the proclamation of the Hluhluwe-Umfolozi and St Lucia GRs. A year later, the cornerstone of the Kruger NP (known then as the Sabie GR) was protected. A gradual jigsaw of protected areas grew throughout the region, reaching its greatest momentum in the last three decades so that today, Southern Africa is home to over 470 parks and game reserves.

The process has seen considerable human casualties. Modelled on the European feudal system of setting aside land for the exclusive use of the gentry, local communities were often forcibly removed and prevented from utilising wildlife. Divorced from their traditional means of subsistence, local people had little incentive to protect it – often seen as one of the forces driving the onslaught of modern commercial poaching which has devastated rhino and elephant populations.

Historically, Southern Africa has suffered less from poaching than East Africa, perhaps because control over protected areas was so absolute. Even so, poaching is widespread and recent initiatives have attempted to return some control to traditional landowners. Among the best-known, Zimbabwe's CAMPFIRE program (Communal Areas Management Program for Indigenous Resources) enables rural communities to manage their wildlife resources and derive economic benefits from tourism and trophy hunting. It works extremely well in some areas, less

Tools of the trade

Compared with potential prey and predators, we humans are physically pretty hopeless. We are slow, not particularly strong and have nothing in the way of natural weapons like horns, claws or fangs. But of course, our dazzling intellect furnished us the means to overcome our feebleness. Ever since *Homo habilis* (Handy Man) first picked up a sharp stone to butcher a carcass 2.3 million years ago, we have mastered nature by making and using tools. Some of the technology hasn't changed for millennia and, in one extraordinary step back in time, is being applied to a very modern problem.

Zoologist Phillip Stander works in northeastern Namibia's remote Bushmanland, studying lions and leopards, but persecution by farmers with modern guns and vehicles is so extreme that the big cats are unapproachable. Which is where the local Ju/Hoan San people step in. Using their exceptional tracking abilities, they can locate and silently approach sleeping cats to within 20m without disturbing them. And, even more remarkably, with modern tranquilising darts fitted to their traditional arrows, Ju/Hoan marksmen sedate the cats so Stander can fit radiocollars. It's a unique partnership of old and new technology, without which the crucial data for cat conservation would be impossible to collect.

so where local corruption prevents the gains being distributed to all members of the village.

The counter argument to CAMPFIRE-type projects cites the extremely high levels of subsistence utilisation in areas adjacent to parks where, typically, wildlife is extremely depleted or eliminated altogether. Issues of ownership and empowerment aside, the main stumbling block is, of course, human population growth. Whether national park, private game reserve or communally controlled, wildlife areas are under relentless pressure from the sheer weight of human numbers. It's a dilemma requiring ever more interventionist conservation solutions. The patchwork pattern of reserves, isolated by farms, cities and fences, means there are very few modern parks that don't require some sort of human management. Translocations, reintroductions, hunting, culling and contraception are all methods used by conservationists to maintain biodiversity in existing natural ecosystems and restore it in damaged ones.

Rather than treating physically separated populations as discrete units, 'meta-population' management tries to mimic normal population processes like emigration, immigration and dispersal as they operated before humanity imposed its physical barriers. The greatest success story of this approach is the white rhino (see the Hluhluwe-Umfolzi GR account in the Parks and Places chapter), but elephants, black rhinos, large carnivores and endangered ungulates are also target species. It is hoped that transfrontier parks (also known as transfrotier conservation areas – see the boxed text) will obviate at least some of the need for meta-population conservation.

Resurrections

Not surprisingly, the extraordinary recent advances in molecular and reproductive technology have been embraced by the conservation arena. Artificial insemination and embryo implantation are already used with some success in zoos; cheetah cubs have been born to captive females inseminated with sperm from wild Namibian males, and domestic cat surrogates have brought African wild cat kittens to term. Neither cheetahs nor African wild cats are anywhere near the point where such triumphs are the final safeguard against extinction, but the same methods could one day help critically endangered species.

Perhaps the most controversial technique in conservation's new toolbox is cloning. The first cloned wild mammal, an Indian gaur (a large wild ox) has already been born to a domestic cow surrogate (although it died shortly after). Cloning has the potential to expand the genetic base of a highly endangered species by resurrecting key individuals for breeding. Imagine if the world's entire population of riverine rabbits were only a dozen individuals and of them, all the males were past breeding age. Cloning could, literally, make new copies of the males which, once mature, could breed. It may seem far-fetched but worldwide, there are dozens of species in such a predicament. One day, the technology may even be able to revive extinct species; if suitably preserved genetic material exists of the blue antelope, there is no reason in theory why the closely related sable antelope couldn't gestate a cloned blue antelope calf.

Other revivals rely on combining more traditional techniques with scientific new ground. Recent genetic analysis revealed that the quagga was a subspecies of the extant Burchell's zebra and not, as long believed, a separate species. Operating on the assumption that the quagga's unique genetic combination still exists locked up in zebra DNA, a new project is using zebras to breed quaggas. Applying millennia-old techniques of selective breeding, zebras showing the characteristic fading of stripes on the rump are being crossed until the phenotype (the outward expression of the genes; in this case, appearance) looks like a quagga. Whether the result is actually a genetic reproduction of the original quagga is questionable but the first generation of quagga facsimiles have already been released into South Africa's Karoo NP.

As methods for conservation in the field, rather than the laboratory, even the sexiest of scientific techniques are still extremely limited. Cloning, assisted reproduction technologies and the best thought-out breeding programs may avert the final demise of endangered species and perhaps even resuscitate extinct ones, but without suitable habitat, the progeny of these schemes will be nothing more than zoo exhibits. The bottom line is that wildlife needs land and plenty of it. In their various forms, modern parks and reserves are the last of these areas (discussed in the next section). None of them will survive in Africa without the continued patronage of you, the visitor.

Transfrontier conservation areas

Also known as peace parks, transfrontier conservation areas (TFCAs) are a recent phenomenon in Africa. The idea is simple enough – linking neighboring wildlife areas separated by international boundaries – but until very recently political instability, bush wars and lack of funds have thwarted any sort of implementation. With the South African–based Peace Parks Foundation taking the lead in fundraising and winning over marginalised local communities, governments are beginning to act. The first Southern African TFCA was formalised in May 2000; straddling Botswana and South Africa, the Kgalagadi Transfrontier Park (TP) consolidates a chunk of the Kalahari larger than the Netherlands (see the Kgalagadi TP account in the Parks and Places chapter). Since then, the Lubombo TFCA merged an L-shape tract along the shared borders of Swaziland, Mozambique and South Africa, and the Gaza-Kruger-Gonarezhou TFCA consolidated a 35,000 sq km area in South Africa, Zimbabwe and Mozambique. Unlike Kgalagadi, both are still only TFCAs on paper and require considerable development for true consolidation. And also unlike Kgalagadi, there are large human populations in both areas that will need demonstrated benefits – such as ecotourism dollars – for these areas to succeed.

PARKS & RESERVES

Around 15.5% of Southern Africa enjoys some sort of statutory protection, but that includes everything from national parks to hunting concessions. Privately owned reserves boost the figure by a few extra percent. At the lower end of the conservation scale but still part of the patchwork are 'game farms', which carry a combination of livestock and wildlife. The contribution to conservation made by each type and their appeal for the wildlife watcher varies considerably.

Abbreviations	
GR	Game Reserve
MR	Marine Reserve
NP	National Park
NR	Nature Reserve
TFCA	Transfrontier Conservation Area
TP	Transfrontier Park

Government

National and provincial parks represent the cornerstone of conservation in Southern Africa. They usually include the largest and oldest protected areas, and the richest wildlife areas typically have a core of state-protected land. Additionally, most governments in the region attempt to set aside a reasonable diversity of ecosystems, so that alongside the Krugers and Chobes, areas of less obvious conservation value are protected. The other great appeal of government parks is their excellent value – generally they are the most inexpensive option.

Private reserves

For visitors from 'Western' countries, it may come as a surprise that private citizens in some African countries can own wildlife land and the wildlife on it. Most of these private plots have a luxury lodge or two and thrive on the demand (mostly international) for five-star bush retreats. The prices can be exorbitant but extremely professional guiding virtually guarantees exceptional sightings. Most numerous in South Africa, excellent private reserves also occur in Zimbabwe, Namibia and southeastern Botswana.

Elsewhere, privately owned reserves are rare and the equivalent is wilderness areas leased by governments to concessionaires. Privately run concessions in Botswana and Zambia generally offer the same five-star treatment but check that you're getting one whose emphasis is photographic, rather than hunting safaris (trophy hunting is the raison d'être for many concessions).

Game farms

These are mostly privately owned and common in South Africa, Namibia and Zimbabwe. They typically carry livestock but also large numbers of wild, free-ranging ungulates; large carnivores, mega-herbivores and any other species that compete with farming are not tolerated. Many game farms run a tourism operation as a sideline but hunting is prevalent and it's an uneasy mix. Trying to view wildlife which has come to associate people with shooting rarely works unless a system of refuges – areas where animals are never hunted – is strictly adhered to. Nonetheless, game farms may have some conservation value; game farmers played a crucial role in the preservation of species like the bontebok, black wildebeest and Cape mountain zebra. ■

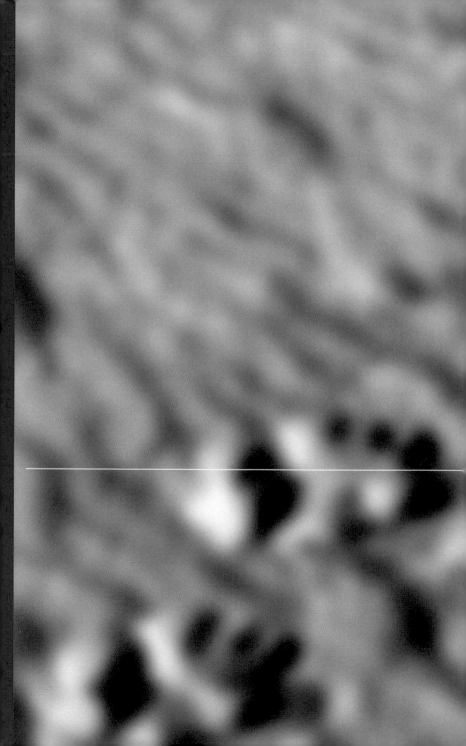

WILDLIFE-WATCHING

*Tips and hints on the art
of watching wildlife*

ONE of the finest prospects in the world for watching wildlife, a safari in Southern Africa ensures some spectacular viewing. Within the many parks and reserves, wildlife is not only abundant and diverse, it's also particularly habituated to the presence of people (in vehicles). Visitors enjoy up-close encounters and the chance of sightings normally reserved for specialists who live and work with animals. Every scale of experience is here, whether you want to see epic seasonal migrations of huge zebra herds, the prolonged grooming sessions of a meerkat colony or a pair of dung beetles resolutely rolling a dung ball to their nest site.

WHEN TO GO

Seasons in Southern Africa are rarely divided along conventional lines and, broadly speaking, fall into a warm, dry period (usually May to October) and a hot, wet one (November to April). Rainfall – and the lack of it – is the single most important factor affecting wildlife behaviour and distribution in Africa. However, don't assume this means a visit is always best timed to coincide with the arrival of the rains. Each season has its attractions (pointed out in detail for each location in the Parks and Places chapter) and regardless of when you go, excellent viewing is possible. However, certain attractions are more likely to be seen at particular times, crucial to keep in mind when planning a visit.

During the dry season, animals usually congregate around dwindling water supplies, making waterholes and permanent rivers productive areas. Carnivores, particularly lions, concentrate their hunting at these points, offering good chances of seeing a kill. The undergrowth is dying off and grass has been heavily grazed in this season which makes spotting game easier, but it can be very dusty and the scenery may look rather stark and barren. This is the coolest period, when days are clear, sunny and warm, and getting around on sand or dirt roads is generally problem-free.

When rains arrive, there is a rapid flush of new life: new grass appears, trees flower and develop fruit, and insects proliferate. Birdlife tends to be best at this time with the arrival of migrants from Eurasia as well as from elsewhere within Africa. Game species disperse because they are no longer tied to restricted water points, but this is usually when large herds of herbivores migrate into open savannas, many species dropping their young. The wet season is the hottest period across most of the region, when temperatures and humidity can be extremely high. In some areas, particularly Zambia, the Okavango Delta and reserves along Namibia's Caprivi Strip, roads become impassable and many lodges close down for the wettest period (usually December to February).

Remember that rainfall across different habitats in Southern Africa is highly variable, so a trip can take in elements of both the dry and wet seasons. For example, late in the dry season in Namibia's Etosha NP when animals congregate in the thousands at waterholes may overlap the arrival of rains in Savute in Botswana, prompting the return of huge herds of zebras. Plan your trip well but don't expect to predict the timing perfectly. Speak to other travellers about destinations they have just left and don't be afraid to change your itinerary when things happen unexpectedly.

HOW TO LOOK

Looking at the right time and place

Visitors are always amazed at the apparent ease with which professional guides locate and spot their quarry. While most of us can't hope to replicate their skills in a brief visit, a few pointers can hone your approach. The Wildlife Gallery and Parks and Places chapters give details for specific species.

Time of Day This is possibly the most important factor determining animal movements and behaviour. Dawn and dusk tend to be the most productive periods for mammals and many birds. They're the coolest parts of the day and also produce the richest light for photographs. The middle of the day is usually too hot for much action but this is when some antelopes feel less vulnerable at water, when many raptors 'thermal' and when reptiles are most obvious. Read up beforehand on desired species so you know what they are likely to be doing when.

Weather Intrinsically linked to this are the prevailing weather conditions. High winds drive many herbivores and birds into cover so concentrate your search in sheltered areas. Summer thunderstorms are often followed by a flurry of activity as insect colonies and frogs emerge, followed by their predators. Overcast or cool days may prolong activity such as hunting by normally crepuscular predators, and extremely cold winter nights might see nocturnal species still active at dawn because they were forced to shelter during their normal active period.

Water Most animals drink daily when water is available so water sources are worthwhile places to invest time, particularly in the dry season. Predators and very large herbivores tend to drink early in the day or at dusk, while a couple of hours after sunrise until midday is usually better for most antelopes. On the coast, receding tides are usually followed by the appearance of wading birds and detritus feeders such as crabs.

The name of the game

The word 'game' actually hails from hunting: originally the game was the thrill of the 'sport', but gradually the quarry itself came to be called game. Derivation notwithstanding, the term pops up regularly in Southern Africa when people refer to wildlife and doesn't necessarily mean that some poor beast is about to receive a lethal dose of lead poisoning. 'Game-viewing' is the most common local term for wildlife watching and is usually done on a 'game drive', a guided tour by vehicle. 'Big game' is, of course, the Big Five (see boxed text later in this chapter) whereas 'general game' collectively refers to the diverse herbivore community, ranging from duikers to giraffes. Of course, while 'game' in its various forms is used widely, hunters also still employ the term, most often as 'Big Game' as well as 'Plains Game,' their term for the herbivores; advertisements for the latter are usually for hunting.

Food Sources Knowing what your quarry eats will help you to decide where to spend time. A flowering aloe might not hold much interest at first glance but knowing that it is irresistible to many sunbird species may change your mind. Fruiting trees attract insects, birds and monkeys while herds of herbivores with their young are a predator's dessert cart.

Habitat Knowing which habitats are preferred by each species is a good beginning but just as important is knowing where to look in those habitats. Animals aren't merely randomly dispersed within favoured habitats. Instead they seek out specific sites to shelter, to feed, to search their surroundings and so on. Hollows in trees, caves, high points on plains – all will be utilised. Many predators use open grasslands but gravitate towards available cover such as large trees, thickets or even grass tussocks. 'Ecotones' – where one habitat merges into another – can be particularly productive because species from both habitats overlap.

Searching for wildlife

As much as knowing where and when to search, finding wildlife is all about recognising patterns and shapes. Shadows in trees and under bushes frequently conceal something that may only be revealed if you're looking for the shape of an ear or the curve of a sleeping body. Pay attention to the behaviour of other animals, often your best indicator of what's around: an entire antelope herd looking in the same direction may indicate a lurking lion.

Walking (see 'Close encounters' under Living With Wildlife later in this chapter) is generally less rewarding than driving in the search for big game but adds an entirely new perspective to searching. Walk quietly and avoid wearing bright colours and strong scents. Approach animals from downwind to avoid alerting them but be careful of 'stalking' too closely – you may surprise your quarry and provoke aggression. Look around in all directions, often. Search for larger game in the distance but smaller creatures may be right at your feet. Look up; in cities, people rarely raise their eyes above ground level but in woodlands and forests, this is where most of the action happens.

Using calls

Vocalisations (or calls) are an important means by which animals communicate and also provide useful information for locating them. Alarm calls often warn of a predator on the move and although it takes considerable experience to be able to identify

---

The Big Five

Throughout Africa, you'll repeatedly hear the phrase the 'Big Five'. It won't take long to work out it refers to the five most sought-after species: lion, leopard, elephant, rhino and buffalo. The term originates from the days of widespread big game hunting when the Big Five were (and still are) considered to be the five most dangerous species to hunt. Now applied more often by lodges and reserves as part of their advertising ('Deep in the heart of Big Five country!'), it's a useful indication of the best-conserved regions: if the Big Five are there, you can generally assume all the species indigenous to the area are still present. Occasionally, you'll hear the 'Big Six', a more precise term indicating both species of rhino (black and white), and just to confuse things, the 'Big Seven', meaning the Big Five plus cheetah and African wild dog.

vocalisations, loud explosive calls are generally alert signals – the snorts of antelopes, braying of zebras and staccato barks of monkeys and baboons.

Calls can also be mimicked to attract wildlife. This technique is most popular with birders and pishing – making the sound 'pish' – will entice many small species. Sucking the back of your hand to make a squeaking noise may do likewise and can also attract small nocturnal predators like genets, foxes and jackals. Using recordings of vocalisations played on portable tape or CD players is another technique, particularly effective for viewing forest and woodland birds. Whether playing back calls or mimicking them, use with discretion. At the least animals may become habituated to calls and ignore them, but at worst it may provoke territorial displays, stress and occasionally aggression.

Tracks and signs

Even when you don't see animals, they leave many signs of their presence. Spoor (tracks), scats (droppings), pellets, nests, scrapes and scent-marks provide information about wildlife and may even help to locate it. Check dirt and sand roads when driving; it won't take long for you to recognise interesting spoor. Elephant footprints are unmistakable and large predator tracks are fairly obvious. Many wild cats and dogs use roads to hunt; look for where the tracks leave the road, often the point they began a stalk or sought out a nearby bush for shade.

Other signs indicate areas to focus your searches. 'Whitewash' on cliff faces usually indicates nesting raptors and clusters of pellets often signify an owl's roost. Stripped bark is a giveaway that elephants have been feeding and polished tree stumps signify regularly used rubbing posts, frequented by buffaloes, warthogs, rhinos and elephants.

There are hundreds of such signs and signals which, even if they don't lead you to the culprit, can enhance your enjoyment of wildlife immeasurably. Identifying species by their spoor is mostly a specialist task but it does help to know what the spoor couldn't be. For example, leopards are far more widespread than lions and the most likely large cat tracks outside conservation areas. Get hold of a field guide to refine your skills (see the Resource Guide).

Wildlife watching furniture: hides, boardwalks and walkways

Apart from camps, the only structures you're likely to encounter in Southern African parks are intended to enhance wildlife-viewing. Probably the most ubiquitous and most rewarding are hides. Also called blinds, hides allow observers to remain hidden and permit close-up viewing of shy wildlife. They take many forms but are usually fairly simple huts which blend into the surroundings and are most often located at waterholes. Game-watching from hides can be exceptional but it requires patience and silence. Arm yourself with a book (it's a good chance to familiarise yourself with your field guides) as well as a small cushion or some padded clothing to sit on; hide seating is 'rustic' and, ironically, not very conductive to prolonged waiting. Hides are usually well designed to use beanbags for photography (see the Photography section later in this chapter).

Walkways are less common but can be found where it's difficult to see much. Boardwalks over wetlands protect fragile habitat and take you deep into otherwise inaccessible terrain. Suspended walkways through forest canopy achieve the same result in very different habitat and are the best way to spot forest birds.

Beyond looking

Most wildlife-watching involves 'collecting' sightings. For many wildlifers, keeping a list of everything seen on safari is irresistible. Over time, lists also reveal which regions and habitats are richest in species and when. Known as twitching or ticking among birdwatchers, it can introduce a whole new element to watching wildlife. Even comparing one day's viewing to the next might reveal the effect of weather, time of day and many other factors not immediately apparent. Many field guides or park brochures include a list of species present to help you keep track (a mammal list is provided at the back of this book).

Beyond keeping a list, look a little closer. Try to identify the sex of animals; ask why male antelopes often appear stuck out on their own; watch the interactions of a baboon troop and observe the dominance patterns. Even for very common species, there is invariably complex behaviour and interaction going on constantly (the Wildlife Gallery chapter provides insights). Sometimes, the key to seeing it is merely being patient.

Equipment

Binoculars and Spotting Scopes Probably the most important piece of equipment for a safari, binoculars help not only to spot wildlife but also to correctly identify it (essential for birds) and to view species and behaviours where close approaches are impossible. There are hundreds of alternatives but a few basic facts simplify the choices.

Firstly, what do those numbers mean? The first number is the magnification while the second refers to the diameter in millimetres of the objective lens (farthest from the eye), an indication of its light-gathering efficiency. Therefore 10x40 and 10x50 have the same magnification (times 10, ie, an object 100m away will appear 10m away) but the 10x50 allows more light to enter, improving the brightness and clarity of the image particularly in poor light. Larger magnifications and in particular, larger objective lenses both contribute to the size and weight of binoculars. Choice is a matter of personal taste. 'Compacts' (usually 8x20 or 10x25) fit into a top pocket, but performance can be poor in low light whereas 10x50s are cumbersome on walks but extremely clear in all light. Intermediate models such as 7x35 or 8x40 are a compromise between the two.

Spotting scopes are essentially telescopes designed for use in the field. They have higher magnification and better clarity than binoculars but usually require the sturdiness of a tripod for use. They are primarily used by birdwatchers and worth considering if you plan on spending a lot of time in hides.

Clothing In closed vehicles, it doesn't really matter what you wear, so long as it's comfortable. On open game drives and while walking, muted natural colours are best; avoid camouflage patterns – it may provoke trouble with the local military or immigrations people. Generally, shorts and light shirts will be fine but long, lightweight trousers (full-length cargo pants are ideal) can be invaluable for avoiding thorns and ticks when walking as well as for protection from mosquito bites after dark. Take a warm jacket for night drives which can be freezing on open vehicles in winter. A lightweight raincoat (the sort that can be rolled up and carried in a belt-bag) is indispensable for unexpected downpours during summer. A hat is a must if you plan on doing any walking, regardless of season. In winter, particularly in the mountains and deserts, temperatures are sub-zero at night – plan accordingly.

Field Guides Field guides are (usually) pocket-sized books that depict the mammals, birds, flowers etc, of a specific area with photos or colour illustrations. Important identification pointers and a distribution map are usually provided for each species; sometimes there are also brief natural histories, summarising breeding, behaviour, diet and the like. Guides to animals are usually organised in taxonomic order, a system that shows evolutionary relationships between species and is generally consistent between guides.

Field guides are a handy tool that have made an incalculable contribution to the popularity of wildlife-watching. But rarely are they the last word on a subject and further reading of weightier texts can provide valuable detail not covered in your field guide – refer to the special sections later in this chapter and the Resource Guide for suggested reading.

GETTING AROUND

Doing it yourself

The ease of getting around on your own in Southern Africa varies considerably. A vehicle is essential to visit parks; motorbikes are usually not allowed and hitching, while feasible to travel in general, usually doesn't work well at park entrances (and is often prohibited). Roads in Namibia, South Africa and Zimbabwe are generally very good and most parks are accessible in normal sedan cars. Car hire is expensive but most companies offer good deals for longer periods and it gives you tremendous flexibility to do your own thing. In Botswana, Malawi and Zambia, virtually all parks are only accessible in 4WDs. Many companies have 4WDs for hire but rates and running costs are considerably higher than for sedans. In Botswana and Zambia, distances between fuel stops can be great: a 4WD (which can carry more fuel) is often necessary just to reach a park, but 4WDs are also much heavier on fuel so be prepared to carry extra. 4WD vehicles are often reserved far in advance especially in peak periods, so book ahead. Keep in mind, some regions and parks are inaccessible even to 4WDs in the wet season; details specific to affected reserves are provided in the Parks and Places chapter.

Guides and tours

The majority of foreign visitors to Southern Africa go on safari with organised tours which are available in every possible permutation and combination. They vary from short (two to three day) trips leaving from the major centres, to extensive, multi-country 'overlanders.' Before you decide anything, try to establish how much time is spent in national parks and reserves and how much time is spent travelling between them. The overlanders often cover an enormous amount of ground but do so at the cost of quality time in reserves. Generally, spending more time at fewer sites is much more rewarding for wildlife-watching than trying to visit many parks.

The standard of tours is generally high in Southern Africa but many guides are in the habit of only looking for the 'charismatic mega-vertebrates' such as the Big Five (largely because that's what many people ask to see). Many guides are bursting for a chance to illustrate their knowledge of less conspicuous species so make sure you speak up. For serious wildlife enthusiasts, specialist companies usually guarantee excellent guides but of course, they are expensive.

Obtaining a guide at park gates rarely works any more; most visitors have (wisely) booked their itinerary ahead of time which usually ensures you'll have already have a guide. Spruikers are not as active in Southern Africa as in East Africa (with the exception of a few places like Victoria Falls) but if you are looking for a guide, ask to see their qualifications and establish what is included in the fee (food, sleeping mats/bags, tents etc). Make sure they have essentials such as a first-aid kit, a reliable vehicle, tools and adequate water. Botswana, South Africa and Zimbabwe have official accreditation protocols but you take your chances elsewhere. If you decide on this option, leave yourself at least a day or two to find a guide and negotiate a fee.

Parks and reserves

Most national and state parks require fees for both entry and accommodation but rates are generally very reasonable in all Southern African countries. Not surprisingly, the more popular (and generally larger) parks are usually more expensive but it can still be cheaper to stay in a park bungalow than in an average hotel room in the large cities. Also keep in mind that the money generated from the popular parks often subsidises less visited ones; for example, by paying the more expensive fees of Kruger NP, you will be contributing to the running costs of all of South Africa's national parks.

Most reserves offer all forms of accommodation. Camping is possible in most and facilities vary from completely undeveloped sites such as in many reserves in Botswana and Zambia to those in most Namibian, South African and Zimbabwean parks

Spotlighting

Although most national parks don't allow tourists to spotlight (unaccompanied driving after dark is prohibited), many reserves offer guided night drives which are highly recommended. Spotlighting is the only way to see nocturnal species such as bushbabies, owls, nightjars and many small carnivores. It also holds the best chance of seeing the larger predators in action, many of which do most of their hunting after dark. Your guide will usually handle the spotlight but you may be offered a stint. When searching, sweep fairly rapidly rather than linger; the greatest giveaway is 'eyeshine' (caused by reflection from the tapetum lucidum, a light-gathering layer of cells on the retina of nocturnal animals), but some species look away if they see the light coming and you'll miss it. When you do spot something, avoid shining directly at it by angling the light towards the nearby surroundings. Apart from potentially being unpleasant for the subject, spotlighting may momentarily disorient animals and may reveal them to predators. In the case of elephants and rhinos, direct spotlighting often annoys them and they generally move off or, occasionally, charge.

which are well serviced by ablution blocks, water and so on. Most camping grounds permit caravans.

More expensive accommodation includes small bungalows or chalets (widespread and excellent value in Namibia, South Africa and Zimbabwe, less so elsewhere) and luxury lodges, usually run by private concessionaires inside or on the perimeter of parks. Privately owned reserves, usually with five-star accommodation, are widespread; see 'Private reserves' in the Nature in Southern Africa chapter for more detail on these fabulously expensive but rewarding options.

LIVING WITH WILDLIFE

Close encounters

Probably more so than any wildlife destination in the world, Africa offers the chance for regular encounters with dangerous species. While small numbers of people are killed by animals each year, this is largely restricted to conflict situations where local people come into regular contact with wildlife. As a tourist, if you heed the regulations and apply common sense, there is very little chance you will be at risk. Safe driving is covered in 'Driving' (later in this section), and unaccompanied walking where dangerous big game occurs is largely prohibited; trail guides will specify what to do if confronted by an angry lion.

Unpleasant encounters with smaller fry are more likely. Most are not life-threatening, though some snakes and scorpions are potentially lethal. Don't walk barefoot at any time (especially in camp after dark when scorpions are active) and handling snakes should be left to the professionals and morons. Malaria is common and precautions should be taken to avoid mosquito bites; prophylactic medicine is advised during the rainy season and long sleeves and trousers are recommended after dark. Ticks are widespread and easily picked up while walking. Again, long trousers are useful but may be uncomfortable in summer (guides will invariably be in shorts). Inspect for ticks after any walk and remove them with a flame or fingernail; be sure to 'dig' in beneath the mouth-parts, don't just pull them off. Lonely Planet's *Healthy Travel Africa* includes comprehensive coverage of these issues.

Driving

In Africa, most wildlife-watching takes place from vehicles which act to disguise the human shape and smell. Animals in reserves are generally very used to cars and tolerate close approaches but the way you drive will affect your success. Firstly, speed is definitely not the essence (see the boxed text). Apart from the safety factor, you will invariably see more if you drive reasonably slowly. When you do spot something, avoid the temptation to accelerate; approach slowly and if the animal looks nervous, stop and wait for it to relax before moving closer. Sometimes, cutting the engine and rolling the final few metres in neutral is helpful. Once you're in place, switch off the engine – animals are more inclined to relax and a running engine can really disturb the viewing experience. However, if you're close

Open vehicles: meals on wheels?

Unlike East Africa, many game-viewing vehicles in Southern Africa are open to the surroundings, begging the question, 'Are they safe?'. Despite affording the clearest of views to people and, seemingly, of them, animals apparently don't perceive the seated figures within as humans and attacks on passengers are extremely rare. In contrast, most animals distinguish an upright human from great distances, but contrary to popular belief, prefer to move away rather than attack. Although modern people rarely see themselves as part of the 'natural order', African wildlife has coevolved with bipedal hominids (which probably hunted for at least two million years) and recognises the form as a predator. Accordingly, there is good reason why the guides of open vehicles will tell you to remain seated. Many species, particularly the big cats, respond instantly when a person stands up in an open vehicle. To avoid frightening animals away or, in extreme cases, provoking an attack, stay seated.

to elephants, buffaloes or rhinos, leaving the engine running may be advisable for a quick getaway.

You usually won't have many options for the approach because it's prohibited to leave marked roads or tracks, but try not to approach animals head-on as they may feel threatened. Most animals will simply move away if nervous of vehicles but be careful of approaching dangerous species too closely. Avoid coming between the members of a group, particularly females and their young. If it happens, as is sometimes the case when an elephant herd suddenly appears all around, don't panic and don't try to manoeuvre out of the way – you may aggravate things. It's usually better to wait quietly until they move on. If carnivores have a kill by the roadside, don't pull up right alongside – give them a little space. Any defensive or aggressive behaviour such as elephants tossing their heads and ear-flapping or big cats growling and lashing their tails is telling you to back off.

Feeding wildlife

Most parks prohibit feeding wildlife with good reason. Animals learn very quickly where hand-outs are given and many become pests at camp sites. Some species, particularly monkeys and baboons, resort to aggression once they lose their natural caution around people and usually end up destroyed. The warnings from camp authorities are clear; if you feed animals, they will be forced to shoot them.

Having said that, authorities often turn a blind eye to feeding less dangerous camp-followers such as birds and small mammals. Indeed many private lodges have feeding stations to attract these species. There is great appeal in sharing your biscuit with a ground squirrel or banded mongoose, but be aware that you may be fostering a dependency or affecting an animal's health or behaviour – probably something to avoid if you can.

Unintentional feeding is also a problem. Dispose of food scraps and secure your supplies carefully. Hyenas are particularly destructive; don't keep anything edible in tents and pack away all food and anything remotely connected to its preparation in your car or trailer. Some parks ask you to leave citrus fruits at the gate because elephants will open a car like a sardine can for them.

Animal welfare

You may be surprised to see ivory, animal skins and other questionable wildlife products on open display, not only at souvenir stores, but also in the reserves and parks themselves. Historically, Southern Africa has experienced fewer problems than East Africa with poaching for high-profile species such as elephants and most of the curios originate from legitimate sources such as culls, problem animal control and hunting. In national parks and reserves (as opposed to private shops), the sale of such items contributes to running costs and hence, to conservation. They will also include certification of origin, necessary for export. Note that many countries will not allow import of certain wildlife products and you would be wise to check in advance. In many countries, attempting to import products like ivory and cat skins is a crime that carries heavy penalties. The meat of many wild species is widely available and readily appears on restaurant menus, including those in the parks. Again, within parks, it is generally the by-product of other activities which (in theory, at least) contribute funds to conservation, as does the sale of the meat itself. If you're tempted but unsure, ask about its origins.

Disturbing wildlife

Given that wildlife here is often very habituated to vehicles, that you can't leave marked roads when you're driving and, if you're not, that you'll usually be with a trained guide, the prospects of seriously disturbing animals are slight. Usually the worst outcome of disturbance is the subject will move out of sight – probably more serious for the viewer than the viewee.

Nonetheless, it's important to remember that people can be an intrusion in the bush and to minimise this where possible. This has already been covered in the sections on 'Driving', and 'Using calls', and the boxed text 'Spotlighting', earlier in this chapter, but a few other pointers should be kept in mind. Be very cautious about picking up animals. Never pick up a young animal that looks 'abandoned'. It almost certainly is not and the mother is probably waiting for you to move away before she returns. People love handling harmless animals like chameleons but this invariably causes the animal stress. 'Getting close to nature' is laudable but wild animals are simply never handled; in their experience, being picked up is life-threatening. Also, don't always assume that your guide is doing the right thing. Sometimes, the pressure to deliver sightings to paying tourists encourages guides to approach animals too closely, to drive off-road, to break speed limits and so on. If you're uncomfortable with something your guide is doing, don't be afraid to speak up and if it's a serious breach, report it to park authorities. ∎

Roadkills

Whether inside parks or driving between them, road vehicles needlessly contribute to thousands of wildlife deaths each year. All reserves specify speed limits (usually 40km/h) with good reason. Speed is the principal factor causing accidents with wildlife, particularly when people are racing back to camp to make gate-closing time at dusk. Allow ample time to return to camp and check along the road edges ahead constantly. Night-driving (outside reserves) is particularly dangerous and is the main cause of mortality for some species such as bat-eared foxes along the final approach to South Africa's Kgalagadi TP. In some cases, the danger for drivers is just as high. Greater kudus are abundant along roads in northern Namibia and collisions with hippos take place on tarred roads heading to the Greater St Lucia Wetland Park in South Africa; both usually result in human as well as animal fatalities.

OTHER SAFARIS

FOR obvious reasons, most game-viewing in Southern Africa takes place from vehicles. Apart from enabling lots of ground to be covered, vehicles shield people from the elements and, like a mobile hide, conceal the human shape from animals, permitting close approaches (see boxed text 'Open vehicles: meals on wheels?' earlier in this chapter). However, there are many alternatives to driving, each of them offering very different wildlife experiences. Contact details for these safaris can be found in the Resource Guide or in the relevant sections of the Parks and Places chapter.

Walking

Although the African wilds may seem the last place you'd be inclined to walk, going by foot introduces a very intimate element to wildlife-watching. Most wildlife gives people a wide berth and doesn't tolerate the close approaches possible in vehicles but the exhilaration of spotting a distant lion or elephant from ground level far surmounts the urge to see them up close. And more so than big game, walking allows appreciation of bush attractions easily missed when driving. Small mammals which disappear at the distant sound of a vehicle – cryptic species like chameleons and tiny ones like dung beetles – are all more likely to be encountered on foot. Walking also immerses the other senses; the musky sage-like smell of giraffes, the rich variety of birdsong and the taste of monkey-oranges or fan palm nuts (but don't sample anything unless your guide tells you it's OK).

No experience necessary. Knowledgeable handlers (called 'mahouts') and the elephant's natural ease in the bush make elephant-back safaris an experience open to all visitors.

Of course, all bush walks should be taken with the greatest of care. Where there are big dangerous species, it's usually mandatory to go with a guide whose experience will ensure you don't become a big cat's breakfast. Unaccompanied walks are generally restricted to regions lacking dangerous game with a few notable exceptions like Mana Pools NP, Zimbabwe where walkers take their chances. Perhaps the most rewarding option is to go on an extended 'Wilderness Trail'. Usually lasting between three and five days, trails are guided and walkers take only food, clothing and a sleeping bag. Sleeping is done under the stars and everyone takes turns at 'watch duty'. The relevant national parks authorities in Namibia, South Africa and Zimbabwe offer some excellent trails in many of their reserves. Also in South Africa, KZN Wildlife and the Wilderness Leadership School conduct trails. Wilderness trails are extremely popular and need to be booked months in advance. Outside Namibia, South Africa and Zimbabwe, government authorities do not conduct guided walks but many tour operators and private camps do.

Mokoro trips in the Okavango usually take the place of a morning or afternoon game drive, but you can retain a poler for as long as you like to further explore the Delta.

On the backs of others

Man has used beasts of burden for centuries but only recently as a means to view wildlife. Horses or elephants, even with riders, are largely ignored by most species, allowing you to move among herds much closer than under your own leg-power. Many parks and reserves offer horseback trails, usually where there are no lions. Riding safaris range from day-trips to 10-day trails, the longer trips usually demanding a degree of riding skill. Trails offered in Botswana's Okavango Delta and Makgadikgadi Pans NP occasionally encounter lions and there-fore are restricted to experienced riders.

While elephant-back safaris are commonplace in India and parts of South-East Asia, there are only a couple of places in Africa where visitors can search for game on trained elephants. In the Okavango Delta, Botswana, the luxurious (and fabu-lously expensive) Abu's Camp is run by the very experienced Randall Moore. Newer but no less rewarding, Elephant Camp near Victoria Falls in Zimbabwe is a far cheaper alternative.

By water

There are many options for safaris by water. Mokoro trips are an intrinsic element of the Okavango Delta and range from morning rides to extended trails where, accompanied by a guide, you can explore the swamps for as long as you like. See the boxed text 'The mokoro' accompanying the Moremi GR account in the Parks and Places chapter. Also in Botswana and neighbouring Zimbabwe, powered boat cruises are popular and skilled pilots drift very close to hippos, Nile crocs, elephants and buffaloes as well as waterbirds. In Lake Kariba (Zimbabwe), Lake Malawi (Malawi) and the Okavango's Panhandle (Botswana), people can stay on houseboats where fishing and birdwatching are the main attractions. Finally, canoe and raft trips are fairly widespread though most offer scenic, rather than wildlife, rewards.

Hands-on

Not a safari in the conventional sense, there are a few select options for wildlifers who want to participate in wildlife research and management. Local wildlife and conservation associations are always keen for volunteers on their trips and professional zo-ologists (best contacted through the relevant university depart-ments) often welcome assistance if planned very well in advance. For a fee, organisations like Earthwatch allow you to join a re-search project, which can be extremely rewarding. A recent in-novation currently only available on a very limited basis in South Africa is the 'darting safari'. Also known as 'green hunts', clients accompany rangers and scientists on wildlife capture operations and pay a hefty fee to dart species such as elephants, rhinos and lions. Ironically, green hunts are proving extremely popular among big game hunters whose trophy is a photograph with their sedated quarry and a fibreglass cast of horns or tusks. Nu-merous operations have sprung up to cash in on the demand; Darting Safaris (PO Box 582, Pretoria 0001, South Africa; ☎/fax 012-305 5840, **e** hunt@dartsafari.com, 🖳 www.dartsafari.com) has the Endangered Wildlife Trust's sanction and is operated by one of South Africa's foremost wildlife vets. ■

Where big game is sparse, such as the Tsauchab River canyon in the Namib-Naukluft Park (pic-tured), walking trails are far more rewarding than driving for experiencing the local wildlife.

BIRDWATCHING

SOUTHERN Africa's bird tally is at least 1075 species, making it one of the prime birdwatching sites in the world. A well-planned four-week trip covering half a dozen key sites can yield half this total and many dedicated first-timers see 250 species in their first four or five days. All 10 of the uniquely African bird families or genera occur in Southern Africa ranging from guaranteed-to-see secretary birds, hamerkops and guineafowl to local specials like nectar-eating sugarbirds found nowhere else. Many groups are particularly well represented including raptors, francolins, kingfishers and, for those who like a challenge, larks, warblers and cisticolas.

How it's done

To ensure the best from a birdwatching trip, a little background research is invaluable. Work through any good field guide (listed at the end of this section) concentrating on the distribution maps: you'll rapidly see patterns of endemism emerging and which areas have the richest diversity. Identify key reserves within these areas where you should plan to spend the most time. Remember that species with a very limited distribution in one country may be abundant in the next so plan accordingly; for example, don't bother travelling to out-of-the-way northern South Africa just to see Meyer's parrots when they're impossible to miss almost anywhere in Zimbabwe.

Binoculars are crucial, and pack some lens tissue to deal with the humidity and dust. Spotting scopes are more cumbersome and require a tripod for easy use, but the many hides in Southern Africa present dozens of opportunities to make their inclusion worthwhile. Scopes are also excellent for wetlands (crucial for Lochinvar NP, Zambia) or watching seabirds from the shore. Some hard-core birders also use a small tape player to call in elusive species like trogons. Scopes and tape players are standard equipment for specialist bird tours and some upmarket lodges, but pack your own if you're travelling independently.

Top spots to go

If you're looking for numbers, bird diversity (like mammal diversity) tends to be greatest in relatively well-watered areas. Taking in just a couple of the major 'bushveld' reserves such as Kruger NP, Moremi GR or Hwange NP will produce hundreds of common species without much effort as well many opportunities for some local specials. Where possible, balance visits to these rich reserves with a few days in more marginal habitats which have fewer species but are known for their endemics and rarities.

South Africa's Western Cape province is a hotspot for specials with over 100 Southern African endemics or 'near-endemics' (occasional vagrants to other areas like southern Angola).

Binoculars are a must for effective birdwatching. They permit close-up views of shy species and allow accurate identification of distant ones.

Quantity and quality are features of birding in Southern Africa: red-billed queleas are widespread and at times can form flocks numbering millions.

They're concentrated in heathlike fynbos (try Cape Town's Kirstenbosch National Botanic Gardens or the Cape Peninsula NP) and the semiarid Karoo (Karoo NP and Namaqua NP, though excellent birding can be had anywhere along the roadside).

Namibia's Namib-Naukluft Park is excellent for desert species including dune and Gray's larks, tractrac chat and Rüppell's korhaan as well as cinnamon-breasted warblers, rockrunners, Herero chats and Monteiro's hornbills in the Naukluft mountains. A very different mix is found in the fertile Caprivi Strip which is extremely rich in species; Mamili and Mudumu NPs are the best. Similarly rich habitat, Botswana's Okavango Panhandle is home to over 400 species including a few that breed nowhere else.

In Zimbabwe, the Eastern Highlands are renowned for specials including many from inaccessible parts of Mozambique like Delegorgue's pigeons, blue swallows, scarce swifts and Taita falcons. These rare falcons can also be seen in the Zambezi Valley (they nest just downstream of Victoria Falls) where other specials include collared palm thrushes, Lilian's lovebirds and Bradfield's hornbills.

Zambia and Malawi together have a suite of species you won't find elsewhere in the region, marking the point where the range of many East African residents peters out. Try Liwonde NP (Malawi), Nyika NP (Malawi) and the Luangwa Valley (Zambia). Bangweulu Swamps in Zambia is famous for its shoebills. For those keen to venture further afield, Northern Mozambique's Mount Namuli is the only place in the world you can see the Namuli apalis as well as Thylolo alethes, dapplethroats and the *belcheri* race of green barbet.

Field guides

As a very popular pastime for local wildlifers, birdwatching in the region is well covered by field guides. The original and still one of the best, *Roberts' Birds of Southern Africa* is almost 900 pages long, making it a little bulky for the field but it has very detailed information and is excellent value. Less weighty, Newman's *Birds of Southern Africa: The Green Edition* and the relative newcomer Sasol's *Illustrated Guide to Bird of Southern Africa* both feature slightly larger illustrations and a very helpful colour coding system for rapid location of families and groups.

While all excellent, these guides only cover the area south of the Zambezi River – traditionally the region known as Southern Africa but less than the scope of this book. *Collins Illustrated Checklist: Birds of Southern Africa* by van Perlo covers the entire region including Malawi and Zambia. Aspinall and Beel's *Field Guide to Zambian Birds not found in Southern Africa* illustrates over 100 species which don't occur south of the Zambezi. For Malawi alone, Newman's *Birds of Malawi* is excellent, especially paired with the original Newman's. Not a field guide but particularly useful for planning a trip, get a copy of Barnes' *Important Bird Areas of Southern Africa*. ■

An African fish eagle with its catch. Southern Africa's larger waterways, especially the Okavango Delta, Lake Kariba and Lake Malawi, are excellent places to watch fish eagles in action.

DOLPHIN- & WHALE-WATCHING

WITH at least 37 cetaceans (the order comprising whales and dolphins) including one found nowhere else in the world, Southern African oceans provide rich rewards for marine mammal lovers. Warm currents and protected bays provide ideal habitat for whales and dolphins to breed and to hunt the productive shallow waters close to shore. Although whale sightings are usually restricted to frustratingly brief glimpses, there are a few spots along the coast where quality sightings are virtually guaranteed at the right time of year. Ranging from the prolonged breaching bouts of southern right and humpback whales to the aerial corkscrew twists of Cape Vidal's spinner dolphins, the most spectacular behaviours are often on display.

Winter visitors, southern right whales are conspicuous along South Africa's Cape Coast between June and November.

How it's done

Apart from patience and binoculars, cetacean spotting doesn't demand much in the way of specialised skills or gear. Shore-based watching is very rewarding, particularly in South Africa where natural cliffs and raised platforms provide excellent lookout posts. Watch for the characteristic 'blows' of whales and for hovering flocks of seabirds such as Cape gannets which indicate large fish shoals, irresistible to many dolphin species.

Since 1998, limited boat-trips allowing close-up whale-viewing have been permitted in South Africa. Licensed boats are restricted from approaching closer than 50m but whales often come closer of their own accord. Strict regulations ensure whales are not harassed although policing originates mainly from tourists; don't be afraid to contact the Ministry of Environment and Tourism (Marine and Coastal Management) if you witness major transgressions such as people touching or swimming with whales, boats pursuing whales, approaching females with calves or remaining with the same individual for longer than 30 minutes. By boarding only government-licensed boats, you can be fairly sure the operator abides by the rules. You'll also get a far superior experience – nonlicensed boats have to stay 300m away.

Namibia's cold coastal waters are surprisingly productive for dolphin-viewing, including bottlenose, common, Heaviside's (pictured) and dusky dolphins.

Whether land-based or by boat, be sure to take a few layers of clothing. Weather is highly changeable along this coastline during the whale season (June through December) and cold sub-Antarctic winds bring fairly miserable conditions. A warm jacket and raincoat are highly recommended.

Top spots to go

Whales and dolphins occur all along the Southern African coast but consistently good sightings are concentrated in a few special sites. Likewise, timing is critical as many species are migratory and congregate for seasonal events such as breeding or localised concentrations of food.

Rapidly becoming South Africa's cetacean capital and providing some of the best whale-watching in the world, Plettenberg Bay is a must. Between June and November, tremendous congregations of southern right whales arrive to court and to give birth. Excellent boat tours virtually guarantee superb breaching displays and other courtship behaviour. Although the southern rights are seasonal, 'Plett' has cetaceans year-round including Bryde's and minke whales as well as bottlenose, spinner and humpback dolphins. Try to get there during peak season when all species are more abundant, but even if you don't you'll probably see something.

For land-based watching, head further west to the coastal town of Hermanus where southern rights are regularly seen from the cliffs above Walker Bay. Other significant whale nurseries include Cape Infanta in De Hoop NR, False Bay (near Cape Town) and Algoa Bay (near Port Elizabeth). Humpback whales also occur in these bays and at Cape Vidal in the Greater St Lucia Wetland Park – they pass close to shore around June and July on their way to breeding waters off Mozambique. In October and November they can be seen on the return trip, often with young calves in tow.

For dolphin-viewing, try to catch the annual 'sardine run'. Actually pilchards, huge shoals of the little fish concentrate between Plettenberg Bay and Durban from June to August providing a feast for huge pods of common dolphins as well as dozens of other species including sharks, seabirds and even people. Another species, the humpback dolphin is associated with river deltas or estuaries and readily seen around Algoa Bay, the Tugela River mouth north of Durban and Mozambique's Maputo Bay.

The west coast of Southern Africa has some unique cetacean attractions including the region's only endemic, Heaviside's dolphin. At 1.8m long, it's also the smallest species in these waters and is usually seen inshore early in the morning. South Africa's Namaqualand coast, Britannia Bay and sometimes the Sea Point lookout over Table Bay offer good odds for this little dolphin and it is regularly spotted along the Namibian coast between Swakopmund and Walvis Bay. Also restricted to the west coast, dusky dolphins are commonly seen and can be identified by their narrow, erect dorsal fin compared with Heaviside's squat, triangular fin.

Bottlenose dolphins are intelligent cooperative hunters, herding shoals of fish into dense masses and then taking turns to plunge into the 'baitball' to feed.

Field guides

Guides on African cetaceans are scanty but *A Guide to Whales, Dolphins and Other Marine Mammals of Southern Africa* by Vic Cockcroft and Peter Joyce includes information on identification, behaviour and where to go. *Whale Watching in South Africa: The Southern Right Whale* by Peter Best is a small but extremely useful booklet with practical tips and behavioural insights into viewing Southern Africa's most visible whale. The Dolphin Action & Protection Group (PO Box 22227, Fish Hoek 7925; ☎ 021-782 5845) based in Fish Hoek near Cape Town produces pamphlets on whale- and dolphin-watching. ■

DIVING & SNORKELLING

LONG summers, warm seas and astonishing diversity makes for superb diving conditions along Southern Africa's coastline. For scuba enthusiasts, dozens of reefs, shipwrecks, kelp forests and inland water-filled caves provide interest for all levels of expertise while snorkellers are able to explore shallow-water reefs, protected bays and warm-water lakes. Some of the world's best diving occurs here, whether it's swimming alongside whale sharks on their annual migration, going eye-to-eye with great white sharks or trying to distinguish between the hundreds of multicoloured cichlids in Lake Malawi.

How it's done

You'll need internationally recognised certification for any scuba diving in the region. For nondivers looking for a course and experienced divers needing local knowledge and equipment, dive schools proliferate along the South African coast between Cape Town and KwaZulu-Natal's north coast. As well as providing instruction and gear for hire, many of them can arrange trips further afield to increasingly popular destinations like South Africa's west coast (try Cape Town) and sites in Mozambique (best arranged from Durban, also from Johannesburg). Instruction and gear is also available at Lake Malawi and the more popular Mozambican spots.

Smallest of Southern African marine turtles, the hawksbill is usually spotted by divers and snorkellers along the east coast.

If you plan on snorkelling, you'll only need fins, mask and snorkel (and a wet suit in winter months), widely available for hire at all dive centres. If you've never snorkelled before, it's hugely rewarding here and extremely easy to learn. The key is to breathe normally through the snorkel; and anticipate a little resistance with the slight change in pressure even just a few inches below the surface. Also, don't panic when the snorkel fills with water as you submerge; simply blow it clear when you reach the surface.

Top spots to go

The South African coast is dotted with dozens of excellent sites. Near Cape Town, the cold Atlantic converges with the warm Indian Ocean, producing a combination of tropical and cold water species with kelp beds, wrecks and seal encounters a regular feature. About 160km east of Cape Town, Dyer Island is the great white shark capital of the world and sightings are virtually guaranteed between May and September. Baiting the sharks ensures spectacular viewing, but is currently the subject of research to determine if it increases the likelihood of attacks on people. Cage-diving allows eye-to-eye experiences, but great whites are surface feeders and nondivers can also get spectacular sightings from the boat. This coastline is the only place in the world where great whites regularly launch themselves up to 3m clear of the water in explosive attacks on their favoured prey, the fur-seal.

Snorkelling close to shore requires no specialised training and gear is widely available in all popular dive spots.

Towards Durban, far less fearsome members of the family can be enjoyed without cages. At Protea Banks and Aliwal Shoal, sponge- and coral-covered reefs are home to breeding colonies of ragged toothed sharks (elsewhere called grey nurses), docile and approachable despite their fierce appearance. North of Durban, the diving becomes tropical at Sodwana Bay, extremely popular for the rich coral reefs inhabited by loggerhead and leatherback turtles, manta rays, sharks, dolphins and, between October and March, whale sharks. Beyond the reach of most divers, submarine canyons here have very recently been revealed to be home to coelacanths (primitive marine fish known only from fossil records until a living specimen was discovered in 1938).

Very similar diving but without the crowds can be found along Mozambique's coastline. Just north of the South African-Mozambican border, Ponto do Oura and Ponta Malongane have Zambezi, hammerhead and whale sharks, many types of rays, potato bass, emperor angelfish and parrot fish. Close to the capital city Maputo, Inhanca Island is known for its whale sharks, rays and dolphins during the summer as well as large schools of barracuda year-round. Five hundred kilometres further north, the Bazaruto Archipelago is known for its pristine reefs although water temperatures approaching 36°C during the 1998 El Nino bleached extensive stands of coral and they'll take some years to renew. Just over 250km south of the Tanzanian border near the town of Pemba, Wimbe reef is close enough to shore that you won't need a boat.

For those with serious experience, Namibia has crystal-clear cave-diving including the largest underground lake in the world, Dragon's Breath Cave. Wildlife is scarce and little-known but some unique species occur in Aigamas Cave and Guinas Lake including endemic catfish and tilapia. Contact the South African Spelaeological Association (PO Box 4814, Cape Town 8000; **e** peters@iaccess.za or peters@datasoft.co.za, 🖳 www.users.iafrica.com/p/pe/peters/sasa/sasahome.html), though expeditions are few and arranged far in advance.

The coral reefs of the east coast attract over 60,000 divers a year. Coral crevices provide countless homes for many colourful sea creatures.

Land-locked Malawi has nothing for marine enthusiasts but the freshwater life in the lake more than makes up for it. Over 600 fish species inhabit the warm waters, the vast percentage of them endemic, brilliantly coloured cichlids. At Nkhata Bay and all around the Nankumba Peninsula they are extremely accustomed to snorkellers and flock around looking for handouts. Otter Point near Cape Maclear has a special snorkelling trail; you'll need the waterproof map included in Digby's *Guide to the Fishes of Lake Malawi*. You might even spot very shy spotted-necked otters, occasionally reported by kayakers around the peninsula.

Field guides

The diver's bible for the region, *The Dive Sites of South Africa* by Anton Koornhof lists attractions and technical information for more than 160 sites along the coast. If you're interested in identification, *Reef Fishes and Corals: East Coast of Southern Africa* (King) illustrates over 200 fish and 32 common coral species from the KwaZulu-Natal and Mozambique coasts. Digby's *Guide to the Fishes of Lake Malawi* by Lewis Digby and co-workers, is invaluable for the lake's 600 plus species. Not a field guide but an invaluable reference, get a copy of *Two Oceans: A Guide to the Marine Life of Southern Africa*. ∎

PHOTOGRAPHY

WILDLIFE photography is a highly specialised field but the quality of today's equipment – even modestly priced, nonprofessional gear – means that excellent results are possible for anyone. In many destinations, wild animals are so used to visitors that exceptional chances for photography arise often. The ubiquitous collection of tourist photos at entrance gates, lodges and park offices shows that having a camera adds a further rewarding element to a wildlife trip, regardless of your expertise.

Equipment

If you're buying your first camera, the selection is mind-boggling. Most professional wildlife photographers use Canon or Nikon, largely because of their formidable lens quality. Cameras essentially all do the same thing, though with varying degrees of complexity and technological assistance. Most modern cameras have a full range of automatic functions but select a model which also allows full manual operation. Once you've mastered the basics of the camera, you'll probably find it limiting if you're unable to begin experimenting with your photography.

Most animals in Southern African reserves – even the most sought-after ones like lions – become astonishingly indifferent to vehicles, providing photographers with terrific opportunities.

More important than camera bodies are the lenses you attach to them, and for wildlife, think long. A 300mm lens is a good starting point though bird portraits require longer. Lenses of 400–600mm focal length are probably out of the price range of most, though 'slower' lenses (that is, lenses with a relatively small maximum aperture) such as a 400mm f5.6 are reasonably priced and very useful when a 300mm just doesn't quite reach. Dedicated (ie, 'brand-name') lenses have superb optical quality and are more expensive than generics but unless you're a pro, the difference is slight.

Zooms are generally not as sharp as fixed focal length lenses (ie, lenses which do not zoom), but the difference is only important if you're thinking about publishing your pictures. Many makes offer zooms around the 100–300mm range which, when paired with a short zoom like a 35–70mm, decently covers most situations for recreational photographers. Recently released 'super-zooms' provide a comprehensive range of focal lengths in one lens. Canon's 35–350mm, 100–400mm and Sigma's 170–500mm are worth investigating. None are cheap but they yield publication-quality results in one versatile package.

To take bird portraits, such as this malachite kingfisher, you'll need to carry a 'super-telephoto' lens with a focal length of at least 500mm.

There are hundreds of accessories photographers use to enhance their shots but one that's vital is the tripod. Many shots are spoiled by 'camera-shake' particularly when using longer lenses. Tripods can be cumbersome to include in your luggage but sturdy, compact models such as Manfrotto's 190 fit into a sausage bag. An excellent alternative for vehicle-based photographers is a bean-bag to rest your camera on while shooting out of windows or from rooftops (although if the vehicle's motor is running camera-shake can still be a problem). A small cloth bag with a zip opening takes up no room and can be filled with ubiquitous raw rice as soon as you arrive at your destination.

In the field

Before you go anywhere, know how your camera works. Visit the local zoo or park and shoot a few rolls to familiarise yourself with its controls and functions. Many good wildlife moments happen unexpectedly and pass in seconds; you'll miss them if you're still fiddling with dials and settings. For the same reason, when in reserves leave your camera turned on (and pack plenty of batteries).

Most cameras will have shutter and aperture priority functions. In shutter priority mode, you set the shutter speed and the camera selects the appropriate aperture for a correct exposure; the reverse applies for aperture priority. These two functions are probably the most valuable for wildlife photographers but you need to know when to use them.

Shutter priority is excellent for shooting action. If you want to freeze motion, select the highest shutter speed permitted with the available light and the camera takes care of the aperture setting. On the other hand, if you're trying to emphasise depth of field in your shot, opt for aperture priority. Large apertures (low 'f-stops') reduce the depth of field, useful for enhancing a portrait shot by throwing the background out of focus. However, if you're shooting a scene where you want everything in focus, such as thousands of wildebeests and zebras on a vast plain, select a small aperture (high 'f-stops').

Composition is a major challenge with wildlife as you can't move your subject around; try different vantage points and experiment with a variety of focal lengths. If you're too far away to take a good portrait, try to show the animal in its habitat. A 400mm might give you a close up of a penguin's face while a 28mm will show the entire colony spread across a pebbly beach receding in the background – all from the same position. Try to tell a story about the animal or illustrate some behaviour. Jackal pups transfixed by nearby springboks might be too shy to approach for a decent close-up but could make a lovely subject if you include the antelopes and surroundings.

Some species which are nocturnal outside reserves (like this spotted hyena) become semi-diurnal in protected areas, permitting daylight viewing and the chance for shots like this.

Unless you're packing very powerful flashes, wildlife photography relies on the vagaries of natural light and the best shots are invariably those taken in the 'golden hour' – just after dawn and just before dusk. Where possible, get into position early, whether it's a bird hide, waterhole or scenic lookout you noted the day before. Don't always assume front-on light is the best. Side lighting can give more depth to a subject and back-lighting, particularly when the sun is low on the horizon, can be very atmospheric.

Above all else, when photographing wildlife, be patient. You never know what will appear at the waterhole next or when a 'snoozing' predator suddenly spots a chance for a kill. You cannot always anticipate when an opportunity will arise but if you're willing to wait, you'll almost certainly see something worth shooting. ■

HABITATS

The Southern African environment and its wildlife

THE ARID LANDS

Desert
Semi-desert

Indian

Atlantic
Ocean

Ocean

ENCOMPASSING western South Africa, much of Namibia and most of Botswana, the great dry tract known as the South West Arid Zone is worthy of the over-used adjective 'unique'. Climatically desolate, this region is actually one of the region's richest centres of endemism. With rainfall averaging between 125 and 250mm, it's correctly known as semidesert but in the far west where it merges with the true desert of the Namib, annual falls rarely top 50mm. While lacking the ecological abundance of wetter habitats, the arid lands distinguish Southern Africa from the rest of the continent probably more than any other habitat. To get a real sense of Southern Africa and tick off many species found nowhere else, the arid lands are a must.

God's sandpit

Dune grasses in the Namib Desert. Long anchoring roots and wind-borne moisture from the Atlantic Ocean enable hardy grasses to grow here year-round.

If there is a single unifying characteristic of the region, it is sand. In fact, the largest expanse of sand in the world occurs here. Resting on a vast ancient basin of rock, it extends from South Africa's Orange River through the entire southern subregion and peters out just shy of the equator. As rainfall increases along a northern gradient, however, vegetation becomes more lush and you wouldn't know it actually sits on a sandy bed. In the south where rainfall is least, desert grasses and shrubs are comparatively sparse, leaving the sand exposed. This is the Kalahari. For hundreds of kilometres, continuous rows of dunes covered in sand-binding grasses create a landscape of parallels. With no permanent lakes or water, a handful of river beds are the point of convergence for ephemeral rainfall and for the desert's wildlife. Arid-adapted springboks, gemsboks and elands extract vital moisture from their diet and can go their entire lives without drinking. But drinking makes sense when water is available and they join water-dependent species like blue wildebeests in the river beds. Unlike true arid-adapted species, wildebeests lack dense, reflective coats and narrow muzzles for selecting the most succulent forage, so they have to work harder to survive here.

Their predators follow (big cats, spotted and brown hyenas) as well as little endemic hunters – Cape foxes, black-footed cats,

Right: Desert trees (like this quiver tree) are ecosystems in their own right, providing shade, food, nesting sites and shelter for a wide variety of animals.

Opposite page: The massive dunes of Sossusvlei in the southeast Namib desert.

Opposite inset: Rarely inhabited by big game, Sossusvlei provides opportunities to view smaller desert life like geckos, desert beetles and horned vipers.

meerkats and yellow mongooses. The body fluids of their prey free carnivores of the need for free-standing water, though like everything here, they drink daily when possible. The open landscape provides relatively few niches for birds but ground-living species like sandgrouse, larks, bustards and coursers occur in abundance. Still one of the most pristine environments in the region, the Kgalagadi Transfrontier Park (TP) and the Central Kalahari National Park (NP) collectively protect a chunk of the Kalahari the size of Portugal.

The desert of rocks

Where the southern extreme of the Kalahari peters out, it blends with a stony semidesert called the Karoo, which then heads northwest in a rocky band through central Namibia until it finally becomes the Kaokoveld and Damaraland. At first glance the vegetation is monotonous, but it's rich in unique succulents, desert grasses and dwarf shrubs providing food for klipspringers, Hartmann's mountain zebras and in the far north, black rhinos.

In South Africa where a vast grassy plateau dominates the landscape, Karoo grazers – springboks, black wildebeests and Cape mountain zebras – occur alongside more widespread species like elands and mountain reedbucks. Less obvious but only found in the Karoo are riverine rabbits, a handful of rare rodents and endemic larks, warblers and korhaans. In the northwest where the Karoo is called Namaqualand, intense spring flushes of desert flowers trigger a flurry of breeding activity for specialised endemics like Karoo bush rats, dassie rats and pygmy rockmice. As well as nectar-lovers like monkey beetles, bees and sunbirds, the floral bounty attracts human admirers by the busload.

The kokerboom or quiver tree, so named because San people (bushmen) used the leathery bark to fashion quivers for their arrows.

The real thing

Technically outside the boundaries of the South West Arid Zone but merging together at its extreme west, the only true desert in Southern Africa lies along Namibia's coast. Stretching over 2000km from the South African border well into Angola, the gravel plains and sienna dunes of the Namib are home to life that depends on fog. The Atlantic Ocean's freezing Benguela Current cools the coastal air as it flows towards Namibia,

The struggle for existence

To our way of thinking, the desert is a desolate place of environmental extremes where life balances on a knife edge. For modern humans, that's essentially apply true, but we all too readily apply it to the desert's natural inhabitants. For desert wildlife, adjectives like 'inhospitable', 'barren' and 'wasteland' are not only irrelevant, they are wrong. Millions of years of evolution has ensured that the desert fauna and flora are suited to their environment in exactly the same way as the inhabitants of rainforests, savannas and wetlands are suited to theirs. Although the paucity of water and other resources means that deserts can never sustain the diversity and density of life that occurs in well-watered habitats, the denizens of the arid zone are as successful in their own specialised way as life anywhere.

forming moisture-laden fogs that are blown up to 80km inland. Fog-basking beetles, trench-digging beetles and zebra-striped tenebrionid beetles harvest the condensing fog and provide the keystone for life. White lady spiders, small geckos and the rapacious Namib dune beetle feed on the fog gatherers and are in turn hunted by predators like the blind Namib golden mole, a miniature sand-swimmer known as the 'shark of the dunes'. Devoid of flora, the dune faces are shunned by larger life but in the broad alleys between dunes, dormant grass seeds respond to rare cloudbursts. As little as 10mm of rain re-animates the seeds and turns the low-lying sand into meadows. Fresh grass, insects and seeds provide a bounty for larks, chats and warblers in the thousands, as well as korhaans, ostriches and desert-adapted antelopes. As the sandy flats dry out, these species disperse back out onto the stony plains, tracking the unpredictable inland thunderstorms that provide patchy relief. ■

Following unpredictable showers, desert plants like these yellow devil's thorns experience a brief and intense bloom.

GRASSLANDS

Grassland
Grassland patches

Indian
Ocean

Atlantic
Ocean

FOR many people, open grasslands epitomise wild Africa. Indeed, there is probably a no more recognisably African habitat than the short grass plains of the Serengeti-Mara ecosystem. But grasslands in Southern Africa were never as extensive as in Kenya and Tanzania, and because of human impact are now rare in their natural state. European colonists sought out the grasslands as productive habitat for their stock and crops, so cattle, sheep and wheat now dominate where huge numbers of wild herbivores once occurred. Nonetheless, numerous reserves like Golden Gate Highlands and Mountain Zebra NPs, as well as many private lands around them, protect significant tracts of the southern grasslands and their representative wildlife.

The highveld

The most distinctive and homogeneous grasslands in the region occur on South Africa's central plateau, known locally as the 'highveld'. Being at high altitudes, these plains experience frosty, dry winters with occasional snow, then endure a drenching from brief but violent storms – which you could just about set your watch to on summer afternoons. Combined with regular grassfires, the battering regime ensures the plains remain mostly treeless except for protected gullies and rocky ridges. Summer fires and rain see the grasslands cloaked in green regrowth but for most of the year they vary in colour from saffron through golden-yellow. They're probably at their most impressive towards the end of winter when tall, straw-coloured stands are buffeted by cold highveld winds.

In winter, grasslands can appear lifeless because large congregations of mega-fauna are absent, but smaller life is everywhere.

Hardy, coarse grasses dominate and most of them are sour tasting like the appropriately named turpentine grass and yellow thatching grass. Local farmers call this habitat 'sourveld', though it hasn't stopped them saturating it with livestock. But even prior to the influx of domestic species, the bitter, nutrient-poor grasslands never carried the diversity and density of herbivores sustained by East Africa's sweetgrass plains. They are, however, notable for the endemic ungulates that once formed massive herds here. A couple of them are now extinct. The quagga, (pronounced 'kwokka' after its braying call) was a

Right: Frequent grassfires help maintain grasslands and stimulate regrowth which attracts herbivores.

Opposite page: Isolated grassland trees are fruitful places to look for wildlife – they provide cover for predators, shade for grazers and perches for birds.

Opposite inset: Lovers of open areas where they can keep an eye out for danger, ostriches are easily viewed on grasslands.

lightly marked subspecies of Burchell's zebra and died out in the wild before 1900. The blue antelope, a relative of sable and roan antelopes, disappeared a century earlier. Other highveld grazers came close to a similar fate but tiny pockets, protected mostly by interested private citizens, have ensured their persistence. Bonteboks, black wildebeests and mountain zebras have now been restored to much of their former range, which they share with more widespread Southern African endemics like springboks. Large carnivores are mostly absent except for isolated populations of the adaptable leopard, but smaller hunters including mongooses, black-footed cats, and Cape and bat-eared foxes are abundant, if mostly difficult to spot. Ostriches are the most conspicuous avian inhabitants of the highveld, but at ground level and often hidden by the long grasses, many different species of longclaws, pipits, widows, bishops, larks and korhaans forage for the teeming seeds and insects.

Islands of grass

Far more widespread than the highveld are the grasslands scattered throughout the woodland-plains mosaic that makes up savanna (see the Savannas section later in this chapter). These patchy open areas are distinct from the unique highveld grasslands and they usually have a moderate scattering of trees and thickets. They also lack the highveld's most characteristic species but because they occur in more fertile, low-lying regions, they sustain a much greater variety of wildlife in far higher concentrations. Black wildebeests are replaced by the more common blue wildebeest, the same species that undertakes legendary migrations in the Serengeti; in Southern Africa they are more sedentary, but readily undertake mini-migrations in search of grazing in the savanna patchwork. Red hartebeests and tsessebes fill the bontebok's niche, hartebeests preferring the dry grasslands in the northwest, while the tsessebe is found in better watered habitat to the northeast. The Cape mountain zebra disappears and Burchell's zebra becomes abundant in areas such as the Botswana's Makgadikgadi/Nxai Pan system

Like many grazing species, white rhinos are often most conspicuous at the ecotone (or boundary) between open plains and savanna woodlands.

The aardvark and the cucumber

The aardvark occurs in many different habitats but where termite mounds reach their highest densities (on open grasslands) so too does the aardvark. This in turn is fortunate for another, very different, grassland species, the aardvark cucumber. A melonlike member of the cucumber family, it's one of the few plant species that bears subterranean fruit, a reproductive strategy called geocarpy. A leathery, water-resistant rind prevents the fruit from rotting in damp soil and the seeds develop 30cm below ground, safe from rodents and other seed-eaters. But germination is triggered by sunlight so as the seeds mature, they have to make it to the surface. Enter the aardvark. Departing from their otherwise wholly insectivorous diet, aardvarks excavate cucumbers and eat them. They excrete the hard seeds undamaged, which can then germinate topside on a bed of nutrient-rich aardvark dung. Why aardvarks eat only this type of cucumber is a mystery but for the plant, it's critical. No other animal is known to eat them and without the aardvark, it would probably disappear.

and Savute region, in which huge herds form that migrate in synchrony with the summer short grass flush.

The richer grazing also sustains 'bulk grazers', ungulates which, by virtue of their size, require huge quantities of palatable grass. Most conspicuous, white rhinos and buffaloes are invariably accompanied by an entourage of cattle egrets opportunistically snapping up disturbed insects. Other insectivorous aeronauts like rollers, whydahs and black-shouldered kites are very common and the rich herpeto-fauna (reptiles and amphibians) attracts snake eagles and secretary birds. Mammalian predators also thrive in the richness of the savanna grasslands, particularly pursuit hunters like cheetahs and African wild dogs. Low in the predator hierarchy, they avoid areas used by the dominant carnivore here, the lion. Spotted hyenas are common on the plains and its less widespread cousin, the brown hyena, occurs in drier areas. Aardwolves, honey badgers, servals, white-tailed mongooses and jackals are widespread, some being more obvious than others. ■

Typically inhabitants of more wooded areas, roan antelopes in Malawi's Nyika NP are surprisingly evident on the grasslands.

SAVANNAS

Moist savanna
Arid savanna

Indian Ocean

Atlantic Ocean

ALTHOUGH the term 'savanna' is often used to evoke an image of open plains, the defining feature of this habitat type is actually bush. Indeed, savanna forms the wooded transition zone between forests and grasslands and it includes 'savanna grasslands', patches of lightly wooded plains within the woodland matrix (covered in the Grasslands section earlier in this chapter). In Southern Africa, savanna is known appropriately as 'bushveld' and is the dominant vegetation type of the region. It covers a vast expanse, beginning as a broad band across the northern reaches of Namibia, Botswana and South Africa and extending though most of Zimbabwe, Zambia and Malawi. Correctly called the Southern Savanna Woodland, it's contiguous with the Northern Savanna of East Africa which includes the great central African bushveld belt that eventually wanes at the Sahara; collectively, savanna is the most widespread habitat on the continent. Of all the Southern African habitat types, savanna is also by far the richest for its variety and abundance of wildlife. Many of the great parks of the region, like Hwange, South Luangwa, Chobe and Kruger NPs, are bushveld parks where the wildlife-viewing is among the best on the planet.

The 'bushveld'. Although it appears too dense for easy wildlife-viewing, most people experience their best sightings in this habitat.

Thornveld

Savanna composition varies markedly across its enormous range but common to all is the thorn tree. At least 25 different species of thorn tree, all members of the genus *Acacia*, make up the different savanna communities of Southern Africa. Among these, the umbrella thorn is easily the most recognisable. Its unmistakable flat-topped crown appears in countless African wildlife documentaries but don't let the cliche deter you; they really are a beautiful tree and when you see one against a setting sun with attendant browsing giraffes, it's only the fussiest of photographers who can keep the lens cap on.

Umbrella thorns and another acacia, the knobthorn with its characteristic knob-covered trunk, are typical of 'sweet' savannas, which maintain high nutritional quality well into the dry winter. This makes them extremely attractive to large concentrations of

Right: The enormous dietary requirements of elephants play a dramatic role in the longevity of savannas.

Opposite page: In Southern Africa, most primates are found in savanna habitat; along with chacma baboons, vervet monkeys (pictured) are guaranteed.

Opposite inset: Despite its extraordinary colours, the lilac-breasted roller is actually a very common savanna species.

browsing ungulates such as giraffes, greater kudus, impalas, black rhinos and elephants. Scattered thickets of buffalo-thorns provide refuges for smaller browsers like grey duikers and bush-bucks as well as a great variety of birdlife including drongos, shrikes, flycatchers and louries. Predators abound, especially lions, leopards and spotted hyenas, as well as many cryptic smaller species like civets and mongooses.

On the poorer soils of northern Namibia, Zimbabwe, southern Zambia and northwest South Africa where seasonally high rainfall leaches out nutrients, savannas are less nutritious and don't sustain such high wildlife concentrations. However, this creates niches for a number of specialised ungulates that thrive at low densities (sables, roans, Lichtenstein's hartebeests and both types of reedbucks), preyed upon by African wild dogs, leopards and the ubiquitous lion. Like sweet savannas, a great ensemble of arboreal as well as ground-roosting birds occur here such as korhaans, francolins, hornbills and larks.

Trees of life

Thorn trees occur throughout savanna but never in isolation and frequently not as the dominant tree type. Accordingly, just as 'thornveld' indicates the predominance of acacias, other savanna types tend to be referred to by the local name of the most numerous or characteristic tree. Thus, the *Baikiaea*-dominated bush of Mozambique is called gusu savanna or simply gusu, the *Brachystegia* woodlands of Zambia are known as miombo and so on. As the most abundant local tree, these diagnostic species inevitably draw a suite of wildlife. Compared with the relatively homogeneous landscape of grasslands and desert, savannas provide a terrific array of niches for an equally diverse fauna. One of the most distinctive savanna trees, the mopane, is a good example. The leaves are highly nutritious and sought-out by browsers ranging from the diminutive steenbok to herds of elephants, which uproot

Southern yellow-billed hornbills regularly perch in trees next to vehicle tracks and game paths looking for insects in the open.

Where the antelope and antelope play

African savannas provide fertile pickings for browsers and grazers, creating many dozens of niches. This helps to explain why savannas have such a terrific variety of herbivores, most of them antelopes – or are they deer? In fact, anything remotely deerlike that you see in Southern Africa, including wildebeests and buffaloes (and very distantly, giraffes), actually belongs to the antelope family, with around 35 species for the region.

Both antelopes and deer have horns but in antelopes, no matter how elaborate the twists and twirls, they always comprise a single, unbranched tine which is never shed. The horns of deer, however, are known as antlers – far more intricate structures with multiple branchings, which are generally shed every year and regrown.

Except for a few introduced species on deer farms (and the inevitable escapers), there are no deer in Southern Africa. The only indigenous deer on the continent is the red deer, a common Eurasian species that colonized North Africa about a million years ago. Far more ancient, the great radiation of African antelopes began at least 20 million years ago.

In open savanna country, white rhinos (pictured) predominate, but as the bush gets denser, the black rhino is more likely to be encountered.

the shallow-rooted mopane to reach the valuable canopy. For less pushy feeders – such as ground-based browsers like greater kudus, impalas and duikers – mopane is still readily accessible because the distinctive butterfly-shaped leaves retain their nutrients after they've fallen to the ground.

Baboons and vervet monkeys do likewise but when foraging in the trees themselves, they often ignore the leaves and search instead for a leaf-resident. A small psyllid insect secretes a tiny, honey-coloured shelter made of waxy scale where the larva develops. Primates turn leaves over and carefully collect the sweet-tasting scale one-by-one and, no doubt, also eat the larvae inside. As well as offering food and safe perches for primates and hundreds of bird species, mopane trees provide sheltering holes for woodpeckers, barbets and hornbills as well as tree squirrels, tree rats and bushbabies. These in turn attract nocturnal predators like owls and genets. On poor soils with limited rainfall, mopane forms a scrubby savanna rarely higher than 3m. But where conditions are particularly favourable such as in Moremi GR, 25m-high trees create a mopane forest and its difficult to believe you're still in savanna country. ■

FORESTS

COMPRISING less than 0.1% of Southern African vegetation, evergreen forests are the region's rarest habitat type. That stems partly from the inevitable human impact but also because Southern African soils and climate are less suitable for forests than more tropical regions. Not surprisingly, the forests that do occur are scattered throughout the highest rainfall areas, ranging from the high montane forests that line the slopes and valleys of the Drakensberg escarpment to the humid coastal dune forests of northern KwaZulu-Natal and Mozambique.

Forests in the mists

Like a series of tree-covered stepping stones, Southern Africa's high altitude forests run in a chain of relict patches starting on South Africa's southern Cape coast and petering out on Malawi's Nyika Plateau. The most extensive stands cover the slopes of the Drakensberg Mountains and the Chimanimani escarpment of Zimbabwe's Eastern Highlands. But regardless of location, they're all similar enough to tropical Africa's upland forests to be tagged with the same 'Afro-montane' label. Indicating true African mountain forest (rather then the dense woodland that creeps onto the lower slopes), Afro-montane vegetation usually grows on high, steep slopes which intercept moisture-laden ocean air. Dense mists and heavy rains are a regular feature, creating a humid, lush environment where everything is damp, from the rotting leaf litter underfoot to the moss- and fungus-covered trunks of 25m-high forest trees.

Unlike equatorial forest, the understorey is usually quite sparse but glades of ferns and forbs choke patches of ground where the canopy admits beams of light. Here, Southern Africa's smallest antelope, the blue duiker, finds refuge and browses the shrubs. A miniature cleaner of the forest floor, it also eats fallen leaves, fruit and flowers, and seeks out monkeys and fruit-eating birds like louries, barbets and parrots in the canopy above (they invariably dislodge and discard fruits to the floor below where the duiker mops up). Anything the duikers miss quickly rots down to become part of the rich cushion of detritus on the forest floor, a breeding ground for thousands of

Even in habitats which are otherwise dry, permanent rivers can give rise to ribbons of riparian (or riverine) forest suitable for forest wildlife.

Right: The leopard is the top predator in forest ecosystems. Its stealthy habits enable it to successfully hunt secretive forest antelopes.

Opposite page: The lushness of riverine forest (here in Chimanimani NP, Zimbabwe) creates ideal habitat for a rich fauna.

Opposite inset: Most forest mammals, like this four-toed elephant shrew, are small and require persistence to spot.

different insect species. Elusive bug-hunters including elephant shrews, two endemic forest shrews and the rare giant golden mole sniff them out but all are very difficult to spot. Fortunately for birdwatchers, avian insectivores like flycatchers, shrikes, robins and bulbuls are hard to miss.

Also conspicuous, the placid samango monkey is the only primate of the southern Afro-montane forests; vervets and baboons venture in from surrounding habitat, but neither are forest specialists. Samangos share the canopy with three species of indigenous squirrel, all of which sunbathe on exposed branches on winter mornings, the only time it's relatively easy to spot them. Even more elusive are the tree civet and tree dassie – you'll need a spotlight to see these two entirely nocturnal canopy residents. Both spend the day asleep in high tree hollows but once night falls, the civet can sometimes be seen foraging on the forest floor for insects, small mammals and fruit. The tree dassie rarely ventures to the ground but its characteristic latrines at the base of huge yellow-woods, teaks or milkwoods are good clues to look up.

Forests in the sand

With an almost completely unbroken canopy and a thick understorey of shade-tolerant shrubs and lianas, the region's coastal forests are denser then their montane counterparts. Also known as lowland forest, they cloak parallel rows of ancient dunes which, over time, have developed a fertile detritus layer. Even so, the soil may be very porous and digging a few centimetres reveals the sandy substrate, so trees maximise their water intake with deep roots which, for a few species, are spread in huge, spoke-like buttresses. Some of them are the tallest trees in the region and the canopy here can top 35m. This is another 10m on the highest montane canopy but it makes little difference to treetop residents, many of which are common to both types of forests. Samango monkeys and tree squirrels are common and, in fact, coastal forests like those surrounding Lake St Lucia are more rewarding sites to look for forest

Smallest of Africa's 19 duiker species, the blue duiker is extremely shy, but its largely diurnal habits provide occasional opportunities for sightings.

The forest elephants of Knysna

The Afro-montane forests lining the mountains of the southern Cape once sustained thousands of elephants during Africa's southernmost elephant migration. Following seasonal rainfall and the new growth which followed, elephants moved down from the Karoo grasslands in the north, over the mountains and into the forests and coastal fynbos. When rains returned to the north, they made the return trip. The migrations ceased during the 19th century as people carved up the Karoo for farms and intensified hunting pressure for ivory. About 600 elephants took refuge in the forests but by 1908, only 20 remained. Ninety years later, that had dwindled to a single female, thought to have been born in the forest near the town of Knysna in the 1940s. An attempt in late 1999 to rejuvenate the population with three young elephants from Kruger NP failed when one died of pneumonia and the other two moved out of the forests onto surrounding farmland. They were removed and the lone cow is again the only reminder of the massive herds which once occupied the forests.

mammals than on the mountains. They also shelter a few species with a distinctly tropical feel like Delegorgue's pigeons, African broadbills and the perfectly camouflaged Gaboon viper, its skin a living reflection of the forest floor's leaf litter.

At the forest edges where the understorey thins out, bushbucks, bushpigs and black rhinos overlap with the blue duiker and forest birds mingle with savanna and woodland species. Red duikers, sunis and a Southern African endemic, the nyala, are also more easily spotted here and attract the only large forest carnivore, the leopard. If the innate shyness of these forest inhabitants doesn't make sighting one enough of a challenge, then the lushness of the habitat will. Where the detritus is sparse, such as around puddles, moist walking trails through forests are an excellent canvas for their tracks and the signs of many other forest creatures. ■

Known for towering trees like Outeniqua yellow-woods, milkwoods and Cape ash, the Cape's indigenous coastal forest is now restricted to a few scattered patches like Tsitsikamma NP.

FYNBOS

In contrast to the summer flush that occurs elsewhere in the region, most fynbos plants flower in spring after the winter rains.

LYING in the extreme southwest of the region between southern Namaqualand and Port Elizabeth, is a habitat found nowhere else on earth. Named after the fine-leaved shrubs that predominate, South Africa's fynbos (Afrikaans for 'fine bush') is one of the richest floral regions in the world. With over 8600 plant species, 70% of them endemic, only a few tropical rainforests can match fynbos for variety, which is sufficient to qualify it for classification as one of the world's six floral kingdoms. A region of cold winter rains and desiccating summers, the heathlike fynbos is resistant to both fire and frost. Often described as Mediterranean or 'macchia' after the scrubby hard-leaved shrubs of Spain, it is far more diverse than any similar European habitat, with characteristically African proteas and cycads alongside hundreds of different sedges, reeds, ericas, lilies and irises.

The fires of creation

Fire is the key to fynbos diversity. The plants here use different strategies to cope with the frequent fires that sweep through in the dry summer and autumn. Likewise, different fires, or even different stages of the same fire, favour species differently. Many proteas and the tall mountain cypress protect their seeds in heat-resistant flowerheads that spring open to disgorge their seed bounty in the relatively cool fires of autumn. Other species have hard-coated seeds that lie dormant in the soil until an intense summer fire triggers their germination. Because the timing and interval between fires is always changing, no single species dominates.

While fire maintains fynbos diversity, ants seem to actually increase it. Over 1400 species of fynbos plant rely on ants to disperse their seeds, a relationship called myrmecochory. The plants 'bribe' ants with elaiosomes, fleshy extrusions on the

Right: Rock dassies are among the many inhabitants of fynbos which use the thick scrub for shelter (shown here at the Cape Peninsula NP).

Opposite page: Cape Peninsula NP. The Cape Peninsula has 2256 plant species – more than Great Britain – in an area the size of Greater London.

Opposite inset: The woody, protective flowers of proteas shelter their seeds from the summer fires that are a common feature of fynbos.

seeds rich in protein, fats, sugars and vitamins. The ants carry the seeds back to their nests to eat the elaiosomes and then abandon the seeds, which germinate safely below ground where they're protected from seed-eating rodents. In addition, ant dispersal may actually isolate seedlings from their parent species. Most myrmecochorous plants are pollinated by insects flying very short distances so germination may be restricted to just a few plants in a very localised area. Over time, this genetic isolation can lead to entirely new species and may explain why some have such restricted ranges; for many fynbos plants, the entire world population occupies an area less than the size of a football oval.

The candy shop

With such an abundance of floral riches, fynbos swarms with nectar- and pollen-eaters. Many thousands of insects occur only here and most of them are still unknown to science. A few such as the protea beetle and carpenter bee are fairly obvious visitors to the flowers but by far the most striking pollinators are the birds. With their vividly coloured bracts (hard, outer petal-like leaves) enclosing a tightly clustered mass of nectar-bearing flowers, the proteas probably evolved to attract birds and most dazzling of them all are the sunbirds. Like Africa's answer to hummingbirds (to which they are not closely related), sunbirds have tube-like beaks, a brush-tipped tongue for mopping up nectar and jewel-like metallic plumage. At least seven different species occur in fynbos; one of them, the orange-breasted sunbird, can be seen nowhere else. Other endemic birds include the Cape sugarbird, a much larger nectar-eater belonging to a unique South African family, as well as Protea canaries, Cape francolins and Victorin's warblers.

Bitter-sweet browsing

Unlike the nutrient-rich flowers, most fynbos plants are fibrous, nutritionally poor and loaded with unpalatable compounds like tannins. As a result, the mammalian fauna is not nearly as diverse but there are a few notable species which characterise the fynbos. The uncommon and timid Cape grysbok browses fynbos with a narrow muzzle, selectively cropping the new growth where indigestible compounds are less dense. With the proliferation of vineyards in the southwest Cape, they also turn readily to grapes and vines. Far more likely to be seen,

Reflecting the spring reproductive bloom of many fynbos plants, the bontebok has a birth peak from September to November.

Ecosystem services

Despite its extraordinary species richness, fynbos actually has much less plant biomass (a measure of the living material per unit area) than similar habitats elsewhere on the globe. Additionally, individual fynbos plants are fairly easy-going on water so slopes covered in undisturbed fynbos serve as excellent catchments. Compared with introduced stands of thirsty alien species like gums, wattles and pine trees, fynbos allows up to 50% more water to reach the streams and rivers that serve the human populations on the Cape lowlands. If its aesthetic beauty and unique ecological make-up is not enough to warrant protection, then surely this crucial 'ecosystem service' is.

the bontebok is another fynbos specialist though it can't subsist on the heath itself and seeks out the open plains known as grassy fynbos scattered throughout the scrub. Cape mountain zebras and grey rhebucks are other distinctive mammals and although leopards were once common here, the role of top predator is now largely occupied by the caracal. Mammals aren't especially abundant or diverse in fynbos but reptiles and amphibians are prolific; collectively there are about 30 species found nowhere else.

The boundaries of the Cape Floral Kingdom encompass around 7% of South Africa's area but only a fraction of that is intact fynbos. Some plant species are so restricted in range they grow only on a single mountain; almost certainly, habitat clearing drove others to extinction before they were even described. Cederberg Wilderness, De Hoop NR, Cape Peninsula NP and Table Mountain are fynbos strongholds. ■

Most fynbos reserves have walking trails, which are by far the most rewarding way to explore this habitat.

THE HIGH POINTS

L YING along a colossal crescent that starts in central Namibia and dwindles in western Mozambique, the mountains and hills of Southern Africa rise abruptly from the surrounding jigsaw of savanna, grassland and semidesert. Technically, mountains are too diverse to qualify as a discrete habitat and harbour a number of distinctive vegetation types including high grasslands, montane forests and mountain fynbos (covered elsewhere in this chapter). But whether it's the sometime snow-covered summits of the Drakensberg Range, Namibia's stony Naukluft Massif or the little rock outcrops that dot Botswana's Savute Marsh, mountains and their hilly offshoots host characteristic fauna and flora worth looking for. Heading to the hills (or in some places, even just scanning them with binoculars from the lowlands) promises a few species found nowhere else and at the very least, increases the chances of spotting some more widespread wildlife which is difficult to find in other habitats.

The mountain bastion

The mountainous spine of Southern Africa's highlands (and by far the highest section), the Drakensberg Mountains form a jagged border between South Africa and Lesotho, which the Zulus call 'uQathlamba' – the Battlement of Spears. At its highest point (on Lesotho's Thabana-Ntlenyana – the Little Black Mountain) the range is just under 3500m high, out of reach to most wildlife except for hovering bearded vultures and hardy little ice rats (the highest living mammal in Southern Africa). Slightly lower down and extending along the escarpment from the Cape fold mountains to the Chimanimani highlands in Zimbabwe, black eagles hunt rock dassies, klipspringers and occasionally rock-dwelling reptiles like rock agamas and adders. Leopards and caracals also hunt here and where the rock gives way to grass-covered slopes, they prey on highland antelopes including oribis, mountain reedbucks and elands.

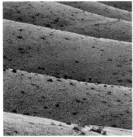

The Bankberg Mountains of South Africa's Eastern Cape province, showing the distinctive 'folds' which give this type of mountain range their name.

Right: The rugged gorges of Chimanimani NP are home to high altitude species like the white-necked raven.

Opposite page: The sandstone cliffs of Golden Gate Highlands NP, South Africa.

Opposite inset: The rock dassie, a ubiquitous resident of all significant rocky areas in the region.

Both rock and grass-covered slopes sustain a liberal scattering of proteas and aloes, attracting sunbirds and sugarbirds as well as baboons, which are equally at home on the steep cliffs, rocky hillsides or grassy slopes. Typical grassland birds like whydahs, warblers, widows and larks are common on the lower slopes and, far more difficult to see, rodents and rodent-hunters like servals and grass owls are also found.

Tablelands and volcanoes

Scattered far from the escarpment and geologically quite different, a few isolated rocky features act like mountain arks for wildlife. Namibia's Naukluft Massif sits on a horizon surrounded by arid gravel plains. Alongside the usual mountain inhabitants – klipspringers, black eagles, baboons and dassies – residents of the gravel plains such as gemsboks and Hartmann's mountain zebras join endemic rock dwellers like Herero chats and Monteiro's hornbills on the plateau in the search for water and food.

A very different plateau straddles the border of northern Malawi and Zambia's easternmost tip. The Nyika Plateau is home to high-living populations of species usually found lower down. Southern reedbucks replace their mountain cousin and the normally shy roan antelope is very conspicuous on the montane grasslands. Leopards, side-striped jackals and, in the high forests, tree civets, are also here.

Not a plateau but a caldera – the rim of a collapsed volcano – Pilanesberg NP has just about everything. In fact, with low-lying valleys, lakes, plains and savannas between concentric rings of rocky hills, it's like a continent in miniature. It provides profitable habitat for characteristic mountain dwellers but because the hills sit in such proximity to other habitats, the mountain ecotone (where it blends with other habitats) is also rich in lowland dwellers. Grazers like zebras, gemsboks, hartebeests and sables move onto the slopes during winter when the low-lying grasslands are spent. Brown hyenas den in the rocks and lions move onto the highpoints to declare territorial rights. You might even see elephants on the red mountains searching under rock fig trees for the ripe, fallen fruits.

The leopard is the top predator of mountain ecosystems, even occurring in the hills above Cape Town and Pretoria.

Border patrol

Although leopards and caracals thrive in mountainous habitat, the most visible top predator hunts on the wing. Killer of klipspringers, hares, monkeys and francolins, the black eagle sits alongside feline hunters at the top of the mountain food web. But, catholic tastes notwithstanding, black eagles mostly kill just two species – rock and yellow-spotted dassies. The most prey-specific of all eagles, its diet throughout Africa comprises at least 90% dassies; in Zimbabwe's Matobo Hills, the figure is 98%. To avoid predation, dassies rely on rocky refuges and if caught in the open, they are almost certainly doomed. This confines dassies to rocky habitats, but where eagles have been wiped out, they range more widely. Minus eagles, dassies can head down onto nearby farms where they raid crops and plunder grazing intended for livestock. Ironically, farmers persecute black eagles because of very occasional lamb-killing but their losses would be far less if the eagles were left to curb dassie wanderings.

Little heads of rock

Like rocky islands, koppies (derived from the Afrikaans for 'little head') can be found in almost any habitat but they provide the greatest contrast, both scenically and biologically, where they jut out of flatlands – the plains, savannas and deserts. Obligate rock-dwellers (those that only live in rocky habitats) like klip-springers, rock dassies and flat lizards occur in little pockets, isolated from one another by the surrounding habitat and only occasionally running the gauntlet to cross to a neighbouring koppie. Rocky recesses provide root-holds for *Euphorbia* trees and rock figs and also give shelter to rodents, rock agamas and snakes. If they're high enough to include a few sheer cliffs, koppies also attract ledge-nesting birds like bald ibises, rock kestrels and rock martins. Invariably, the rock specialists share these outcrops with occasional visitors from the encircling habitat. Lionesses venture into them to give birth and elands and greater kudus move onto the lower slopes to feed. In the past, koppies were equally as important to humans and on a few, the evidence still remains. In the Gubatsa Hills in Chobe NP, rock paintings of elands, sables and other antelopes are thought to have been left by the San people around 4000 years ago. ■

Hosting the highest points in Southern Africa, the Drakensberg Mountains are also among its most scenic.

AQUATICA

Following the summer rains, areas like Namibia's Caprivi Strip and Botswana's Okavango Delta may be accessible only by aircraft and boat.

EVERY habitat relies on water to sustain life. For some Southern African habitats, water is scarce enough that its arrival brings about a transformation and even well-watered habitats here endure a dry season. But for some species, water is a daily feature. Indeed, they depend on a continuous supply and would perish without it. To get a reasonable look at those species that never leave the water, you'll need snorkelling or scuba gear (see the Diving & Snorkelling section in the Wildlife-Watching chapter) but for many watery habitats a boat trip, hired canoe or even a pair of gumboots is all it takes.

Inland

Hugely variable in character and configuration, inland waters include everything from rivers to lakes, marshes and ponds. Surrounding many a wetland or river, water-loving trees like wild figs, fever trees and jackalberries give away the presence of water even before you see it. Trees mean food and shelter, and with water so close, they become a fertile focal point for wildlife congregations. Weaver birds and foam-nest frogs nest in the branches overhanging the water, perhaps as insurance against land-based predators but not enough to deter snakes and genets. Constantly available fruit in sycamore fig trees attracts fruit-eaters on every level: barbets, hornbills and monkeys in the branches; duikers, bushpigs and civets below and even fruit-eating fish and terrapins in the water. Like a floating tree raft, another species, the water fig, provides nest sites for storks and cormorants, and cover for hippos, Nile crocodiles and sitatungas. Elephants even wade in to browse its leaves.

Other water plants from the prolific reed family are generally less palatable but provide perches and 'bolt-holes' for kingfishers, herons and grebes. Marsh mongooses, servals and Nile monitors hunt among them for crabs, frogs, wetland rodents and tiny musk shrews. Waterbucks, lechwes and reedbucks take refuge in the reeds while high above them, African fish eagles find a high waterside perch to wait for barbel (catfish) to venture near the surface and occasionally even take ducks, dabchicks or flamingos.

Right: Nile crocodiles are well-known residents of lakes and rivers. They can be hard to spot, often resting motionless below the water's surface with only their eyes exposed.

Opposite page: The Okavango Delta, Botswana. In summer it's the region's largest waterway.

Opposite inset: The African wild dog, one of many large mammal species which reach high densities in the rich habitat at the edge of major waterways.

The coast

Where the land meets the sea, life has to endure a constant pattern of inundation and evaporation. But the ocean's warm shallow waters ensures a daily delivery of rich planktonic soup to the shore inhabitants. Sparking an entire food web, the plankton supports marine worms, limpets, mussels and crabs which themselves sustain battalions of shorebirds like sand-pipers, greenshanks and stints as well as Cape clawless otters. Coastal fishers like noddies, gulls, terns and jackass penguins vie with fur-seals just offshore and jostle for space on the beach to breed. Their colonies attract the hunters and the scavengers; great white sharks patrol the shallows and beachcombing brown hyenas and jackals look for lost seal pups and carcasses spewed up by the waves. After dark, smaller predators like mongooses, honey badgers and monitor lizards search for the eggs of shorebirds and marine turtles. Female leatherbacks and loggerheads lay their eggs along the east coast and then abandon them to their fate; many will be discovered by the beachcombers long before hatching.

Estuaries

Immutably linked to the coast, some inland waterways also receive a twice-daily deluge of salt water. Known as estuaries, the water here experiences a constant seesaw in salinity levels. This regular mixing of freshwater and saltwater gives rise to a nutrient bounty but also provides constant challenges for wildlife. Water temperature fluctuates enormously and the soup of suspended sediments restricts the penetration of light for photosynthesis and clogs up gills and filter-feeding apparatus. This means that wildlife is constantly moving around, seeking the best balance for their requirements. Flamingos follow the mobile waves of algae and zooplankton, and kingfishers, herons and terns hunt for fish. Nile crocodiles prefer fresh water but make occasional excursions into the estuarine zone and, more unex-pectedly, Zambezi sharks sometimes make the opposite trip.

A few species always stay put in the region between high and low tide. Mangrove trees use tendril-like buttress roots for

The only penguin to nest on the African continent, jackass penguins are unperturbed by people at a few key sites, such as Boulders Beach, South Africa.

The endangered mermaid

Thought to be the inspiration for mariners' tales of mermaids, the dugong is in danger of becoming just as mythical. Living entirely off shallow-water sea grasses, they often browse the same meadow for days, making them vulnerable to human hunters. Despite weighing up to 400kg, they have no defence and once caught, people simply hold them underwater until they drown. Long lived and slow to reproduce, females might not breed until their 15th year and the interval between calves is as long as seven years. Such a slow reproductive rate means that even subsistence hunters probably kill more than are replaced. In the Southern African region, they only occur along the Mozambique coast but the population is now much reduced and fragmented. Probably the best place to see them is the beautiful Bazaruto Archipelago. If you go there, ask the locals if you can see dugongs; you might not succeed but if enough people ask, a local dugong-based economy might ensure their preservation.

support in the erratic muddy floor and a few species grow snorkel-like roots clear of the mud for 'breathing'. Mudskippers, fiddler crabs and mangrove snails shelter among the roots, and emerge at low tide to forage on the algae-coated mud, never straying far from a burrow; jackals, otters, marsh mongooses and aerial predators also move in as the water recedes.

Cape fur-seals, the most common seal species in Southern African waters and the only one likely to be encountered close to the continental shore.

Oceans

Even if you're not a diver, the open ocean can boost your species count. There are more than three dozen species of whale and dolphin here, many of them visible from shore or on short boat trips (see the Dolphin and Whale-Watching special section in the Wildlife-Watching chapter). Likewise, pelagic (sea-going) birds like albatrosses, petrels and shearwaters abound though none of them breed in the region. However, tours to a number of small islands like those off Cape Town and West Coast NP reveal huge breeding colonies of Cape gannets, cormorants, gulls and jackass penguins as well as the most visible great white sharks in the world. The warmer, eastern coastline is home to many easily seen marine attractions including whale sharks by the dozen and nesting sea turtles. Far less likely to be spotted despite its preference for shallow waters, the dugong is now one of the most endangered denizens of Southern African waters. ■

THE HUMAN LANDSCAPE

EVEN in Africa, there are few environments that haven't felt the touch of humans. Indeed, given that our ancestors were here at least five million years ago, bipedal hominids have been an agent of change in Southern Africa for millennia. For most of that time, human modifications to the landscape have been gradual and insignificant, and only in our very recent history have people actively changed habitats on a far-reaching, destructive scale.

Thankfully in today's parks and reserves, the human influence is largely a benevolent one and for a few places like the Central Kalahari and North Luangwa, aside from a few vehicle tracks and scattered camps, they are probably much as they were thousands of years ago. People are more evident in other parks like the carefully managed Kruger or Etosha NPs, but a permanent human presence here is necessary to balance the demands of intense tourism with the fundamental rationale for reserves – that of maintaining diversity in a properly functioning ecosystem. In modern Africa, large reserves simply could not exist without people. Of course, outside protected areas, human impact on habitats has been far greater and damaging, but even where the most abundant species is *Homo sapiens*, wildlife can be surprisingly resilient.

Farmlands

Whether it's for cattle, sheep, wheat or corn, huge areas of natural habitat have been cleared and converted in order to feed Africa's humanity. Farming is relentlessly incompatible with the needs of large mammals so don't expect to spot lions, elephants and rhinos once you depart a park or reserve. But wildlife that doesn't interfere with farming interests is usually left alone and in some cases, may actually be better off than inside reserves. Big carnivores are usually the first to go, which can alleviate the impact of predation on smaller species. Known as 'predator release', it means that species like Cape ground squirrels, meerkats, oribis and steenboks may thrive – they even learn to spend less time looking for danger and more time feeding. In Namibia, where an estimated 95% of the

Many African species are extremely tolerant of human activity so long as they're not persecuted: here, visitors get close-up views of a Cape fur-seal colony.

Right: In South Africa, jackass penguins still come to Boulders Beach to nest, despite encroaching human settlement.

Opposite page: In parts of the Namib Desert, the human footprint is slowly being eroded as people abandon towns to the dunes.

Opposite inset: A number of cities in Southern Africa are close to natural features with wildlife attractions, like Table Mountain near Cape Town.

cheetah population occurs outside conservation areas, predator release helps these fast cats (see the boxed text).

Other predators, particularly raptors, caracals and jackals, benefit from the boom in rodent numbers that inevitably accompanies cultivation. Its an uneasy balance, though, and population increases are often offset by human hunting and poisoning. For larger birds of prey, such persecution may outweigh the benefits and the distribution maps of many eagles and vultures eerily match the pattern of farmlands in reverse. For other birds, the secondary growth that springs up around agriculture creates niches for waxbills, canaries, robins and prinias, and open cultivation itself attracts whydahs, bishops, guineafowl, cranes and korhaans.

Farmlands are hardly a wildlifer's delight, but it's worth keeping your eyes peeled while driving between reserves. There are some stretches through farming country with almost guaranteed sightings of blue cranes, yellow mongooses, hovering black-shouldered kites and long-crested eagles.

Living in the city

Except for very occasional intrusions by dog-hunting leopards, urban environments have little in the way of big game. But for smaller, more generalist species – those able to exploit a wide array of habitats – cities are as profitable as anywhere. Garden birds like hoopoes, bulbuls and barbets are common and markets attract hadeda ibises, pied crows and yellow-billed kites. Large city parks and the grounds of universities sometimes harbour more elusive wildlife like tree squirrels, genets and the slender mongoose. In Durban, vervet monkeys roam the botanic gardens and the Kirstenbosch Botanic Gardens in Cape Town are rich in sunbirds, flycatchers and sugarbirds. Isolated koppies scattered throughout Johannesberg and Pretoria have dassies, rock agamas and kestrels.

Johannesburg, South Africa. Most large cities are fairly barren places to look for wildlife but urban birds and a few mammal species can be spotted.

Cheetahs on farmlands

Namibia is the world's cheetah capital; with an estimated 2000 to 3000 animals, no African country has more. However, only about 5% of them inhabit reserves. The rest live on farms – huge ranches that mostly run domestic stock but are undeveloped enough for thousands of greater kudus, springboks and gemsboks – cheetah prey – still to persist. Cheetahs prefer their natural prey over livestock so they're less likely than other big carnivores to incur the farmer's wrath. Not so the cheetah's natural enemies – lions, leopards and spotted hyenas – which are hunted relentlessly. Ironically, this actually helps the cheetah – in protected areas, other carnivores contribute to cheetah cub mortality rates as high as 95%, but on farms, their absence means many more cheetah cubs survive. Even so, it's an imperfect sanctuary. Cheetahs do occasionally kill calves and farmers retaliate. Also, the wild antelopes on farms belong to the landowner and most stock farmers are also game-farmers; they sell game for restocking elsewhere, for hunting or for the widespread (and legal) game meat market. So, even if cheetahs stick to their normal prey, it might 'belong' to someone else and many hundreds of farmland cheetahs are still killed every year.

Invaders

Wherever people settle, there will always be the exotic animals we brought along for the ride. Whether it's for food, 'sport', companionship or simply to remind us of home, some of them invariably escape and establish free-living or feral populations. With such a rich complement of indigenous wildlife, Southern Africa provides relatively few niches for invaders so the region has suffered far less than many other places. Nonetheless, alongside the ubiquitous house mouse, house rat and feral cat, you may see a few species that are a long way from home.

On Cape Town's Table Mountain, there are around 100 Himalayan tahrs, all descended from a pair that escaped in 1935. Native to India, Nepal and Bhutan, this member of the goat clan has the family's ability to eat almost anything and is denuding the mountain of its natural fynbos. A recent plan to cull them may soon see the mountain returned to the klipspringers. Also in Cape Town and its surrounds, the North American grey squirrel is a very common sight in parks and leafy suburbs, so much so that many locals mistakenly consider it a native. More widely spread is the European fallow deer, the only deer in Southern Africa (see the boxed text 'Where the antelope and the antelope play' in the Savanna section earlier in this chapter) and a fairly common sight on game farms throughout the Cape and Free State. Introduced birds are numerous but most of them – like Indian mynahs, house sparrows and feral pigeons – are commensal with humans and are restricted to urban or rural habitats. ■

Farmland at the base of the Drakensberg Mountains, South Africa: no place for big game but often very good for grassland birds and smaller mammals.

PARKS AND PLACES

*The best wildlife-watching
destinations in Southern Africa*

INTRODUCTION

SOUTHERN Africa has almost 500 different protected areas, ranging from little nature reserves tucked away in city suburbs to some of the finest and largest national parks in the world. Collectively, around 642,000 sq km of Southern Africa enjoys some form of statutory protection – that's a little more than the size of Spain and Portugal combined – and there is also a fair chunk of privately owned land under conservation (see the Parks and reserves section in the Nature in Southern Africa chapter for a description of the different types).

Of course, there are very few of us with the time, money and dedication to attempt to visit every park in the region so this chapter picks out the finest from the hundreds of options. Taken one country at a time, we've selected a range of the very best wildlife-viewing destinations.

National and state parks dominate: not only do the government-run parks represent the largest protected areas and, consequently, the greatest diversity and concentrations of wildlife, but they also rely on gate takings to survive. As clichéd as it sounds, your visitor fees help protect Southern Africa's wildlife.

Where space permits, we've also listed a few of the more exclusive options; these appear at the end of each country account in the Other Sites section, which also details more specialised destinations such as over-wintering wetlands for migratory birds, locations known for sightings of difficult-to-see species and a few sites close enough to major cities for day-trips.

For each featured park, we detail its specific wildlife attractions and show you how to find them. Although nobody can predict exactly where or when a particular species might appear, we provide a few tips that maximise your chances. Regardless of the time of year, the wildlife in Southern Africa is extraordinary, but sightings vary according to season, so details are also included on seasonal events like migrations, breeding periods and birth flushes. Generally, the larger and more diverse the park, the more space is devoted to its description.

Finally, suggested itineraries are included to help planning. Remember, when it comes to wildlife, it is invariably more productive to spend more time at a few sites than vice versa.

Itineraries

One week You could easily spend a week in any of the region's large parks and not get bored (except perhaps the Namib-Naukluft Park, unless you're a true desert-lover and don't mind long spells between wildlife sightings). Kruger, Etosha, Chobe, Hwange and Kafue NPs are all huge – greater size generally translates to greater diversity. Take your time exploring one of these parks, moving between different camps to take in a number of different habitats. Virtually all the large parks have small, usually privately run, reserves on their borders – if you miss a particularly elusive species, the excellent guiding of the private reserves often produces rare sights, even if you only stay a night or two (but they're expensive). Alternatively, devote a week to exploring the reserves of a region, such as South Africa's KwaZulu-Natal (Greater St Lucia Wetland Park, Hluhluwe-Umfolozi GR and Itala GR all have different attractions) or Zimbabwe's eastern boundary (Gonarezhou to the Eastern Highlands).

Two weeks Distance is still against you, but two weeks does allow a lot of ground to be covered. In South Africa, you could drive from Kruger NP south to some of the KwaZulu-Natal sites and then along the coast to take in Addo Elephant NP and a fynbos reserve in the Cape. Or else, also starting at Kruger, head north into Zimbabwe for Hwange and Victoria Falls NPs, stopping off at Matobo NP on the way.

Namibia's excellent roads also make for speedy travel; you could explore much of the west coast (Namib-Naukluft Park and Skeleton Coast NP) then head to Etosha NP. Or, you could team Etosha and perhaps Waterberg Plateau Park with a trip over the South African border into Augrabies Falls NP and Kgalagadi TP. Malawi is small enough to travel its entire length; Liwonde NP followed by Lake Malawi and then put in some solid driving to reach Nyika NP and Vwaza Marsh WR.

Botswana's and Zambia's roads eat up travel time so don't expect to cover as much ground. In Botswana, start at Makgadikgadi and Nxai Pans, before heading out to Moremi and then Chobe; or team Makgadikgadi/Nxai Pans with the Central Kalahari. Alternatively, from Chobe, you could head into Namibia's Caprivi Strip to see Mamili NP and end up in Kaudom GR. In Zambia, stick to the north or south: combine Kafue NP with Lochinvar and Lower Zambezi NPs, or North/South Luangwa NPs with Kasanka NP and Bangweulu Swamps.

Four weeks Probably the ideal duration to really get a sense of the region's diversity. It doesn't really matter how you spend it, but again, don't be tempted to cram in dozens of sites. Rather, use the extra time to get to some different habitats by allocating a few days for some long-distance travel between key sites.

You could start at Hwange (Zimbabwe) heading through Victoria Falls, to Chobe NP and Moremi GR, before heading back north into Namibia's Caprivi Strip to Kaudom GR and Etosha NP. Or begin the other way from Etosha NP heading east into Zambia to take in Kafue and Lochinvar then do some solid driving north to Kasanka and Bangweulu. Depending on time, head east into Malawi or down into Zimbabwe for Mana Pools and Matusadona NPs.

Alternatively, you could start in KwaZulu-Natal, heading down to the Cape then north from Cape Town to Namaqua and Augrabies Falls NPs. Cross the border into Namibia for the Namib-Naukluft and Etosha. Of course, if you can afford the luxury of flights (and dozens of light planes hop between sites every day), you can cover more ground and use less time travelling and more looking for wildlife. However you do it, good luck! ■

SOUTH AFRICA

Highlights

- Feeling the spray from breaching southern right whales off the Cape coast
- Klipspringer lambs play-chasing with their parents among the rocks of the Karoo's Nuweveld Mountains
- Calling narina trogons with taped playback in Zululand's humid sandforest
- Watching a cheetah in a 100km/h sprint after a springbok along the Auob riverbed in the Kalahari
- Swimming among little jackass penguins at Boulders Beach in Cape Peninsula NP
- Tracking black rhinos by foot in KwaZulu-Natal's thorn tree woodlands

Inset: Wild animals and native vegetation can be seen right next to a major city – Cape Town – on the slopes of Table Mountain.

Bushveld paradise

DOMINATED by interwoven mosaics of woodland, savanna and the dry, rocky shrublands known as the Karoo, most of South Africa looks very different from the iconic grasslands many people associate with Africa. Indeed, the largest diversity and density of South African wildlife occurs not on open plains but in the woodlands of the north and east, known locally as bushveld or 'the lowveld'. The country's premier reserve, Kruger NP, protects an expanse of bushveld the size of Israel and is also where the main populations of large mammals occur, including eminently viewable Big Five. One of them, the rhino, owes its existence to South Africa: countrywide, there are more white rhinos here than in the rest of Africa combined; and Kruger protects just under half the continent's black rhino population.

Away from the bushveld, wildlife is thinner on the ground, but a further 19 national parks and countless provincial parks offer a huge variety of wildlife habitats, a few of which shouldn't be missed. The Kalahari Desert experiences seasonal congregations of nomadic herbivores and is also excellent for seeing predators, both mammalian and avian. The far more temperate Drakensberg Mountains are also known for raptors, including the region's only population of bearded vultures. Other Drakensberg specialities include increasingly rare antelopes such as mountain reedbucks, grey rhebucks and oribis. Where the mountains give way to the highveld grasslands and the Karoo, endemic black wildebeests, Cape mountain zebras and dozens of bird rarities can be seen.

South Africa also harbours unique smaller attractions and is the only country on earth to have one of the world's six floral kingdoms entirely within its boundaries. The southwest Cape's fynbos has the highest concentration of plant species on earth, more than two-thirds of which are endemic. Fynbos wildlife is not as diverse, but this is the only place to see bonteboks, Cape grysboks, and six endemic bird species including Cape sugarbirds, orange-breasted sunbirds and protea canaries.

Most significant wildlife populations in South Africa are enclosed behind fences, intended to prevent conflict with the substantial human communities which now abut most parks. But don't let this deter you; many parks are vast and you'll only see fences when you drive through the gates. Rest assured, the animals within are wild and everything from weavers fashioning their intricate nests to a leopard feeding on its tree-cached kill can be spotted. ∎

KRUGER NP

A massive, wild bushveld expanse: Big Five, cheetahs, African wild dogs and dozens of herbivore species; diverse birdlife

GREATER ST LUCIA WP

A vast estuary with fringing woodlands and dune forests; black rhinos, somango monkeys, crocodiles and rich waterbird life

PILANESBERG NP

Sitting inside a collapsed volcano, a mix of arid and bushveld species; elephants, white rhinos and antelopes

KGALAGADI TP

Southern Africa's first 'Peace Park'; rolling red dunes and parched riverbeds with gemsboks, springboks, wildebeests and all their predators

DE HOOP NR

A coastal fynbos strip bordered by high dunes and wetlands; bonteboks, grey rhebucks and blue cranes; southern right whales offshore

KAROO NP

Highveld grasslands, rocky gorges and mountain drives; klipspringers, Cape mountain zebras and black wildebeests; rich in endemic birdlife

Suggested itineraries

One week From Jo'burg head straight to Kruger NP, which could easily occupy a week's exploring. Alternatively, drive east from Cape Town along the coast to take in De Hoop NR (1 night), Tsitsikamma NP (1 night), Addo Elephant NP (3 nights) and Mountain Zebra NP (1 night).

Two weeks Team the Kruger NP option above with KwaZulu-Natal or, KwaZulu-Natal with the Cape reserves (driving Cape Town to Durban or vice versa). Alternatively, from Cape Town head north through Namaqualand to Augrabies Falls NP and then onto Kgalagadi TP (4 nights); return via Karoo NP.

One month From Jo'burg, a month will give you time to explore the two finest reserves, Kruger and Kgalagadi; with Blyde River Canyon NR, Augrabies Falls, Pilanesberg and Tswalu all close enough for side-trips. Otherwise, driving between Jo'burg and Cape Town (or vice versa), head to Kruger (4 nights) then south to St Lucia (2 nights), The Drakensberg (2 nights), Addo (3 nights), Mountain Zebra (2 nights), Tsitsikamma (5 nights for the Otter Trail), De Hoop (2 nights) and Bontebok NP (1 night), then spend a few days in Cape Town exploring Cape Peninsula NP and Kirstenbosch National Botanic Gardens.

KRUGER NATIONAL PARK

The bushveld's bounty

Wildlife highlights

South Africa's richest park with more mammal and bird species than any other in the country. Sightings of the Big Five are frequent and uncommon species often encountered include cheetahs, African wild dogs, roan antelopes, sables and nyalas. Guided night drives are excellent for small carnivores, owls, nightjars and a chance of seeing big cats hunting. Birdlife is prolific.

SOUTH Africa's largest and most diverse reserve is also one of the oldest. Free from persecution for more than a century, the animals are often extremely accepting of vehicles and Kruger offers exceptional opportunities for close-up wildlife-watching. Almost the size of Israel, it has a diversity of species unmatched elsewhere in South Africa, drawing more international tourists than any other destination in the country. Its popularity has led to inevitable development, often criticised by the purists. Kruger has 24 camps and the most extensive road network of any Southern African national park, but don't let this put you off: it is justifiably famous for very regular viewing of the **Big Five** as well as rarer highlights such as **cheetahs** and **African wild dogs**. Most visitors will see 30 mammal species in a three-day visit (particularly if you join one of the excellent guided night drives) and birdlife is prolific with more species recorded here than in any other park in South Africa. For many people, the key to enjoying Kruger is simply to avoid the main roads as far as possible.

Private reserves

Like all reserves in South Africa, Kruger is entirely enclosed, but along its western boundary 100km of fences have been removed to merge with numerous, adjoining privately owned reserves. While the wildlife is the same as Kruger's, the private reserves offer a very up-market wildlife experience in which viewing of the Big Five and other 'specials' is virtually guaranteed. Moreover their 'ethical' standards are generally very high. Unlike Kruger, visitors don't drive themselves and the guided game drives leave the roads, following predators on the hunt or moving in on rare species to have a closer look. The guides (called rangers) work very hard at habituating animals to vehicles so that viewing of normally elusive species such as leopards, cheetahs and African wild dogs is unsurpassed. Such superb sightings come at a price though and a night at one of these luxury lodges can cost 10 times as much as Kruger. The experience, however, is unforgettable.

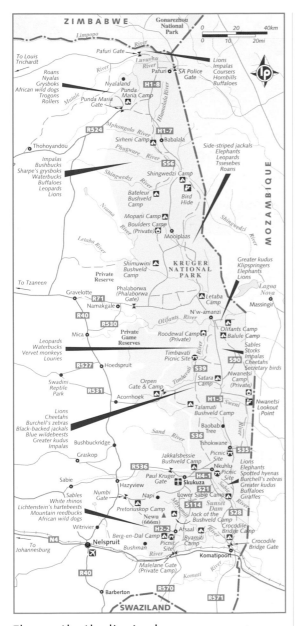

Location Skukuza is 462km east of Pretoria. Sealed roads accessible year-round but Crocodile Bridge Gate can be underwater during the summer.

Facilities 800km of game-viewing roads, hides, Braille Trail at Berg-en-Dal Camp, Elephant Hall at Letaba, Stevenson-Hamilton library/museum at Skukuza, 78 cultural heritage sites through-out the park. Guided day and night drives available at most camps. Skukuza, Berg-en-Dal and Letaba Camps offer specialist 'bush drives'.

Accommodation Camps (24) capable of sleeping close to 6000 people per night. All types of accommodation available at these: guest houses, chalets, bungalows, camping grounds and caravan sites.

Wildlife rhythms During summer many herbivores drop their young and birding is at its richest with the influx of summer migrants, particularly insect-eaters. March through May is the period when impalas, blue wildebeests and warthogs rut and their vulner-ability to predators increases. Visibility is best and wildlife concentrates at water sources during winter (May to October).

Contact SANP (☎ 012-343 1991, fax 343 0905, e reservations@parks-sa.co.za).

The south: the lion's share

Almost all visitors begin exploring Kruger at the southern end of the park (the most accessible section). With the highest rain-fall in the park, the vegetation here can be correspondingly dense, particularly in the rainy months (October to March)

With perhaps as many as 2500 lions, Kruger NP has one of Africa's highest densities of these big cats.

when new growth makes game-viewing difficult. But this is also the best region to look for both **rhino** species, and **elephants** and **lions** are abundant. Base yourself at Lower Sabie Camp for almost assured viewing of lions and their main prey species, **buffaloes**. The Lower Sabie Road (H4-1) heading towards Skukuza is justifiably nicknamed Lion Drive and the thorn thickets lining the eastern side of the road are favoured habitat of **black rhinos** as well as **bushbucks** and **grey duikers**. If you don't find any **lions** yourself, book a guided night drive at Lower Sabie (or any of the major camps) for a chance of seeing lions on the hunt, plus **small carnivores, owls** and **nightjars**.

Giraffes are most common in the south, readily seen along a narrow band of open savanna between Crocodile Bridge Gate and Lower Sabie Camp (take the S28). **Burchell's zebras, blue wildebeests** and **tsessebes** are also common here, especially in the dry winter when migratory herds from further north swell the resident herbivore populations. Rarer species concentrate in the woodlands of Kruger's southeastern corner. The mountain bushveld around Berg-en-Dal Camp is the only place in the park where you can see **mountain reedbucks**. Their slightly larger cousin, the **southern reedbuck**, occurs on the moist grasslands between the hills. Their Zulu name 'Mziki' mimics their distinctive high-pitched alarm whistle: if you hear it, search the hills for **leopards**. **White rhinos** are also common on these grasslands. Along the H2-2 (near Pretoriuskop Camp), chances are very good for **sable antelopes** and for one of the rarest mammals in the park, **Lichtenstein's hartebeest**. Reintroduced from Malawi when Kruger's indigenous population became extinct, this is the only national park in South Africa where you can see them. This area is also known for good **African wild dog** sightings. During peak periods, the main routes can be very busy, so if seeing other cars bothers you, take the less travelled, unsealed roads such as the S114, the S21 and the S128. As an alternative, consider taking a guided day drive: these have access to areas closed to self-drive visitors and the guides are generally excellent.

Central: the wildlife heartland

The geographical centre of the park is also the heart of its best game-viewing and you can be reasonably sure that a few days spent here will be rewarded with sightings of all the **Big Five** (though **rhinos** are scarce: try the S36). Grasslands, which begin as a ribbonlike strip on the southern boundary, fan out here across open basalt plains, providing excellent visibility for spotting numerous grazers and the predators that follow them. Take the main H1-3 road or the gravel S35 and S41 for a good chance of seeing **cheetahs**, rare in the park due to the very high densities of **lions** and **spotted hyenas**. Rich sweetgrass savanna along the road between Satara Camp and Orpen Gate is another excellent area to search for them. You'll see **impalas** by the hundreds (Kruger has more than 100,000) – spend extra time watching them on these open areas, particularly during the rut in April and May. Where there are impalas there are **cheetahs** and **leopards**, and the intense social activity of the breeding season distracts the antelopes from their normal vigilance, making them vulnerable to predators.

Keep a look out on the plains for **red-billed queleas**, which arrive in vast swarms during the summer to nest in stunted thorn tree thickets dotting the savanna (December to April). With as many as 500 nests in a single tree, hundreds of the nestlings fall to ground, attracting **raptors, snakes, monitor**

The greater blue-eared starling is probably the most common starling in the park and a guaranteed camp site visitor.

The view from a bridge over Olifants River. Lookouts over Kruger's many river crossings allow visitors to scan for hippos, crocs and waterbirds.

The northern part of Kruger is the driest section and the sandy riverbeds are often used as animal 'highways'; stop on bridges (where permitted) and spend some time waiting for something to appear.

lizards and small carnivores such as **slender mongooses**. Drive the Old Main Road (S90) between Satara and Olifants Camps – also excellent for **secretary birds, white storks** and plains **antelopes**.

Game-viewing along Kruger's numerous rivers can be excellent and one of the best routes in the entire reserve follows the Timbavati River (the S39). Check large riverine trees for snoozing **leopards** (sometimes a dangling leg or tail gives them away) which cache their kills among the branches to avoid losing kills to other predators. **Elephants, buffaloes** and numerous herbivores are common along the rivercourse and during the winter, wait at Piet Grober Dam for superb views of animals congregating at the water. Early in the morning, **vervet monkeys** and **chacma baboons** warm up on sunlit trees along the rivercourses. In particular, spend some time watching sycamore figs, which fruit all year round: in addition to primates, they attract **tree squirrels**, fruit-eating birds such as **purple-crested louries** and **African green pigeons**, and insect-eaters like **chinspot batises** and various **starlings** drawn to the swarms which feed on the figs. If you miss them on the drive, Letaba Camp is rich in fig trees and their attendant fauna.

Thrill of the unexpected

The Gomondwane Road, south of Lower Sabie Camp, on the dirt track to Crocodile Bridge. Vegetation sparkling after the morning's heavy rain; open grassland, interspersed with small shrubs, and the occasional marula tree. The low hills of the Lebombo Mountains a backdrop to the east. Suddenly, I shout 'stop!' A cheetah, lying against the base of a tree, her mouth open, and definitely short of breath. Then, about 5m away, three young cubs holding onto an impala. We had arrived seconds after a mother cheetah had dragged an impala down for her cubs. The cubs are tugging at the impala, but not getting very far, and have to wait until the mother catches her breath and can walk across to open up the soft underbelly for the youngsters. She shows them how, patiently teaching them important survival skills. A grisly act to watch but we feel privileged to witness a process which has remained unchanged for hundreds of thousands of years.

Rob Slotow, Durban, South Africa

The north: arid refuge for rarities

The northern section is the driest part of the park and game is best along the rivers and at waterholes. Leave the main tarred road (H1-7), which follows the rivers only for brief intervals, and take gravel roads such as the S52 and S56 which explore alluvial plains near Shingwedzi Camp. The north is dominated by mopane trees, a favourite browse of **elephants** and if you haven't already encountered them further south, you will see them here. Baobab trees also become common as you head north, many of them showing the destructive mark of elephants, which gouge out their water-rich bark and inner wood to eat, particularly during the very dry winter.

The aridity of the north makes it less attractive to common herbivores such as **Burchell's zebras** and **blue wildebeests**, which tend to be semi-nomadic or migratory here. This creates a refuge for rarer antelopes including **Lichtenstein's hartebeests** (the only place other than the far southeastern corner where they may be seen), **roan antelopes**, **sables** and **elands**: the area around Bateleur Bushveld Camp is an excellent place to look. This is the best part of the park to search for **nyalas**, particularly along the Luvuvhu River at the very northern tip of Kruger, also renowned for excellent birdwatching: notable specials include **Pel's fishing owls**, **silvery-cheeked hornbills**, **narina trogons**, **broad-billed rollers** and **swallow-tailed bee-eaters**. The mopane shrubveld along the H1-8 between Punda Maria Camp and Pafuri Gate is the only place in South Africa you're likely to see **three-banded coursers**.

The far north area is also well-known for **African wild dogs** which, like the rare herbivores that prosper here, find a retreat from dominant species. **Lions** – their main predator – are fewer, making the north ideal for denning. Termite mounds are worth a second look: dogs use them as dens when they pup during May to July, the only time they are resident in an area for any length of time. If you see them, take lots of photos: Kruger researchers rely heavily on tourist photos to monitor numbers and distribution of wild dogs and run yearly competitions for the most valuable submissions. ■

Expect to see large herds of impalas (below) in Kruger's heartland. Impalas and other herbivores in turn support good populations of predators.

Watching tips

Some terrific views of animals can take place at camps and picnic areas where otherwise shy species have become used to people. At Letaba Camp, for example, very tame bushbucks wander between the chalets and even females with lambs approach to within touching distance (but don't!). Check the disused termite mound at Afsaal picnic area for a very tame colony of dwarf mongooses. Any eating area in the main camps will attract tree squirrels, glossy starlings, hornbills and crested barbets looking for scraps. Dams, viewpoints and picnic spots close to the camps make ideal spots to prolong the afternoon before heading back before gate-closing time. Sunset Dam is only two minutes away from Lower Sabie Camp, and offers excellent close-up viewing and photo opportunities of birds such as kingfishers, African darters and storks. Nwanetsi lookout point overlooking the central plains is less than 2km from Nwanetsi Camp and is one of the best viewsites in Kruger.

HLUHLUWE-UMFOLOZI GAME RESERVE

Royal hunting grounds of the Zulu

ONCE the private hunting grounds of King Shaka Zulu, Hluhluwe-Umfolozi is the largest big game reserve in KwaZulu-Natal and, along with sections of the Greater St Lucia Wetland Park, jointly the oldest park in Africa. The permanent water of the Hluhluwe and the Black and White uMfolozi Rivers combined with an abundance of high quality vegetation sustains large populations of **giraffes**, **blue wildebeests**, **Burchell's zebras**, **impalas**, **nyalas**, **greater kudus** and many other herbivores. Additionally, it's the only reserve in the province with a full complement of the 'Big Six' – **lions**, **leopards**, **elephants**, **buffaloes** and both **rhino** species. While the cats are infrequently seen, Hluhluwe-Umfolozi is an excellent reserve to view elephants, buffaloes and, a species which owes its existence to the park, the **white rhino**.

Rhinos for Africa

Hluhluwe-Umfolozi was set aside with the specific purpose of protecting Africa's tiny relict population of **southern white rhinos**, an action which saved the species from certain extinction. In the sanctuary of this single location, white rhino

Osteophagia

Like this female nyala (inset), many herbivores occasionally gnaw on bones. Known as osteophagia, the behaviour arises among animals whose diets are deficient in phosphorus, calcium or other trace elements. It is particularly prominent where there are sandy soils which, being very permeable, are poor at retaining minerals. As a result, 'sandveld' plants tend to be low in vital elements and herbivores are forced to seek them elsewhere. Winter is the most likely time to observe osteophagia; as plants on poor soils ripen and dry, they translocate minerals to the roots leaving the above-ground foliage with as little as one-tenth the normal level of phosphorus and calcium. Animals resorting to bone-chewing may satisfy their nutritional requirements, but the behaviour carries a high cost. Bones often harbour the bacterium which causes botulism, a disease which results in paralysis of all the muscles and eventual death.

numbers have blossomed; from only 25 at the end of the 19th century, there are now over 9000 in South Africa alone, all of them descended from Hluhluwe-Umfolozi stock. Hluhluwe-Umfolozi itself is home to 1800 – far more than the combined total of all other African countries – and visitors are virtually guaranteed to see some. They are more or less evenly distributed throughout the reserve, favouring low-lying wooded grasslands and 'vleis' (seasonally flooded wetlands) rather than the park's many hills and high points. Among the best spots to look are the chain of grassland waterholes along the main route from Memorial Gate to Hilltops Camp (in the Hluhluwe section).

Elephants and **buffaloes** are also easily seen. Try the Sontuli, Ngolotsha and Okhukho Loops in Umfolozi. The loops follow the course of the Black uMfolozi River, often used as a highway by elephants moving in their regular pattern between Umfolozi and Hluhluwe. The lookout points along the rivers are productive spots to wait for them with binoculars, particularly towards sunset when they are more active: sometimes the main breeding herd of more than 100 animals passes beneath the patient observer. Buffaloes, particularly bulls in small bachelor groups or alone (known in South Africa as 'dagha boys') also use the rivercourses. During the heat of the day, dagha boys take refuge among the reeds and African date palms lining the riverbanks: keep watch for them when driving through river crossings such as those along the Hippo Pools Road (in Hluhluwe) and along the main circular road in Umfolozi.

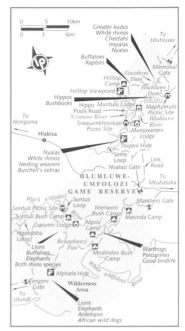

Hides, hills and high places

The dense bush and widespread waterways makes viewing of less conspicuous wildlife more of a challenge. Most of the common herbivores – **giraffes**, **blue wildebeests**, **Burchell's zebras**, **waterbucks**, **impalas**, **nyalas**, **greater kudus** and **warthogs** – can be seen anywhere in the reserve but the hides

Location 247km northwest of Durban. Sealed road accessible year-round.

Facilities 200km of game-viewing roads, guided drives (day and night: book at Park Office), lookout points, hides, self-guided trails, guided day walks.

Accommodation 2–6 person chalets, tented camps, private bush camps, luxury lodges.

Wildlife rhythms Summer is very hot and also the main rainfall period so widespread water and lush bush makes game-viewing difficult. It is, however, when seasonally breeding herbivores such as impalas and blue wildebeests drop their young. June to October is the dry period when animals are generally more visible, particularly at waterpoints.

Contact KZN Wildlife (☎ 0331-845 1000, fax 1001).

The Nzimane River. Hluhluwe-Umfolozi's rivers are popular commuting routes for elephants as well as favoured hide-outs for small bachelor groups of buffaloes.

are probably the most rewarding way to observe them. The dry season (between June and October) when the rivers are low is the best time to invest effort in the hides – assuming they have water (ask staff members at the camp reception desks before setting out). Thiyeni Hide (in Hluhluwe) is probably the best and is situated ideally for early morning photography. It's also a favourite site for **rhinos** to wallow in the mud and take advantage of the scratching post on the opposite bank – two activities which play an important role in controlling ticks and other external parasites. **Warthogs** and **buffaloes** indulge in the same behaviours. It pays to make a brief reconnaissance trip to the waterholes on nearby Seme Loop: if there is plentiful water around, waiting at the hide is far less productive.

Umfolozi is more prone to water shortages than the Hluhluwe section and in very dry periods, Mphafa Hide may be the only water source between the White and Black uMfolozi Rivers. As well as visits from the large browsers and grazers, it sometimes delivers sightings of **lions**, more abundant in Umfolozi than Hluhluwe. Carnivores can survive for long periods without drinking because the body fluids of their prey satisfy their requirements, but most cats will drink daily if water is

Fever trees

Clustered wherever there are well-watered soils (along rivers, around pans and on floodplains) the yellow-barked *Acacia xanthophloea* is better known by its common name, the fever tree. So convinced were early explorers that the tree's powdery, yellow-green bark harboured malaria, that men would cover their faces with handkerchiefs as they passed the trees. In fact, the fever tree's peculiar bark is harmless and its unusual colour arises from photosynthetic pigments rather than pathogens. Even so, it does have an association with malaria, albeit a blameless one. Fever trees grow best in a moist humid environment, the same conditions that the malaria-carrying *Anopheles* mosquito relies on for breeding. So wherever people encountered malaria at its worst, fever trees were typically abundant. Today, except for rare and isolated cases, Hluhluwe-Umfolozi is largely free of malaria but the beautiful fever tree is still widespread.

available. Lions usually drink early in the morning or late in the afternoon but they readily spend the entire day sleeping near waterholes. Look carefully under bushes and trees around waterpoints: sometimes, only the flick of an ear or tail-tip reveals their presence. If you don't see any, book a guided night drive at any of the camps to search for hunting lions, as well as **leopards**, **spotted hyenas**, and small carnivores including **large-spotted genets** and **white-tailed mongooses**.

There are many high points and lookout points in the reserve, another fruitful tactic for spotting wildlife. From the lookout points near Hilltops Camp, you are likely to see **buffalo** herds and enjoy excellent viewing of many raptors, including **jackal buzzards**, **martial eagles**, **crowned eagles** and various **vultures**, which ride the thermals in their search for prey and carcasses. The spotting scope in front of the Hilltops restaurant is well-worth the nominal fee. The lookout points along the Hluhluwe River near Sisuzu are the most likely points to see **hippos** (which only occur in Hluhluwe) and **bushbucks** can be found in the tall reeds along the river banks.

Giraffes have no specific birth season at Hluhluwe-Umfolozi so calves can be spotted year-round.

New additions

African wild dogs are an Umfolozi special, the only protected population in the province. Once reduced to single figures in the region, a reintroduction project initiated in early 1998 is proving to be very hopeful and by the start of 2000 there were three resident packs, all of them successfully breeding. Wild dogs can move enormous distances in a day and only localise their movements when there are young pups in the den. Your best chance of seeing them is to ask of recent sightings at camp reception or else look out for the marked wild dog research vehicle; researchers radiotrack them daily and are happy to provide tips of places to look. They may also have information on **cheetahs**, another species whose numbers have been recently replenished and whose movements are difficult to predict. The open low-lying areas in Hluhluwe near Memorial Gate are good cheetah habitat. ∎

> ### Watching tips
> Mpila Camp (especially around the permanent tents) is renowned for nocturnal visits from Africa's largest rodent, the Cape porcupine. Normally very shy, they are emboldened by attractive smells issuing from the open-air kitchens. Turn off all lights and sit on the open verandahs to listen for the snuffling, foraging sounds that announce their arrival. Living in extended family units, some groups number as many as 14 – view them by soft torchlight. Avoid the Link Road between Hluhluwe and Umfolozi in the early mornings and late afternoons: it's the main thoroughfare for staff vehicles heading to work at the lodges and the traffic tends to frighten off animals.

KGALAGADI TRANSFRONTIER PARK

Bridging boundaries across the Kalahari

Wildlife highlights

Excellent for predators – aerial and terrestrial. Lions, spotted hyenas and brown hyenas are readily sighted, and the Auob riverbed is excellent for cheetahs. Cape foxes, African wild cats and numerous other small carnivores are exceptional. Unparalleled chances to view birds of prey with 52 species of raptor. Impressive summer congregations of antelopes – springboks, blue wildebeests and gemsboks – along the riverbeds.

COMPRISING the Kalahari Gemsbok NP on the South African side and the Gemsbok-Mabuasehube complex in Botswana, this is the first Southern African 'peace park' (see the boxed text 'Transfrontier conservation areas' in the Nature chapter). Most tourism activity happens on the 2WD-friendly South African side but If you have a 4WD and are entirely self-sufficient, visitors can stay on the Botswanan side. Take note though, aside from a newly opened 3-day 4WD wilderness trail (advance bookings essential), there are presently no roads on the Botswanan side except in the Mabuasehube section. Logistical constraints aside, the aridity of the Kalahari forbids intensive human occupation, resulting in one of the most pristine areas in Southern Africa. Excellent visibility and wildlife congregations along the relatively fertile riverbeds provide some of South Africa's most rewarding viewing, and it is a favourite park for wildlife photographers and other visitors seeking moments of action and interaction.

Tsama melons and gemsbok cucumbers

In a land of so little water, two unusual plants provide the inhabitants of the Kalahari with vital moisture. The fruits of the watermelon-like tsama (inset), and the deep-rooted gemsbok cucumber comprise 95% water and are sought out by many Kalahari creatures. Birds such as glossy starlings, grey hornbills and pied crows eat the flesh, as do desert rodents which consume the nutrient-rich seeds. Large herbivores in the Kalahari also eat the fruit and even consume the cucumber's extremely bitter roots in their efforts to gain moisture. When water is particularly scarce, even meat-eaters may resort to frugivory (eating fruit) and hyenas, honey badgers and occasionally, the large cats devour tsamas during the dry winter. Even when eaten, a dead tsama melon can be a source of water. Dried, eaten-out tsama shells act as mini-reservoirs for rainwater – a bounty in a place where puddles seldom form.

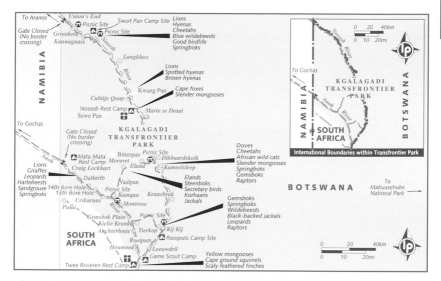

Abundance among the red dunes

Despite its inhospitable appearance, the enduring presence of arid-adapted vegetation ensures there is abundant life. In the central and eastern areas of the park, extensive duinriet grasslands bind the sand, providing a firm foundation for low bushes and ground-hugging shrubs such as the brandy bush and tsama melon. With little available cover, the few large acacia trees scattered among the dune vegetation are worth a closer look. They provide much needed shade for Kalahari animals (look carefully – during the heat of the day, animals usually lie down and are easily missed) and in some cases, also harbour important food sources. Most common of the dune trees, the widely dispersed shepherd's tree with characteristic pale whitish-grey bark bears highly nutritious leaves year-round, attracting **antelopes** which also relish the flowers. Look near the trees for the **eland**, (males weigh up to 900kg), predominantly a browser

Winter mornings in the Kalahari can be subzero, an excellent time to look for predators warming themselves up after a cold night.

Location 920km west of Johannesburg. Entry from South Africa, Namibia or Botswana. Namibian routes involve at least 300km of gravel as does final 60km from South African side but are negotiable by 2WD. All Botswanan routes require 4WD.

Facilities Guided night drives, information centre and photography display at Twee Rivieren, Predator Information Centre at Nossob.

Accommodation Three permanent camps (Twee Rivieren, Mata Mata and Nossob), with a variety of accommodation on the South African side. Botswanan side has four basic camp sites (Two Rivers, Rooiputs, Polentswe and the Game Scout Camp in the Mabuasehube section) with no facilities.

Wildlife rhythms Wildlife congregates in the riverbeds following rain (February to May). December to January marks the birth peak of the springboks, attracting a great variety of predators. This is also the period some small carnivores have their litters.

Contact South Africa: SANP (☎ 012-343 1991, fax 0905). Park Office (☎ 054-561 0021/2/3/4, fax 0026). Botswana: Parks and Reserves Reservations Office (☎ 580 774, fax 775, **e** dwnp@gov.bw). Prior bookings (with relevant country authority) are required.

and able to feed on leaves beyond the reach of other antelopes. Restricted almost exclusively to the dunes and rarely seen in the riverbeds, their herds may number in the thousands where there is a high concentration of browse.

The dunes are most productive for game-viewing from June through to the first rains in February, but the large herds tend to be widely dispersed. During this period, rather than driving long distances, it is often more rewarding to wait at dune waterholes: try Vaalpan, Moravet and Kielie Krankie. The largest Kalahari resident, the **giraffe**, has recently been reintroduced and the small herd appears to have settled around the Craig Lockhart waterhole near Mata Mata Rest Camp.

Life along the riverbeds

Less scenic than the dunes, the two main riverbeds of the park – the Nossob and the Auob – are the real focal points for wildlife-viewing. The rivers rarely flow but deep groundwater allows long-rooted blackthorn trees, raisin bushes and other desert plants to persist year-round. Drivers usually hurtle past them on their way to waterholes, but each is a mini-ecosystem in itself. Small clusters of **pale chanting goshawks**, particularly when perched low on bushes or fallen trees, usually indicate a small hunter on the prowl. Most often it will be a **honey badger**, frequently active during the day, particularly when it is cool. The

---

The spring in springbok

If you spend any time watching springboks, particularly youngsters, you'll probably see them stotting. This is the name given to the stiff-legged, bouncing gait adopted by a number of antelope species, apparently when they spot predators. In the springbok, stotting is raised to spectacular heights in which they arch the back and bounce on all four legs at once in gymnastic 3m-high leaps. Completing the display, they flare the white, erectile dorsal crest known as the 'pronk,' which is why South Africans call the behaviour 'pronking'. Terminology aside, what function does it play? The most commonly cited theory says that stotting signals to a predator that it's been seen and that the stotter is too fit and agile to bother wasting energy trying to catch. But while predators do elicit the display, springboks pronk at almost anything that causes tension or excitement. A wave of pronking often ripples through a springbok herd as it approaches water and young animals pronk repeatedly in exuberant play with one another or perhaps simply to gain bearings on unfamiliar surroundings. Even distant thunder and lightning heralding a brewing storm can be enough to set off a chain reaction of bouncing springboks.

goshawks follow the badger, gathering around as it digs for rodents or reptiles and snapping up anything that escapes the badger's notice. Occasionally the solitary **slender mongoose**, distinctive with its rich ruddy-brown fur and black-tipped tail, attracts the goshawks' opportunistic attention. Aside from the goshawks, the riverbeds are excellent for raptor-viewing, including **bateleur** and **martial eagles**; **secretary birds**; **lanner, red-necked** and **pygmy falcons**; and **white-backed** and **lappet-faced vultures**.

During the rainy season, usually between February and May, a spectacular eruption of flowering and growth in the riverbed plants draws animals in from the surrounding dunes where they spend the dry winter searching for sustenance. Large aggregations of the nomadic antelope species – **springboks, gemsboks, red hartebeests** and **blue wildebeests** – converge on the riverbeds in this season of plenty. Breeding males often remain in the riverbed year-round, defending their territories in anticipation of the arrival of the herds. Contrary to the popular belief that they have been evicted from the herd, this explains why single male springboks, blue wildebeests and red hartebeests are found spaced evenly along the riverbeds, often with no other antelopes in sight. With the arrival of immigrants from the dunes, they attempt to herd females into their patch and mate with any that are receptive, while also driving off challenging males. The 'rut', as it is known, is a period of intense activity sometimes restricted to only one to two weeks. Never predictable, it generally happens following the rains – a rich time to visit.

The giant communal nests of sociable weavers attract numerous predators including gymnogenes, pygmy falcons (which often inhabit the nests), and cobras.

A land of hunters

The bounty of prey species in the riverbeds inevitably attracts their predators, most conspicuously, **lions**. The absence of dense, thorn-ridden vegetation frees their coats of the burrs, scars and knots inflicted on their bushveld cousins and Kalahari lions are often considered the most beautiful of their species. **Leopards** (easily missed unless one looks carefully) use the tangled camelthorns along the riverbeds to cache their kills, while **cheetahs** hunt **springboks** establishing their breeding territories following the rains. Clans of **spotted hyenas** are here – usually seen on early morning visits to waterholes. Their largely solitary cousin, the **brown hyena**, is restricted to Southern Africa's semiarid regions and the Kalahari is one of the best places to see them.

Less obvious predators are easily viewed here also. During early summer, **black-backed jackals, Cape foxes** and **bat-eared foxes** den along the riverbeds, providing excellent opportunities to see newly emerged pups playing outside their sandy retreats. The Kalahari is also a haven for the **African wild cat**. This progenitor of the domestic cat is threatened by interbreeding with its tame cousin, and it is only in very isolated regions where the pure African wild cat persists. Look carefully among the calcite ridges lining the riverbeds (especially along the Nossob near the picnic area south of Dikbaardskolk waterhole): wild cats and other small hunters are readily seen searching the little caves and crannies for prey. ■

Watching tips

Don't be afraid to sit and wait in the Kalahari. In winter, wildlife is drawn to the numerous pans and artificial boreholes (with attendant windmills), particularly the 'sweetwater' waterholes – as opposed to the brackish, less palatable ones. Good places to try include Leeuwdril, Kij Kij, Rooiputs, Union's End, Cubitje Quap, Kwang and Kannaguass in the Nossob, and most windmills in the Auob. Ask at the camp offices which waterholes are active. Smaller attractions abound in the camps. Nossob Rest Camp is one of the best places to see Cape foxes, which hover around the camp ground at night, while ground squirrels will come running at the sound of an opening food packet at all the camps. Twee Rivieren Rest Camp has extremely tame scaly-feathered finches.

PILANESBERG NATIONAL PARK

Life in the volcano

Wildlife highlights

Variety is one of Pilanesberg's great attractions, with a mixture of arid and moist woodland species, including over 20 species of ungulates, all readily viewable. Viewing the Big Five is very productive, though buffaloes are uncommon and mostly inhabit out-of-the-way areas. Cheetahs and African wild dogs have been reintroduced, and brown hyenas are very common. More than 300 species of bird recorded and, like the mammal fauna, they represent a rewarding combination of arid-zone and bushveld species.

THE entire boundary of this national park is formed by the rim of an extinct 1300 million-year-old volcano. Rising 600m above the flat bushveld plains, concentric rings of mountains created when the volcano collapsed inwards provide the setting for one of South Africa's most diverse and accessible reserves. Founded in 1979, the park is the site of one of Africa's largest wildlife restocking efforts – almost 6000 animals were translocated here in a venture called 'Operation Genesis' in the 1970s. The project was highly successful and today Pilanesberg is not only one of the best places in South Africa to see wildlife, it is also a source of animals for capture and translocation to other young reserves.

Where desert and bushveld merge

Lying at the confluence of two major vegetation zones, Pilanesberg's fauna is an unusual combination of the arid-adapted inhabitants typical of Kalahari thornveld and the bushveld species occurring in moist woodland savanna. The wide valleys between the concentric mountains provide excellent vistas for spotting a terrific diversity of species. This is one of the few parks in South Africa where **springboks** (an arid-zone species)

Pachyderms as peacemakers

Like numerous South African reserves re-establishing wildlife, most of Pilanesberg's founding elephants were juveniles when released and they matured without the normal social interactions of complete herds. Lacking the stabilising influence of mature dominant bulls, young males reach sexual maturity prematurely and occasionally display aberrant behaviour misdirected at rhinos. Often the bulls simply associate with them but in at least 40 incidents, they have attacked and killed rhinos. Today, improved drugs and capture techniques enable the translocation of fully grown elephants – impossible when the first introductions were made two decades ago. In a fascinating experiment aiming to establish a normal dominance hierarchy and suppress the young males' unruly behaviour, six huge males captured in Kruger NP were released in 1998. Since the arrival of the 'peace keepers', the rhino-killing has stopped. Keep a special look out for the new males – apart from towering above all other elephants, they have been radiocollared to monitor their progress for the first few years of the experiment.

and **impalas** graze in mixed herds or where **gemsboks, greater kudus, elands** and **sable antelopes** share the gentler hillsides; rockier hills are home to **mountain reedbucks** and **klipspringers**.

In the summer (November to January), low-lying areas in the valleys receive abundant water, giving rise to nutrient-rich 'sweetveld' grasslands which attract many grazing species. Large congregations of **Burchell's zebras** (one of the most abundant ungulates in the park), **blue wildebeests, red harte-beests, tsessebes** and **warthogs** collect in the valleys, particularly in the central area around Mankwe Dam. By winter, these areas tend to be overgrazed and animals disperse onto the hillsides – still easily seen but in smaller, less conspicuous herds.

Location Approximately 110 km northwest of Pretoria. All access routes are tarred, internal roads are tar or well-maintained gravel.

Facilities Over 180km of game-viewing roads, guided night drives, guided and self-guided walks, lookout points, hides, bird aviary at Manyane Complex, sunken hide at water level at Kwa Maritane Lodge.

Accommodation Various chalets, cottages and lodges. Camping ground and caravan site at Manyane and Bakgatla. The Sun City Complex with hotel accommodation for hundreds is located on the southern boundary.

Wildlife rhythms Between September to November, a flush of new growth following annual burning produces excellent game-viewing in the open areas. Over summer (November to January) the grass is longer but many herbivores drop their young and the birding is excellent with arrival of many migratory bird species.

Contact Bookings Office (☎ 014-555 5351/2/3/4/5/6/7, fax 5525).

Mankwe Dam, in the centre of Pilanesberg, guarantees hippos as well as dozens of waterbird species.

From bishops to bustards

Pilanesberg's range of environments also provides suitable habitat for a diverse bird fauna. The world's heaviest flying bird, the **kori bustard**, shares the grasslands with **ostriches**, **secretary birds** and many smaller species such as three species of **whydahs** (**pin-tailed**, **shaft-tailed** and **paradise**) and the similar looking but not closely related **long-tailed** and **red-collared widows**. **Lesser masked weavers** and vivid **golden** and **red bishops** inhabit vleis (seasonally flooded wetlands) while **masked weavers** build their nests in trees overhanging the water (there's a good example of this at Tilodi Dam).

At Mankwe Dam, a hide built out over the water provides viewing of **hippo** pods and **waterbucks**, and sightings of **waterbirds** are excellent. A dozen species of the **heron** and **egret** family have been recorded here as well as ubiquitous **African fish eagles**, **hamerkops**, **white-faced ducks** and **Egyptian geese**. **Pied, giant**, and **pygmy kingfishers** also occur and if you're very early in the morning, you might see **Cape clawless otters** from the hide. Other notable birds among the 300-odd species total include four species of **francolins**, (Natal, Swainson's, **crested** and **coqui**), all readily seen along the roadside, and **blue cranes**, **chinspot batises**, **pearl-spotted owls** and **Kalahari robins**.

Night sights

Pilanesberg's guided night drives provide excellent chances of observing nocturnal predators on the prowl. To spot them, the rangers will be looking for eyeshine as shown in this lioness (inset). Eyeshine is created by a reflective layer of cells called the tapetum lucidum which rebounds 'missed' light to the retina for a second grab at imaging. Many diurnal species, including most antelopes, have a tapetum layer (don't be fooled by eyeshine alone when spotlighting!) but it's best developed in night-time hunters like the cats which have as many as 15 layers of the mirrored, tapetal cells. No-one has tested exactly how effective it is in wild species but the humble domestic cat can see six times better in darkness than people.

Even more basic than the reflective refinement of the tapetum, good night vision requires rhodopsin or 'visual purple,' a light-sensitive compound produced with vitamin A. But the best source of vitamin A is in plants and tubers like yams, beyond the dietary reach of most meat-eaters. So they rely on herbivores to process vitamin A into conveniently accessible packages stored in the liver, lungs and other tissues. By doing so, the prey unintentionally equips the predator with its nocturnal advantage.

Dangerous liaisons

Really big game is easily spotted; aside from the large parks of KwaZulu-Natal, Pilanesberg is one of the finest places to view both **rhino** species. The largely solitary and retiring **black rhino** is the more difficult to find, favouring gully thickets (dense forests growing where two hillsides meet) and the thick vegetation along the base of the hills during the day. They are readily seen in more open habitat at night – book a guided night drive. The more common **white rhino** is abundant here and it is not unusual to see upwards of 20 in a single day, particularly if you spend an entire day driving during the mild winter when they are more active on the open grasslands.

Elephants are a common sight anywhere in the park; stop at the lookout points (particularly along Lenong View) with some good binoculars, and scan the wooded savannas if you don't encounter them while driving. Pilanesberg is unusual in that some male elephants occasionally form associations with rhinos – extraordinary to observe but apparently the undesirable result of the historical translocations.

New blood and night drives

Large carnivores are well represented at Pilanesberg, though some are very recent arrivals. **Lions** reintroduced from Namibia's Etosha NP have only been resident since 1994 but have thrived since their re-establishment. The pride territories meet around the game-rich central region; check the large dams (Mankwe, Makorwane, Lengau, Malatse and Batlako) especially during the dry months (April to October). Rangers post recent sightings at the Manyane Gate and Pilanesberg Centre, and in the early morning territorial roars can help pinpoint their location. Far less vocal, **leopards** are abundant at Pilanesberg. The red rocks at the junction of Mankwe Way and Kubu Drive produce the most consistent sightings – stop and scan with binoculars. They can be difficult to spot during the day, but night drives (available at all camps) see them frequently and another nocturnal predator, the **brown hyena**, is virtually guaranteed. Brown hyenas also regularly visit the Scavenger Hide at Mothata and there has been an active den in the rocky hillside along Ntshwe Drive for a number of years. Another hyena species, the entirely insectivorous **aardwolf**, is often seen among the clustered termitaria (termite mounds) near the junction of Nkakane and Tshepe Drives and along Mankwe Way.

Night drives reveal other rarely seen species. **Lesser bushbabies** perform extraordinary acrobatics on the tips of thorn trees in their efforts to capture insect prey. They readily hunt moths and other insects attracted to the glow of spotlights but rarely sit still for long: branch tips, while good for hunting, are exposed and they risk attack from **spotted eagle owls** and two **genet** species, the **large-spotted** and **small-spotted** (distinguishable by their tail tips, which are black and white respectively). **Cape porcupines**, the largest rodent in Africa are frequently seen and stocky **Jameson's red rock rabbits**, rarely spotted elsewhere, are common in the rocks along the road up to the Fish Eagle picnic area overlooking Mankwe Dam. ■

> ### Watching tips
> Stop every so often and scan the rocky hillsides with binoculars, particularly along Nkakane and Dithabaneng Drives. Lions use high points to search the valleys for prey and leopards are most often seen in the hills. Other inhabitants of rocky hills including caracals, klipspringers and black eagles, are very easily missed unless you spend a bit of extra time searching. Fascinating research projects on lions, rhinos, African wild dogs, cheetahs and elephants are conducted at Pilanesberg. Look for the research vehicles with distinctive 'Ecological Monitoring' stickers and ask the researchers for information; they are very approachable and a great source of recent sightings.

ADDO ELEPHANT NATIONAL PARK

Last stand of the Cape elephants

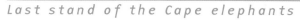

Wildlife highlights
Viewing of elephants at close quarters virtually guaranteed. Ostriches, secretary birds, Burchell's zebras, red hartebeests and tame meerkats are easily seen while black rhinos and buffaloes occur but are shy. Bushbucks, yellow and small grey mongooses and many unusual reptiles, including Southern dwarf chameleons and the endemic Tasman's girdled lizard occur here. The best place in Africa to view unique flightless dung beetles.

A S its name suggests, **elephants** are the great attraction of this park, home of the last remaining population in the Eastern Cape. Largely devoid of tall trees, Addo's low-canopy forest of thornbush and succulent shrubs affords excellent viewing prospects for the park's namesake as they browse on densely clustered spekboom – the dominant plant and the elephants' main food source. Although the reserve now includes the separate Zuurberg section (on the other side of the railway), there are no public roads there and the best game-viewing – particularly of elephants – is in Addo proper.

Sanctuary for mega-herbivores

Originating from only 11 animals – the survivors of intense persecution by ivory hunters and farmers – the **elephants** here can probably recognise every other individual in the population, creating remarkable opportunities to observe social interactions at key points. In the summer waterholes (especially Hapoor Dam) attract family after family, which meet in a kind of social 'congress' and take their turn at the water. From near-extinction earlier this century, there are now more than 270 elephants in Addo, making it one of the densest populations in South Africa: on a hot afternoon, you could easily see half the entire population in two to three hours at the pans.

Rolling in it

Once widespread in South Africa, the unique flightless dung beetle or scarab (*Circellium bacchus*) is now restricted to a few scattered populations in the Eastern Cape, the largest at Addo. The only scarab that has lost the power of flight, it thrives in Addo, which lacks flying competitors. They eat mainly elephant dung but prefer the more pliable droppings of buffaloes for 'brood balls'. The female constructs and rolls the ball (with the male following) to a suitable site where it is buried and subterranean mating follows. A single egg is laid and following hatching, the larva feeds in the dungball for four months until it emerges as an adult. Elephants readily walk along the roads and drop large deposits of dung – irresistible to the beetles. Flightless dung beetles are endangered and one of their main enemies is man – in cars! Please heed the signs and avoid driving over beetles or the dung which may harbour dozens of them.

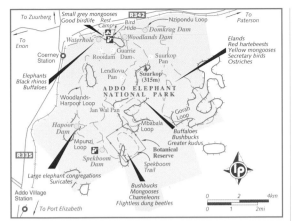

Map labels:
To Zuurberg — Small grey mongooses, Good birdlife
R342 — Rest Camp
Bird Hide — Domkrag Dam
Nzipondu Loop
To Paterson
To Enon
Coerney Station
Waterhole — Woodlands Dam
Guarrie Dam — Rooidam Dam — Suurkop Pan
Elands, Red hartebeests, Yellow mongooses, Secretary birds, Ostriches
Elephants, Black rhinos, Buffaloes
Lendlovu Pan
Suurkop (315m)
ADDO ELEPHANT NATIONAL PARK
Woodlands-Harpoor Loop
Jan Wal Pan
Gorah Loop
Hapoor Dam
Mbabala Loop
Buffaloes, Bushbucks, Greater kudus
Mpunzi Loop
Botanical Reserve
R335
Spekboom Dam
Spekboom Trail
Large elephant congregations, Suricates
Bushbucks, Mongooses, Chameleons, Flightless dung beetles
Addo Village Station
To Port Elizabeth
0 2 4km
0 1 2mi

Other Cape mammals reduced to relict populations find refuge here. The **buffalo** is usually a grazer, but in the spekboomveld thicket it survives largely by browsing the thick bush. Unlike the huge herds seen on open plains elsewhere, Addo buffaloes form small, matriarchal family groups periodically joined by the largely solitary males. Look out for nocturnal visits of these unusual social groups at the spotlit waterhole near the main reception complex at the rest camp. This is also a good site for watching endangered **black rhinos**. Originally reintroduced from Kenya in the 1960s, modern genetic analysis revealed them to be a distinct subspecies and the population is gradually being replaced with Namibian rhinos – genetically identical to the 'Cape' rhino originally inhabiting this area until the last one was shot in 1853. Other mammals to look out for are the very tame **meerkats** easily seen along the Woodlands-Harpoor Loop. The Gorah Loop grasslands are scenically dull but home to **Burchell's zebras, elands, red hartebeests, bat-eared foxes** and **black-backed jackals** as well as **ostriches, secretary birds,** and South Africa's national bird, the endangered **blue crane**.

Addo's dense, hedge-like bush includes over 500 species of plant, best experienced on the Spekboom Trail. Established as a botanical reserve, the trail was fenced off from elephants, rhinos and buffaloes in the 1950s. Freed from browsing pressure for over 40 years, the vegetation here looks quite different to the rest of the park. The walk also reveals some smaller residents, easily missed when driving. Look out for the **flightless dung beetle** and giant **golden orb-web spiders**, whose unruly webs span the bush paths in the early morning – the female spider is 10 times the size of the male and most likely to be seen. Addo is rich in tortoises and while the 15 to 20kg **leopard tortoise** is readily seen from vehicles, check the herbaceous ground-cover for less conspicuous **angulate tortoises** and the tiny **parrot-beaked tortoise**. At head height, the canopy shelters other secretive reptiles including **southern dwarf chameleons** and endemic **Tasman's girdled lizards**. Walk quietly to improve your chances of encountering **yellow** and **small grey mongooses** and elusive, small antelopes including **bushbucks** and **grey duikers**. ∎

Location 72km northeast of Port Elizabeth. Sealed road accessible year-round. Internal roads are well-maintained gravel.

Facilities 75km of game-viewing roads, lookout points, hide at Spekboom waterhole, 12km walk in botanical reserve, waterhole (spotlit at night) and birdwatching hide at reception building. Guided night drives (book at Park Office).

Accommodation Variety of 2–6 person huts and cottages, camping ground and caravan site.

Wildlife rhythms The spring flush of flowers (September to November) creates unforgettable scenes of elephants grazing in fields of daisies. Birding is best from September to April when summer migrants arrive.

Contact SANP (☎ 012-343 1991, fax 0905, e reservations@parks-sa.co.za).

Watching tips

Spend time around the main reception complex and waterhole-hide for some excellent birding opportunities. Malachite, black and double-collared sunbirds feed on flowering aloes from May to September while the summer months (November to February) bring breeding Cape weavers and red bishops to the reeds around the pan. Others such as African sedge warblers, malachite kingfishers, spotted-backed weavers and black-crowned night herons are regularly seen at the waterhole.

AUGRABIES FALLS NATIONAL PARK

Place of great calm

THE original human inhabitants of this area, the Khoi people, called the Augrabies Falls 'Akoerabis' (the place of great noise). Applying only to the 56m-high Main Falls themselves, this is a park where silence dominates. The isolation and endless rocky desert environment makes Augrabies one of the most peaceful locations in South Africa and it is worth a visit even just to enjoy the total quiet at Oranjekom or Arrow Point lookouts with their spectacular dawn and dusk views.

Moonscape mammals

Tourism activities in the park centre on the Orange River Gorge – 18km of steep-sided canyons and ravines that can be seen from various lookout points or explored more closely by canoe. Wildlife congregates along the rivercourse though you are more likely to see it from the game-viewing roads which traverse numerous small tributaries on the southern side of the gorge. This area is one of the finest sites in South Africa for viewing **klipspringers**. These stocky little antelopes mate for life, so when you see one it's virtually certain that its mate is nearby. Early mornings, especially when they lamb in spring and early summer (September to January), reveal them to be surprisingly playful.

Augrabies flat lizards

With its spectacular colouring and existing at one of the highest densities recorded for any lizard in the world, the Augrabies flat lizard (*Platysaurus broadleyi*) is impossible to miss. Easily overlooked once their sheer abundance no longer surprises, the apparent lizard chaos at the falls is actually a complex society based on 'dear enemies' and discriminating females. The flamboyant males (inset) establish territories where the black fly (their main food source) emerges from the river in swarms. Territories are fiercely contested but males don't waste energy confronting neighbours who can maintain the status quo – the 'dear enemy'. Instead, they continually repel intrusions by 'floater' males – individuals without a territory. Flashing them with a vivid orange, sometimes yellow, abdomen indicates their dominant status and floaters are wise to retreat or risk being attacked. And the reason territories are so important? Females, of course. They congregate where flies are most abundant, so males with good territories inevitably attract more mates.

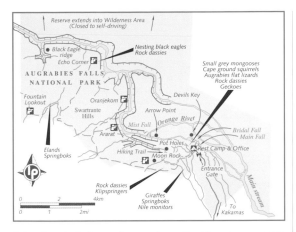

Reserve extends into Wilderness Area
(Closed to self-driving)

Black Eagle
ridge
Echo Corner

Nesting black eagles
Rock dassies

AUGRABIES FALLS
NATIONAL PARK

Small grey mongooses
Cape ground squirrels
Augrabies flat lizards
Rock dassies
Geckoes

Fountain
Lookout

Oranjekom

Devils Key

Swartrante
Hills

Arrow Point

Mist Fall   Orange River

Ararat

Bridal Fall
Main Fall

Elands
Springboks

Hiking Trail

Pot Holes

Moon Rock

Rest Camp & Office

Entrance
Gate

Rock dassies
Klipspringers

Giraffes
Springboks
Nile monitors

To
Kakamas

Main stream

0   2   4km
0   1   2mi

Location 130km west of Upington. Sealed road accessible year-round.
Facilities Game drive network, lookout points, 3-day hiking trails, short walks. Combined canoe/cycling/walking excursions and guided night drives (book at Park Office at the rest camp).
Accommodation 2–4 person chalets, camping ground and caravan site.
Wildlife rhythms The falls are most spectacular following the rains in January to April – also when most plants flower, attracting pollen and nectar eating birds.
Contact Park Office (☎ 054-451 0050/1/2, fax 0053) or SANP (☎ 012-343 1991, fax 0905, e reservations@parks-sa.co.za).

Pale-winged starlings often perch on the klipspringers, using their long beaks to probe ears and under tails for ticks.

Springboks, **ostriches** and **giraffes** (the latter is recently re-introduced) are also frequently seen along the roadside close to the rest camp and create some unique photo opportunities against the moonscape-like backdrop. Take the drive over the scorched-looking Swartrante Hills to Echo Corner and Fountain Lookout for a chance to see **elands** and **gemsboks**. Augrabies is also home to the 'desert' **black rhino**, largest of the four black rhino subspecies and adapted for extreme aridity.

The main viewing area around Main Falls offers smaller but no less rewarding attractions. It's worth spending an hour or two at the numerous **rock dassie** colonies on the paths between the reception complex and the Main Falls. **Small grey mongooses** hunt among the reeds here, subsisting largely on small rodents such as **striped mice**, seen darting across the paths. However, they also make regular forays into the dassie colonies, presumably looking for unguarded youngsters born around December. Adult dassies, however, are vigorous defenders of their offspring and have modified incisors which act as defensive tusks – more than a match for any mongoose. If discovered in the colony, dassies band together and chase mongooses furiously, an extraordinary scene sometimes played out in front of the main restaurant.

In winter, the bright yellow flowers of the quiver tree (kokerboom) attract a rich variety of birds including **lesser double-collared sunbirds**, **dusky sunbirds** and **scimitar-billed woodhoopoes**. Also in and around the camp, Augrabies' reptile fauna is best seen during the short self-guided walks. Apart from very conspicuous **Augrabies flat lizards**, most species are shy but walkers occasionally encounter **sand snakes** and **black-necked spitting cobras**. **Puff adders**, **horned adders** and **Cape cobras** may also be seen, particularly on cold mornings when they are sluggish and sun themselves on the rocks. The short Dassie Trail between the rest camp and Moon Rock crosses numerous reed-lined streams where **Nile monitors** up to 2m long are sometimes seen. ■

Rivalled only by Karoo NP, Augrabies Falls is Southern Africa's klipspringer capital.

Watching tips

The gorge near Echo Lookout has had a resident pair of black eagles nesting for some years. They are readily seen if you wait patiently at the lookout. The breeding season (April to June) is particularly rewarding as they make frequent passes at eye level carrying nesting materials. Check the camping ground shower blocks at night for a giant of the gecko family – Bibron's thick-toed gecko.

GREATER ST LUCIA WETLAND PARK

A wetland mosaic

> ### Wildlife highlights
> Excellent for shy sand-forest specials including red duikers, samango monkeys, sunis and Tonga red squirrels. Hippos, Nile crocodiles and wetland birds are abundant in the estuary and general birdlife is prolific. Nyalas, warthogs and southern reedbucks are very common and Burchell's zebras, buffaloes and black rhinos can be seen.

ACTUALLY comprising 10 separate protected areas linked to the 60km-long St Lucia estuary, this is one of Southern Africa's most important coastal wetlands. The administrative boundaries are inconsequential to visitors as there are no fences and wildlife moves freely over the entire park. The reserve protects diverse land and water habitats, all interlinked but each with distinctive faunal attractions.

From reed beds to coral reefs

Of the discrete land ecosystems surrounding Lake St Lucia, the richest in wildlife are the Eastern Shores where the highest vegetated dunes in the world tower over adjacent swamp and grassland. The dune forest is home to **Tonga red squirrels** which often reveal their presence by extraordinary tail-flicking displays and trilling contact calls. Occasionally they accompany 'bird parties'. Generally a winter phenomenon, bird parties comprise some local specials: **Knysna louries**, **Woodward's batises**, **puffbacks**, **wattle-eyed** and **blue-mantled flycatchers**, **Natal robins**, **white-eared barbets**, **tambourine doves** and others. **Black rhinos, buffaloes, Burchell's zebras, waterbucks, greater kudus, nyalas, bushbucks, warthogs** and the largest population of **southern reedbucks** in Southern Africa also occur on the Eastern Shores. The best way to explore is on the Emoyeni Trail, a five-day hike starting at Mission Rocks. Or for those with less time, choose from a series of circular day hikes on the self-guided Mziki Trail.

The yawn chorus

Apart from physiological reasons, hippos use yawns to intimidate one another. Yawning is a ritualised threat which displays the massive recurved canines – capable of inflicting serious damage. Despite living in close social groups, hippos value their own small 'personal space' and constantly yawn and grunt at one another to maintain it. If the yawning display is ignored, the conflict may escalate and it occasionally ends in death, particularly when territorial bulls fight. They also yawn at other threats, humans included. Hippos at St Lucia are very used to the high amount of water traffic and rarely pay much attention to boats. However, when they emerge to feed along the obvious paths surrounding the Lake, they are extremely dangerous. Short-sighted and nervous on land, they are quick to attack and their massive jaws are quite capable of biting a human in two. If you find yourself the recipient of a hippo yawn, retreat!

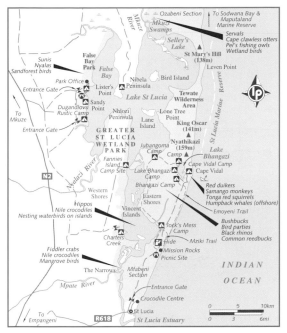

To Sodwana Bay &
Maputaland
Marine Reserve

Location 245km north of Durban. Sealed road accessible year-round: beware of hippos on the R618 tar road after dark.

Facilities Game-viewing roads, guided ferry trips, turtle drives, lookout points, 5-day self-guided hiking trails, many short walks, Crocodile Centre.

Accommodation Numerous camps within the park offering a full range of huts, cottages, camping grounds and caravan sites.

Wildlife rhythms Late spring through summer (October to March) is best for humpback whales, whale sharks and nesting turtles.

Contact KZN Wildlife (☎ 0331-845 1000, fax 1001).

Only 15km away, the Western Shores of the lake receive less than half the rainfall, so the vegetation is dominated by dry woodlands and savannas. Wildlife is not as prolific but it's easier to see. Patches of sandforest are sanctuary to **Neergaard's sunbirds**, **African broadbills**, **green coucals** and at least 111 species of **butterfly**, possibly more than any other reserve of its size in Southern Africa. **Sunis** and **red duikers** are common and frequently seen around the camp sites at False Bay Park – also where **nyalas** were first described to science over 150 years ago.

Lake St Lucia itself is home to 800 **hippos** and at least 1000 **Nile crocodiles** over 1m long, most of them congregating in The Narrows and along the eastern shore of the estuary. You can hire boats in St Lucia town or else join a guided launch with KZN Wildlife. The launch is also the best way to view St Lucia's abundant birdlife including **black egrets** (with their 'canopying' feeding display), **black-crowned night herons**, **goliath herons**, **woolly-necked storks**, **African fish eagles**, **greater flamingos**, **African spoonbills** and **eastern white pelicans**.

The estuary is linked to the offshore St Lucia Marine Reserve which, with the adjoining Maputaland MR, forms the largest coastal reserve in Africa. The reefs here offer spectacular diving, best experienced at Sodwana Bay. Apart from the profusion of vibrant **reef fishes** and abundant **coral**, the warm water also attracts **humpback whales** and **whale sharks**. Sodwana Bay is also a key nesting site for **loggerhead** and **leatherback turtles**. On night drives, **honey badgers** and **side-striped jackals** are sometimes seen raiding their nests. ■

Watching tips
The camp ground and cabins at Cape Vidal are excellent for viewing samango monkeys; they often enter huts looking for food (even while people are inside), so lock up. Similarly, the camp site at Sodwana Bay attracts very tame troops of banded mongooses looking for handouts. Just north of St Lucia town on the road to Cape Vidal, the Crocodile Centre has detailed information and feeding displays of St Lucia's top predator – it's worth a look.

ITALA GAME RESERVE

Life under the iron mountain

> **Wildlife highlights**
> Very good for viewing both rhino species. Giraffes, Burchell's zebras, blue wildebeests, impalas, red hartebeests and tsessebes are all common. Local specialities include oribis and, nesting bald ibises and black eagles. Excellent for birdlife with 400 species on record.

EXTREMELY rugged and scenic terrain is Itala's hallmark and its steep mountain roads are the closest two-wheel drivers can come to the feeling one gets from four-wheel driving. It is also an important reserve for high altitude grasslands, which are heavily effected by intensive agriculture and forestry and now survive in a handful of protected areas. Grasslands and mountains alike extend far into the distance here and a pair of binoculars will greatly enhance your chances of spotting wildlife from the numerous lookout points.

The mountain grasslands

Itala's high plains give sanctuary to a rich assemblage of grazers, ranging in size from numerous and easily seen **white rhinos** down to the slender **oribi**. This little orange-brown antelope has disappeared from much of its range where habitat clearing for crops and plantations has destroyed its habitat. Easily alarmed and considered the fastest of the small antelopes, they are not easy to see: scan the grasslands around the airstrip and along Bergvliet Loop with binoculars and watch for its characteristic rocking-horse running motion. Grass fires usually laid towards the end of winter provide new growth which they find irresistible. If you miss them in the park, the small Vryheid Nature Resort near the town of Vryheid (70km to the west) is a good place to look for them.

Tsessebes also occur in Itala, the only population in KwaZulu-Natal and at the extreme southern limit of their range. They spend most of their time on the plains near the airstrip. **Blue wildebeests**, **Burchell's zebras**, **elands**, **red hartebeests** and

Aloes

Favouring rocky soils and abundant on mountainsides, the mountain aloe (*Aloe marlothii*) is an important source of food during Itala's lean winters. Unlike most plants, aloes flower from June to August, producing prodigious amounts of nectar and pollen when other food sources are barren. Vervet monkeys and over 40 species of bird are attracted to the plants – their orange pollen-coated faces bear testament to the aloes' bounty. The Zulu people are well aware of its value during the lean period and, in addition to delighting in the nectar (the orange faces of children will greet you along the road to the park in winter!), they fashion delicate snares of goat-hair tied to the flowers to trap feeding birds. They also pound the dead, dried leaves to make a potent snuff and use the spiny 'trunk' to make kraals for livestock. Aloes are protected from human utilisation in Itala but are well worth watching for visits from other inhabitants.

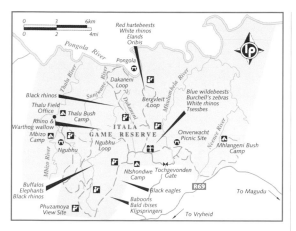

Location 400km north of Durban. Sealed road accessible year-round.
Facilities 80km of game-viewing roads, short 4WD trails, lookout points, self-guided nature trails, waterhole hide, short guided walks, guided day and night drives.
Accomodation 2, 4 and 6 person chalets, luxury lodge, 3 private bush camps and camping ground (no caravans).
Wildlife rhythms High winds are a feature of winter (June to August) driving animals to seek cover and generally be less visible. The warm spring and summer months tend to be more productive and are when most young herbivores are born (November to January).
Contact KZN Wildlife (☎ 0331-845 1000, fax 1001). Park Office (☎ 0388-75239).

southern reedbucks can be seen on the plains and look for pairs of **secretary birds** striding through the long grass in search of snakes, lizards and small rodents. In the early morning, you might be lucky enough to catch **servals** or **African wild cats** out hunting. They readily walk on roads, probably because these are noiseless and improve their chances of hearing rodents and ground birds in the grass. By keeping your speed below 20km/h, you are less likely to happen upon them suddenly and startle them into cover. Also keep a look out for their prey including seven **cisticola** species, **Cape** and **bully canaries** and two **long-claw** species (**orange-throated** and **yellow-throated**).

Providing protection from the frequent winds that buffet the plains, both the high cliffs and wooded valleys of the Ngubhu Basin and Dakaneni Loop can be rewarding for big game watchers. **Elephants** and **buffaloes** favour the watercourses deep in the Basin and are best spotted from the lookout points along the Ngubhu Loop. **Black rhinos** occur here, one of the few species that can safely utilise poisonous candelabra-like *Euphorbia* (candelabra) trees. Look for discarded segments of the cactus-like stems for signs of recent feeding activity: if they are still oozing the toxic, white latex-like sap, it means a black rhino isn't far away. Candelabra trees are prominent near the junction of Ngubhu Loop and the 2WD road to Thalu Bush Camp, along the descent into the Dakaneni Loop and above Ntshondwe Camp. Other inhabitants of the Basin, **greater kudus**, **impalas** and **giraffes** (Itala's emblem) are common among the sweet-thorn woodlands lining the valleys.

High above, the cliffs of the Basin are home to rare **southern bald ibises**. Restricted to a narrow band of montane grasslands in eastern South Africa, they form breeding colonies of up to 100 birds on the safety of steep mountainsides. During July to October look for their untidy, platform-like nests clustered on ledges and in clefts. Also seen on the cliffs, **chacma baboons** make excellent sentries. Their booming alarm bark carries widely in the mountains and usually means one of two things – intrusion by another troop or a sighting of a **leopard** (Itala's top predator is most often seen along the Ngubhu Loop). ■

Poisonous candelabra trees cover the lower cliffs surrounding Ntshondwe Camp.

KAROO NATIONAL PARK

Rock-hoppers and plains game

> **Wildlife highlights**
> A great place for watching klipspringers, which are very tame. Black wildebeests, red hartebeests, springboks and mountain reedbucks are common and the second-largest remaining population of the Cape mountain zebra lives here. Buffaloes and black rhinos also occur but are rarely seen. Birdlife includes over 20 breeding pairs of black eagles and numerous Karoo endemics.

As one of the last protected vestiges of the Great Karoo plains this park is an excellent site for viewing large herbivores that formerly existed here in huge migratory herds. Most of these representative Karoo species can be seen on the grasslands in the southeast of the park (take the Lammertjiesleegte Loop). Mixed herds of **springboks**, **Burchell's zebras**, **red hartebeests**, **elands**, **Cape mountain zebras** (the second largest remaining population) and **black wildebeests** as well as **ostriches** give some idea of the sight that must have greeted early European hunters and explorers – though, sadly, at a much reduced scale. Birdlife, however, is largely undiminished and aside from many species of **raptors** and all three Southern African **bustards** (**kori**, **Stanley's** and **Ludwig's**), it includes Karoo endemics such as the **Karoo korhaan** and **Sclater's** and **Karoo larks**.

Cliffside ballerinas and aeronauts

For those interested in mammals, the greatest attraction here is the ease of viewing normally timid **klipspringers**. Monogamous and territorial, pairs of these extraordinarily sure-footed antelopes dot the scree slopes of the 150 million-year-old Nuweveld Mountains. Driving along the well-named Klipspringer Pass as it heads to the Middle Plateau of the Nuweveld, watch out for them browsing the scrubby anchor Karoo bushes and young

The riverine rabbit

Alternatively classified by early naturalists as a hare (due mostly to its prominent, elongated ears) or a rabbit, modern genetic analysis confirms the riverine rabbit is a true rabbit and also one of South Africa's most endangered mammals. Never widespread (it has always been restricted to the central Karoo region), the species has lost over half its original range to farming and now numbers less than 1500. Breeding projects have reintroduced the species to Karoo NP, the only protected area open to the public where it can be seen. Just as important, projects outside the park with local farmers are fostering awareness of the species' rarity and pride in those property owners with rabbits on their farms.

sweet-thorn trees. Although unusually tame here, they have a habit of freezing as cars approach and are easily missed, so drive slowly. Small family groups of **mountain reedbucks** also occur; however, they are not nearly as confiding as klipspringers and often only announce their presence with a shrill alarm whistle and by flashing the white underside of their tail – a danger signal which, if you're very fortunate, might reveal the presence of a hunting **caracal**.

Raptors are often seen up on the Middle Plateau and the gorge beneath the Rooivalle Lookout is frequently occupied by **black eagles** using the ravine currents to hunt their main prey species, the **rock dassie**. **Peregrine falcons**, **lanner falcons** and three species of **kestrels** (**rock**, **greater** and **lesser**) also favour the rocky cliffsides as do **rock martins**, cruising effortlessly at 80km/h in the canyon below as they search for insect prey. They are often seen flying in

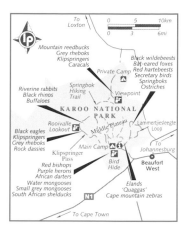

mixed flocks with members of the similar but separate swift family. Five species – **European**, **black**, **white-rumped**, **little** and **alpine swifts** – inhabit the gorge. Book a 4WD trail at the reception office (Rest Camp) to venture further onto Middle Plateau for a chance to see **black rhinos** and **buffaloes**.

Night sights

Even before colonisation by European farmers, large carnivores were never plentiful in the relatively barren Karoo and today, only the adaptable **leopard** still persists here. Guided night drives are well-worth taking for a chance (albeit, very slight) to spot these elusive cats. Smaller hunters, however, are regular sights. On the grasslands **bat-eared foxes** and diminutive **Cape foxes** hunt for small rodents and the seven species of **shrews** and **elephant shrews** that occur here. The endemic **black-footed cat** is a special nocturnal find but you need to be alert to thwart its habit of squatting low in the grass and slinking off when detected. Occasionally, the presence of **owls** perched on low bushes or in the grass gives them away. Owls sometimes follow the cats as they forage, opportunistically taking small birds that the hunters flush from their night-time roosts in the Karoo grass.

Aardwolves, the smallest member of the hyena family, are most abundant where there are congregations of termite mounds; despite their carnivorous ancestry, they subsist entirely upon termites, consuming up to 250,000 each night. Sometimes, they can be spotted trailing another nocturnal termite specialist, the **aardvark**. With their long tubular snout, oversized ears and tapered tail, aardvarks resemble no other mammal and use their prodigous strength and bearlike claws to rip open termite mounds. Aardwolves mop up afterwards, lapping the exposed insects from the soil surface.

Spotlighting is also the only way you're likely to see the most endangered mammal in the park, the **riverine rabbit**. They are entirely nocturnal, solitary and favour the dense riverine scrub lining the Karoo's seasonal rivers – all conspiring to make a sighting a rare and special event. ■

Location 4km southwest of Beaufort West. Sealed road accessible year-round.

Facilities 25km of game-viewing roads, 4WD day trails, guided night drives, birdwatching hide, information centre and two interpretive nature trails including one equipped for wheelchairs and blind visitors.

Accomodation 3 and 6 person chalets, 12 bed huts, camping ground and caravan site.

Wildlife rhythms Spring to early summer (September to December) marks the lambing peak for many Karoo herbivores and is also when most Karoo bushes and plants bear their flowers, attracting birdlife.

Contact SANP (☎ 012-343 1991, e reservations@ parks-sa.co.za). Park Office (☎ 0201-52828/9, fax 51671).

Watching tips

Some of the more wary herbivores spend the daytime in the mountains and only emerge around sunset. Allow a little extra time to make it back to camp before gate-closing and look out for elands, grey rhebucks and Cape mountain zebras in the foothills close to the Rest Camp.

MKUZI GAME RESERVE

The north-south divide

FORMING part of a vast coastal expanse called the Mozambique Plain, Mkuzi lies in a rich transition zone where northern tropical species mix with temperate forms from further south. The park protects the southern fringes of the Makatini Flats, an extensive floodplain formerly home to large numbers of elephants and migratory herbivores making their seasonal movements into Mozambique. Bounded by the Mkuze River in the east and the Lebombo Mountains in the west, a rich blend of habitats including grasslands, acacia woodlands, ancient sand dunes, rivers and pans, and two rare types of forest are home to an equally varied fauna.

Last stand of the tropics

If you imagine the Mozambique Plain 'squeezed' between the Lebombo Mountains and the coast, Mkuzi lies at the narrowest end of the funnel. Suitable habitat for many tropical species is suddenly telescoped down and many tropical species, particularly birds, have their southernmost distribution here. Rare birds you won't see further south include **Jameson's firefinches** (look for them in the foothills of the Lebombos near the Emshopi entrance gate), **purple-banded** and **Neergaard's sunbirds**, **yellow white-eyes**, **Woodward's batises** and **purple rollers**. Some species migrate from Mozambique to breed here including

The fig bounty

One of the rarest forest types in Southern Africa, the sycamore fig forest at Mkuzi is the largest remnant in KwaZulu-Natal and home to hundreds of mammals, birds and insects. The key to its richness is a year-round abundance of fruit. The sycamore produces fruit at least twice a year and different individual trees bear figs in different months. This dependable food supply attracts a tremendous variety of fruit-eating species: in the canopy, vervet monkeys (inset), baboons and tree squirrels compete with African green pigeons, louries and brown-headed parrots for the ripest fruits. Fallen figs are eaten by bushpigs, porcupines and red duikers, and even fish feed on fruits dropping into the Mkuze River. Insects literally infest the figs which, in turn, attract avian and mammalian insect-eaters alike, including paradise and blue-mantled flycatchers, various bats and four-toed elephant shrews, which search for prey among the leaf litter and fallen fruits.

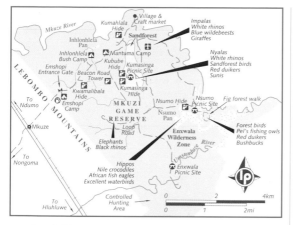

grey-hooded kingfishers, which nest from February to April, and flocks of up to 30 broad-billed rollers which are visible during September until December.

One particularly productive habitat here is sycamore fig forest, a very rare forest type under intense pressure from habitat destruction for farming. The fig trees attract a great variety of species and there is a very rewarding self-guided walk (Fig Forest Walk) you can take to look for them. It begins where the Mkuze River flows into Nsumo Pan (near the Nsumo picnic site) – itself prime habitat for birds including many different herons, ducks, waders, flamingos and a breeding colony of pink-backed pelicans, as well as hippos. The fig trees along the river are home to Pel's fishing owls, African fish eagles and at least five species of kingfisher, which perch on the branches to search for fish, frogs and crustaceans. Crowned eagles, with talons powerful enough to crush a man's arm, hunt in the forest canopy for vervet monkeys, while shy and secretive southern banded snake eagles fly from tree to tree searching for reptile prey. The calls of purple-crested louries, green-spotted doves, trumpeter hornbills and red-billed woodhoopoes (to name just a few) are constant companions during the walk. The lush canopy makes them difficult to spot but their calls assist greatly, particularly if you choose a spot to sit and wait.

Birds aside, Mkuzi is home to a rich community of mammals, best seen from the numerous hides. Between sunrise and midday at Kumasinga Hide is very productive and virtually guarantees sightings of white rhinos, nyalas, red and grey duikers and greater kudus, particularly during the dry winter (June to October). Blue wildebeests, Burchell's zebras, impalas and warthogs are very common and shy bushbucks and sunis also drink at Kumasinga. If you are extremely lucky, the reserve's top predator, the leopard, might come for an early morning drink. Mkuzi is a sanctuary for black rhinos, which outnumber the less threatened white rhino here. They are sometimes seen along the Loop Road and the drive to Enxwala viewpoint, also good sites to search for Mkuzi's small population of reintroduced elephants. ■

Location 309km north of Durban. Sealed roads except final 25km – call ahead after heavy rain.

Facilities 100km of game-viewing roads, hides, Fig Forest Walk, guided night drives, bird walks and game walks (book at Park Office).

Accommodation Various bungalows, cottages and tented camps. Camping ground and caravan site at entrance gate.

Wildlife rhythms Game-viewing from the numerous hides is best between June and October. Game is more widely dispersed during the rainy season (November to February) and is less likely to be seen from the hides (however birdlife is more varied).

Contact KZN Wildlife (☎ 0331-845-1000, fax 0331-845 1001).

Watching tips

The picnic site near Kumasinga Hide offers good viewing of difficult-to-see sandforest birds which look for possible hand-outs. A morning at the hide followed by lunch at the picnic benches can be a very rewarding way to experience sandforest fauna.

DE HOOP NATURE RESERVE

Life at the tip of Africa

Wildlife highlights
Excellent for rare Cape 'specials' including bonteboks, Cape mountain zebras and grey rhebucks. Thirteen species of marine mammal, including the southern right whale. 260 bird species, including African black oystercatchers and blue cranes.

Location 50km east of Bredasdorp.
Facilities Game-viewing roads, education centres, mountain biking trails (book ahead), coastal and wetland walking trails.
Accommodation 4 person cottages (supply own bedding), camping ground and caravan site.
Wildlife rhythms Most southern right whale calves are born in August, also the wettest and windiest month.
Contact Park (☎ 028-542 1126, **e** dehoopinfo@sdm.dorea.co.za).

Watching tips
This region is home to the greatest numbers of endangered blue cranes in the world. If you don't see any on the grasslands near Potberg Centre, look for them on the agricultural lands just outside the park boundaries.

AT first glance, the heathlike fynbos of the Southwest Cape appears rather drab but this region has the highest concentration of plant species in the world, many of which are found nowhere else on earth. Under tremendous pressure from surrounding agriculture, there are few intact stands of this diverse floral kingdom remaining. De Hoop protects one of the largest and gives sanctuary to a unique community of coastal wildlife.

With its very high tannin content and tough texture, fynbos is unpalatable to many antelopes but a few species thrive here. The largest remaining population of **bonteboks** inhabits the grass-covered plains running from the limestone hills at the entrance gate to the coastline. Once reduced to only 17 individuals, all bonteboks in the world originate from the nearby Bontebok NP (only 60km from De Hoop, it's well worth a day-trip) and re-introduced populations are ensuring the species' survival. Another rare antelope, the **grey rhebuck**, occurs at De Hoop – one of the few reserves where these normally shy South African endemics are visible. The waterhole on the road to the office is an excellent place to wait for other plains game, including **elands**, **greater kudus**, **ostriches** and endangered **Cape mountain zebras**.

With 40km of coastline, an offshore marine reserve and a major wetland, De Hoop also protects a very different fauna to that seen on the coastal plain. **Southern right whales** swim inshore during July to October when they arrive to give birth and to mate – Cape Infanta at the eastern end of De Hoop is one of the most important calving grounds. Small family groups of **Bryde's whales** are a special sight, sometimes surrounded by **common** and **bottlenose dolphins**. The permanent wetland De Hoop Vlei attracts over 100 species of **waterbird** – take the 5km Vlei Walking Trail and binoculars to view rare **African black oystercatchers**. ■

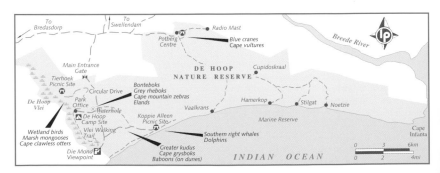

THE DRAKENSBERG

Along the dragon's back

KNOWN for superb mountain scenery, the Drakensberg Range (called 'The Drakensberg' in South Africa) is essentially a scenic and recreation reserve. Hundreds of trails and climbs traverse the mountains and only the Golden Gate Highlands NP (and adjoining Qwa-Qwa Highlands NP) in the northern Drakensberg has a road network where visitors can view **black wildebeests, Burchell's zebras, blesboks, elands** and **mountain reedbucks** by car. The Drakensberg's wildlife is not prolific but aside from the magnificent setting, there are some special attractions making a visit worthwhile. Throughout the mountains, there are a few sites where bones are set out to provision one of Southern Africa's rarest raptors, the **bearded vulture** (or lammergeier). At Giant's Castle GR, visitors can hike from the Main Camp to a specially constructed stone hide (booking is essential), one of the few places in the world where sightings of lammergeiers are almost certain. Nearly always accompanied by scavengers such as **house crows** and **white-necked ravens**, these unusual-looking birds also have an unusual feeding strategy: they drop bones onto a favourite rock (called an ossuary) until they shatter and the birds can reach the marrow inside. **Cape vultures, black eagles, yellow-billed kites** and **jackal buzzards** are also regular diners at the 'vulture restaurant'. Golden Gate Highlands NP also has a vulture hide, about 2km from Brandwag Camp, where raptors (mostly Cape vultures but also some lammergeiers) may congregate in the hundreds.

Arguably in the most beautiful section of the 'Berg, the Tugela River walks in the Royal Natal NP pass through grasslands and forested gorges where **mountain reedbucks, oribis, pin-tailed whydahs, Gurney's sugarbirds** and many species of **widows, cisticolas, pipits, warblers** and **larks** are readily seen. In the summer, look out for **puffadders** and **Berg adders** sunning themselves on the paths. Both species are very placid and bite only if highly provoked (such as when trodden on!). At Tendele and Mahai Camps, **chacma baboons, grey duikers, helmeted guineafowl,** and **red** and **golden bishops** are common visitors. Main Camp in Giant's Castle has regular visits from very tame **large-spotted genets**. ∎

Wildlife highlights

Reliable site for viewing bearded vultures. Mountain reedbucks and oribis are two uncommon species seen fairly often. Chats, cisticolas, warblers, pipits and raptors well represented.

Location Golden Gate and Qwa-Qwa Highlands NPs: 330km south of Johannesburg. Royal Natal: 270km north of Durban. Giant's Castle: 190km north of Durban.

Facilities Bearded vulture viewing hides, game-viewing roads and hiking trails.

Accommodation A great variety.

Wildlife rhythms Summer (December to March) is best for birdlife. In winter (June to August), game concentrates on the lower slopes. The vulture restaurant at Giant's Castle is only open on weekends from May to September (book far in advance).

Contact Golden Gate: SANP (☎ 012-343 1991). Qwa-Qwa: Ecotourism Officer, Agri-Eco (☎ 058-713 4444). Giant's Castle and Royal Natal NPs: KZN Wildlife (reservations: ☎ 0331-845 1000).

Watching tips

At Golden Gate Highlands NP, the eastern loop road encompasses the home range of a female African wild cat.

MOUNTAIN ZEBRA NATIONAL PARK

The zebras' arena

Wildlife highlights
The best reserve in which to see Cape mountain zebras. Excellent for red hartebeests, springboks, black wildebeests and ostriches. Visible predators include bat-eared foxes, four mongoose species and occasionally caracals. Bird highlights include black eagles, blue cranes and many small grassland species.

Location 280km north of Port Elizabeth.
Facilities 42.5km of game-viewing roads; also lookout points and walking trails. Horse-riding trail and 3-day hiking trail (book at Park Office).
Accommodation 4 and 6 person chalets, camping ground and caravan site.
Wildlife rhythms Most Cape mountain zebra foals are born between October and March. Mares with newborns are extremely protective of their offspring, leading to intense social activity in the herd during the birth season.
Contact SANP (☎ 012-343 1991, fax 0905, e reservations@parks-sa.co.za). Park Office (☎ 0481-2427/86, fax 3943).

Watching tips
White-browed sparrow-weavers, pale-winged starlings and fiscal shrikes are virtually guaranteed visitors to the chalets if you take meals on the verandah.

L IKE many parks of the Cape Province, this reserve was established as a sanctuary for an endangered endemic mammal (after which the reserve is named). The surrounding slopes of the Bankberg Mountains create a natural amphitheatre in which to view the largest remaining population of the **Cape mountain zebra**. Once reduced to 91 individuals, Mountain Zebra NP is one of only three naturally surviving populations and this is the best place to see them.

Dwellers of the high plateaus
The Rooiplaat Loop in the north takes you through a scenic pass onto the best game-viewing areas. In spring and summer (September through March) most Cape mountain zebras congregate on these grassy plateaus, favouring their palatable grasses. Although non-territorial, stallions violently defend their harems from challenging males and Rooiplaat's open plains offer excellent chances to view the clashes. Naturally migratory, they tend to move into the mountains in winter when grazing on the plains is poorest. The Rooiplaat Plateau also shelters herds of common elands, red hartebeests, black wildebeests, blesboks and springboks as well as bat-eared foxes. Ostriches and blue cranes are seen on the plateau as well as dozens of grassland bird species including quail finches, pin-tailed whydahs, Cape canaries and southern ant-eating chats.

Cliffside cat watchers
Deep valleys running into the seasonal Wilgerboom River provide habitat for a very different fauna to the plains. Set out along Kranskop Drive as early as possible for the best chance to see the park's top predator, the tuft-eared **caracal**. The chattering bark of **rock dassies** and the alarm screams of resident **black eagles** act as valuable cues to stop and scan the rocky slopes for this cat. Highly adaptable, caracals also live in densely wooded watercourses where the herbivores range from the tiny (**grey duikers**) to the huge (**buffaloes**). But cat-

spotters occur everywhere: **greater kudus**, **klipspringers** and **mountain reedbucks** live on the lower slopes and their respective alarm calls (a booming bark, a trumpetlike whistle and a shrill nasal whistle) usually mean 'caracal!'. ■

NDUMO GAME RESERVE

Subtropical profusion

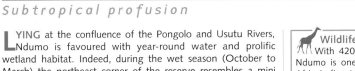

LYING at the confluence of the Pongolo and Usutu Rivers, Ndumo is favoured with year-round water and prolific wetland habitat. Indeed, during the wet season (October to March) the northeast corner of the reserve resembles a mini Okavango Delta where the two rivers meet in a swamp of channels and pans. A mosaic of dense mahemane bush, open floodplains and riverine forests of fig trees, fever trees and ilala palms provides habitat for many subtropical species that are difficult to see elsewhere in Southern Africa.

Hide and peek

Large mammals tend to be shy and difficult to spot but **nyalas** number in the thousands, forming unusually large herds. They rarely venture far from the protection of thick bush but with relatively few predators here, they congregate on the floodplain to graze the rich grasses. The hides overlooking Nyamithi Pan in the early morning and evening offer the best chance for viewing large aggregations as well as numerous **giraffes, greater kudus, waterbucks, impalas, bushbucks** and **red duikers**. Late in the afternoon, **bushpigs** sometimes appear in their small family groups known as sounders. Primarily nocturnal, they occasionally venture out at sunset when they wallow in mud to remove parasites and regulate their temperature – particularly during the summer. Some 700 **Nile crocodiles** larger than 2m and over 300 **hippos** inhabit the rivers and pans and cannot be missed from the hides.

Most visitors are attracted to Ndumo for its prolific birdlife. **African fish eagles, Pel's fishing owls, palmnut vultures, southern banded snake eagles** and **pygmy geese** are plentiful around the pans. Many **kingfisher** species also occur including **giant, brown-hooded, woodland, malachite** and **pied,** the last distinctive for their hovering hunting patterns. Patches of threatened sandforest are home to rare trees and rare birds alike. Among huge Lebombo wattles, wild mangoes and Mozambique coffee trees, look for **narina trogons, African broadbills, broad-billed rollers, pink-throated twinspots** and **yellow-spotted nicators**. Ndumo has 85% of the bird species found at Kruger NP yet it is only 0.5% the size. ∎

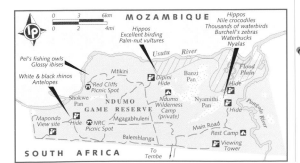

Wildlife highlights
With 420 bird species, Ndumo is one of Southern Africa's finest birding sites. Abundant hippos, nyalas, impalas and Nile crocodiles. Bushpigs, red duikers, bushbucks and sunis are all common but can be difficult to see.

Location 409km north of Durban. Tarred all the way except for the last 15km – check ahead after heavy rains. **Facilities** Game-viewing roads, guided game drives, guided walks, numerous hides and viewing towers, viewsites. **Accommodation** 3 person cottages, camping ground and caravan site. Luxury tented accommodation at Ndumo Wilderness Camp (book through Wilderness Safaris). **Wildlife rhythms** The mild, dry winters (March to October) when water levels are lowest are best for game-viewing on the floodplain. Birding is excellent year round but reaches its peak in summer. **Contact** KZN Wildlife (☎ 0331-845 1000).

Watching tips
Accompanied walks are perhaps the best way to spot tiny suni antelopes. They're abundant here but freeze at the sound of footfall and are difficult to spot in the dense bush. They constantly flicker their tails – a giveaway if you watch for it.

PHINDA RESOURCE RESERVE

Luxury and lifers

Wildlife highlights
Easily the best place in South Africa to see cheetahs. Excellent Big Five and good general game including easily seen subtropical antelopes like nyalas, red duikers and sunis. Prolific birdlife includes those to be found in an extensive patch of rare sandforest habitat.

Location 300km north of Durban. Access for 2WD but call ahead in the rainy season (December to February).
Facilities Guided game drives and walks, bird hide, boat cruises, river canoeing, scuba diving and snorkelling (off-site).
Accommodation Four luxury lodges.
Wildlife rhythms Winter is the dry season when undergrowth is sparse: the best time for clear sightings. Summer is when migrant birds arrive and many antelopes give birth.
Contact Bookings with CCA (☎ 011-809 4300, fax 4400).

Watching tips
Phinda's rangers and trackers will find everything for you but ask about guided day-trips (which they call 'adventures') to wildlife attractions nearby, including black rhino walks in Mkuzi GR, diving on the east coast coral reefs and guided flights over Greater St Lucia Wetland Park.

AMONG the finest of South Africa's many privately owned reserves, Phinda is adjacent to Mkuzi GR but about 10 times as expensive to visit. The wildlife is essentially the same (though Phinda has **lions** and lacks black rhinos) but in contrast to the Mkuzi's self-drive experience, Phinda's rangers promise exceptional guided sightings. If your list is missing a few 'lifers' (species you have never seen in your life) like **cheetahs**, **sunis** or **African finfoots** and you've got the cash, Phinda virtually guarantees them.

Return of the wildlife

Phinda's full name, Phinda Isilwane, is Zulu for 'the return of the wildlife'. Prior to 1990, the most abundant large mammal here was the domestic cow but, along with miles of barbed wire fencing, Phinda's owners removed them and restored the full complement of KwaZulu-Natal mammalian megafauna. As well as over 1000 head of various **antelope** species, 56 **elephants** and more **white rhinos** than remain in most African countries, they reintroduced the top predators. Today, **Big Five** sightings are standard game drive fare and this is one of the few reserves in Africa where **cheetahs** are a certainty. Their numbers are modest but like most big cats here, the cheetahs are indifferent to safari vehicles, and permit terrific chances for watching behaviour – mothers with cubs are exceptionally viewable.

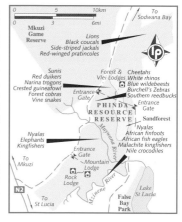

Buck and birds

Local herbivorous specials include the **suni**, tame **red duikers** (keep an eye for them on the paths of Forest Lodge) and **nyalas** in abundance as well as more widespread species like **blue wildebeests**, **Burchell's zebras**, **impalas**, **greater kudus** and **giraffes**. Although the game drives invariably focus on mammals, ask the rangers to show off their considerable birding knowledge. There are more than 360 species here and some people come to Phinda for the birdlife alone. If you're a birder, be sure to tell reception when you check in and they'll make sure you get time with specialist birding guides who can show you rare species like **narina trogons**, **African finfoots**, **black coucals** and sandforest specials like **African broadbills** and **Neergaard's sunbirds**. ■

TEMBE ELEPHANT RESERVE

War refugees never forget

ESTABLISHED to protect the survivors of intense poaching in neighbouring Mozambique, Tembe is sanctuary for about 130 **elephants**. Formerly ranging freely over the border, their seasonal migrations carried them through the crossfire of Mozambique's civil war until elephant-proof fences restricted them to the protected South African side. After a decade in safety, Tembe's elephants are beginning to relax, but combined with the scars of AK-47 fire (still visible on some individuals) the years of persecution have left them nervous, aggressive and prone to charging with little provocation. Although there are many places in Southern Africa where elephants are easier to see, Tembe's war refugees are truly wild and dangerous – if you see them, leave the engine running and treat all charges as genuine.

Seeking the safe ground

All Tembe's roads are 4WD and only five vehicles per day are admitted, so you may not encounter another vehicle in the course of a day's exploration. And with the possibility of a belligerent elephant just around the next corner, Tembe really conveys a sense of wilderness. Unfortunately, except for the Tembe Safari Camp there is at present nowhere to stay and self-driving visitors have to leave Tembe before the sun sets. Nonetheless, a day-trip can be rewarding, particularly if you use nearby Ndumo GR (35km away) as a base. The thick subtropical bush makes game-viewing difficult from vehicles, especially in the lush summer, and time is best spent at hides. Ponweni Hide overlooking Muzi Swamp is an excellent (and safe!) place for spotting **elephants**, particularly during the driest period, May to October, when they share the limited water with herds of **nyalas**, **buffaloes**, **waterbucks** and **impalas**. Rare elsewhere, **red duikers**, tiny **suni** antelopes and **crested guineafowl** are abundant; they are often seen on the enclosed Ngobozana Sandforest Trails near the Main Gate, but you need to walk quietly and look deep into the undergrowth. The trails are also excellent for birdlife including **African broadbills**, **narina trogons**, **Neergaard's sunbirds** and, a very occasional visitor, the **blue-throated sunbird**. ∎

> ### Wildlife highlights
> Home of South Africa's wildest elephants. Nyalas, impalas, waterbucks and red duikers are easily seen, and Southern Africa's largest population of suni occurs here. Abundant birdlife similar to that at Ndumo but not as diverse; the blue-throated sunbird is a notable special.

Location 415km north of Durban. Entrance road is tarred but all internal roads are 4WD. **Facilities** Self-guided sandforest walks, hides, elephant museum at Main Gate. **Accommodation** Private luxury camp (Tembe Safari Camp) only, contact Maputa Safaris. Nearby Ndumo GR offers alternatives. **Wildlife rhythms** Although wary, elephants (and most other large mammals) are readily seen at waterholes in the dry season (May to October). **Contact** KZN Wildlife (☎ 0331-845 1000, fax 1001). Park Officer (☎ 035-592 0001, fax 0240).

> ### Watching tips
> For day-trippers who have to leave before sunset, maximise your visit by ending at the viewing tower 4km from the Main Gate. It's an excellent site for watching antelopes and birdlife at sunset and is only a five-minute drive from the gate.

OTHER SITES – SOUTH AFRICA

Austin Roberts Bird Sanctuary

Sitting in Pretoria's quiet eastern suburbs, this small sanctuary is home to 170 species of bird, including virtually guaranteed viewing of South Africa's national bird, the blue crane. Entry to the hide is free but it's only open on the weekends and holidays. Otherwise, the suitably named (and very good) Blue Crane Restaurant overlooking the main dam attracts a hopeful avian retinue including its rare namesake at touching distance (but don't!).
Boshoff St, New Muckleneuk, Pretoria,
☎ *012-433 3480*

Bird Island

Scattered along South Africa's stormy west coast, numerous islands act as breeding colonies for seabirds but most are inaccessible. Joined to the mainland by a breakwater, Bird Island is the easiest to reach. About 5000 pairs of Cape gannets build their guano mound nests here between October and December and year-round residents include four species of cormorants (Cape, crowned, white-breasted and bank), plus jackass penguins, Hartlaub's gulls and Cape fur-seals. A new and excellent gannet observatory overlooking the colonies enables some superb viewing. Only 10km south, a bonus attraction for birders is Wadrif Saltpan where huge numbers of flamingos, terns, waders and ducks congregate with occasional rarities including American (lesser) golden plovers, Pacific golden plovers and pectoral sandpipers.
Lambert's Bay, ☎ *02625-727*

Blyde River Canyon Nature Reserve

Conveniently on the way to Kruger NP's Orpen Gate, this stretch of the Drakensberg is renowned for its rugged, chiselled scenery, waterfalls and rough-hewn cliffs. All five of Southern Africa's primates occur here as well as good populations of otherwise uncommon antelopes, such as rhebucks, Sharpe's grysboks and oribis. The birdlife, particularly birds of prey, is excellent.
130km north of Nelspruit,
☎ *013-769 6019*

Cape Peninsula National Park

An easy day-trip from Cape Town, this finger of land protects a sizeable chunk of coastal fynbos and its distinctive fauna. Big game isn't prolific but Cape mountain zebras, bonteboks, elands and red hartebeest are easily seen, especially around the Sirkelsvlei waterhole, accessible only on foot or bike. Chacma baboons are extremely tame (heed the warning signs: they'll come through an open car window if given a chance) and birdlife is good. Between June and November, southern right whales are virtually guaranteed from the many lookout points across False Bay. As well as hiking, you can cycle, fish (from shore or launch a boat) and swim. Take the Simon's Town Rd back to Cape Town to include a stop-off at The Boulders where you can swim with jackass penguins from the nearby colony.
57km south of Cape Town,
☎ *021-706 2405*

Cederberg Wilderness

Notable as South Africa's only reserve set aside specifically for leopards, Cederberg is better known for its scenery. A network of hiking trails (and very limited road access) traverses South Africa's largest remaining patch of montane fynbos where Cape grysboks, grey rhebucks, grey duikers and chacma baboons occur. In the spring, the flowering fynbos attracts sunbirds and sugarbirds. Klipspringers, black eagles and rock dassies as well as San paintings occur among the rocks. This is a true wilderness area where you are allowed to explore where you like.
210km north of Cape Town,
☎ *027-482 2812*

De Wildt Cheetah Research and Breeding Project

Not a game park in the normal sense, De Wildt is a breeding project for endangered South African wildlife. Famous for finding the key to breeding captive cheetahs (housing males and females separately until the female comes into heat), they were also the first to breed 'king' cheetahs, a beautifully marked variant which is otherwise no different from the normally spotted form. As well as the cheetahs, guided tours take in captive African wild dogs, brown hyenas, caracals, riverine rabbits and a number of raptors including visitors to a very well-patronised 'vulture restaurant'.
65km northwest of Pretoria,
☎ *012-504 1921*

Kirstenbosch National Botanic Gardens

If you miss the larger fynbos reserves scattered throughout the Cape, be sure to stop at the Gardens. Sitting at the eastern base of Table Mountain, over 9000 indigenous plant species attract orange-breasted sunbirds, Cape sugarbirds, Klaas' cuckoos and Cape francolins to name only a handful. Sit near a flowering protea for unsurpassed, close-up photographic opportunities.
Constantia, Cape Town,
☎ *021-761 4916*

Kosi Bay Nature Reserve

Actually a series of four estuarine lakes, Kosi Bay is surrounded

by dune forest, raffia palms, mangroves, swamps and fig forest, best explored by the guided four-day Kosi Trail. Mammals are elusive but hippos inhabit the lakes, and the thick coastal bush makes excellent habitat for vervet and samango monkeys as well as bushbucks, blue duikers and red duikers. Birdlife is prolific and the raffia palm forest is probably the best place in South Africa to see palmnut vultures.
450km north of Durban,
☎ 0331-845 1000

Marakele National Park
Although least developed of South Africa's national parks and seldom visited, Marakele is ideal for the self-sufficient. You'll need a 4WD to find game which, except for lions, includes the Big Five (both rhino species) and over a dozen antelope species including fairly easy-to-spot roans. The world's largest Cape vulture colony nests in the splendid mountain surrounds of the Waterberg Range and close to 300 other bird species have been recorded here.
240km northwest of Pretoria,
☎ 012-343 1991

Namaqua National Park
Launched only in August 1999, South Africa's twentieth national park hosts a spring wildflower flush that draws people from around the globe. As well as the flowers, Namaqualand protects a rich diversity of endemic desert life: many succulents, lizards, tortoises, mole-rats, bees and scorpions are found

nowhere else. More widespread and conspicuous life includes ostriches, korhaans, larks and arid-adapted antelopes.
550km north of Cape Town,
☎ 012-343 1991, fax 0905

Nylsvlei Nature Reserve
A visit here during the summer when a huge wetland forms following the rains guarantees superb bird-viewing. In good seasons 60,000 wetland birds of 100-plus species have been recorded here and a further 300-odd species occur in the surrounding mixed bushveld. Mammals aren't abundant but tsessebes, southern reedbucks and roans are among the normally elusive species seen fairly often.
130km north of Pretoria,
☎ 014-743 1074

Tsitsikamma National Park
With a Cape clawless otter as its emblem and a 46km walking trail named after them, you could be forgiven for thinking that you'll bump into these amphibious mammals at every

turn. However, otters are extremely shy and you'll need to be out early and keep very quiet for a chance to spot one. The challenging Otter Trail takes you though prime otter habitat but mostly it is renowned for its scenery and the chance to glimpse dolphins offshore. Tame rock dassies, small grey mongooses and sunbirds frequent the camp sites and short walks through beautiful indigenous Cape forest hold a chance for blue duikers and Knysna louries. Tsitsikamma is very busy on weekends and holidays.
56km east of Plettenberg Bay,
☎ 012-343 1991, fax 0905

Tswalu Private Desert Reserve
The largest privately owned reserve in Southern Africa, Tswalu is as expensive as it is huge. But for people wanting a luxury Kalahari experience, it's unrivalled. Typical desert species like springboks, gemsboks and red hartebeests are here (as well as a few which don't belong, like roan and sable antelopes) and most notably, the desert race of the black rhino. Guided night drives offer excellent chances of spotting many of the Kalahari's rich carnivore community, from Cape foxes to lions. And birdlife is excellent, particularly raptors, bustards, finches, queleas and weavers.
650km west of Johannesburg,
☎ 053-781 9311

Weenen Nature Reserve
Rolling terrain lightly covered in thornveld and grasslands ensures good visibility of a surprisingly rich mammal fauna. There's nothing here you can't see in the larger KwaZulu-Natal reserves, but usually you're free to hike without guides in search of wildlife including both rhinos, buffaloes, giraffes, elands and mountain reedbucks. Birdlife is very good and includes a 'vulture restaurant'.
180km north of Durban,
☎ 0363-41809

NAMIBIA

Highlights

- The unrelenting assault on the senses of Cape Cross's 80,000 Cape fur-seals
- Summer flocks of flamingos numbering in the millions when Etosha Pan is filled
- Following the tracks of desert elephants along the dry Hoanib and Hoarusib riverbeds
- Being woken by the echo of distant lion roars and attendant jackal barks at Etosha's Okaukuejo Rest Camp
- Encountering pairs of Damara dik-diks on the short walks close to camp at Waterberg Plateau
- Seeing gemsboks in single file scale the massive saffron-coloured dunes of the Namib

Life in the extreme

THE driest country in the Southern African region, Namibia is a land dominated by deserts, rocky canyons, arid savannas and acacia woodlands. Wildlife is most abundant in the north where the most fertile habitats lie, ranging from the seasonally inundated Etosha NP to the relatively lush reserves along the Caprivi Strip. For big game watchers, there are really only three significant areas in Namibia: Kaokoland, where elusive desert elephants and black rhinos follow the rivercourses running to the Skeleton Coast; the isolated and rarely visited Kaudom GR where Namibia's last African wild dogs find refuge; and Etosha NP, one of the world's finest game reserves. With easily observed Big Five (except for buffalo), an unusual blend of arid-adapted herbivores (alongside typical bush and plains dwellers), abundant birdlife and unlimited visibility, Etosha is invariably the highlight of a Namibian safari.

Further south is the largest game reserve in Africa, the Namib-Naukluft Park, which covers an astonishing 6% of Namibia's area. Much of it is true desert and large mammals occur in extremely low densities, though local specials include Hartmann's mountain zebras as well as more widespread Southern African endemics like springboks and gemsboks. For aficionados of smaller life, the Namib is an endemism hotspot: on the dunes, Gray's larks, dune larks, slip-face lizards and fog-basking beetles are found, while the scattered rocky plateaus host long-billed larks, rockrunners and Herero chats.

The similarly severe Namibian coast is no place to expect abundant big game though it's the only spot in the world where massive fur-seal colonies are patrolled by hunting brown hyenas and black-backed jackals. The coast also hosts massive flocks of summer waders including sanderlings, turnstones and grey plovers, while Heaviside's and dusky dolphins can often be seen in the shallow offshore waters.

The driest parts of Namibia are best visited during the summer rainfalls when large pools form in the desert, attracting brief but unusually large congregations of all forms of desert wildlife. Conversely, Etosha and Kaudom are most productive during the dry winters, when animals collect at the limited waterpoints. Etosha, in particular, is extremely rewarding during the winter and a day spent at the waterholes can see an endless procession of thousands of animals ranging from banded mongooses to elephants. ∎

Inset: Massive sand dunes tower 200m above the valley floor at Sossusvlei in Namibia's extensive Namib-Naukluft Park.

SKELETON COAST NP
A sandblasted desert wilderness;
Cape fur-seals and brown hyenas;
black-backed korhaans, rufous-tailed
palm thrushes and nesting Damara terns

ETOSHA NP
A massive saltpan surrounded
by plains and woodlands;
black rhinos, elephants, lions
and arid-adapted antelopes;
raptors, quelas and doves

MAMILI NP
Secluded, little-visited and remote;
red lechwes, sitatungas,
waterbucks, buffaloes and hippos;
Namibia's richest birding region

WATERBERG PLATEAU PARK
A 200m-high plateau protecting
rare species; rhinos, buffaloes,
roan antelopes and Damara dik-diks;
endemic birds plus a Cape vulture colony

NAMIB-NAUKLUFT PARK
A desert colossus; gemsboks, springboks
and Hartmann's mountain zebras;
endemics including Gray's larks,
tractrac chats and slip-face lizards

Suggested itineraries

One week From Windhoek, head to Etosha NP for the entire week! Okonjima is a very worthwhile detour on the way. Alternatively, use Swakopmund as your base and explore the Namib, taking in the Welwitschia Plains Drive, Sandwich Harbour and working down to Sossusvlei; otherwise do the Welwitschia Plains Drive, Cape Cross and the southern Skeleton Coast.

Two weeks Starting in Swakopmund, spend a day exploring the northern Namib then head north to the Skeleton Coast, taking in Cape Cross on the way. Stay a few nights at the Torra Bay camp site then head northeast to Etosha for 3–4 nights. Head south from Etosha, taking in both Okonjima and Waterberg Plateau Park for 2 nights each before finishing in Windhoek.

One month Combine the 2 week main wildlife areas with time to spend at smaller attractions like Waterberg Plateau and Okonjima. For the intrepid, leave from Windhoek direct to Etosha for 5 nights, then 4WD east to Kaudom GR for 4 nights. Spend a week exploring the Caprivi Strip, then drive back via Waterberg Plateau and Okonjima to finish at Windhoek.

ETOSHA NATIONAL PARK

The great white place

Wildlife highlights
Namibia's number one wildlife reserve and one of the best parks in the world for wildlife-watching. Lions, leopards, elephants and black rhinos are commonly seen. Very large congregations of blue wildebeests, Burchell's zebras, springboks, gemsboks and elands, especially in the winter, and black-faced impalas and Damara dik-diks are endemic. Birdlife is excellent, particularly during the summer when European and intra-African migrants arrive. Viewing birds of prey is good throughout the year.

WITH little more than a low stone fence separating you from the surrounding white plains, a thermos of early morning coffee and cameras ready, there are few places which can match the wildlife prospects of dawn at Etosha's Okaukuejo waterhole. The jewel in Namibia's wildlife crown, Etosha NP is undoubtedly one of the best reserves in the world. Although the stark Etosha Pan occupies almost a third of the park and gives the reserve its name, it's the surrounding sweetgrass plains and mopane woodlands that sustain large numbers of game. A network of artificial waterholes and naturally upwelling springs scattered along the southern boundary of the pan ensure large congregations of wildlife, and even one day at a single waterhole such as Okaukuejo can produce literally thousands of animals.

Wealth at the waterholes

Once the bed of a vast inland lake, Etosha is now bone dry for much of the year: indeed, the bleached calcite soils and emaciated thorn trees give winter a still, skeletal air. However, this is when waterholes are at their most productive, drawing in prolific wildlife from the dry plains. Perhaps more so than anywhere

Etosha's endemic antelopes

Etosha is home to two antelopes which occur only in northwestern Namibia and across the border in Angola (where the prolonged civil war has left their populations uncertain). Both are easily overlooked – one because it seems familiar, the other due to its diminutive size. At first glance, the black-faced impala looks no different to the common impala, but it is a unique subspecies with slightly darker colouring and a purplish-black facial blaze. Very difficult to see outside Etosha, it is common around Halali and Namutoni Rest Camps. Also near Namutoni, one of Africa's smallest antelopes, the Damara dik-dik (inset) occurs at densities of 90 every square kilometre – one of the densest concentrations of any small antelope in Africa. Along Dikdik Drive (Bloubokdraai) they ignore vehicles, making this one of the best places to observe the monogamous pairs; they mate for life, so if you see one cross the road, be sure to wait for its partner to appear.

else in Southern Africa, Etosha's waterholes during the dry season assure exceptional sightings. In the morning, arrive as early as possible at a waterhole and wait. Milling around in the pre-dawn shadow, throngs of **blue wildebeests, Burchell's zebras, giraffes, springboks, gemsboks, elands** and others wait for first light. Coming down to water is dangerous even when visibility is good and herbivores try to avoid nocturnal drinking, when predators have the advantage of night. Virtually the moment the first splinter of sun appears above the horizon, the procession begins. Row upon row of animals move down to the water, most taking their fill quickly and then moving off into the surrounding scrub, inevitably to be replaced by another herd.

The dense concentration of animals invites constant activity around the water. **Zebra** stallions herd their small harems when another group appears and opposing males sometimes clash in furious bouts of kicking and biting in defence of their mares. Young male antelopes, typically springboks and gemsboks, lock horns and spar, practising the skills which one day may win them dominance. Flocks of **Cape turtle doves, red-eyed doves** and three species of **sandgrouse** (**Namaqua, Burchell's** and **double-banded**) circle constantly, attracting raptors such as **pale chanting goshawks, Ovambo goshawks, lanner falcons, bateleurs** and **martial eagles,** and the chances of seeing an aerial kill are high at the waterholes. Everything makes way when **elephants** arrive, particularly a bull in sexual readiness. Known as musth and obvious by the copiously oozing temporal gland on the temples, bulls in this state are aggressive and intolerant. Other drinkers are chased and vehicles should keep their distance.

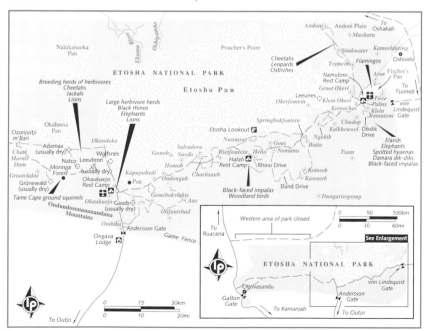

Giraffes are very common in the east of Etosha (around Namutoni camp), but sightings get progressively less frequent the further west you travel.

The early bird catches the cats

The waterhole procession continues for most of the morning so, although the best light for photography is in the early morning, you won't be disappointed if you arrive late as an entire day can pass at a waterhole without a lull in activity. Take note though, except for ubiquitous **black-backed jackals** trotting nimbly among the herds, the chances of viewing predators at the pans are better early in the day, particularly of shy species such as **leopards**, which seek cover as it warms up. **Cheetahs** also drink early, though they are rare in Etosha despite the suitable habitat and high numbers of **springboks**, their main prey. Competition from **lions**, which also concentrate heavily on springboks, keeps cheetah numbers low: most sightings are around Namutoni, Andoni and Charitsaub. Like other cats, lions generally drink early or towards sundown but they readily rest near waterholes throughout the day. With no natural enemies aside from other lions, they can relax at waterholes which also provide excellent chances for an ambush. Waterholes with suitable cover around them are worth a second look – try Chudop, Kalkheuwel, (also very good for **leopards**) and the Salvadora-Charitsaub-Sueda triangle in between Halali and Okaukuejo. Okondeka near Okaukuejo Rest Camp is a focal point for the Okondeka pride.

Patience breeds a vision splendid

'Who knows who will turn up next?' We had just experienced an incredible early morning rendezvous with a clan of hyenas, a troop of banded mongooses, a gang of skittish zebras, a kudu family and a herd of wildebeests on the banks of Chudop Dam. In the emptiness of their departure, a car pulled up beside ours and we were asked if we had seen any big cats. We hadn't but after listing with joy the procession we'd already seen, I added what I thought was a tantalizing piece of wisdom, 'Who knows who will turn up in the next 10 minutes?' Well, our impatient friend took no heed and off he drove. Not five minutes later, drinking our coffee in the first quiet moment of the morning, I looked across the dam and realised our hyenas were back. As they moved out of the surrounding bush and walked towards us, my companion cried, 'Wait a second, they're not hyenas. It's a pride of lions!'

Sophie Wise, Melbourne, Australia

Other productive waterholes are Klein Namutoni and Twee Palms (both are excellent for afternoon photography), Aus and Gemsbokvlakte. However, you needn't even leave camp to enjoy the waterholes. All the rest camps have a waterhole within walking distance, perhaps the best of them the famous floodlit waterhole at Okaukuejo. Apart from very regular visits by **elephants** and most of the **antelope** species, this is an excellent site for **black rhinos**. Virtually assured during winter if you sit up during the night, you can see more black rhinos in a single sitting than the numbers surviving in most other African countries.

Floods and flocks

In a region of such little water, Etosha is transformed during the short, wet summer. Most rain falls between January and March, arriving in violent, thunderous squalls and filling much of Etosha Pan with a shallow, life-giving layer. This is one of the most important breeding grounds of **greater** and **lesser flamingos** (the latter more striking in its pinker plumage and dark red bill)

Location 435km north of Windhoek on tarred road. Internal roads are very well maintained gravel.
Facilities Extensive game drive network, lookout points, spotlit waterholes at each camp site.
Accommodation 3 camps (Okaukuejo, Halali, Namutoni) all with 2–4 bed bungalows, camp sites and rooms in a former German fort at Namutoni. Numerous luxury lodges outside the park such as Ongava, Aoba, Mokuti and Hobatere.
Wildlife rhythms No rain falls between July and September – this is when game concentrations around waterholes are at their peak. Summer is best for birding as well as large congregations of grazers with young (but temperatures can be oppressive).
Contact MET (☎ 061-236 975, fax 224 900, **e** reservations@ iwwn.com.na). Namibia Tourism (Windhoek ☎ 061-284 2111, fax 2364; Johannesburg ☎ 011-784 8024, fax 8340, **e** namtour@citec.co.za; 🖳 www.tourism.com.na/ office.html).

Elephants occur throughout the park but the waterholes in the east and in the mopane woodlands surrounding Halali camp provide virtually assured viewing.

During the winter, large congregations of zebras at waterholes result in inevitable clashes between stallions.

which arrive at the pan in the thousands. Huge numbers are attracted to the shallow water of Fischer's Pan near Namutoni where they build their conical mud nests on the mudflats. In summers of particularly high rainfalls, up to a million flamingos may spread themselves across the pan and the colonies are sometimes raided by **spotted hyenas** and **black-backed jackals**. Large numbers of **eastern white pelicans** also breed here in good years.

For many Palaearctic migrants, the flooded Etosha Pan provides an opportune stopover, so they tend to be visible at the start of summer rains (November) and towards the end (March to April). Waders such as **sanderlings**, **Caspian plovers**, **grey plovers** and **marsh sandpipers** join breeding migrants from equatorial Africa including rare **dwarf bitterns** and non-breeding intra-African visitors such as **Abdim's storks** and **open-billed storks**. Migratory birds of prey including **steppe buzzards**, **African**

Blue wildebeests trek between the eastern and western boundaries of Etosha, tracking rain and the new growth that it brings.

hobbies, Montagu's and **pallid harriers, western red-footed falcons** and **lesser kestrels** swell the raptor species count; in all, 35 species are known from the park. Less reliant on rainfall for their life cycles, raptor sightings are rewarding all year due to the constant supply of carcasses.

New life

Water everywhere means that other wildlife is not tied to the waterholes and disperses to utilise grasslands which are unproductive during the winter. With so much water around, there isn't much point waiting at waterholes and summer is best spent driving in search of animals. Large herds of **blue wildebeests, springboks, gemsboks** and **Burchell's zebras** move to the sweetgrass plains to the north and west of Okaukuejo. This is where summer breeders such as springboks and blue wildebeests drop their young and the plains near Okondeka waterhole and at Grootvlakte (head west from Okaukuejo Rest Camp as far as permitted – beyond the Ozonjuiti m'Bari waterhole is only open to registered tour operators) are usually excellent for seeing herds with newborn young. The birthing flush attracts large numbers of predators and this is probably the best time to see **cheetahs** on these plains. Opportunistic **jackals** are everywhere, searching relentlessly for unattended young or dogging larger hunters in the hope of a kill. **Honey badgers, bat-eared foxes** and troops of **banded mongooses** search among the new grass for newly emerged frogs and insects attracted to the flush of wildflowers. Endemic **black-faced impalas** also drop their young at this time (late December and January), though the largest concentrations occur far to the east near Namutoni Rest Camp.

Summer days can be extremely hot and, more so than in winter, it is important to be looking for wildlife at the crack of dawn (when the gates open) or late in the afternoon. Once the day begins to heat up, most animals take cover and even if you do spot something, it's unlikely to be doing much more than resting. ∎

Watching tips

While sitting on the benches around Okaukuejo waterhole at night, keep an eye on the large camelthorn trees that line the path along the stone wall. Arboreal black-tailed tree rats emerge at night to forage on young shoots, buds and the outer tunics of seedpods. Shine with a flashlight into the trees to show up the distinctive white belly. Occasionally, small-spotted genets can be seen hunting the rats and other nocturnal denizens such as Bibron's thick-toed gecko, also readily seen on the chalet walls at night. Close to the spotlights, watch the branch tips for lesser bushbabies and fork-tailed drongos as they snatch moths and other insects from the air. At Namutoni Rest Camp, huge numbers of red-billed queleas roost in the reedbeds near King Nehale waterhole. Watch them from the fort tower as the flocks return from the plains at sundown, so dense they resemble smoke clouds.

NAMIB-NAUKLUFT PARK

Cryptic inhabitants of a desert giant

Wildlife highlights

Wildlife highlights

Wildlife is thinly spread but the Namib is excellent for some intriguing arid-zone Namibian/southern Angolan endemics – including Hartmann's mountain zebras, Herero chats, and Gray's and dune larks. Unusual reptiles include Peringuey's adders, dune-plated lizards, slip-face lizards, web-footed geckos and barking geckos. Gemsboks, springboks and ostriches are fairly common and Namibia's only population of wild horses occurs here. The welwitschia plant is a unique floral highlight.

AFRICA'S largest park is also one of the most arid and much of the Namib-Naukluft appears to have no life at all. However, coastal fogs (born when moist Atlantic air meets freezing Antarctic currents) provide critical moisture and allow wildlife to persist in barren, moonscape-like conditions. Nowhere in this vast wilderness is wildlife abundant but there are few places on earth where the sense of life's persistence is as palpable. From the vast central dune sea, whose northward progress over the gravel plains is checked only by occasional flows down the Kuiseb River, to the relatively lush Naukluft mountain plateau, the Namib's wildlife requires patience and insight to enjoy.

Gravel plains and watery havens

Bordered by the Swakop and Kuiseb Rivers, the Namib section of the park is the most accessible and the scenic Welwitschia Plains Drive provides an excellent introduction (permits available at Swakopmund or Windhoek and ask for the informative brochure). Life is hardly noticeable here, but look around the base of drought-resistant dollar bushes and ink bushes for signs of **beetles**, **spiders** and the **Namaqua chameleon**, top predator

Baboons of the Namib

Making their home in the most arid region in the world to be inhabited by any primate (aside from humans), the chacma baboons of the Namib live a perilous existence. Water is so scarce here that they may go without drinking for months (116 days is the record) – people would perish after about a week. To be able to survive here, the Namib baboons have learned a unique suite of adaptive behaviours. Showering themselves with shaded, cool sand from under trees, taking single bites from poisonous but moisture-filled plants and limiting social activity to the cool hours of the early morning all serve to lower a baboon's body temperature. Even so, their temperature may vary 5–6°C in a day, regularly topping 42°C. While this would ultimately prove fatal for humans, overheated baboons simply lie down with splayed arms and legs, passively dissipating heat until it is cool enough to resume foraging.

of the shrub mini-ecosystems. Don't be surprised if inquisitive **tractrac chats** suddenly appear from nowhere at the designated stopping points: in this place of extremes, people are a profitable source of easy pickings. Less confiding are endemic **Gray's larks**. Small and stone-coloured, they crouch when alarmed and are extremely difficult to see. Search the gravel with binoculars: they frequently hide close to the road until the disturbance of a vehicle has passed. North of the Swakop River, the plains are strewn with ancient **welwitschia** plants which, by absorbing condensation from coastal fogs, can survive any drought and live for thousands of years.

More conspicuous wildlife congregates along the two riverbeds. The Kuiseb Bridge camp site allows exploration of the canyon, home to **klipspringers**, **steenboks** and small troops of arid-adapted **chacma baboons**. The canyon walls are home to cliff-breeding birds such as **black eagles**, **black storks** and **rosy-faced lovebirds**, while the comparatively lush vegetation of the riverbeds attracts **swallow-tailed bee-eaters**, **cardinal woodpeckers** and **brubrus**. **Lappet-faced vultures** nest in large camelthorn trees from May to September.

Gemsboks can survive in the Namib's driest areas, but they come to standing water when it is available.

On the coast and accessible only by 4WD, Sandwich Lagoon was formerly Namibia's most important coastal wetland for seabirds and shorebirds. The sheltered lagoon once attracted an estimated 200,000 birds but increased siltation of the wetland is forcing birds elsewhere. September and October still see the arrival of Palaearctic waders such as **Arctic terns**, **curlew sandpipers**, **sanderlings**, **little stints**, **turnstones**, and **bar-tailed godwits** (albeit in reduced numbers). Flocks of **greater** and **lesser flamingos**, **eastern white pelicans**, **black-necked grebes**, **chestnut-banded plovers** and **Hartlaub's gulls** also occur. Check the MET offices in Swakopmund for updates on the birdlife before you decide to make the trip.

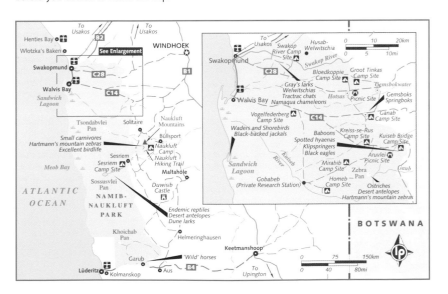

Location Multiple entry points, most accessible by 2WD. Sandwich Lagoon is only accessible by 4WD and the last 4km to Sossusvlei are negotiable by 4WD or on foot.

Facilities Numerous walks in the Naukluft section including short walks and day trails from the camp site or the very challenging Naukluft Hiking Trail which takes 4–8 days (self-guided and book well ahead). Also a 2-day 4WD route, otherwise the massif is inaccessible to vehicles (but the camp site can be reached by 2WD).

Accommodation 8 basic camp sites in the Namib section. Sesriem camp site and luxury hotel (Karos Lodge) near Sossusvlei. Koedoesrus camp site at Naukluft entrance. No accommodation at Sandwich Lagoon.

Wildlife rhythms The rains are unpredictable but usually occur in summer (December to February), if at all, transforming parts of the Namib (particularly the dunes at Sossusvlei where wildlife congregates). September to October onwards is best for birds at Sandwich Lagoon.

Contact MET (☎ 061-236 975, fax 224 900, e reservations@iwwn.com.na).

Mountain oasis

Rising unexpectedly from the flat gravel plains in the east, the Naukluft Massif is a high plateau cut by narrow gorges, waterfalls and freezing mountain pools. This is the richest area of the Namib for wildlife, though even here it is widespread and scarce. You are almost certain to see **Hartmann's mountain zebras**, a distinct race restricted to western Namibia and southern Angola and for which this section of the park was proclaimed. Largest of the three races of zebras occurring in Southern Africa, they are most active early in the morning and after 3pm; on cold mornings, look for them on east-facing slopes where they sun themselves. Ubiquitous **gemsboks** and **springboks** occur on the plateau flats, while **klipspringers**, **greater kudus** and **grey duikers** inhabit the wooded gorges. **Leopards**, **caracals** and numerous other carnivores occur but most are very rarely seen. Colonies of **meerkats** and **yellow mongooses** are the most visible predators, often sharing their burrow systems with **Cape ground squirrels**.

The Massif's varied habitats are rich in birdlife, marking the transition zone between the Namib's gravel plains and less arid Karoo savanna to the southeast. February is usually the best month, when rains on the plateau attract **African black ducks**,

Welwitschias

Found only on the gravel plains running from the northern Namib to southern Angola, the extraordinary *Welwitschia mirabilis* is often classified in the same group as pine trees because of its reddish-brown, coniferlike cones. However, with equally valid similarities to the flowering plants and mosses, many botanists believe it has no close relatives and has an ancestry as unique as its appearance. Resembling a huge, shrivelled lettuce, their tangled, multiform appearance is actually created by two enormous, leathery leaves. Growing from opposite sides of the woody stumplike stem, the leaves put on about 10cm a year but the ends spilt and wilt in the Namib's harsh conditions, giving the illusion of many fronds. Regardless, the large surface area of the leaves is an effective sponge for fog-borne moisture, enabling the welwitschia to weather the aridity here for millennia. At more than 1500 years old, the Husab welwitschia at the end of the Welwitschia Plains Drive is the grand-daddy among those easily reached, but a number of plants over 2000 years old also exist here – their locations are kept secret to avoid vandalism.

Karoo robins, pin-tailed whydahs and **cinnamon-breasted warblers** along with **Rüppell's korhaans** and rock dwellers such as **long-billed larks, Herero chats, rockrunners, Monteiro's hornbills** and **chestnut weavers.** The well-vegetated valleys are home to **swallow-tailed bee-eaters, long-billed crombecs, Layard's titbabblers, golden-tailed woodpeckers** and **lesser honeyguides,** while above in the cliffs, look for **black eagles, lanner falcons** and **augur buzzards.**

Dune dwellers

Probably the most recognisable icon of the Namib, the apricot dunes of the vast central dune sea harbour a very different fauna. In contrast to the epic scenery of the dune surrounds, the wildlife here is inconspicuous and cryptic. Reliant on the coastal fogs, the dune community engages in unique moisture-collection rituals. **Fog-basking beetles** line up on dune crests, their posteriors raised skywards to intercept the incoming fog, which condenses on their smooth carapace. **Button beetles** have a different tactic, excavating neat, parallel trenches which act as fog-traps from which they drink their fill. **Web-footed geckos** also rely on condensation, using their long tongue to collect moisture beads from the head and snout. Most likely to be seen in the early morning, follow their tiny, fig-leaf tracks. You may also encounter their main predator, **Peringuey's adder** which submerges itself beneath the sand, leaving only its face protruding – keep an eye out for its distinctive side-winding track. Appropriately named dune endemics, **dune-plated lizards, slip-face lizards** and **dune larks** are other specials to watch out for.

The fauna of the dunes is probably best seen at Sossusvlei, where a huge clay-bottomed pan can hold water for months following good rainfall (in summer, if does occur), attracting larger game such as **gemsboks, springboks** and **ostriches.** Further south, the windmill at Garub is the only source of water for **wild horses.** Probably descended from mounts kept by occupying German troops in the late 1800s, the horses are a unique component of the Namib. Watch for them along the tarred road between Lüderitz and Aus and pay particular attention at night: second to droughts, road deaths are the main cause of mortality to the desert horses. ■

Trails through the Naukluft Plateau permit close-up views of the Namib's unique plant life as well as birds and reptiles.

> ### Watching tips
> An artificial waterhole on the gravel plains near Ganab camp site attracts Hartmann's mountain zebras, springboks, gemsboks and ostriches. Other waterholes, Zebra Pan and Hotsas, are further afield from camp sites but still worth visiting. Found throughout the Namib, the barking gecko unleashes its squeaking vocal repertoire just as the sun is setting. Wait patiently with a flashlight near the source of the 'barks', particularly in the Sesriem camp site.

SKELETON COAST NATIONAL PARK
& KAOKOLAND

Resilient fauna along the 'coast of hell'

Wildlife highlights
Home of the much publicised desert elephants and rhinos. Gemsboks, springboks, ostriches and greater kudus are fairly common and Cape fur-seals form massive colonies on the coast. Notable bird specials include rufous-tailed palm thrushes, Rüppell's parrots and Gray's larks; wetland birdlife at the Uniab Delta is excellent.

Location 200km north of Swakopmund (Ugab River Gate) or 170km west of Khorixas (Springbokwasser Gate). Salt/gravel road accessible year-round.
Facilities Hide at Uniab Delta.
Accommodation Bungalows, camp site, tented camp and lodge.
Wildlife rhythms October to May is consistently sunny with clear skies and also encompasses most migratory bird arrivals (September to February). Winter (April to May) experiences dense fogs and cold westerly winds when wildlife tends to seek cover.
Contact MET (☎ 061-236 975, fax 224 900, e reservations@ iwwn.com.na).

NAMED not only for the many mariners who perished here, but also for the numerous shipwrecks and whale remains that litter this desolate stretch of northern Namibian coastline, the Skeleton Coast is one of Southern Africa's most remote parks. Stretching almost 500km from the Ugab River mouth to the Angolan border in the north, the barren coastal desert forbids large congregations of wildlife and this is not a place to expect encounters with teeming herds. However, the arid-adapted wildlife inhabits surroundings unlike any other and for those prepared to invest some extra effort, there are unique viewing and photographic opportunities here.

Life at the oasis

A few kilometres north of the Torra Bay camp site, the mouth of the Uniab River spreads out into a series of reed-fringed freshwater pools where wildlife seeks respite from the arid desert. Small groups of **springboks**, **greater kudus** and flocks of

Amputees for freedom

Kaokoland (and adjoining Damaraland) is home to the world's last free-ranging population of black rhinos (all other populations live in protected areas) but its isolation leaves them vulnerable to poachers from neighbouring Angola and Zambia. Beginning in the late 1980s, the Ministry of Environment and Tourism embarked on a program aimed at removing the incentive for killing rhinos by sawing off their horns – a stategy also used on white rhinos (inset) elsewhere. Rhinos are darted from helicopters and, using a small chain saw, both horns are removed just above the bone. Released with an antibiotic coating of Stockholm tar on the stump, the rhinos apparently suffer no ill effects – but their calves might. Researchers found that although dehorned rhinos forage and interact with other rhinos normally, mothers were probably less capable of defending calves from predators. Combined with the fact that horns regrow as much as 6cm a year – necessitating frequent and expensive trims – the controversial scheme was eventually abandoned.

up to 50 **ostriches** are drawn from the gravel plains to the pools, while the permanent water permits normally nomadic **gemsboks** to occur here year-round.

However, more so than occasional sightings of large game, the birdlife of the delta is its most rewarding feature. Large aggregations of **flamingos**, **black crakes**, **Egyptian geese**, **Cape shovelers**, **Cape teals**, **avocets** and **purple gallinules** are commonly seen from the elevated parking area above the fifth delta. During the summer, **little stints** and **wood** and **curlew sandpipers** occur while residents of the arid plains such as **tractrac chats**, **black korhaans** and **Gray's larks** (a Namibian endemic) make regular visits. Around sunset, flocks of **Namaqua sandgrouse** arrive daily from as far as 60km away to drink and, in the case of the male, to soak their absorbent belly feathers to carry water back to the chicks. A 6km self-guided trail takes walkers along a narrow canyon of the Uniab towards the coast where you should watch out for rare **Damara terns** on their nests (little more than a shallow scrape in the gravelly soil). From September through to May, tens of thousands of Palaearctic migrants such as **sanderlings**, **turnstones** and **grey plovers** congregate on the beach.

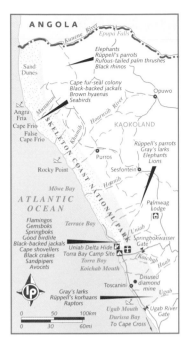

Wilderness within the wilderness

The entire northern section of the park (starting 14km north of Terrace Bay) has been set aside as a wilderness area and is closed to self-driving tourists. However, organised tours enable visitors to explore the region by guided walks and 4WD tours. The huge **Cape fur-seal** colony at Cape Frio is the main wildlife attraction but all along the coast, beached seal carcasses attract **brown hyenas** and **black-backed jackals**. The only seal-hunting **lions** in the world occur along the Skeleton Coast, even preying on the bulls – which may weigh as much as 350kg – as well as scavenging the occasional beached **whale** or **dolphin**. Nobody is sure if lions still occur as far north as Cape Frio but there is a large pride just outside the park boundary between the Hoanib and Uniab riverbeds in the south. Privately owned Palmwag Lodge (☎ 061-259293) is in the pride's territory.

Although not abundant, other big game occurs in the wilderness area and outside the park in Kaokoland. The much publicised desert **elephants** use the Hoanib and other major rivercourses to move between patches of vegetation and water. Scarce and capable of covering large distances daily, they are difficult to find. The best chance of seeing them is probably with a tour by the very experienced Skeleton Coast Fly-in Safaris. **Black rhinos**, **giraffes**, **chacma baboons**, and **klipspringers** inhabit the tree-lined watercourses as well as many small birds including **mountain chats**, **rockrunners**, **titbabblers**, **white-backed** and **red-faced mousebirds** and **Rüppell's parrots** (the range of the latter is restricted to Kaokoland and neighbouring southern Angola). The tours camp on the Kunene River, the only place in Southern Africa with recorded sightings of **rufous-tailed palm thrushes**, **Cinderella waxbills** and **grey kestrels**. ■

Cape fur-seal colonies occur all along the Skeleton Coast. Guided tours take in the colossal one at Cape Frio.

Watching tips

Following tracks is rewarding for revealing how animals eke out an existence here. Try following brown hyena tracks to fathom the distances these animals cover to survive. But don't expect to catch up with anything: beachcombing hyenas may walk 50km a day. For the more sedate, the hide at the Uniab Delta is surprisingly under-utilised by people and is a good place to invest time waiting for large mammals and birds.

CAPE CROSS SEAL RESERVE

Pandemonium on a sand-blasted coast

Wildlife highlights
Close-up viewing of a huge Cape fur-seal colony. Predators such as black-backed jackals and brown hyenas are common, especially from November to January when young pups are present. Large flocks of white-breasted and Cape cormorants; common terns are regularly seen offshore.

Location 115km north of Swakopmund. Compacted salt road accessible year-round to all vehicles.
Facilities Sealing museum.
Accommodation None. Camp site Mile 72 is 20km south and has fuel and toilets. Swakopmund is an hour's drive away and has a variety of accommodation.
Wildlife rhythms 90% of pups are born in a 34-day period from late November to early December.
Contact MET (☎ 061-236 975, fax 224 900, **e** reservations@iwwn.com.na) or the Namib info tourist office in Swakopmund (☎ 064-404 827/402 224, fax 405 101).

Watching tips
Rather than walking the length of the viewing wall expecting to see something different, choose a spot and sit for a while: no matter where you are, there is constant interaction and behaviour.

THE only pinniped (which encompasses seals, sea lions and the walrus) that breeds on continental Africa, the **Cape fur-seal** is restricted to about 25 colonies. Most occur on inaccessible islands but a handful of extremely large mainland colonies provide extraordinary viewing opportunities. En route to the Skeleton Coast NP lies one of the most accessible, Cape Cross. Between 80,000 and 110,000 fur-seals live here in a dense, seething mass. Unlike some seal species which huddle closely, Cape fur-seals vigorously defend their own small personal space. They wage a perpetual growling, bleating battle for resting spots, creating a staggering din which never subsides. Combined with the colony's pungent aroma, the effect is truly breathtaking.

There is endless activity and interaction in the colony – adults fighting for space, lost pups looking for mothers, yearling seals playing in the surf – so visiting at any time is fruitful. However, the social bedlam reaches a violent high during the breeding season when adult males begin arriving in mid-October to stake out territories. Their patch may only be a few metres wide but they defend it fiercely from other males and clashes are occasionally fatal. Territories are constantly disputed, peaking in mid-November when pregnant females 'haul out' to look for birth sites. Males gain mating 'rights' with females that pup in their territories, so their arrival at the colony intensifies the already high levels of aggression.

Like males disputing territories, females fight over pupping sites – each prefers a position close to the water. But despite the female's strong maternal bond and vigorous defence of her offspring, unattended pups are vulnerable to predation from **brown hyenas** and **black-backed jackals** (active early in the morning and late afternoon). Combined with abandonment and being crushed by adults –

particularly bulls in the frenetic defence of their harem – over one-quarter of pups die in their first year. Please do not contribute to pup deaths by walking among the seals and creating a stampede. If you get tired of seal-watching, scan the water with binoculars for various seabirds including **white-breasted** and **Cape cormorants** and **Arctic** and **common terns**. ∎

KAUDOM GAME RESERVE

A wilderness challenge

PROBABLY Namibia's richest wildlife area after Etosha NP, Kaudom is also one of the most challenging. Deep sandy roads crisscrossed by fossil river valleys (called omiramba), which become boggy marshes during the wet season, restrict access to 4WD only and vehicles must travel in pairs. There are few places in Southern Africa which evoke Kaudom's sense of wilderness and for the adventurous wildlife-watcher, it has much to offer.

A refuge for predators

Aside from Etosha, Kaudom is Namibia's most important reserve for large carnivores. One of only two protected populations of **lions** occurs here and it is the only place in Namibia where **African wild dogs** can be spotted. They regularly visit Sikereti Camp in the south, but these nomads range widely and frequently wander over the border into Botswana. Tsoana waterhole and waterholes along the eastern side of the reserve (such as Baikiaea, Leeupan and Tari Kora) are good places to look for wild dogs as well as **spotted hyenas**, **leopards** and **cheetahs**. In the drier winter months, many species of herbivore concentrate at the waterholes, including large herds of **elephants**, **buffaloes**, **giraffes**, **Burchell's zebras**, **blue wildebeests**, **greater kudus** and **tsessebes**. The extensive floodplains around Kaudom Camp in the north attract large herds of grazers and hold very good prospects for spotting **roan antelopes**.

In contrast to the other wildlife which disperses during the wet summer, a flush of migratory birdlife is attracted to Kaudom in the rainy season. Woodland residents such as **Meyer's parrots**, **Bradfield's hornbills**, and **Senegal** and **coppery-tailed coucals** are joined by over 70 migrants including **open-billed storks**, **African crakes**, **dwarf bitterns** and **African golden orioles**. Migratory raptors such as **lesser spotted eagles**, **western red-footed falcons** and **Montagu's** and **pallid harriers** can be seen in the summer while year-round residents include **pygmy falcons**, **red-necked falcons**, **Dickinson's kestrels** and rare **western banded snake eagles**. ∎

Map legend:
- FRV: Fossil River Valley
- To Katere & Rundu
- Cwiba FRV
- Kaudomn FRV
- Greater kudus, Roan antelopes, Blue wildebeests, Cheetahs
- Kaudom Camp
- Burkea WH
- Kaudom WH
- Doringstraat WH
- To Xaideng
- **KAUDOM GAME RESERVE**
- Elandsvlakte WH
- Tsau WH
- Leeupan WH
- Lions, Elands, Giraffes, Tsessebes, Elephants, Greater kudus
- Dussi WH
- Eland Plains
- Chadom FRV
- Kremetart WH
- Soncana WH
- Tsoana WH
- Khaudum FRV
- Tari Kora WH
- Baikiaea WH
- To Samakaikai
- Sikereti Camp
- Sikereti Pan
- Tsoanadom FRV
- Lions, Raptors, Coucals, Hornbills, African wild dogs
- To Tsumkwe
- BOTSWANA

Wildlife highlights

Outside Etosha, the only reserve in Namibia where you can see lions. Also home to African wild dogs, spotted hyenas, leopards and cheetahs. Good viewing of roan antelopes and elephants. A rich area for birds with 320 species – about a third of them summer visitors.

Location 796km north of Windhoek. Only accessible by 4WD and vehicles must travel in pairs.

Facilities 300km game drive network.

Accommodation Two camps, each with huts, camp sites and shower blocks.

Wildlife rhythms June to October is best for seeing large mammals, which congregate around the waterholes and along the omiramba. November to April is the richest time to visit for birdwatchers.

Contact MET (☎ 061-236 975, fax 224 900, e reservations@ iwwn.com.na).

Watching tips

Unlike most big game reserves, you can leave your car at any point. Use this privilege judiciously to check the muddy edges of waterholes: fresh tracks of lions, African wild dogs and other predators indicate areas in which to invest some time. Exercise extreme care when searching around waterholes and never alight from a vehicle alone.

MAMILI NATIONAL PARK

Return of the wildlife

Wildlife highlights
Namibia's richest birding region, this is the place to look for rare and uncommon species, including western banded snake eagles, wattled cranes, slaty egrets, white-crowned plovers, brown fire-finches and a host of others. Lions, elephants, buffaloes and semi-aquatic antelopes are fairly common on the main islands.

Location 155km southeast of Katima Mulilo, access only by 4WD.
Facilities None.
Accommodation 5 undeveloped camp sites: visitors need to be entirely self-sufficient. Huts are available in nearby Mudumu NP.
Wildlife rhythms Birding is best in summer but the rains (mostly between December and March) make much of the park inaccessible. Game-viewing is better during winter (June to August), particularly on the two islands.
Contact MET (☎ 061-236 975, fax 224 900, **e** reservations@ iwwn.com.na). Chief Conservation Officer, Katima Mulilo (☎ 067-352 27).

Watching tips
Nearby Mudumu NP is the only location in Namibia where the coppery sunbird has been recorded, though there is no reason why it should not occur in Mamili – keep a look out, particularly on the edges of riverine forest.

Aprotracted history of cross-border conflict, resettlement and heavy poaching has severely effected the wildlife of the Caprivi Strip, Namibia's 500km long fingerlike extension in its extreme northeast. Sitting in the massive Linyanti Swamp and the site of Namibia's largest protected wetland, Mamili has escaped the worst and although antelope numbers were devastated during the 1980s, the wildlife is recovering and approaching the richness of the nearby Okavango Delta. Seldom-visited due to its isolation and difficult roads, the birdlife alone warrants a trip.

Year-round water creates fertile habitat for birds and nearly 70% of Namibia's total have been recorded from this region. **Wattled cranes** breed on the expansive floodplains, while the waterways are home to **slaty egrets**, **rufous-bellied herons**, **African** and **lesser jacanas**, **pygmy geese** and **swamp boubous**. Seven species of cisticola occur including the papyrus-dwelling **chirping cisticola** and the very similar **black-backed cisticola** (the alarm call of the latter, which sounds like a machine-gun, is the easiest way to differentiate them). **Greater** and **lesser blue-eared starlings**, **western banded snake eagles**, **brown firefinches**, **collared palm thrushes** and **eastern bearded robins** are among the many other specials you might see, while **Bradfield's hornbills**, **three-banded coursers** and **white-crowned plovers** are common. Both **yellow-billed** and **red-billed oxpeckers** occur.

Despite heavy poaching in the past, Mamili's rich habitats have remained essentially undiminished and mammal populations are beginning to flourish again. **Red lechwes**, **sitatungas**, and **waterbucks** were formerly the poachers' main targets but, except for the shy sitatungas, they are easily seen in the park today. Hundreds of **hippos** and **Nile crocodiles** inhabit the permanent channels, while **elephants**, **buffaloes** and **lions** are common on the two main islands, Lupala and Nkasa. Other predators include **leopards**, **spotted hyenas** and **African wild dogs**. The Mashi River is home to **spotted-necked otters**. ∎

WATERBERG PLATEAU PARK

A tableland refuge

RISING 200m above the surrounding flat terrain, the Waterberg Plateau is a natural geological sanctuary. The steep cliffs of the plateau create a barrier to migration and game-viewing is best in the plateau's open woodlands. Visitors cannot take up their own vehicles, but guided game drives usually produce a wide variety of game species including some rare species, particularly **roan** and **sable antelopes**. However, seats are limited (book ahead or as soon as you arrive), game is generally shy here and the tours tend to be rather rushed. By far, the best way to experience Waterberg is by its numerous walking trails.

Two extended walks – one accompanied by an armed ranger, the other self-guided – allow the adventurous to explore. There is always the chance of encounters with some dangerous species including **black** and **white rhinos**, **buffaloes** and **leopards** so only experienced bushwalkers should attempt the four-day self-guided trail. Wildlife is generally less approachable by foot than in vehicles, but **giraffes**, **tsessebes**, **greater kudus**, **warthogs** and **chacma baboons** are common sights on the walks. The top predator, the leopard, apparently numbers 70 which, if accurate, makes it one of the highest densities in Southern Africa, but the rangers count themselves lucky if they see two a year.

Birding during the walks is excellent. The foothills are preferred habitat of four Namibian endemics: **Hartlaub's francolins**, **Monteiro's hornbills**, **rockrunners** and **short-toed rock thrushes**. Namibia's sole breeding colony of **Cape vultures** roosts in the cliffs of Waterberg's Karakuwisa Mountain; the Vulture Hide at the foot of the mountain offers excellent viewing of these and other birds of prey including **booted** and **black eagles**, **peregrine** and **lanner falcons** and **augur buzzards**. Carcasses are replenished every Wednesday to attract raptors. Even the short walks around the rest camp can be rewarding and **Rüppell's parrots**, **Carp's tits** and **Bennett's woodpeckers** are specials that can be seen on the Kambazembi Walk. ■

Wildlife highlights

A refuge for rare species including black and white rhinos, and roan and sable antelopes. Birding is very good: attractions include seven Namibian endemics and Namibia's only breeding colony of Cape vultures. Excellent for Damara dik-diks.

Location 97km east of Otjiwarongo. Final 25km on gravel/sand – check ahead following rain.
Facilities Guided game drives, hides, vulture hide, self-guided short walks and 4-day self-guided or guided trail.
Accommodation 2, 3 and 5 bed chalets, primitive huts for trailists, camping ground.
Wildlife rhythms Game-viewing is most productive during the dry season (April to October).
Contact MET (☎ 061-236 975, fax 224 900, **e** reservations@ iwwn.com.na).

Watching tips

Take time to explore the short tracks around Bernabé de la Bat Rest Camp – early mornings are excellent for viewing pairs of Damara dik-diks close to camp – the only place in Southern Africa aside from Etosha where they are likely to be seen.

Karakuwisa Mountain
Cape vulture colony
Raptors
Kiewietdrink
Elandsdrink
Waterberg Wilderness
Vulture Hide & Restaurant
WATERBERG PLATEAU PARK
Antephora Wilderness Trail Camp
Viewing Hide
Sables
Tsessebes
Roan antelopes
Securidaca
Hartlaub's francolins
Short-toed rock thrushes
Rockrunners
Viewing Hide
Bergtuin
Duitsepos
Viewing Hide
Dinosaur Footprints
Etjokuil
Huilboom Wilderness Trail Camp
Huilboom
Otjozongombe Shelter
Otjomapenda Shelter
To Grootfontein
Geelhout Mountain View
Sables
Tsessebes
Roan antelopes
Onjoka Park Headquarters (closed to public)
Bernabé de la Bat Rest Camp
Carp's black tits
Damara dik-diks
Rüppell's parrots
Banded mongooses
Bennett's woodpeckers
Omuverume
D2512
Little Waterberg
To Otjiwarongo & Okakarara

OTHER SITES – NAMIBIA

Brandberg
Like a smaller version of the Naukluft Massif, Brandberg rises abruptly from the Namib Desert and at its highest point towers 2.5km above the gravel plains. Wildlife is very sparse but you will see some painted on the walls: Brandberg preserves an extraordinary gallery of San paintings an estimated 15,000 to 16,000 years old including the famously enigmatic White Lady. Endemic birds such as Rüppell's korhaans, Herero chats and Monteiro's hornbills occur here as well as small numbers of chacma baboons, klipspringers and steenboks.
140km west of Omaruru,
☎ *061-236 975, fax 224 900,*
e *reservations@iwwn.com.na*

Bwabwata National Park
Combining the former Caprivi GR with the Mahango GR and the Kwando Triangle near Kongola, Bwabwata aims to rehabilitate a wilderness that has been heavily affected by poaching. Mahango and Kwando are core conservation areas and also the only spots with any sort of facilities but you'll need a 4WD regardless. Wildlife in Mahango and Kwando is similar to the Okavango's and is good in winter when waterholes and rivers are low.
220km east of Rundu,
☎ *061-236 975, fax 224 900,*
e *reservations@iwwn.com.na*

Cheetah Conservation Fund
To the east of Otjiwarongo and with almost identical aims of big cat conservation as Okonjima (see the Okonjima account), the Cheetah Conservation Fund has a research centre and an excellent Cheetah Museum. Displays and interactive exhibits illustrate the ecology of the cheetah in Namibia as well as the conservation problems it faces. Visitors are shown cheetahs rescued

from conflict situation on farms, many of which are destined for relocation into safe conservation areas and Chewbaaka, CCF's tame 'ambassador' cheetah, might also make a thrilling appearance. The Centre does not have overnight accommodation, but it's in the middle of the Waterberg Conservancy – a unique alliance of 10 privately owned farms promoting cheetah conservation. A number of the farmers operate beautiful and very hospitable guest houses – by staying with them, you directly support their efforts to conserve the cheetah. CCF doesn't charge for visits to the cheetah museum but donations are their lifeblood.
50km east of Otjiwarongo,
☎ *067-306 25,*
e *cheeta@iafrica.com.na,*
🖳 *www.cheetah.org*

Daan Viljoen Game Park
Just outside of Windhoek and on the road to Swakopmund, the camp site and bungalows at

this beautiful little park make a rewarding overnight alternative to the capital. There's only a handful of big game species here but one of them is the endemic Hartmann's mountain zebra, far more visible here than in the rest of their scattered range throughout the Namib. Springboks, red hartebeests, greater kudus, elands, gemsboks and over 200 bird species occur at Daan Viljoen GP. It gets very busy on weekends and holidays.
25km west of Windhoek,
☎ *061-236 975, fax 224 900,*
e *reservations@iwwn.com.na*

Fish River Canyon Park
For absolute quiet and otherworldly views, the 2600 million-year-old Fish River Canyon is hard to surpass. It is widely cited as the world's second-largest canyon after the Grand Canyon, but it depends on your criteria (length, depth or width): even Ethiopia's Blue Nile Gorge is far deeper. Regardless, the scenery is quite spectacular and is the main attraction. Wildlife is difficult to see here but during winter when the Orange River dwindles to a few waterholes is the best time. It's also when the outstanding 5-day Fish River Hiking Trail is open (May to September). Natural 60°C hot mineral springs soothe aching

muscles at the end of the trail at Ai-Ais which is set up as a spa resort. There's another up-welling of hot springs at the Palm Springs camp site at the start of the trail, accessible also to day walkers. If you spot en-terprising locals along the road-side with hand-written signs of the park's name, by all means pay their small fee but they'll show you a miniature tributary at the edge of the real thing.
94km west of Grünau,
☎ *061-236 975, fax 224 900,*
 e *reservations@iwwn.com.na*

Hobatere Lodge

A privately run concession on the western boundary of Etosha NP, the wildlife is similar but the experience and expense is typical of luxury lodges across Southern Africa. Guided game drives ensure you'll see pretty much everything you might en-counter on your own in Etosha and they also operate after dark with chances for nocturnal sightings of leopards, small car-nivores and owls. The lions and leopards here are the object of a fascinating study to determine how big cats live in extremely arid areas – ask owner-manager Steve Brain about it. For lovers of smaller game, Steve is also an excellent birder and there are few people in Southern Africa who can match his butterfly knowledge. Hobatere also has access to the tourist-restricted western half of Etosha.
70km northeast of Kamanjab,
☎*/fax 067-330 261*

Mudumu National Park

Similar to nearby Mamili NP (see account earlier in Namibia section), Mudumu was former-ly a hunting concession. Pro-tected now for over a decade, wildlife is recolonising this park and is as diverse as the nearby Okavango Delta, albeit in much smaller numbers. The birdlife is more rewarding with western banded snake eagles, rufous-bellied herons, wattled cranes and coppery and purple-banded

sunbirds among the local spe-cials you might spot.
50km south Kongola,
☎ *061-236 975, fax 224 900,*
 e *reservations@iwwn.com.na*

Okonjima

Owned by farmers-turned con-servationists, the Hanssen family, Okonjima is famous for its cats. As much refuge as reserve, they rescue cheetahs and leopards which would otherwise end up shot by stockmen. Orphaned cubs are hand-raised, which means a few tame big cats wander around – exhilarating but extremely dangerous and children under 12 are forbidden. However, wild-caught adults are relocated to safe reserves else-where and the Hanssens are doing much to reduce the con-flict between farmers and preda-tors – their work is well worth supporting. They also virtually guarantee wild leopard sightings on a backdrop of Namibian red rocks. The photographic oppor-tunities are unique, so long as you don't mind bait-style feeds to attract these normally ex-tremely elusive cats.
55km south of Otjiwarongo,
☎ *067-304 566/306 585,*
 e *africat@natron.net,*
🖳 *www.africat.org*

Tsaobis Leopard Nature Park

The only park in Namibia set aside specifically to protect leop-ards, you'll need considerable luck to see one here. They're very shy and cross the reserve's fence as they please, but the resident Hartmann's mountain zebras, greater kudus, gemsboks

and springboks ensure that there's usually a few around. Best places to look are along the Tsaobis and Swakop riverbeds. You're free to explore on foot here and although you probably won't find any big cats, the rugged scenery and herbivore sightings are rewarding.
35km west of Otjimbingwe,
☎ *062 252 ask for 1304*

Walvis Bay Nature Reserve

Encompassing a massive lagoon and the Kuiseb River Delta, this is one of the most important wetlands in Southern Africa for migrating waders from the northern hemisphere. Between 100,000 and 150,000 birds of 45 species arrive here during the summer months to feed before returning to Eurasia for the breeding season. As well as vis-iting species like sanderlings, Arctic terns and little stints, Damara terns nest here year-round. A saltworks operates here but seems not to worry the birds: their numbers have been steadily growing in the last decade as nearby Sandwich Lagoon silts up (see the Namib-Naukluft account).
18km south of Walvis Bay,
☎ *061-236 975, fax 224 900,*
 e *reservations@iwwn.com.na*

BOTSWANA

Bountiful wildlife in wide open spaces

WITH a human population around 1.5 million – most of it along the eastern border – vast tracts of Botswana are still largely occupied by wildlife alone. Tour guides are quick to apply adjectives like 'unspoiled', but while Botswana is far from pristine, wildlife populations are huge and, in much of the country, unconstrained by fences, roads and towns. In an increasingly populated continent, Botswana is one of the few places where ancient migratory patterns and seasonal movements are still able to cover great distances. With an excellent conservation record and an official policy of minimal development in parks, this is a place where superb wildlife-viewing is guaranteed. However, you'll need 4WD or an organised tour to enjoy it.

There are not many reserves in Botswana but most of them are huge. Officially protected areas constitute more than 17% of the country – one of the world's highest percentages of land devoted to conservation. Furthermore, parks are linked by largely uninhabited habitat corridors (which allow wildlife to move freely between reserves) and 'wildlife management areas' (where tourism, some hunting and other human activity is permitted), which effectively more than double the amount of land available to wildlife.

With such a large percentage of land area dedicated to conservation, Botswana protects critically important populations of many large animals. Elephants number 120,000 and other mega-herbivores, like gir-

affes, hippos and buffaloes, occur in the thousands. Lions, spotted hyenas and leopards are very numerous and Southern Africa's largest population of the endangered African wild dog occurs here. Huge seasonal congregations of Burchell's zebras and blue wildebeests follow nomadic pathways between Nxai Pan and Chobe NP, while resident aquatic antelopes such as red lechwes, pukus and sitatungas remain in the well-watered Okavango and Chobe riverfront year-round.

With 80% of the country covered in dry Kalahari sands, water is the critical resource for wildlife. The wet season between October and April sees the arrival of migratory birds and is when the herds congregate on the fertile marshes and plains. The desert also blooms and huge herds of springboks, gemsboks and red hartebeests coalesce in the Central Kalahari GR and Kgalagadi TP – followed by their predators. The dry season is less spectacular but limited waterpoints in the Kalahari and Nxai Pan areas produce excellent opportunities for witnessing ambushes by carnivores. Along the Chobe River, the dry season aggregations of elephants are among the largest anywhere in Africa. ∎

Inset: Explore avenues of water by mokoro (a traditional dugout canoe) through Botswana's Okavango Delta for outstanding views of animals large and small.

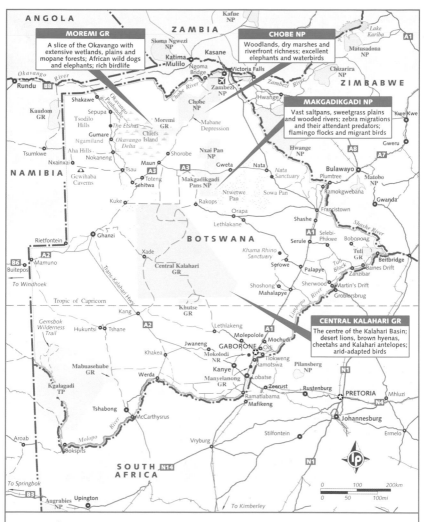

MOREMI GR
A slice of the Okavango with extensive wetlands, plains and mopane forests; African wild dogs and elephants; rich birdlife

CHOBE NP
Woodlands, dry marshes and riverfront richness; excellent elephants and waterbirds

MAKGADIKGADI NP
Vast saltpans, sweetgrass plains and zebra migrations and their attendant predators; flamingo flocks and migrant birds

CENTRAL KALAHARI GR
The centre of the Kalahari Basin; desert lions, brown hyenas, cheetahs and Kalahari antelopes; arid-adapted birds

Suggested itineraries

One week Botswana's huge conservation areas and relative inaccessibility means a week is best spent at one site. From Maun, explore any one of the following by 4WD: Central Kalahari GR, Makgadikgadi Pans and Nxai Pan NPs, the Okavango Delta or Chobe NP. An organised safari might be able to combine a couple of these if you can afford internal flights.

Two weeks Various paired combinations of the above sites work well, all from Maun and all requiring 4WD. Team Makgadikgadi and Nxai Pans (including a trip to Nata Bird Sanctuary) with the Central Kalahari, or Makgadikgadi and Nxai Pans with Moremi. Moremi/Chobe is also an excellent combination, and equally possible beginning at Kasane rather than Maun.

One month A month is sufficient to take in all four main wildlife areas mentioned in the one-week itinerary, allowing a week for each site and the day's driving required between them. Starting from Kasane means you don't have to backtrack, but it is possible from Maun in two stints. Otherwise you can try Maun-Makgadikgadi and Nxai Pans-Chobe-Moremi-Maun.

CHOBE NATIONAL PARK

The elephant's playground

KNOWN largely for enormous congregations of **elephants** and **buffaloes** along the Chobe River, this is actually one of Botswana's most diverse reserves. Encompassing wildlife-rich riverine woodlands, the Okavango-like Linyanti Swamp and the dry savanna-forest mosaic of Savute and Ngwezumba, game and birdlife here is both varied and abundant. Each area holds distinct attractions which fluctuate according to the cycles of rain and regrowth. Chobe's diversity and abundance ensure first-class viewing but the seasonal differences from one area to the next means that timing can make all the difference.

Along the river of many names

Forming the reserve's northern boundary as well as the international border between Botswana and Namibia, the Chobe River (also called the Kwando, Linyanti, and Itenge) is undeniably the most popular part of the park. Even before you see **elephants** here, it's clear they are abundant. Depending on seasonal movements, between 35,000 to 55,000 live inside the park and the damage to vegetation is severe. In the winter, the destruction looks stark but this is unquestionably the best time to see the herds as thousands line up along the river each morning and evening. They are exceptionally tolerant of vehicles (but be sure

Elephant damage

Driving along the Chobe River, the destructive power of elephants is starkly apparent. Tree destruction is actually normal behaviour and not restricted to periods of food shortage. Elephants fell trees for leaves otherwise out of reach and to avoid unappetizing foliage. Many trees mobilise unpalatable compounds such as tannins where browsing is greatest – usually lower down the tree where most species feed – and this is the reason elephants and many other species feed briefly before moving on. Knocking over the entire tree makes more palatable leaves accessible, though even uprooted trees produce more toxins when browsed (at least until they die). Although apparently wasteful, uprooting trees opens up dense habitat and promotes soil turnover. However, in enclosed conservation areas where elephant densities can be very high, they can completely destroy woodland with serious consequences for diversity. Woodland dwelling birds and mammals may eventually be driven to extinction – and this is the core of the ongoing controversy about the need to cull.

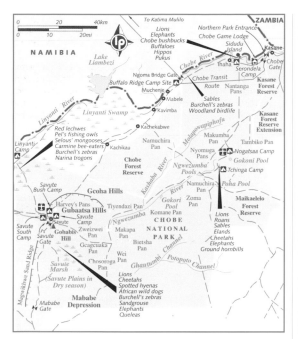

you maintain a reasonable distance) and close-up viewing of elephants interacting, swimming across the river and feeding on the riverine woodland is unsurpassed.

Other land leviathans are here in numbers. Herds of up to 1500 **buffaloes** occupy the riverfront, preferring the tall grass growing on the various 'flats' (where the river spreads out in summer flood). Leave camp early to catch them moving off these floodplains into the woodlands where they spend the day ruminating. The **lions** here know the pattern and the riverfront offers fine chances to witness a kill. Buffaloes have the advantage in the open but once they reach the wooded bushline, the dense cover allows the lions to isolate a target. Frequently they pick out a youngster (born between January and April) but

Location Chobe Gate is 6km west of Kasane (79km west of Victoria Falls); access is on tar, but internal roads are 4WD. Mababe Gate is 143km north of Maun on sand roads requiring 4WD.

Facilities Game-viewing road network and lookout points. River cruises and motorboat hire available from numerous operators in Kasane. San (Bushman) paintings on Tsonxhwaa Hill at Savute, south of Savute Gate.

Accommodation Five public camp sites and various upmarket camps within the park. Numerous options in Kasane and surrounding the park.

Wildlife rhythms The dry season (August to October) is best along the riverfront and around waterholes at Savute and Ngwezumba. The summer rains (December to February) attract massive Burchell's zebra migrations to Savute Marsh, which move to Linyanti from April onwards. For photographers, winter along the river is thick with dust and the smoke of intentionally-set fires on the Namibian side: it can make conditions very hazy but the sunsets are extraordinary.

Contact Parks and Reserves Reservations Office (☎ 661 265, fax 264, PO Box 20364, Maun, Botswana). Prior bookings are required.

Lion prides can tackle adult buffaloes, but during the summer birth season calves make up the bulk of their kills.

adults are not invulnerable and the protracted struggle between a bull buffalo and a lion pride is absolutely compelling to witness.

Hippo pods and puku pockets

Large pods of **hippos** are common in the river (one of which is invariably found near Sedudu Island) and the various boat cruises available are an exhilarating way to view them. This is the only place in Botswana where you can see the **puku**; common in Zambia and the DRC, a small enclave of this semi-aquatic antelope occurs here in isolation. The richly marked Chobe subspecies of the **bushbuck** is another riverfront special and **red lechwes**, **greater kudus** and **impalas** are common.

Aside from **elephants** and **buffaloes**, there is another major mammal species you will see in abundance here – people. The superb wildlife-viewing and proximity to Victoria Falls (90km away) attracts high numbers of visitors, most of them concentrated between the entrance gate and Serondela Camp. Venture further west towards Ngoma Gate to avoid the traffic. During the winter, you can drive all day and animals will still be found. This is the best time to look for **Burchell's zebras**, **sables** and **roan antelopes** which generally drink from mid-morning onwards when the elephants have moved off. For birdwatchers, the quieter areas along the riverfront and surrounding woodlands are the park's richest areas for birdlife and include numerous species at their southernmost limit such as **African skimmers** and **Souza's shrikes**. Some unusual raptors occur in the woodlands, among them **red-necked falcons** and **African hobbies**, while unexpected pockets of **Knysna louries** and **Natal nightjars** are also found here. Woolly caper bushes at the edge of the floodplains attract **common waxbills**, **swamp boubous** plus **yellow-bellied** and **black-eyed bulbuls**. **Pink-throated longclaws**, **giant kingfishers**, **slaty egrets** and **white-fronted bee-eaters** are often seen on boat trips, and **half-collared kingfishers** and **white-crowned** and **long-toed plovers** are other notable specials among the 450 species that have been recorded.

Spotted hyenas and white-backed vultures feed on a carcass, Savute Marsh. This region of the park provides some of the best predator viewing in Southern Africa.

Chobe's buffalo herds regularly number over 1500 and lions are never far away.

Savute: life and death on the dry marsh

Almost a day's drive from the Chobe River, Savute is the other major centre of wildlife activity in the park. Frequently likened to the Serengeti Plains for its similar scenery and cycles of migration, the experience here is very different to the riverfront. Once a rich marsh fed by the Savute Channel (which hasn't flowed since the 1980s) the Savute Marsh is now dry for much of the year and wildlife congregates around the waterholes. Late in the dry season (August to October), the larger natural pans, particularly Harvey's Pans and the artificial waterholes near the camp sites, offer superb viewing. The huge herds of **elephants** are gathered further north along the Chobe at this time but bulls remain here year-round, constantly jostling for dominance at the water and chasing **lions** away. Being one of the few regions in Africa where lions regularly prey upon young elephants, their intolerance for the big cats is unequivocal.

Although winter viewing of carnivores at the waterholes can be excellent, summer viewing offers even more opportunities as their numbers increase following the arrival of the migratory herds. When the rains arrive (usually November to December),

Sink or swim

One evening we stopped near the old Serondela camp site to watch a small family of elephants swimming across the river. Reminiscent of whales, the adults seemed to 'float-sink' the crossing, while the youngsters were discernible only by their small trunks snorkelling the water's surface. After most of the family had docked on the other side we noticed a mother and calf still struggling in the middle of the river. The calf seemed to have lost his bearings and was beginning to swim back to the shore they had just left. An exhausted mother had swum half the width of the river to help him. Now she guided the calf with her trunk as best she could, trying desperately to keep him afloat. The drama was so riveting we had to remind ourselves to breathe. Finally they reached the shore where they recovered in the shallows for what seemed an eternity before joining the others.

Robyn Keene-Young, Johannesburg, South Africa

Game-viewing by boat is an excellent way to see elephants, hippos, crocs and waterbirds.

thousands of **Burchell's zebras** move into the area from the north, seeking the new growth out on the Marsh. Since the Savute Channel dried out, the numbers have dwindled but they're still impressive. **Lion** and **spotted hyena** numbers swell on the zebra feast, and most foals are born during this period providing a glut of suitable prey for other predators that can't tackle the adults. **Cheetahs** and **African wild dogs** are most common during this period – the open areas of the marsh are the best places to look for them. Smaller hunters, particularly **black-backed** and **side-striped jackals**, contest kill remains and afterbirth with four **vulture** species (**hooded, white-backed, lappet-faced** and **white-headed**) and numerous other **raptors**. Although Savute's drier habitat does not support the diversity of birds seen along the river, an additional summer bonus is the arrival of many migratory species including **Abdim's storks, carmine bee-eaters, Caspian** and **ringed plovers**, various **sandpipers**, and **black-winged pratincoles**. Take note, although the sand roads around Savute are compacted and easy to traverse in the summer, the Marsh roads become extremely boggy, sometimes necessitating road closures between December and March – check ahead.

Far from the madding crowd

Although the Chobe River is the only part of the reserve which can be called crowded, for those looking for really quiet spots,

Use binoculars to check under the fronds of the real fan palm for nesting palm swifts; they glue their eggs to the palm leaves using their sticky saliva.

Elephants are intolerant of other drinkers, a great source of exciting and often amusing sightings.

two other regions in the park are worth exploring. The Ngwezumba region between Savute and Chobe has very little development and is largely ignored by most of the commercial tours. Clay-bottomed pans hold water well into the winter and the two camp sites (Nogatsaa and Tchinga) sit on the edge of pans, allowing some excellent viewing of **elephants**, **buffaloes**, **lions** and numerous species of **antelope** literally from your tent. Nogatsaa Camp acts as a Botswana Defence Force post and can be noisy sometimes but Tchinga is totally undeveloped (except for an unreliable water pump: carry your own supply).

Very different habitat occurs in the northwest corner of the park at Linyanti, the name given to this stretch of the Chobe River which forms part of the Linyanti Swamp in summer. Like a pocket of the Okavango, a mosaic of savanna, papyrus reeds and mature forest creates an environment particularly rich in birdlife. **Pel's fishing owls**, **slaty egrets**, **rufous-bellied herons**, **white-backed herons**, and **African skimmers** are among the species recorded along the river while the forests are home to **Meyer's parrots**, **black-headed orioles** and **green-capped eremomelas**, to name just a few.

Game-viewing peaks from April onwards when huge **Burchell's zebra** herds return from Savute to congregate at Linyanti and while only 7km of the river is accessible to self-drive tourists, the various lookouts over the river produce some excellent viewing. More animals arrive as the winter progresses so it's better to arrive late in the dry (September to October). Aside from **lions** and reasonable chances for **leopards** and **African wild dogs**, this area is rich in small carnivores which are very difficult to see elsewhere, including **servals**, **zorillas** and **Selous' mongooses**. However, most of them are active after dark. Private concessions along the river conduct excellent night-drives, but you need to be an overnight guest. Kwando Wildlife Experiences are excellent (see Botswana's Other Sites section). ∎

Watching tips

In winter, elephants are so abundant along the Chobe they tend to monopolise the river and other game can be a little sparse. The waterhole just inside the entrance gate attracts more retiring species such as sables, greater kudus, Chobe bushbucks and sometimes leopards. If you don't see any Chobe bushbucks when driving around or at the waterhole, some very tame ones loiter at Chobe Game Lodge. Various camp sites are renowned for their regular visitors: Serondela has a very tame (and destructive) troop of banded mongooses while Savute has spotted hyenas and elephants. Nogatsaa and Tchinga camp sites have visits from very bold lions: occasionally, they lie down literally at the fringes of the camp fire.

CENTRAL KALAHARI GAME RESERVE

Botswana's desert heart

Wildlife highlights
A true wilderness, the Central Kalahari is home to huge populations of blue wildebeests, springboks and gemsboks which congregate during the summer. Lions, cheetahs and spotted hyenas are often seen here and smaller predators such as meerkats, honey badgers and bat-eared foxes are very common. Raptors are diverse, and insectivorous and seed-eating birds such as finches, larks, flycatchers and weavers are abundant during the summer.

LOCATED in the most extensive expanse of sand found anywhere in the world lies Botswana's largest game reserve, a vast tract of arid wilderness in the centre of the country three times the size of Swaziland. Originally established to enable the Khwe people to maintain their traditional way of life, it has been opened to tourism only very recently and is still largely undeveloped. The Central Kalahari is one of the most remote destinations in Southern Africa – some of its tracks don't see a vehicle for months – and it requires self-sufficiency and experience to explore. Located in Botswana's centre, this immense expanse is home to huge populations of large herbivores and the predators which subsist on them, but for most of the year, wildlife is widely dispersed and can be difficult to see. To experience the Kalahari at its most productive requires that a visit is well-timed to coincide with the summer rains, when thousands of animals congregate in the richest parts of the park.

Valley of the hyenas
Made famous by Mark and Delia Owens who studied **brown hyenas** here for seven years, Deception Valley in the northern part of the park is a fossil riverbed that hasn't flowed for 16,000 years. However, the valley is peppered with open pans which become the wildlife focus of the park following the rains.

People of the Kalahari
Unique among African reserves, the Central Kalahari was originally proclaimed to protect the hunting-gatherer existence of the indigenous Khwe ('Bushmen') who have lived here for at least 30,000 years. Together with more recent arrivals, the Bkagalagadi people, you can still encounter their villages in the park. Until 1997, almost 2000 people lived here, but against their wishes the government has begun resettling them outside the reserve, ostensibly to improve their access to amenities, though cynics believe the move clears the way for large-scale mining of extensive diamond deposits. There are now only around 200 to 300 people living in villages clustered in the east and south of the park. Extremely friendly, they welcome visitors but please observe proper etiquette: wait at a respectable distance from the houses until the occupants greet you and ask before taking any photographs.

Location 170km south of Maun (to Matswere Game Scout Camp) or 215km north-west from Gaborone to Khutse. Only accessible by 4WD.

Accommodation None. Numerous undeveloped camp sites, some with pit latrines. Visitors must be entirely self-sufficient here. Water can be obtained at the gamescout camps but also take plenty.

Wildlife rhythms Summer rains (usually around December to March) make animals concentrate in the pans systems and is also the period many herbivores drop their young. Roads during the wet can be very boggy and hard-going.

Contact Parks and Reserves Reservations Office (☎ 580 774, fax 775, **e** dwnp@gov.bw, PO Box 131, Gaborone, Botswana). Prior bookings are required.

Columns of herbivores move in from the surrounding woodland and scrub, seeking the flush of young, sweet grass growing on the pans. Driving the length of the valley, it is possible to see thousands of herbivores in a single day – **blue wildebeests**, **springboks**, and **gemsboks** dominate but **red hartebeests**, **greater kudus** and **elands** are also common.

The profusion of meat-on-the-hoof means that predators will be nearby and chances are very high for seeing Kalahari **lions**. This is also a fairly reliable time for **cheetahs** and the open terrain offers superb scope for viewing a 100km/h hunt. During December and January, their quarry will almost invariably be the springboks' newborn young. If you are fortunate enough to encounter a mother cheetah with cubs, she may release the young alive for the cubs to practice their hunting skills – sometimes distressing to watch, but crucial experience for the young cheetahs and fascinating to witness. **Spotted hyenas** are often seen in the early mornings and **brown hyenas** (on which Deception's reputation was founded) are common. However, being largely

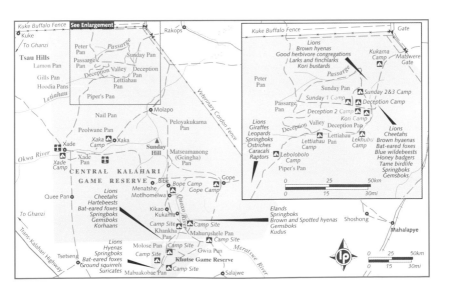

The summer flush of grass in the Central Kalahari provides rich pickings for many grazers including gemsboks.

nocturnal and shy, you may only catch a glimpse of a brown hyena on your way back to camp at dusk.

The burst of green also brings hordes of insects and other invertebrates, a rich food source for aerial and terrestrial hunters alike. **Honey badgers, bat-eared foxes, yellow mongooses** and **meerkats** dig relentlessly in the sandy soil, often for **scorpions** which are prolific in summer. The most forbidding-looking ones with over-sized pincers are actually relatively harmless but beware of the smaller species with thick tails and small pincers (family Buthidae): their poison is extremely dangerous. **Kori bustards, red-crested** and **black korhaans** and **secretary birds** stride through the short grass, snapping up insects as well as lizards and the occasional rodent, while bug-and-seed specialists such as **Marico flycatchers, chat flycatchers** and 10 species of **lark** and **finchlark** are abundant. Raptors include **martial eagles, bateleurs, black-breasted snake eagles, pale chanting goshawks,** numerous **falcons** and **black-shouldered kites.**

In the winter, wildlife in Deception Valley can be as thin on the ground as in the rest of the park but if you do visit in the dry, drive the length of the valley to Piper's Pan where you can also camp. With its solar-powered pump, it is far more reliable

Veterinary fences

If you approach the Central Kalahari from the north or east, you'll have to pass through the Kuke veterinary fence to enter the park. In fact, veterinary fences (intended to isolate supposed disease-carrying wildlife from cattle) crisscross the entire country, carving up Botswana into livestock and non-livestock areas. Fences are nothing new to Botswana's cattle ranchers but during a severe drought in the 1980s, their effects on wildlife reached catastrophic levels. When the Central Kalahari's blue wildebeests attempted to migrate from the park to better grazing in the north, an estimated 65,000 to 70,000 died against the Kuke Fence. Similar fences prevent migrations between Nxai Pan and the Okavango, between northern Botswana and Namibia's Caprivi Strip and elsewhere around the country, including the arid northwest where three new fences have been erected since 1995.

Even so, despite the indisputable costs to wildlife (an estimated 1.5 million head of large ungulates have been killed since 1960), the fences also work the other way. They exclude cattle from core wildlife areas, often the only barrier to wilderness being converted to farmland by relentless encroachment. In a country where cattle numbers only continue to escalate, fences may be the ultimate hope for maintaining wildlife areas.

than the erratic water supplies at other artificial waterholes (Sunday, Letiahau and Passarge) and offers the best chances for wildlife-viewing. **Springboks**, **gemsboks** and **ostriches** are assured, though in much smaller numbers than the summer herds, and other species such as **blue wildebeests**, **giraffes** and **greater kudus** have usually dispersed.

Khutse: game-viewing by camp chair

The maps show the Khutse region as a separate game reserve but this applies on paper only. Forming the southernmost extension of the Central Kalahari, it was once part of an ancient river system that held enough surface water to give rise to its name, which means 'where one kneels down to drink'. Nowadays, as in the north, it is dry for most of the year but during the wet summer, its scattering of about 60 pans are focal points for wildlife activity. The concentrations rarely reach the densities in Deception but the same species are present. Predators tend not to be as commonly viewed as in the north (perhaps because the number of people is greater around Khutse), but it is well-known for its **lions**, which make regular visits to the permanent waterhole at Molose.

Almost all the camp sites in Khutse are situated close to pans, many of them right on the pan's edge which means you don't have to travel far to see animals. Some of the sites are ideally placed to sit in camp and wait for game to arrive. If you're reasonably quiet and avoid standing or moving around (animals are very wary of the human shape but don't appear to recognise it if you stay seated) you can see just about everything from the comfort of your camp chair. If you do decide to drive around, it's possible to cover Khutse's entire network (about 160km) in a day but it's generally far more rewarding to focus activity in one area. Overlapping the border of Khutse and the Central Kalahari are a series of closely clustered pans (most with camp sites) where, if there's nothing at one pan, there'll probably be something at the next. Khutse is easily reached from the south providing you have a 4WD, but if you're planning on driving through the reserve don't expect to see much wildlife on the 290km arid stretch between Xade and Khanke Pan on the Central Kalahari-Khutse border. ■

Watching tips
Perhaps because people are so scarce here, the birds in some of the camps show little fear and are quite tame. At Owen's Camp in Deception Valley, Kalahari robins, titbabblers, southern masked weavers and scaly-feathered finches will approach visitors closely. Strangely, the leaflet to Khutse suggests leaving some fruit out for the birds to attract them in the camp sites, though it is against park regulations to feed animals. Providing slivers of fruit for birds is probably not too serious, but bear in mind that every action that alters an animal's behaviour, however slight, should be viewed with a critical eye.

MAKGADIKGADI PANS & NXAI PAN NATIONAL PARKS

Front row seats to life and death

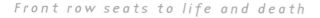

Wildlife highlights
Summer brings thousands of migratory Burchell's zebras and blue wildebeests to Nxai Pan, joining winter residents that include springboks and giraffes. Viewing of lions is good and this is one of the best places in Botswana to see cheetahs. Elephants are normally seen (best in summer), and giraffes, red hartebeests and impalas are numerous. Excellent birding particularly in the wet season, a highlight being huge flocks of flamingos on the pans.

DEEP Kalahari sands surrounding endless saltpans hardly seem a likely habitat for abundant wildlife and perhaps for this reason, these parks experience moderate tourist traffic. However, while lacking the richness of the Okavango Delta or Chobe NP, open scenery and perfect visibility offers rare chances to view seldom-seen wildlife events such as predators making kills and the birth of herbivores. Makgadikgadi Pans and Nxai Pan are divided only by the tarred Maun-Nata highway – be alert driving this stretch as there are no fences and animals move freely between the two reserves. Never predictable, wildlife movements may cover huge distances and the key to enjoying these reserves is knowing where to be when the rain comes and where to be when it doesn't.

Makgadikgadi Pans: migrations and congregations

Dominated by the massive Ntwetwe and Sowa (or Sua) saltpans, Makgadikgadi can be rather lifeless during the dry winter. The pans themselves are too salty to support any vegetation or much wildlife but for unparalleled, moonscape-like vistas, they are best visited in the Dry (May to November) when it is safe to drive on them. Most wildlife action occurs in the west where

Why do zebras have stripes?

Watching the huge zebra herds at Makgadikgadi and Nxai, it's difficult not to ponder the most obvious question: why do they have stripes? There are many theories and no single answer is entirely satisfactory. The most enduring suggests that stripes break up the zebra's outline, disorienting predators during the hunt. However, given that many carnivores easily capture zebras, the effect, if any, must be minimal. Rather than confuse predators, the stripes' function may be directed towards other zebras. Highly attracted to stripes (even painted on safari trucks), zebras might rely on them to maintain contact. Contrasting bands are a clear visual signal in dark, dusty conditions (such as during a nocturnal hunt), possibly assisting zebras to avoid being separated and becoming an easy kill. Stripes are also thought to be a mechanism for foals and mothers to recognise one another but, like most of the theories, this has never been verified.

the national park actually begins, with its western boundary (the Boteti River) forming the main focus for much of the year. Here, the pans and dry grasslands give way to riverine woodlands where animals congregate looking for pools in the riverbed. The build-up takes place gradually from about May. By October, the congregations of **Burchell's zebras**, **blue wildebeests**, **giraffes** and **greater kudus** can be massive and **lions**, **spotted hyenas** and **leopards** are regularly sighted. Khumaga Camp overlooks the Boteti and the river road offers numerous lookout points to spot game.

As soon as the rains arrive, the herds are no longer tied to the river and begin to disperse. Usually from December onwards, they begin the search for new growth carpeting the plains and you need to travel further afield to find them. Njuca Hills Camp makes a good base to explore the grasslands. The drives are very long unless you double back but well worth the effort to catch the migration as it heads south. By about March, the herds are concentrated in the southeast of the reserve or have moved out of the park altogether, moving back towards the Boteti in May.

Highly variable, it's easy to miss the throng of herbivores, but equally breathtaking congregations take place on the flooded pans themselves. Tens of thousands of **greater** and **lesser flamingos** arrive, drawn to millions of tiny crustaceans (which remained dormant in eggs during the winter) and the algae,

Location 162km east of Maun. Only accessible by 4WD.

Facilities Game-viewing hide and Baines' baobabs at Nxai Pan NP.

Accommodation 4 basic camp sites. Nxai Pan sites and Khumaga have shower blocks with water; Njuca Hills has pit latrines and no water.

Wildlife rhythms Summer rains (usually around December to March) concentrate animals at Nxai Pan and is also the period many herbivores drop their young. Game-viewing is best at Makgadikgadi late in the dry (October). Massive flamingo flocks arrive at the saltpans following the rain but roads during the wet can be very boggy and driving on the pans is extremely dangerous.

Contact Parks and Reserves Reservations Office (☎ 661 265, fax 264, PO Box 20364, Maun, Botswana). Prior bookings are required.

Baines' baobabs. Originally referred to as the Sleeping Sisters, they were immortalised in oils by Thomas Baines in 1862.

which flourishes in the warm, shallow water. The location of the huge flocks varies, but probably the most reliable place to see them is actually outside the national park at the Nata Bird Sanctuary on the northeastern side of Sowa Pan. Other summer migrants include **African fish eagles**, **saddle-billed storks**, **wattled cranes** and many species of **wader** and **plover**.

Nxai Pan: abandon hope, ye who drink here

Unlike the bare, salt-encrusted pans of Makgadikgadi, Nxai Pan itself supports a layer of sweet grass and is surrounded by mopane woodland, providing a mixture of habitats for grazers and browsers. During the long dry winter, many herbivores leave the park but arid-adapted **springboks** usually remain, becoming the main food source for Nxai's carnivores. In particularly dry winters, the artificial waterhole just north of South Camp holds exceptional opportunities to watch interactions between predators and prey. Despite virtually no cover, **lions** position themselves around the pan, knowing that the springboks will inevitably attempt to drink. Equally aware of the lions' presence, the springboks are extremely cautious but invariably, one lingers a fraction too long at the water when the lions unleash their rush. In the course of a single winter's day at the waterhole, it is quite possible to witness three or four kills.

Cheetahs enjoy ideal habitat at Nxai: the savanna-woodland mosaic is ideal hunting terrain and also offers refuges for females to raise their cubs. The resident springbok herds provide a year-round larder but cheetahs don't wait at waterholes like lions. Drive the roads which crisscross the pan and make frequent stops to scan for them with binoculars. Be out searching at dawn when, in addition, you are almost certain to see numerous smaller predators including **bat-eared foxes** huddled together in the winter sun or **honey badgers**, sometimes accompanied by **pale chanting goshawks** hoping for a mouse or lizard escaping the badger's attention. Other raptors such as **kestrels**, **red-necked falcons**, **martial eagles** and **bateleurs** are common. **Kori bustards**, **black korhaans**, **red-billed francolins**

Safe by seconds

'Cheetahs.' The call came from our hawk-eyed tracker, Moffat. Across Nxai Pan, I could just make out four shapes silhouetted against the dawn sun. They could have been impalas for all the detail I could see but Moffat's eyes never lied. As we approached, he and fellow ranger Seagal conferred briefly in Setswana then Seagal turned to us, his excitement transparent. 'Four males, probably brothers. And they're hunting.'

Sure enough, we'd no sooner pulled alongside the coalition when they spotted a distant herd of springboks. Switching suddenly to an intent trot, the four brothers began closing the gap. Suddenly a springbok's piercing alarm whistle broke the still, winter air: spotted! As though connected, springboks and cheetahs exploded. Three of the brothers were too slow off the mark but the leading male had chosen his target. Incredibly, as the cheetah narrowed the quarry's lead, the springbok turned in a great arc straight towards our vehicle, thundering past us within metres. Then, as quickly as the chase began, the cheetah gave up! 'Too long', said Seagal. 'Cheetahs can only sprint for about 15 seconds, then…exhaustion!' As the springbok sped to safety, the panting cat flopped down. Moments later, his lagging brothers trotted up and joined him in the dust, the chase forgotten.

Sophie Wise, Melbourne, Australia

Real fan palms at sunset, Makgadikgadi: they're also known in Botswana by their Tswana name, the Mokolane palm.

and four different **coursers** (**Burchell's**, **Temminck's**, **double-banded** and **bronze-winged**) are just a few of the other birds commonly seen. At South Camp there are very visible **blue**, **violet-eared** and **black-cheeked waxbills**.

Summer's flood of life

For all the rewards of winter at Nxai, it's during the wet summer that the park erupts with life. Beginning around December, the rains bring a green flush to the heavily grazed vegetation and thousands of herbivores move to the pan. Probably the closest thing in Southern Africa to the Serengeti migrations, huge herds of **Burchell's zebras** and **blue wildebeests** accompanied by smaller numbers of **elands**, **red hartebeests**, **impalas** and **giraffes** join the **springboks**, many of them to drop their young.

Plentiful water means that predators have to wander further to hunt but the sheer abundance of animals, particularly young vulnerable ones, means that success is virtually assured – though of course, it might occur anywhere and seeing the action is less predictable than during winter.

Summer also brings the return of **elephant** herds. While small groups of bulls can be seen year-round, breeding herds with calves require the flush of summer growth. They are hard to miss, but if you don't see them in the open, drive the roads through the mopane woodlands near North Camp and to Kgama-Kgama Pan. Other summer visitors include **Abdim's storks**, **European bee-eaters** and **dusky larks**. ■

Watching tips

Hollows in the isolated baobabs scattered thoughout Nxai Pan and Makgadikgadi make perfect roosts for various birds. Barn owls nest in one such hollow of Baines' baobabs (the famous trees painted by explorer Thomas Baines during his 1862 expedition) and southern yellow-billed hornbills, lilac-breasted and purple rollers in the baobabs on Kubu Island. The deep folds in their massive trunks attract bees which nest in the crevices: such as in the single baobab on Baobab Loop at Nxai Pan. When this nest is active, people have experienced the terrific privilege of being guided to the nest by a greater honeyguide.

MOREMI GAME RESERVE
Wealth in the swamps

THE only part of Botswana with abundant, year-round water, the Okavango Delta is a massive oasis where the density of many wildlife species reaches its peak for the entire country. Protecting almost one-third of the Okavango, Moremi GR encompasses some of the most productive areas of an inherently bountiful region. Except for rhinos, the **Big Five** are abundant and Africa's largest and most southern population of the semi-aquatic **red lechwe** occurs here. Their abundance (there are over 30,000 in the Delta) as well as extremely high densities of **impalas** contribute to making this ideal habitat for Southern Africa's most endangered large carnivore, the **African wild dog**. Aside from the multitude of other wildlife species that can be seen here, many people visit Moremi because it is the best place in Southern Africa to see them.

The painted wolves of winter
The Okavango contains one of the largest remaining populations of **African wild dogs** in Africa, many with permanent home ranges inside Moremi (there are no fences in the reserve and they are free to roam throughout the Delta). They have become inured to the constant presence of vehicles and their indifference permits rare encounters, including witnessing hunts and watching young pups at den sites. You're unlikely to stumble upon an active den without some local knowledge, but even if you don't see puppies, the packs make morning and evening forays onto the game rich floodplains and woodland edges in the Xakanaxa area, on Mboma Island (particularly the Northern Loop) and along the Khwai River.

The mokoro
Appearing on every tourist brochure ever produced on the Okavango and suffering slightly from a 'must-do' tag, the dug-out mokoro (plural: mekoro) has actually been used by Delta fishermen since the mid-1700s. Fashioned by hand using small axes, their manufacture can take as long as five months, a back-breaking task because rot-resistant hardwoods such as kiaat and jackalberry trees are preferred. Even so, mekoro only last for a few years and with the increase of tourism in the Okavango, mokoro-making is threatening the hardwood trees and placing demands on many other species which, traditionally, were never used. Many lodges and operations now offer trips in fibreglass mekoro or conventional-style canoes. Don't be disappointed; regardless of the material used, the trips are a silent, intimate way to explore the Okavango's waterways and the fibreglass option is doing much to conserve the Delta's large trees.

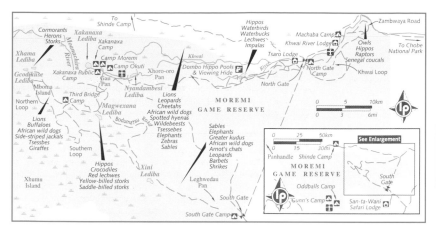

Midwinter, when the pups are born, coincides with peak prey concentrations along the permanent water sources. Abundant water in Moremi means cyclical wildlife movements are less pronounced than elsewhere in Botswana but as the smaller pools dwindle, large herds of **red lechwes**, **impalas**, **waterbucks** and **blue wildebeests** congregate near the deeper channels and pools. The dry winter also experiences an influx of **elephants**, **buffaloes** and **Burchell's zebras** from drier regions outside the Delta, augmenting the resident herds which remain year-round. Although wildlife exists in profusion all year, it is generally best viewed in winter.

Streams and extremes

Although much of Moremi is permanently underwater, the main land mass in the east and extensive sandy islands provide far more diverse habitats than the constantly flooded central Delta. Forests of mature mopane trees (characterised by small butterfly-shaped leaves) are dominated by the constant presence of two mammalian extremes: **elephants** and **tree squirrels**. Virtually everything in between also occurs in the forests, but for better viewing, head towards the floodplains where the mopane gives way to open woodlands of knobthorns (with very distinctive knob-ridden trunks) and rain trees, named for the mist-like droplets exuded by frog-hoppers (spittle bugs), which siphon off the sap and excrete the excess fluid – the 'rain'.

Location 97km north of Maun (to South Gate) – all roads in Moremi require 4WD.

Facilities Extensive game drive network, hide at Dombo Hippo Pool. Mokoro rides and boat trips available at many lodges and camps.

Accommodation 4 public camp sites in Moremi and 2 on the periphery (Gunn's Camp and Oddball's, both private concessions), also 3 camp sites in the Panhandle (Drostsky's Cabins, Shakawe Fishing Camp and Makwena). 5 lodges operate inside the park but there are many on the periphery and throughout the Okavango.

Wildlife rhythms The dry season is generally the most productive because summer rains make many areas inaccessible and dense vegetation impedes viewing. Additionally, while less pronounced than elsewhere, animals congregate at permanent water during winter. Late in the Dry (September to October) is best but temperatures can be high.

Contact Parks and Reserves Reservations Office (☎ 661 265, fax 264, PO Box 20364, Maun, Botswana). Prior bookings are required.

These edge woodlands are the richest wildlife habitat and apart from being favoured by **African wild dogs**, hold excellent chances for **lions** and **leopards** as well as most of Moremi's large herbivores. Birdlife is prolific and includes very common **Arnot's chats, black-collared barbets** and **arrow-marked babblers** and some rarer specials such as **Bradfield's hornbills**. As these woodlands open further onto the floodplains, check the reedbeds and woodlands lining the channels for three species of **coucal** (**black, coppery-tailed** and **Senegal**).

Life of the lagoons

With water in such abundance, it's no surprise that wading birds are prolific. Eighteen different members of the heron family occur here, including **goliath herons, slaty egrets, black egrets, white-backed night herons, rufous-bellied herons,** and all three Southern African **bittern** species. While the more secretive species are largely solitary, communally roosting species such as **grey herons, black-headed herons** and **little egrets** as well as various **storks** and **cormorants** form large breeding colonies. During the breeding season from August to November (peaking September to October), over a thousand birds of various species can be seen in a few hours at one of these 'heronries'. The best sites are Xakanaxa Lediba, Gcodikwe Lediba and Xobega Lediba (lediba means 'lagoon' in Setswana), all of them along the Moanachira River – you'll need to boat or mokoro to reach them. Along the permanent pools and waterways, viewing of **wattled cranes, saddle-billed storks, pygmy geese, fulvous ducks, darters** and dozens more species is excellent – the hide at Dombo Hippo Pool and the inter-connected Gau, Mokutshumu and Mmalwswana Pans near Xakanaxa are prime spots.

Raptors over the river Khwai

In addition to ever-present waterbirds, the Khwai River is also well known for congregations of raptors. During the dry season (July to November), the northern reaches of the river are particularly rewarding: take the Zambwaya Road to see large

The carnivore chain of command

With such an abundance of large carnivores, Moremi is one of the finest reserves for witnessing interactions between the super-predators. As competitors for the same resources, they share no affinity and encounters between them are typically hostile. By far the largest African carnivore, the lion (inset) sits largely unchallenged at the top of the pecking order. Lions usually kill anything they can and that includes all other large predators if they get hold of one. Adult lions in turn mostly only worry about other lions but large spotted hyena clans occasionally kill injured or subadult lions and are certainly able to drive small prides off their kills. Spotted hyenas also dominate the other hunters and Moremi is excellent for observing them trailing African wild dogs on the hunt, hoping for a free meal. Again, weight of numbers is a factor: a few spotted hyenas can lord over an entire African wild dog pack but a single spotted hyena is easily harassed into retreat. Both spotted hyena clans and wild dog packs also dominate leopards, but individuals do so at their peril: leopards sometimes kill lone spotted hyenas and wild dogs. At the very bottom of the hierarchy sits the cheetah. They've sacrificed brute force for speed and can't physically overpower the other super-predators. Further, they simply cannot afford the risk of injury and invariably give way to other large predators, regardless of numbers.

The central Okavango is permanently inundated. Most game-viewing takes place on the periphery where terrestrial life is more abundant.

numbers of **bateleurs**, **African fish eagles**, **tawny eagles**, **black-breasted snake eagles**, **martial eagles** and many smaller species. Ten species of **owl** occur in the reserve: four species (**giant eagle**, **spotted eagle**, **white-faced** and **pearl-spotted**) are often seen in daylight if you look carefully in the woodland trees. The Okavango is also arguably the best place in Africa to view the rare and secretive **Pel's fishing owl**: at sunset, they perch on the poles marking the various river stream crossings but for the best chances, take a boat or mokoro very early in the morning or at dusk – also your best chance to catch a glimpse of the very elusive **sitatunga** (best seen in the Jao area).

Besides aerial predators, the Khwai region produces excellent viewing of terrestrial hunters. **Lions** and **spotted hyenas** are common and the floodplains here are probably the best place in Moremi to look for **cheetahs**. **Leopards** and **African wild dogs** are regularly seen and the well-watered grasslands are optimum habitat for **servals**. Long-legged rodent specialists, servals are more crepuscular (active at dawn and dusk) than most small cats, so keep a careful look out when departing and returning to camp. Moremi is also excellent for **side-striped jackals**. Less common and less studied than the abundant black-backed species, they look very similar from a distance but their white-tipped tail is a giveaway (black-backed jackals have a black tail tip). ■

Watching tips

Most camp sites have very distinctive sausage trees, which are irresistible to flocks of Meyer's parrots that open the bulbous fruits for their seeds. During spring many species feed on the fallen flowers, including nocturnal specials such as bushbucks, Cape porcupines and African civets: camp near one (but not underneath, the fruits weigh in at 4kg) and watch with a torch from your tent. For birders looking to top Moremi's avian wealth, a trip north into the Panhandle (the park's northwestern extension) will improve your chances of seeing black-faced babblers and Cape parrots, and is also very good for African skimmers and Pel's fishing owls.

MABUASEHUBE GAME RESERVE
Place of red earth

Location 82km north of Tshabong, 4WD access only.
Facilities None; water for cooking available at the gamescout camp.
Accommodation Undeveloped camp sites at Khiding, Lesholoago, Mabuasehube and Mpaathutlwa Pans.
Wildlife rhythms December to March is the rainy season when newly sprouted grass and water give rise to congregations of herbivores and their hunters around the pans.
Contact Reservations Office (☎ 580 774, fax 775, e dwnp@gov.bw, PO Box 131, Gaborone, Botswana).

Watching tips
If a productive-looking pan (ie, lots of grass and/or water) seems lifeless, take a closer look before racing off to the next one. Lions resting in the surrounding wild sesame bushes or under the acacia trees could be the reason.

ADJOINING the Kgalagadi TP, Mabuasehube is shown as a separate entity on most maps but is now officially part of the KTP. Even so, except for the extremely sandy and remote track along the KTP's southern boundary, there is no link for vehicles between the two and most people visit Mabuasehube as its own destination. With seven large pans and a legion of smaller ones clustered into an area only 5% the size of the KTP, Mabuasehube is a hotspot for wildlife activity.

The red circuit
Encircling the pan system, Mabuasehube's road network is all on Kalahari red sand (mabuasehube means 'the place of red earth'). Strictly 4WD, the circuit is best during the rainy season when the sand is compacted. This is also the best time for game-viewing, when water-filled pans and the new grass around them attract large herds of **gemsboks**, **springboks**, **elands** and **red hartebeests**. **Big cats**, **spotted hyenas** and occasionally **African wild dogs** follow them. Bosobogolo and Mpaathutlwa Pans have excellent grass cover in summer. The white clay pan at Mabuasehube is mostly bare of vegetation year-round but the mineral-rich soil attracts the herds for another reason: they lick the surface for supplementary salts or drink them in solution after a downpour. Thousands of **African bullfrogs** emerge from this pan-bed to breed following the first rain. At up to 2kg, the adult males are extremely aggressive and even attack **lions** in defence of their tadpole brood.

With basic camp sites overlooking four of the pans, sometimes you needn't even leave camp for some excellent viewing. It's illegal to drive after dark here but armed with a fold-out chair and a decent torch (spotlights are prohibited), you can illuminate a few nocturnal sights from the comfort of camp. **Brown hyenas** and **black-backed jackals** usually won't be far away if you've been cooking meat, and at both the Mabuasehube and Lesholoago camp sites **honey badgers** and **Cape foxes** will sometimes wander in. And although they won't be interested in your cooking, insectivorous **aardwolves** are another possibility, especially when the rain brings a breeding flush of **termites** to the surface. ∎

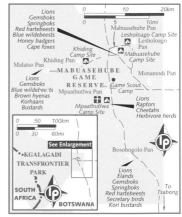

OTHER SITES – BOTSWANA

Gcwihaba Caverns (Drotsky's Cave)
Because they're remote and completely undeveloped, you shouldn't venture too deeply into Gcwihaba Caverns unless you're an experienced caver. But one of the easiest routes (beginning at the lower entrance, halfway up the hill at the end of the entrance road) is a boon for bat-lovers: thousands of Commerson's leaf-nosed bats, Egyptian slit-faced bats and Dent's horseshoe bats roost here. Outside the caves, arid-adapted antelopes as well as the very occasional lion and African wild dog pack pass through.
331km east of Maun

Khama Rhino Sanctuary
Established to protect the few remaining rhinos in Botswana, the Botswanan Defence Force patrols here 24 hours a day to thwart would-be poachers. Both white and black rhinos occur, but collectively they number less than a dozen. Nonetheless, it holds the best chances in Botswana of spotting one, along with Kalahari wildlife like red hartebeests, elands, brown hyenas, bat-eared foxes and ostriches. The minimal gate fee is excellent value and contributes directly to rhino conservation. Khama's camp site, Mekonwa, (again, ridiculously affordable) makes an excellent overnight stop on the way to the Central Kalahari GR or Makgadikgadi Pans NP.
20km northwest of Serowe,
☎ *430 713*

Kwando Wildlife Experiences
For the well-heeled, Kwando offers a combination of fabulous wildlife-viewing and luxury accommodation in one of the most remote places in Southern Africa. Still wild enough to lie in the path of Botswana's dwindling migrations, Kwando's swamp habitat also ensures high numbers of resident game so viewing is superb year-round. Everything on the species lists for Moremi GR and Chobe NP is here and guided game drives virtually guarantee you'll see them. Carnivore sightings are exceptional; African wild dogs den here annually and for small predator aficionados, Kwando delivers views of the rare Selous' mongoose without fail.
185km east of Kasane,
South Africa ☎ *011-880 6138,*
e *kwandojnb@global.co.za*

Manyelanong Game Reserve
This reserve protects Botswana's largest Cape vulture colony, once numbering in the thousands but now a few hundred. It's worth a stop for die-hard raptor fans, especially between April and July when they nest, but a folding chair and binoculars are a must.
45km south of Gaborone (just south of the village of Otse)

Mokolodi Nature Reserve
A peaceful alternative to staying in Gaborone, Mokolodi is a combination of game reserve, environmental education centre and animal rehabilitation facility. Numerous antelopes as well as hippos, Burchell's zebras, giraffes and a few white rhinos can be seen, and guided night drives sometimes glimpse a brown hyena or honey badger. There is also a small herd of semi-tame young elephants here which are stabled by night but free to roam during the day. For a fee, visitors can walk with them for a unique insight into an elephant's day.
12km south of Gaborone,
☎ *353 959*

Tuli Game Reserve
Lying at the very eastern extremity of Botswana, this collection of private reserves shares its boundaries with South Africa and Zimbabwe. Elephant sightings are excellent, general game is good and while large predators are elusive, lions and leopards are fairly common. Bird sightings are excellent (over 375 species) and two species of dassie occur in mixed colonies on the Limpopo River cliffs.
335km southeast of Francistown, South Africa
☎ *011-789 2677*

ZIMBABWE

Highlights

- Stalking rhinos, buffaloes and lions on an adrenalin-charged walking safari at Matusadona NP
- Weaving past hippos, Nile crocodiles and colonies of bee-eaters as you canoe along the Zambezi River
- Watching herds of elephants amble in to drink, bathe and dust-bathe at a Hwange waterhole
- Listening to the thunder of Victoria Falls while searching for birds such as Taita falcons, trumpeter hornbills and Schalow's louries
- Hiking the Eastern Highlands in search of Swynnerton's robins, Chirunda apalises and other specials
- Scanning Mahenye Forest in Gonarezhou NP for narina trogons and Angola pittas
- Following an African wild dog pack as it courses through the woodlands of Hwange NP
- Seeing an elephant stand on its hind legs to strip a winter-thorn acacia of its pods at Mana Pools NP

Valley haven pulsing with life

MOST of Zimbabwe spreads across a series of plateaus, affording it a temperate climate although it lies entirely within the tropics. Zimbabwe's highveld (1200 to 1700m) extends from the southwest across to the Eastern Highlands, separating the Zambezi and Limpopo–Sabi Basins. Its middleveld (900 to 1200m) comprises 40% of the country and is dominated by miombo woodlands, interspersed with koppies, settlements and cultivation. However, it's Zimbabwe's low-lying regions that attract most wildlife-watchers. The Zambezi Valley's mopane woodlands, riverine forests and grasslands support high numbers of mammals, and this is where most of the national parks are located. The Zambezi flows over Victoria Falls (a World Heritage Site), winds through deep gorges then enters Lake Kariba before continuing east – providing year-round water for the region's wildlife. In the south, Zimbabwe's arid lowveld slopes down to the Limpopo and Save Rivers, an area of mopane woodlands, savanna and the gateway to the recently established Gaza-Gonarezhou-Kruger TP.

Around 13% of Zimbabwe consists of national parks and safari areas. The 11 national parks, run by the Department of National Parks and Wildlife Management, protect a large proportion of the country's 84,000 elephants as well as healthy populations of lions, leopards, buffaloes, antelopes, hippos and endangered African wild dogs. Zimbabwe's dry winter (June to October) is the time to see animals congregating at water sources – canoe trips provide good vantage points for this, particularly at Matusadona and Mana Pools NPs (the latter a World Heritage Site). Walking safaris and rhino-tracking are popular, although rhino numbers have dwindled in recent decades because of poaching.

Zimbabwe's premier park, Hwange NP, houses one of the world's highest concentrations of elephants and its battered mopane woodlands bear testament to their ability to transform habitats. At least 20% of its woodlands have already been destroyed and the park's at more than twice its elephant-carrying capacity. Elephants devour over 70% of all plant matter consumed in Zimbabwe's parks and managing their activity is a constant source of controversy.

The Eastern Highlands, which form the spine of south-east Africa, house endemic subspecies of Cape buntings and bokmakieries. Highland forests feature Afro-tropical flora and fauna, and near-endemics such as Swynnerton's robins and red-faced crimsonwings. Montane grasslands spotted with ericas, aloes and proteas (typical of Cape fynbos) attract Gurney's sugarbirds and sunbirds, while waterside sward provides breeding sites for endangered blue swallows. In November and December pockets of evergreen forest in the Eastern Highlands and Gonarezhou NP attract migrants such as Angola pittas and African broadbills. This is the best time to search for Zimbabwe's 666 bird species. ∎

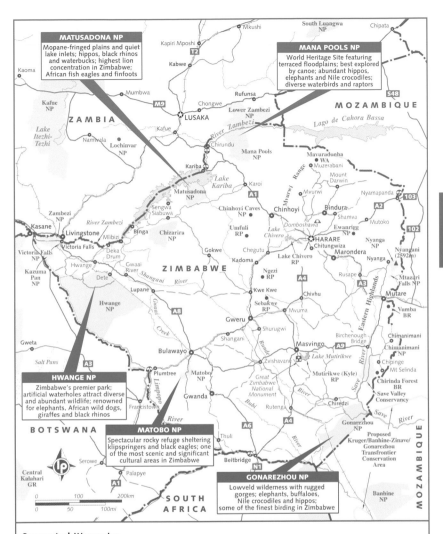

MATUSADONA NP
Mopane-fringed plains and quiet lake inlets; hippos, black rhinos and waterbucks; highest lion concentration in Zimbabwe; African fish eagles and finfoots

MANA POOLS NP
World Heritage Site featuring terraced floodplains; best explored by canoe; abundant hippos, elephants and Nile crocodiles; diverse waterbirds and raptors

HWANGE NP
Zimbabwe's premier park; artificial waterholes attract diverse and abundant wildlife; renowned for elephants, African wild dogs, giraffes and black rhinos

MATOBO NP
Spectacular rocky refuge sheltering klipspringers and black eagles; one of the most scenic and significant cultural areas in Zimbabwe

GONAREZHOU NP
Lowveld wilderness with rugged gorges; elephants, buffaloes, Nile crocodiles and hippos; some of the finest birding in Zimbabwe

Suggested itineraries

One week Explore Victoria Falls and Zambezi NPs to search for finfoots and Taita falcons and to check out the falls (1 day). Drive to Hwange NP for black rhinos and giraffes and explore the Main Camp area (2 days), then take a walking safari at Sinamatella or Robins Camps (2 days). Drive to Matobo NP for a night before returning to Victoria Falls.

Two weeks Starting at Victoria Falls, fly or drive to Kariba and join a Zambezi canoeing safari through to Mana Pools NP for elephants and Nile crocs. Head on to Matusadona NP for walking safaris and lion tracking, before scooting up to Hwange NP. Swing across to Matobo NP for dassies and black eagles before driving to Victoria Falls NP.

One month From Harare, head up to Vumba Mountains and Nyanga NP, then Chimanimani NP. Visit Gonarezhou NP and cross over to Bulawayo and Matobo NP. From there explore Hwange NP, fly or drive to Kariba and take a safari through Mana Pools and Matusadona NPs, ending in Victoria Falls NP. Explore the Upper Zambezi area then return to Harare.

HWANGE NATIONAL PARK
Zimbabwe's premier park

Wildlife highlights

The greatest and most accessible national park in Zimbabwe: 107 species of mammal, 435 birds, 104 reptiles and more than 116 butterflies have been recorded. The 30,000-strong elephant population is the world's second most dense after neighbouring Chobe NP. Plains game includes blue wildebeests and Burchell's zebras, and antelope specials are sables, roans and elands. Buffaloes occur in great herds in the dry season. Lions are in good number and the area is a major stronghold for African wild dogs. Hwange is one of the few places to see giraffes and black rhinos in Zimbabwe.

THE size of Northern Ireland, Hwange is the largest and best known of Zimbabwe's national parks. The construction of 60 artificial waterholes in Hwange – an area that has few permanent sources of water and a low rainfall of 620mm per year – has helped create a game-rich park that boasts the greatest diversity and abundance of animals in Zimbabwe. It is also an important breeding area for the endangered **African wild dog** and **black rhino**. The park is regionally and administratively divided into three parts – Main Camp, Robins and Sinamatella.

You are likely to encounter animals before you get into Hwange. The 20km stretch of road into the park is flanked by msasa, mnondo, false mopane and Zimbabwe teaks – the teak's big mauve flowers that bloom in the late rainy season are popular with **giraffes**, **chacma baboons** and birds. The classic plains animals – **blue wildebeests**, **Burchell's zebras** and **impalas** – are likely to be seen grazing side by side in the patches of open ground. Even **lions** might be observed before entering the park (one guide recounted seeing a hitchhiker thumbing into the park while being watched by a group of lions on the other side of the road).

Necking giraffes

Hwange is Zimbabwe's premier park for giraffe-watching and you might get to observe giraffes 'necking' (inset). This is not necessarily affection. Males gently neck with females during courtship, but males also get into a rough version with each other as a way of sorting out dominance. The males twist their necks around each other and arch their necks to sledge the other on the body with their horns. It seems like a gentle dance because the giraffes take a while to swing their neck and build up momentum. But the thump likely packs a punch because it can be heard 100m away and a struck giraffe usually jumps on impact. These bruising displays can go on for half an hour. You may notice that the ends of the horns of male giraffes lack the turfs of hair visible on the females' horns – this is rubbed off during fighting.

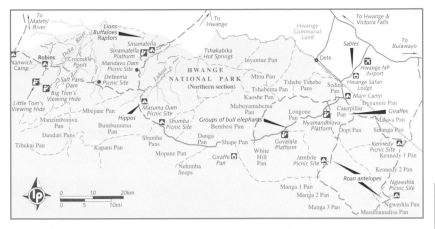

Flying bananas

Around Main Camp, semitame birds await you near the cafe tables including friendly **white-browed sparrow-weavers** and **glossy starlings**. There are seven hornbill species in the park, including a Hwange speciality, **Bradfield's hornbill**, which reaches the eastern edge of its range here. The largest hornbill is the turkey-sized **ground hornbill**, which is typically seen feeding in open areas in groups of five to six. The **southern yellow-billed hornbill** ('the flying banana') is found in thornveld, the **red-billed** and **crowned hornbill** are associated with the mopane woodlands in the northwest of the park, and **grey hornbills** can be found throughout. Hornbills have a lolloping, 'drunken' flight pattern so are easy to identify on the wing. In the leaf litter **kurrichane thrushes** peck for worms, while flocks of **southern pied babblers** chatter incessantly. Mammals aren't abundant in Main Camp, except chirrupy groups of **banded mongooses**. However, long-term staff witnessed a few **lion** kills inside the camp before the new electric fence was constructed around it.

Only the northern third of Hwange is open to the public yet few visitors see more than a fraction of this: most vehicles concentrate on the crowded 'Ten-Mile Drive'. There are many other dirt road loops, each taking several hours, perhaps a day, to negotiate. Waterholes are on average about 10km apart, and

The Linkwasha floodplain in summer is dense with grazing species such as buffaloes, Burchell's zebras and blue wildebeests (pictured).

Chacma baboons are ubiquitous at Hwange and easily ignored, but troops are fertile ground for observing constant interaction.

the terrain is mostly flat and carpeted by deep, pale Kalahari sands. Teak woodlands dominate much of the Main Camp section, and it is in the denser vegetation that stately **greater kudus** will often be seen browsing.

Areas of acacia savanna are favoured by **giraffes** and the trimmed bases of the camelthorn trees are the work of their 45cm tongue. Very little habitat in Zimbabwe is suitable for giraffes, and this is one of the few places they can be seen – the Main Camp region is said to have the highest density of giraffes in Africa. While watching them also keep an eye out for **red-billed** and **yellow-billed oxpeckers**. Although yellow-billed oxpeckers also perch on buffaloes, warthogs and hippos, giraffes are the red-billed oxpecker's favourite host.

Too many elephants?

Further south, the trees give way to patches of leadwoods; tall trees with tangled, dendritic branches. The solitary dead leadwood standing in the middle of the Makwa Pan supports a large **red-billed buffalo weavers'** nest. In the pan lurk **terrapins**; one was spotted snatching a **wattled starling** and taking it under. There are five species of **tortoise** and terrapin in Hwange. In the rainy season (November to April) two types of terrapin can be seen moving between water points as they disperse to colonise new areas.

While much of Hwange is thick woodland, massive floodplains and grasslands provide superb viewing opportunities.

This open area is good for seeing plains animals as well as **lions** and **elephants**. The feeding pressure of too many elephants is immediately apparent around Sinanga Pan (and other waterholes). Their destructive foraging has killed trees, and the woodland has been broken off to a uniform head-height for half a kilometre in every direction. The elephant problem in Hwange is vexing. The provision of artificial water supplies has resulted in a population of 30,000 elephants, which is over twice the number that the park's food supply can support. The elephants are not only eating themselves out of food; they are eating out the food supply of other animals. Control of elephant numbers seems imperative for the long-term survival of the park and its flora and fauna.

Although the chance of seeing the elusive and nocturnal **leopard** is remote (night drives are not routinely permitted), listen for its distinctive sawing cough if staying over at the Ngweshla picnic site. In the height of the dry season, when elephants monopolise the waterholes, one leopard regularly climbed under the fence to drink out of the camp's birdbath. Leopards have also been to known to park their dead prey in the branches of the tall trees around this camp. Up high their food is safe from theft by lions and hyenas. The vlei and waterhole here is also especially good for seeing **waterbucks**.

The **roan** is a species not often encountered in Zimbabwe. The best places in the Main Camp region to see them are on the southern loop around Ngweshla, and towards the three Manga Pans and Jambile Pan. Further north, the camelthorn-dominated

Location Main Camp 288km northwest of Bulawayo; 199km from Victoria Falls (sealed road). Robins 93km south of Vic Falls. Sinamatella turn-off near Hwange town, then 45km of dirt (4WD best).

Facilities Stores, fuel, viewing platforms, Main Camp museum, night drives on full moon, walking safaris and hides.

Accommodation Camping grounds, caravan sites, self-catering chalets and lodges (book in advance). Numerous private luxury lodges on edge of park.

Wildlife rhythms Best April to October (dry season); very cold May to August. Game-viewing roads around Robins closed November to April; others may close during rainy season. Excellent birding November to February.

Contact National Parks Central Booking Office (☎ 04-706 077/8, fax 04-726 089, 724 914).

Permanent water at Hwange has doubled the natural numbers of elephants, making them impossible to miss.

Lions are abundant at Hwange and can be encountered anywhere in the park.

area around Dopi Pan is a quiet spot to see herds of **elephants** during the dry season. The Guvalala Platform, located at a vlei surrounded by *Terminalia*, is a good place to see a diverse array of species; large groups of bull elephants often gather here. From there, heading west, the road soon deteriorates into potholes and the landscape turns from scrub into mopane woodland as you venture towards Robins and Sinamatella (this is good habitat for **Arnot's chats**).

Granite lookouts and rhino-tracking

Those 'in the know' escape busy Main Camp and journey to the northwestern border to see **black rhinos** and take in the view from Sinamatella Camp. Sinamatella sits 55m above a waterhole so you actually look down on the birds and mammals coming in to drink and bathe: at the height of summer, great clouds of dust tumbling across the floodplain herald the arrival of 1000-strong **buffalo** herds to the waterhole. A tail thrashing under a shady bush may reveal **lions** (lions and **spotted hyenas** are plentiful). **African wild dogs** are in good number, but because of their large home ranges, sightings are unpredictable.

Elephant recycling

A glance at any Hwange waterhole is enough to convince most visitors that there are too many elephants in the park. While elephant overpopulation is a concern, the park's vegetation is being recycled, not trashed. At Hwange elephants eat woody vegetation faster than it can regenerate, bulldozing woodland into savanna. However, about 80% of what is consumed is returned to the soil in the form of dung.

Many species actually benefit from the elephants' activity. Ilala palm nuts germinate after passing through an elephant's digestive tract and being deposited in a pile of fertiliser. Battered mopanes burst into leaf after the rains, sprouting new branches out of wounds; and the felling of trees (and branches) provides small ungulates, like impalas and bushbucks, with access to browse. So elephant feeding need not be viewed as purely destructive. Whether Hwange's elephants are decreasing the number of other browsers is a matter of contention, but if resources are short – are they really the species to blame?

Visitors can go on guided walking safaris of several days duration – this provides the best chance of seeing **black rhinos**. Also, there are several picnic spots, viewing platforms and dams; Mandavu and Masuma Dams are favourite viewing spots among many (Mandavu, the largest, is home to **Nile crocodiles** and Masuma has **hippos**).

In contrast to the Kalahari sands that cover two-thirds of Hwange, the Robins and Sinamatella areas are rockier. Granite outcrops around Sinamatella are good places for spotting **tawny** and **martial eagles**. At nightfall Sinamatella becomes a hunting ground for **honey badgers**.

Most visitors come to Hwange during the dry winter season. During the rains, when the vleis fill and the Deka and Lukosi Rivers flow, the animals disperse and the long grass makes viewing difficult. Even the **elephants** seem to vanish, probably migrating south into the wild and inaccessible part of Hwange. Yet for birders and **butterfly** enthusiasts this is one of the best times to visit the north of the park. The top time for birding is from November to February; Salt Pan Dam near Robins is a favourite spot for viewing **waders** and **waterbirds**. ∎

A linkwasha tree (below) graces one of Hwange's waterholes at dusk.

Watching tips

Nyamandhlovu Platform is a human circus at sunset, so if you want to visit, see it at sunrise. When the animals retire to siesta in the middle of the day, the waterhole at Hwange Safari Lodge (open to all) is a reliable place to see sables. This spotlit waterhole is also a top place to spend the evening. Night drives are only allowed in the park for three to four nights during full moon (best July to October), but private lodges outside the park run them. Elias, who is an institution at Main Camp, conducts excellent daily walks to Sedina Pan, near Main Camp. For tranquillity, book one of the park's seven exclusive camp sites (located at picnic points) or head to Robins and Sinamatella.

GONAREZHOU NATIONAL PARK

Embattled wildlife re-emerging

Wildlife highlights
Elephants, crocs, hippos, buffaloes and fabulous birds (400 species). Outstanding for raptors, such as bateleurs, lanner and peregrine falcons, and lappet-faced vultures. Angola pittas, narina trogons, and mottled spinetails are specials. Among 108 reptile species are two endemics – Warren's girdled lizard and the marbled tree snake. Nearby Save Valley Conservancy has black rhinos and African wild dogs. Roans and nyalas are occasionally seen.

GONAREZHOU is Zimbabwe's wild frontier – fiercely hot in summer with a low and erratic rainfall, this park is part of the parched, harsh lowveld, and contains rugged, spectacular gorges. While mammal diversity is high and elephants occur in large numbers, animal numbers are low – this is not a place to rush about and tick off big game. But birding here is some of the finest in Zimbabwe and you often have much of the park to yourself.

Some 30 years ago, the park was devastated by ill-conceived management practices (the shooting of thousands of animals in an attempt to control tsetse flies), by poaching during war, and by the worst drought in Zimbabwe's history in 1992. But Gonarezhou reopened in 1994 and is now recovering.

Gonarezhou is divided into two areas, which are named after rivers – the Save-Runde subregion in the north and the Mwenezi subregion in the south. The Save River holds a **Nile crocodile** density second only to the Zambezi. The rivers contain **hippos** and large numbers of freshwater fish including the **tiger fish** and endemic **black bream**. Marine fish sometimes venture up the Save from the Indian Ocean and even **Zambezi sharks** have been recorded. **African fish eagles** are ever present near

---

Gaza-Kruger-Gonarezhou Transfrontier Park

In November 2000 Mozambique, South Africa and Zimbabwe agreed (in principle) to remove the barriers between Kruger and Gonarezhou NPs and the Gaza wildlife management area to form one transfrontier park. Animals – particularly elephants, buffaloes and antelopes – traditionally moved across these political boundaries with the changing seasons, but these migratory pathways have been blocked by fences and animal numbers controlled by controversial culling and translocation programs. With ecotourism being a major earner, the project has the potential to aid not only the migratory animals but also the communities in and around these areas. However, some conservationists claim that this will create a poachers' paradise, while other critics have expressed concern about the flow-on effects of the 'war veteran' land appropriation in Zimbabwe's lowveld. Only time will tell.

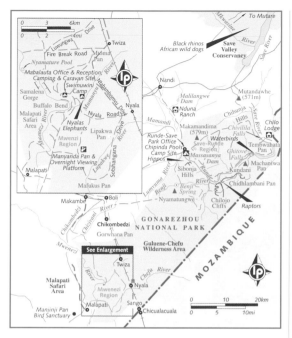

Location Chipinda HQ 550km south of Harare, Mabalauta HQ 667km south of Harare.
Facilities Viewing platforms, NP driver and vehicle for hire at Chipinda.
Accommodation Camping grounds; luxury accommodation outside park.
Wildlife rhythms Best for mammals September to January, as rivers dry up to form pools. Narina trogons and Angola pittas breed January to February.
Contact National Parks Central Booking Office (☎ 04-706 077/8, fax 04-726 089, 724 914).

the rivers and **Pel's fishing owls** occur at Runde and Mwenezi, best seen during the rains when pools form.

Convergence of waters and wildlife

The highest concentrations of animals are found in the north, especially near the pans, rivers and around the junction of the Save and Runde Rivers – a tangle of ilala palms, fever trees and nyala berries. **Green coucals** skulk through thickets and the descending *du-du-du-du* call of **blue-spotted doves** continues throughout the day. Between mid-November and late January at Mahenye Forest, migrant **narina trogons** are vocal in the early morning and evening before breeding in February. **Angola pittas** arrive between late December and early January and have even noisier courtships. Both species disappear by late March. Tembwahata and Machaniwa Pans contain numerous **ducks**, **storks**, **geese**, **herons**, **ibises**, and **pipits**, plus an occasional **hippo**.

Away from the rivers and pans, the bush turns into endless *Combretum* and mopane woodlands. The congregation of **elephants** in this area is evident by the broken-off, stunted mopane trees. The park has more than 5000 elephants, which is around carrying capacity. However, part of the hunting legacy remains: many of Gonarezhou's elephants still associate vehicles and people with trouble, and elephants here have a reputation for being extremely dangerous.

Impalas are found throughout the park, and herds of up to 150 **buffaloes** can be encountered. Of the smaller animals, the quivering tail of **tree squirrels** will readily catch your eye.

At rest, the bateleur eagle is easily sexed: the male (pictured) has all-black secondary (lower) wing feathers compared with the female's greyish ones.

Probably the most common large carnivore in Gonarezhou, spotted hyenas are visible here during the day – early mornings and evenings are best.

Scrutinise the trees that they dash up and you will often find their grass nests (dreys) sticking out of trunk hollows. **Southern yellow-billed hornbills, long-tailed starlings, lilac-breasted rollers, hoopoes** and **red-billed woodhoopoes** are common in this area. On the ground, **Natal francolins** wander across the road, and camouflaged **double-banded sandgrouse** break with a flurry of wing beats if you get close. Clouds of tiny **queleas** and **waxbills** fly up from feeding on seeds and the deep *oomph, oomph-oomph* signals that **ground hornbills** are nearby.

Raptures for raptors

Gonarezhou is outstanding for raptors, especially at Tembwa-hata Pan. **Martial eagles, tawny eagles** and **bateleurs** are common and the park contains a substantial breeding popula-tion of **lappet-faced vultures**. This is the largest African vulture and is less frequently seen than most others – its size and red face are distinctive. The most common vultures are **white-backed vultures** and their nests – an untidy mass of sticks – are commonly seen in baobab trees. Also in baobabs are the large thorny nests of **buffalo weavers**. Throughout the park you will see an enormous number of baobabs, including a 'forest' just east of Tembwahata Pan. Within their hollows, limbs, and from their flesh, fruit and flowers, some baobabs have provided animals with refuge and food for hundreds of years. These are one of the few trees able to withstand ringbarking by elephants – although some botanists argue that they are succulents, not trees. **Squirrels, parrots** (**Cape, Meyer's** and **brown-headed**) and **hornbills** all use the baobabs' hollows. Rare swiftlike

The trogons must be crazy

One morning, I took a group to look for narina trogons in Mahenye Forest. We walked for hours with no success, but saw lots of other birds. Deciding to call it quits we headed back to the Land Rover. While we were having drinks, a fellow guide was playing around with an empty Coke bottle trying to imitate a trogon call – and guess what? Seven trogons flew out of nowhere to the tree above us, paused there for quite a while, then flew off. I've never seen so many of them together. That same afternoon we went looking for Pel's fishing owl. While searching, we saw an immature fish eagle dive for a fish. As it swooped, so too did a fishing owl – both were going for the same fish.

Humphrey Gumpo, wildlife guide

mottled spinetails nest at Shadreck's Office, an open baobab that used to house a poacher.

The famous Chilojo Cliffs, layered red and ochre sandstone rock faces, stretch for about 30km along the Runde River. **Lanner** and **peregrine falcons** breed in the cliffs, and holes in the exposed river bank house noisy **white-fronted bee-eaters**. **Sables** are often seen below the cliffs, and waterholes on the plateau above the cliffs are excellent places to look for **roan antelopes**.

Nyalas reach the major northern edge of their African range here (also occurring in Mana Pools NP and Lengwe NP – the latter in Malawi). Herds of up to 20 might be seen around the Chipinda Pools and the Benji area – the shaggy manes, and greyer colour of males distinguishes them from **greater kudus**. **African wild dogs** are a highlight in the park, but their home ranges are so vast that sightings are pot luck. However, the Nyavasikana River area can be a good spot to check. Early morning drives to the cliffs from Chipinda can be rewarding as **cheetahs** sometimes sun themselves on the main track. Everywhere **hyena** numbers are good. Unlike most species, these scavengers benefited from the 1991–92 drought.

Mwenezi region

The southern section of Gonarezhou is dominated by the meandering Mwenezi River, which snakes through dry woodland and ridges topped by baobabs and ironwoods. In winter wildlife focuses on the tiny pools that dot the region. Buffalo Bend on the Mwenezi River is particularly good during dry season; Swimuwini Camp overlooks the Bend and **elephants** and **nyalas** visit its small pond. **Cheetahs** are uncommon at Gonarezhou – the best place to see them is around the Mabalauta area, where **lion** numbers are low. ∎

If you don't pick out the martial eagle (below) by its great size and powerful build, its white breast with dark flecks are diagnostic characters.

> **Watching tips**
> Try to visit the Save Valley Conservancy, 60km north of Gonarezhou. In the early 1990s poor farming returns and drought convinced 23 ranchers to invest in photographic tourism and sustainable hunting. Fences were pulled down, stock removed and wildlife reintroduced. Animal numbers are greater than in Gonarezhou, with black rhinos and African wild dogs the highlights. Under the care of so many landholders their movements are known, so early morning tracking can lead to seeing either species; the best time to visit is from June to August when the dogs are denning. The Senuko Lodge staff are expert birders. Malilangwe is another private conservancy Bordering Gonerazhou and Nduna Lodge has excellent birding guides.

MANA POOLS NATIONAL PARK

Wanderings of the Zambezi etched on riverbanks

Wildlife highlights
The Zambezi abounds with hippos and Nile crocs, and is great to explore by canoe. Elephants and buffaloes are abundant and African wild dogs occur in the park. Hyenas, baboons and vervet monkeys are common; impalas, elands and greater kudus are widespread, and Burchell's zebras occur near the pools. This is one of only two places to see nyalas in Zimbabwe. Highest concentration of lions and leopards may be in the south, although Ruckomechi boasts good leopard sightings. Waterbirds feature among 387 recorded bird species; and other avian attractions include 52 species of raptor and owl, and two 'specials' are Shelley's sunbird and Lilian's lovebird.

WITH the Zambezi River as its northern boundary, the terraced floodplains of Mana Pools rise behind pods of **hippos** and basking **Nile crocodiles**. Marshy areas support a profusion of **birds**, and **elephants** and **buffaloes** graze along the riverbanks. This World Heritage Site is usually explored by canoe safaris.

Paddling among hippos

Canoe safaris range from a short paddle to a safari that lasts for days – starting in Kariba and ending on the Mozambique border. One of the first things you are told is to avoid Mana's abundant **hippos** at all cost. This entails zigzagging along the river to stay out of their fiercely defended territories. Pods of up to 60 stay submerged during the day to protect their delicate skin from the sun – often only eyes, ears and nostrils show above the water. Most snort, grunt and submerge as you pass, but if they feel threatened they may attack – canoeing is not

---

Butterfly leaves and mopane worms

Mana is covered in endless mopane woodland. This hardy tree is easily recognised by its butterfly-shaped leaves, which fold together and hang vertically during the heat of the day to reduce water loss. The leaves are packed with protein and phosphorus – even after they have turned russet and fallen, they retain some nutrients and ensure a winter source of food for many animals. At times the leaves become covered in waxy psyllids, which baboons and monkeys carefully pick off. But the invertebrate most associated with this tree is the 'mopane worm' (inset) – these large hairless caterpillars occur in the thousands in the rainy season. Parcels of fatty protein, they are great pickings for birds, monkeys, baboons and even people. Mopane wood hollows easily, often due to elephant damage, and provides nest sites for hornbills, woodpeckers, barbets and tree (Smith's bush) squirrels, which cache food over winter in them.

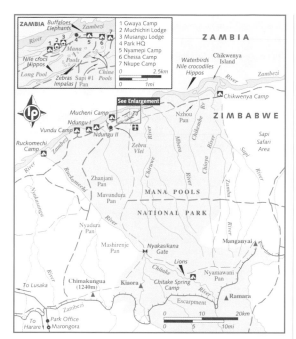

Location Nyamepi HQ is 388km from Harare. Mostly off-limits to vehicles November to April, otherwise boat, fly or canoe in – 4WD is best.
Facilities No fuel or stores. Nyamepi HQ sells a bird list and map; canoes and game scouts for hire.
Accommodation Around 10 camping grounds along the river and 2 at Chikore. Come self-sufficient. Four self-catering NP lodges with facilities. Three all-inclusive private luxury lodges.
Wildlife rhythms Good game-viewing May to September, but best in October (although hot). Migrant birds present August to April.
Contact National Parks Central Booking Office (☎ 04-706 077/8, fax 04-726 089, 724 914).

for the faint-hearted! The Zambezi also teems with **Nile crocodiles** which bask on sand bars, especially during winter (June to August).

On shore, **elephants** and **buffaloes** drink, wallow and rub parasites off their hides. High banks often house colonies of **white-fronted bee-eaters**, which are joined by **blue-cheeked bee-eaters** between October and April. The striking **carmine bee-eaters** arrive in August, departing in December. Ternlike **African skimmers** rest on sandbanks, and fish by trailing their lower bill through the water. Among 90 waterbird species are **woolly-necked storks**, **rufous-bellied herons**, **pygmy geese** and **white-crowned plovers**. **Long-toed plovers** wade through weedy channels. Fifty-two of the area's 400 bird species are raptors and owls, with the most conspicuous being the **African fish eagle**. **Pel's fishing owl** might be seen perched cryptically in dense overhanging foliage. In the riverine scrub the 'big twitch' is **Shelley's sunbird** – previously unknown south of Zambia, during summer it has been found here.

Wheels and walking

'Mana' means four and refers to four pools close together at the northern end of the park. These pools, especially Long Pool and Chine Pools, are the prime animal-viewing spots during the height of the dry season (July to November). Long Pool is usually occupied by **hippos** and **Nile crocodiles**, and **Burchell's zebras** and **impalas** graze in the surrounding open areas.

The flat 'floodplain' here is actually river terracing, caused by the Zambezi receding as its course changes over time.

Africa's largest lizard, the Nile monitor or water leguaan, forages in and around water for frogs, small crustaceans, insects, eggs and birds.

Effectively, the pools are remnant oxbow lakes. Tall Natal mahoganies and winter-thorns grow on the alluvial soils of these flats. The foliage of the broad-leafed mahogany is trimmed at head-height by **impalas, greater kudus, elands** and **nyalas**; the winter-thorn's browse-line is up high, courtesy of elephants. Between August and October, when few trees fruit and most are losing their leaves, the pods and leaves of the winter-thorn (or apple-ring acacia – its pods are coiled like apple peelings) provide a vital winter food source. Elephants ringbark these trees but leave the evergreen mahogany alone. Its scientific name, *Trichilia emetica*, refers to the protective emetic (nausea-inducing substance) contained in the bark. Away from the river, sandy areas are dominated by jesse bush – a tangle of shrubby *Combretum* and *Terminalia*.

From the lodges and camping grounds near the river you can observe the goings-on along the Zambezi. **Elephants** spied on the Zambian side may cross and wander past during dinner. During the night **hippos** come ashore and munch on grass only 20m away from campers. At the popular Nyamepi Camp anything left out at night will be pinched by fearless **honey badgers** or **spotted hyenas**. During the day the **baboons** and **vervet monkeys** fill that role. In the morning you may wake up to find your tent being used as a trampoline by young vervets.

The dirt on Mana Pools

The history of Mana Pools is etched on its soils: shaped by water, wind and humans. The valley is marked by wide floodplain terraces, dry channels and pools – all remnants of the Zambezi River's gradual movement northwards. Sandy soils adjacent to channels support winter-thorns, while older 'islands' are covered in woodlands of sausage trees, rain trees and Natal mahoganies. Mana's low-lying floodplains have not been subject to major flooding since 1958, when the Kariba Dam was completed upstream. As a result, the floodplain soils are not seasonally replenished with alluvium, leading to gradual soil degradation.

Soils differ across the valley, giving rise to various layers of vegetation. Browsers such as greater kudus and nyalas feed on mopane woodlands, which dominate clay soils, and spiky jesse. During drier months, grazers such as buffaloes and zebras concentrate on the floodplains, also utilising grassed miombo woodlands. In wet season, most grazers disappear from the floodplains, exploiting fresh graze further afield. With such diverse 'layers' of grasslands and browse, it's no surprise that elephants – the quintessential mixed feeder – are abundant here.

Game-viewing by canoe provides a unique perspective, which affords great opportunities for taking photographs.

Elephants abound at Mana and while here look closely at the females. Many of them have no tusks – probably a genetic anomaly that has been exacerbated by the selective hunting of elephants with tusks. Mana's cows have a reputation for being aggressive – little wonder when they are without the protection of tusks – but 'Agatha' is an exception. This matriarch has been bringing her herd through Chikwenya Camp for years and they are a daily sight during the height of dry season. Here too are some very relaxed **buffaloes** – old 'dagha boys' (males in bachelor herds) often used to snooze in front of doorways, refusing to budge even when nudged by a Land Rover. The buildings are now raised so tripping over buffaloes is less of a problem.

Southwards

The park's southern reaches are much drier. The area's clay soils are dominated by mopane and giant baobabs dot the horizon. **White-browed sparrow-weaver** nests dangling from the mopanes are clustered on the western side where they are protected from the weather. During summer, male **broad-tailed paradise whydahs**, with their dramatically long tail, display for their mates. **Lilian's lovebirds** mass in large flocks in the mopane – Mana is one of the few places this lovebird occurs south of the Zambezi.

The southern boundary of the park cuts through the mountainous Zambezi Escarpment. This is the watershed of the Chitake River, where the adventurous can embark on walking safaris. It's hot, dusty and uncomfortable during November, but this is the best time for walking safaris. By August, the small water pans have dried up and in the south the only water source is the Chitake, a tapering, 1km-long stream where everything comes to drink – large herds of **elephants**, **antelopes** and **buffaloes** are readily seen. For predators the riverside is easy pickings: Chitake is the place to see **lions** in action and they are regularly found within 200m of the river during the height of the dry season. Guided walks in other areas of the park can also be undertaken from private lodges. Incomprehensibly, visitors are allowed to walk unescorted in Mana. Given the numbers of elephants and buffaloes in the park, this is only for those with a death wish. ■

Watching tips
A crack-of-dawn drive between Vundu and Nkupe camps may reward you with lion sightings. Zebra Vlei, below Mucheni Camp, is the place to search for African wild dogs, especially between August and October.

MATUSADONA NATIONAL PARK

Lakeside ark

MATUSADONA stretches up from the shores of Lake Kariba and over the rugged Zambezi Escarpment. Two-thirds of the park are largely unexplored jesse-tangled hills and most visitors confine their activities to the lake's inlets and mopane-fringed plains near the shore. The foreshore is rich in **waterbirds** (around 200 species recorded), and there are plenty of **hippos**, **Nile crocodiles**, **elephants** and **buffaloes**. Matusadona has the highest density of **lions** in Zimbabwe and is also one of the few reserves containing **black rhinos**.

Refuge for escapers

Matusadona is bounded by the Ume River to the west and the deep Sanyati Gorge to the east; many visitors travel along these and the lake in boats or view wildlife from moored houseboats. Craggy dead mopane trees, drowned when the Zambezi River was dammed to create Lake Kariba, dominate the lake's edge (as the water level rose, 5000 marooned animals were rescued and resettled in Matusadona NP). Perched on these are **cormorants**, **darters** and an enormous population of **African fish eagles**. The lake teems with **vundu**, **barbel**, **bream** and **tiger fish**, which attract anglers from far and wide.

Torpedo grass dominates the shoreline, attracting **buffaloes**, **elephants** and **antelopes** throughout the dry season (June to December). **Waterbucks** and **impalas** are common, while **roans**, **sables** and **elands** occur in inaccessible miombo woodlands and ridges, coming to water in the drier months. **Saddle-billed storks** and **plovers** are abundant along the shore, and **malachite kingfishers** perch on stumps and reeds. **Pied kingfishers**, which

Floppy trunk syndrome

Floppy trunk syndrome (FTS) is a condition of progressive paralysis of the elephant's trunk, principally affecting older males. First observed in East Africa, FTS appeared among Matusadona's elephants in 1989. Since then about 40 cases have been reported. In the worst situations loss of trunk function interferes with the elephant's ability to feed and drink and they eventually die. But others can be minimally affected and survive; some even recover. Considerable research has been undertaken and Fothergill Island at Matusadona is heavily involved – you may see elephants there sporting radio-collars. Scientists examine vegetation, soil and water for likely culprits such as pesticides, heavy metals and toxins. The exact cause is uncertain but it appears to be a toxin. FTS appeared in Kruger NP in 1993 (also affecting elephant's limbs) and researchers pinpointed the cause as long-term exposure to a neurotoxin – elephants recover once removed from the area but the exact nature of the neurotoxin remains unknown.

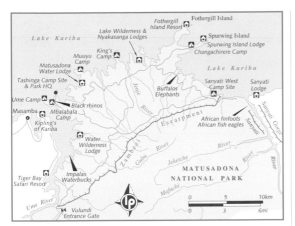

Map labels: Fothergill Island Resort, Fothergill Island, Lake Wilderness & Nyakasanga Lodges, Lake Kariba, Spurwing Island, Spurwing Island Lodge, Changachirere Camp, Muuyu Camp, King's Camp, Matusadona Water Lodge, Tashinga Camp Site & Park HQ, Lake Kariba, Ume Camp, Black rhinos, Buffalos Elephants, Sanyati West Camp Site, Sanyati Lodge, Masamba, Mbalabala Camp, Kipling's of Kariba, Escarpment, African finfoots African fish eagles, Sanyati Gorge, Water Wilderness Lodge, Zambezi River, Gubu River, Jeketche, River, Jenje River, MATUSADONA NATIONAL PARK, Tiger Bay Safari Resort, Impalas Waterbucks, Mufuchi, Ume River, Vulundi Entrance Gate, 0 5 10km, 0 3 6mi

normally feed along shorelines, fly well out over the lake to catch the introduced kapenta (sardine), and **grey-headed gulls** and **white-winged terns** whisk over the water. A journey through the dramatic Sanyati Gorge is a way to see **African fish eagles** and their nests, and **bee-eaters** nest in the banks. The shy, darterlike **African finfoot** also inhabits this area.

To see **black rhinos** visit park HQ at Tashinga. From here rangers will guide you to the young rhinos that were brought to Matusadona. This is not the average encounter with a black rhino; although 'don't touch' is the rule some of the friendlier young ones often come over and rub their stubby horns against your thigh – and will even jut their horn up billowing shorts. Matusadona is one of the few Zimbabwean IPZs (Intensive Protection Zones) – to date seven orphaned rhinos have taken part. Under guard but free-ranging during the day, they are enticed with rhino-treats back into protective 'bomas' at Tashinga each night. One rhino has graduated and roams free; characteristically unpredictable, she readily chases people.

Unlike the orphaned youngsters, the cautious, wild black rhinos in Matusadona are rarely seen and are usually found only on walking safaris – the ultimate African adventure. The 'Daily News', as guides call the sandy tracks and riverbeds, tells a new story each morning and broadcasts the night's events. In sand, signs may be as obvious as firm hoof prints but on stony ground they can be as subtle as a stone polished by the brush of a hoof. Aerial signs such as bent grass or freshly broken branches also lead the way. Tracking is done at first light when the rhinos are still active. The alarm hiss of **oxpeckers**, frequent companions of rhinos, may be the first clue that you are near. The sound of the rhino's big molars chewing may be the next – in the still of the morning this sound can carry 50m or more. A rhino's senses of smell and hearing are acute, so from here it is a downwind, stealthy approach to get close. Exciting stuff! Short walking safaris (conducted by lodges and camps) often get you close to **elephants** and tracking **lions** is a major draw of the park. Alternatively, game drives will get you even closer to lions and **buffaloes**, while keeping you within your comfort zone. ■

Location 468km northwest of Harare. Boat or fly in from Kariba (18km away). Drive in is back-breaking, 4WD only. Inaccessible by road in wet season.
Facilities No fuel or stores. Maps, guides (if available) and canoes from Tashinga.
Accommodation Excellent camp site (Tashinga), small camp site at Sanyati West, also camp sites without facilities. Several luxury lodges surround the park. Houseboats moor at park's edge.
Wildlife rhythms Best game viewing June to November.
Contact National Parks Central Booking Office (☎ 04-706 077/8, fax 04-726 089, 724 914).

Watching tips

If travelling independently, consider hiring a game scout from the Park HQ at Tashinga so you can get out on foot. Cheetahs have been released near Fothergill Island and are being monitored by researchers, who advise the cats' whereabouts to lodge drivers.

VICTORIA FALLS & ZAMBEZI
NATIONAL PARKS

Mosi-ou-Tunya – the smoke that thunders

Wildlife highlights
Elephants, lions, sables, buffaloes and African wild dogs in Zambezi NP. Zambezi River good for hippos and Nile crocs, as well as birding highlights such as African finfoot, collared palm thrush, rock pratincole and Schalow's lourie. Taita falcon at Batoka Gorge, trumpeter hornbills at Victoria Falls.

Location 875km west of Harare, 448km from Bulawayo.
Facilities Everything at Vic Falls. Night drives, horse trails and walking safaris in and around Zambezi NP.
Accommodation Camp sites, lodges and hotels at Victoria Falls. Camp sites, lodges in Zambezi NP.
Wildlife rhythms Best game in dry season (July to September) although good any time.
Contact Victoria Falls Publicity Association (☎ 013-4202). National Parks Central Booking Office (☎ 04-706 077/8, fax 04-726 089, 724 914).

CENTRE stage are the Falls – a World Heritage Site and one of the natural wonders of the world – where 550,000 cubic metres of water hurtle over each minute, plummeting more than 100m and sending up a plume of spray that can rise 500m above. Victoria Falls comprise five separate falls and there are pathways that provide a view of each. The spray nurtures a rainforest area surrounding the Falls, replete with figs, twisted vines, ferns and orchids. Mammals are scarce but you may encounter **baboons**, **vervet monkeys**, **banded mongooses** and **Chobe bushbucks**. Small birds such as **waxbills**, **firefinches**, **mannikins** and **whydahs** (distinguished by their long tails in the wet season) inhabit open grassy areas. Viewpoint Number IV is a reliable spot to look for large **trumpeter** and **crowned hornbills**, but the species to watch for is **Schalow's lourie**; in Zimbabwe it is restricted to this area. Despite its conspicuous size and brilliant green coloration it's not readily seen – a walk upstream is your best bet.

Away from the Falls, most people head upstream and explore the palm islands and channels by canoe, motorboat or barge. Although busy on the water this is a good way to see **hippos**, **Nile crocodiles**, **white-crowned plovers**, **African finfoots** and **rock pratincoles**. The rare **Taita falcon** has breeding sites in the Batoka Gorge below the Falls. Indeed the whole 120km stretch of gorge is a dream for raptor lovers – 36 species include **African hawk-eagle**, and **black** and **crowned eagles**.

Taita falcon

The gorges below Victoria Falls are home to the rare Taita falcon. This small peregrine-like falcon has a discontinuous distribution stretching from Ethiopia to South Africa, but it doesn't appear to breed in East Africa and is incredibly rare throughout its range. The falcon's stronghold is the gorges and mountains of Zimbabwe, where it estimated to have about 50 breeding sites (breeding between July and October). A good lookout for this species is near the Victoria Falls Hotel; but you'll need a falcon's-eye to distinguish it from male peregrines. Why this falcon is so rare is uncertain – it's been suggested that their breeding sites are so inaccessible that the birds aren't being recorded. This seems unlikely and a more common view is that they suffer competition for nest sites from the larger lanner and peregrine falcons.

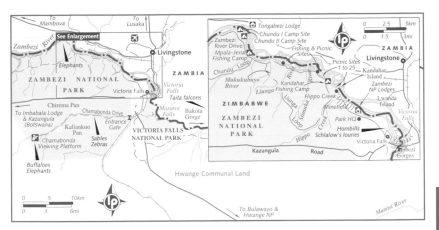

Victoria Falls town has a surprising number of animals venturing through. **Elephants** wander about and **buffaloes** are occasionally encountered. During a walk on the Elephant Hills golf course you should encounter **impalas**, **waterbucks** and **greater kudus**. It's also good **birding** territory and **warthogs** dig up the putting greens with their snout. A journey around Zambezi Drive will typically reveal **greater kudus**, **elephants**, **buffaloes** and **impalas**. The 'Big Tree' is a good place for elephants and buffaloes in the dry season (as is the waterhole at Victoria Falls Safari Lodge). A walk along the river (at your own risk) usually reveals **collared palm thrushes** and **tropical boubous** flittering amid the wild date palms.

Just 4km from town, the Zambezi River forms Zambezi NP's northern boundary and numerous picnic spots and fishing camps are located along the river's edge. This northern section is dominated by mopane woodland and riverine vegetation (apple-ring acacia, figs and ebony). This is a good place to find **elephants**, **buffaloes**, **waterbucks**, **impalas** and **greater kudus**. Over 400 bird species have been recorded and the river has throngs of **herons**, **egrets**, **storks** and **ibises**. **Pel's fishing owl** is a sought-after treat and **African skimmers** are present between August and December. A road follows the river and there are a couple of loops (inaccessible in wet season). The Liunga Loop is a good area for **giraffes** and occasionally **lions** are seen. **Hippos** wallow near Picnic Site 23, especially during dry season. For **elephants** visit Chundu I and II. You can take guided walks near Hippo Creek and along its spring lines. **African wild dogs** occur in the park and the best opportunity to see them is between May and August when they den.

A single road crosses the centre of the southern part of the park through the Chamabonda Vlei to the Njoko Pan and its game-viewing platform. The south is dominated by teak, but the road follows a stretch of grassland and this is the place to see **Burchell's zebras** and the regal **sable**. **Elephants** frequent waterholes, there are reasonable **buffalo** herds and you are more likely to see **lions** here than in the riverine area. **Stanley's bustard**, a rarity in Zimbabwe, has been seen here occasionally. ∎

Watching tips

Birders should consider staying at (you can't just visit) Imbabala Lodge about 70km west of town, near the intersection of Namibia, Zimbabwe, Botswana and Zambia, and home to several 'Okavango specials'. Slaty egrets are resident, rufous-bellied herons are regular visitors, coppery-tailed coucals occur among the reeds and white-rumped babblers are found in woodlands. Other specialities include chirping cisticola, red-shouldered widow and long-toed plover. Ruddy turnstones and grey plovers are common migratory visitors.

CHIMANIMANI NATIONAL PARK
& VUMBA MOUNTAINS

Zimbabwe's highlands

> **Wildlife highlights**
> The Eastern Highlands is the only area in Zimbabwe where you'll see samango monkeys. Vumba has 249 bird species including 48 specials and four near-endemics. Highlights include Chirinda apalis, red-faced crimsonwing, blue swallow, Gurney's sugarbird, Taita falcon and a new bokmakierie subspecies.

MOUNTAIN mists, evergreen forests and elements of West, East and Southern African montane flora and fauna characterise the Eastern Highlands. Vumba is a trove of birdlife, Chimanimani a mountain wilderness.

The Vumba Mountains contain the whole range of Zimbabwe's Afro-tropical highland bird species. In addition to birds, **samango monkeys** forage in trees at Vumba Botanical Gardens and Reserve. There are birdfeeders at Tony's Coffee Shop while White Horse Inn and Eden Lodge are favoured places to search for samangos, birdwatch in gardens and take walks to local forests. Birding can also be done by horseback at Fern Gully New Forest Stud. Proteas are farmed in the region and these attract **sunbirds** and **Gurney's sugarbird,** which breeds here in winter.

For specialist birding everyone heads to Seldomseen Bird Study Station for guided birding with world-renowned Peter Mwadziwana. Near-endemics include **Swynnerton's robin,** which hop along the forest floor and **Roberts' prinia,** which is usually located by its loud *cha-cha-cha-cha* call. The **Chirinda apalis,** another near-endemic, forages high up in the canopy, which is also home to the **stripe-cheeked bulbul.** Other specials include **forest weavers, white-tailed flycatchers, orange ground thrushes** and **black-fronted bush shrikes.** The finchlike **red-faced crimsonwing** can be spied feeding on seeds on the ground.

Between March and May, noisy flocks of **silvery-cheeked hornbills** fly in through the mountains at dawn and dusk. After feeding during the day, they return to their roosts in the nearby

Haroni–Rusitu junction

Keen birders should visit the nearby, though hard to get to, lower-lying Haroni and Rusitu reserves. This is one of the most biologically complex areas in Zimbabwe because its forest has affiliations with Mozambique coastal forests and Congo forests. Haroni Forest Botanical Reserve is mostly cleared so Rusitu Reserve is the area to visit. This is the only Zimbabwe locality for several tree, fern and orchid species and is home to special reptiles, amphibians and mammals – including a rare East African fruit-bat (the collared fruit-bat), Grant's bushbaby and the tree civet. Among 233 bird species are nine East African coastal species, 10 Afro-tropical highland species and seven Zambezian species. These include barred cuckoo, silvery-cheeked hornbill, little spotted woodpecker, African broadbill, slender bulbul, Vanga flycatcher, Mozambique and Woodward's batises, black-headed apalis, Delegorgue's pigeon, chestnut-fronted helmet-shrike, Nyasa seedcracker and the prized Angola pitta, which breeds here in December.

mountains, after May they return to Mozambique. With them go the **red-chested, Jacobin, Klaas'** and **emerald cuckoos,** which breed here during summer. They return in August, at the same time as the endangered **blue swallow** – its metallic dark blue plumage and streaming paired tail feathers distinctive as it hawks for insects low over open montane scrub. About four to six pairs are known to visit Vumba and it remains a mystery where this swallow goes to when it departs in autumn. Vumba also has a variety of **butterflies** – many of Zimbabwe's 500 species occur here, including several rarities.

This rugged wilderness, with it peaks, gorges, and plateau grasslands is the spot for serious hikers. Chimanimani is a village and nearby is an eland sanctuary (there are no elands but **samango monkeys** climb the soaring trees with buttressed roots) and the Bridal Veil Falls. Around the village you'll readily see the **white-necked raven**, a high altitude species. Its massive bill distinguishes it from the common pied crow.

About 17km from the village is the base camp for hikes into the park. From there it is a three-hour hike to the mountain hut, from where hikers take various routes over the mountains. Mammals are not readily visible although **elands, sables, roans, blue duikers** and **bushbucks** are present. While there is plenty of evidence of **leopards**, they are rarely seen. Of the 186 recorded bird species on the mountain, nearly 30 have a restricted range or assemblage; two are East African coastal specials and seven are Zambezian. The **blue swallow** visits during the rainy season and the most reliable place to see this rarity is around Sawerombi (although this area is being consumed by timber plantations).

The Bundi Valley's meadows are interspersed with heathers and ericas; **Shelley's francolins** flutter up from rocky scrub. **Gurney's sugarbirds** can often be seen feeding on proteas and the wooded streambeds are the place to look for **malachite sunbirds.** Haroni River Gorge is a well-known site for **kingfishers, wagtails** and **louries.**

Among a variety of birds of prey in these mountains is one of the rarest, the **Taita falcon.** They turn up with some regularity on the telephone lines that run right along Roy Bennet's tobacco field, which is easily seen on the road to base camp. About 60 plant species are restricted to this mountain range, as well as over 300 **orchids** and several **amphibians.** ■

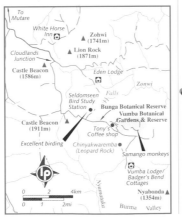

Location Vumba: 28km southeast of Mutare. Chimanimani NP: 157km southeast of Mutare.

Facilities Vumba: Bird study centre, horse riding trails. Chimanimani: Maps from tourist office (in village), no facilities in park.

Accommodation Vumba: Camping ground, cottages and hotels. Chimanimani: Hut, camp site, caves, camping permissible anywhere.

Wildlife rhythms Vumba: Blue swallows and cuckoos return August. Chimanimani: Best June to September.

Contact Curator, Vumba Botanical Gardens (☎ 020-2722). Chimanimani Tourist Association (☎ 126-2294).

Watching tips

One of the rarest highland birds is not found at Vumba, but at Chimanimani. This area is the only known location of a recently described subspecies of bokmakierie. It is actually quite commonly seen and the *Philippia*-covered rocky hillsides are a good place look.

MATOBO NATIONAL PARK
Life in the balance

Wildlife highlights

More than 300 birds recorded – 32 raptor species breed here. White rhinos, elands, giraffes and hippos at Whovi. Dassies and klipspringers common in rocky areas. Waterbirds excellent at Toghwana and Mjelele Dams. Black eagles and leopards also fairly common.

Location 53km south of Bulawayo; year-round access, some roads 4WD only.
Facilities Guided walks in Whovi (book ahead), interpretation centres, horseback safaris, walking trails in wilderness areas.
Accommodation Camping, caravan sites, NP self-catering chalets, lodges nearby.
Wildlife rhythms Best April to October.
Contact National Parks Booking Office, Bulawayo (☎ 09-63646) or Harare (☎ 04-706 077/8).

Watching tips

From 'View of the World' scan for crowned eagles, and lanner and peregrine falcons.

DOMES of weathered granite balancing on top of each other form giant koppies that rise above the msasa and munondo mosaic to give Matobo its unusual beauty. Streaks of yellow lichen stain the rock faces and pairs of **klipspringer** stand stock-still on boulders. Above, **black (Verreaux's) eagles** spiral in the thermals as the day heats up, hunting for their favoured prey, rabbit-sized **dassies** that live among the rocks.

One of the most scenic and significant cultural areas in Zimbabwe, Matobo is also home to the elusive **leopard, rhinos,** and the world's highest concentration of **black eagles.** Driving at dawn and dusk to spot a leopard is worthwhile here (night drives are not permitted) – one ranger reported seeing four different leopards within 3km. To the west, inside the Whovi GP, is Zimbabwe's greatest number of **white rhinos** and some **black rhinos.** Relaxed in the safety of this Intensive Protection Zone, the sociable whites often graze or snooze under the trees around the water trough just past the entrance. Whovi's boundaries are no barrier to **purple-crested louries,** but **giraffes, elands,** most of the **Burchell's zebras** and all **hippos** are restricted to the game park. Hippos are found only in Mpopoma and Chintampa Dams, and at all the dams the cry of the **African fish eagle** can be heard.

Whovi is open only to vehicles, but in the rest of Matobo you can walk to caves and Bushman paintings. Walk carefully: Matobo boasts a large population of **black mambas,** growing up to 3.5m and with a reputation for aggression. **Greater kudus, sables, blue wildebeests, impalas** and **waterbucks** can be seen when walking or driving, and **baboons, vervet monkeys** and **warthogs** keep campers company – warthogs at Maleme Dam camp site are outrageously tame. The park is topped off by the panoramic Malindidzimu or 'View of the World' lookout. Here the famed 'Lizard Man' trained rainbow-coloured **agama lizards** to come out to take food; he recently died aged 97, but there is a trainee in place! ■

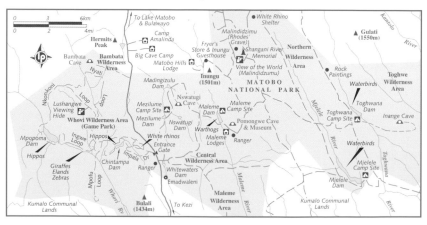

NYANGA NATIONAL PARK

Montane grasslands, evergreen forests

THE section of the Eastern Highlands closest to Harare, Nyanga is a popular retreat with fabulous views, gorges and waterfalls. Home to Zimbabwe's highest mountain (Mt Nyangani, 2593m) and Africa's second highest waterfall (Mtarazi Falls, 762m), relatively few mammals occur in this highland park.

Bird specials and roaring waters

The park's three main dams are good places for birding. the Rhodes Nyanga Hotel's gardens attract lots of birds, some of which breed in the surrounds. **Waterbucks** are sometimes seen around the hotel and park HQ. Antelopes, including **greater kudus**, visit nearby Udu Dam at dusk. This dam is a good spot to observe noisy **Natal francolins** and **little bee-eaters**; and **red bishops** and **orange-breasted waxbills** breed among the reeds.

The rare **blue swallow** might be seen in the grasslands during the rainy season – when insects are hatching up to eight have been observed in the evening on some dams (such as Troutbeck). **Black-collared** and **crested barbets**, and the flashy **purple-crested lourie** can be seen in woodlands.

Mtarazi Falls is a good place to look for bird specials such as the **orange ground thrush**, **starred robin**, **Chirinda apalis**, **red-faced crimsonwing** and **striped-cheeked bulbul**. If you hike up Mt Nyangani, watch for **Gurney's sugarbird** on the lower reaches. This bird is attracted to aloes (flowering between June and July), heather and proteas.

Nyanga seems an odd environment to encounter **secretary birds** but you may see them stalking through the mountain grasslands. **Blue wildebeests** seem out of place here, but they were introduced to Nyanga and are regularly seen around the Troutbeck Road.

Next to Nyanga NP is the Nyazengu NR, a popular birding area. East of Mt Nyangani, the Honde Valley is another excellent birding area, famous for the presence of the **marsh tchagra**. The rare **palmnut vulture** is often seen in the *Raffia* palms near the Aberfoyle Country Club; ask at the Club for a bird guide who can show you the birds of the nearby Gleneagles Estates. ■

Map: Connemara Lakes; World's View; Troutbeck Dam; Troutbeck; Blue swallows; Nyamhuka; Nyanga; Wildebeests; Gleneagles Mountain Reserve; NYANGA NATIONAL PARK; Udu Dam; Park HQ; Aberfoyle Country Club; Nyanga Dam; Mare Dam; Mare; Mt Nyangani (2593m); Purdon Dam; Nyazengu Falls; ZIMBABWE; Palm-nut vultures; Nyazengu Nature Reserve; Eastern Highlands Country Club; Juliasdale; To Rusape & Harare; Pungwe Falls; 0 3 6km; 0 2 4mi; Mtarazi Falls National Park; Mtarazi Falls; Honde Valley; Odzi River; Starred robins; Orange ground thrushes; To Mutare; Chirinda apalises; Honde River; Hauna; MOZAMBIQUE

Wildlife highlights
Great for birding in general, with at least 276 species recorded. Specialities include blue swallow, red-faced crimsonwing, orange ground thrush, starred robin, Chirinda apalis, Gurney's sugarbird and . Three *Protea* species are endemic to the Eastern Highlands.

Location 100km southeast of Harare.
Facilities Park HQ, museums at Ziwa site, bird list at Rhodes Hotel, horse riding. Signposted walks at Nyazenga NR.
Accommodation Camping, caravan sites, upmarket hotels and lodges.
Wildlife rhythms Best November to May.
Contact Nyanga Tourist Association (☎ 029-8435).

Watching tips
November is the height of breeding activity for birds in evergreen forests. Forest edge and woodland birds breed a little later. A visit during early summer (November to December) could be the most rewarding to hear the birds calling, in breeding plumage and displaying. Migrants are also present at that time. Birds seasonally cross borders and change altitudes, so walks in different habitats and altitudes should yield the greatest variety.

MALAWI

Highlights

- Gliding past hippos, Nile crocodiles and cormorant colonies on a Shire River boat trip
- Cantering past Burchell's zebras, roan antelopes and reedbucks on a horseback safari across Nyika's rolling grasslands
- Snorkelling through schools of shimmering cichlids in Lake Malawi
- Relaxing at Mvuu Camp at Liwonde NP as brown-breasted barbets, collared palm thrushes and green coucals fossick nearby
- Sitting and waiting at a hide in Lengwe NP to catch a glimpse of nyalas, sunis and bush shrikes
- Hearing African fish eagles ('Malawi sparrows') cry in duet while paddling a kayak across the waters of Lake Malawi NP
- Having a herd of elephants to yourself; then spotting a bird 'feeding flock' in the Vwaza Marsh WR
- Endangered wattled cranes and Denham's bustards strutting across the grassy Nyika Plateau

Lakeside wonderland

MALAWI stretches 900km along a trench formed by the Rift Valley system. Dominating this long, thin country is sealike Lake Malawi, which covers 20% of the country's total area. In the northwest, a narrow strip of shoreline gives way to steep escarpments which rise to the Nyika and Viphaya Plateaus. South of these highlands is a series of plateaus undulating between 760 and 1370m. Lake Malawi (Africa's third-largest lake) has only one outlet – the Shire River, which courses south to the Zambezi in Mozambique. East of the Shire is the Zomba Plateau and Malawi's highest point, Mt Mulanje (3001m).

Lake Malawi is famous for its cichlids, a tropical freshwater fish family numbering over 1000 species here. Lake Malawi NP (a World Heritage Site) is one of several places where you can snorkel and scuba dive among these colourful fish – visibility is best between August and October.

Malawi's dramatic variation in altitude has given rise to diverse soils, vegetation and climatic zones. Overall, the climate is equatorial with a dry season (May to August), a hot humid period (September to October) and a wet season (November to April), with temperatures lower in the highlands. Rich plateau soils are mostly cultivated; poor escarpment soils are covered in miombo woodlands, giving way to evergreen forests at higher altitudes. One exception is the Nyika Plateau, which Malawi shares with Zambia. Here, above 2000m, rolling montane grasslands support roans, elands and other mammals, 435 bird species (including four endemic subspecies) and a rich montane flora including 200 orchid species (12 endemics), proteas, lobelias and juniper forests.

Less than 40% of Malawi is woodlands and over 50,000 hectares of this is cleared each year for human exploitation, while many parks suffer from poaching and population encroachment. Malawi's premier 'island' of wildlife is Liwonde NP, located on the Shire River. Surrounded by a density of over 130 people per sq km, Liwonde's riverine vegetation and mopane woodlands support elephants, Nile crocodiles, hippos, sables and a few reintroduced, but seldom seen, black rhinos.

Light on mammals, Malawi's big drawcard is its 645 bird species: around one-tenth occur nowhere else in Southern Africa, including 30 specialities (with limited distributions elsewhere). Liwonde specials include Pel's fishing owls, brown-breasted barbets and Lilian's lovebirds. Vwaza Marsh WR is good for waterbirds and miombo specials and another twitching site is thicket-filled Lengwe NP.

Malawi's five national parks and four wildlife reserves are administered by the Department of Parks and Wildlife. In major parks, accommodation is provided by private operators. In fact the department encourages inquiries to be made directly to these companies. While facilities and roads have improved, some parks are inaccessible in the wet season. ∎

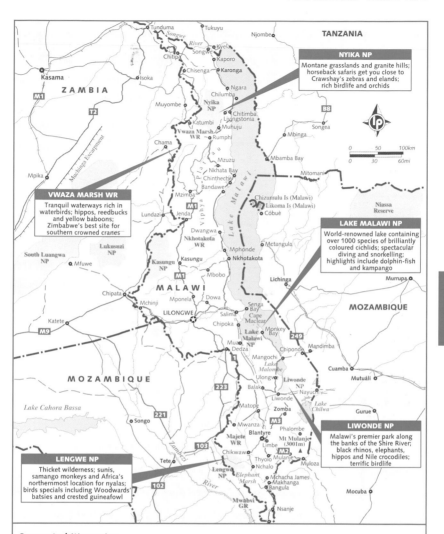

NYIKA NP
Montane grasslands and granite hills; horseback safaris get you close to Crawshay's zebras and elands; rich birdlife and orchids

VWAZA MARSH WR
Tranquil waterways rich in waterbirds; hippos, reedbucks and yellow baboons; Zimbabwe's best site for southern crowned cranes

LAKE MALAWI NP
World-renowned lake containing over 1000 species of brilliantly coloured cichlids; spectacular diving and snorkelling; highlights include dolphin-fish and kampango

LIWONDE NP
Malawi's premier park along the banks of the Shire River; black rhinos, elephants, hippos and Nile crocodiles; terrific birdlife

LENGWE NP
Thicket wilderness; sunis, samango monkeys and Africa's northernmost location for nyalas; birds specials including Woodwards' batsies and crested guineafowl

Suggested itineraries

One week From Lilongwe, forge up to Nyika NP for horseback safaris, hikes and game drives (3 days) then explore Vwaza Marsh WR, looking for elephants and birds (2 days). Scoot down to the lakeside Nkhata Bay and Chintheche areas (2 days) to spend time birdwatching, snorkelling or scuba diving before heading back to Lilongwe.

Two weeks Visit Lengwe NP for sunis and crested guineafowl, then go down to Liwonde NP for birding, game-viewing and boat trips. Head north to Lake Malawi NP for snorkelling or scuba diving then skirt the lakeshore to either Chintheche or Senga Bay. From here, head up to the montane grasslands of Nyika NP, then visit Vwaza Marsh WR.

One month An extra fortnight will give you time to winkle out Malawi's endemic specialities. Explore Elephant Marsh and Lengwe NP, then visit Liwonde and Lake Malawi NPs (include Domwe and Mumbo Islands). Skirt the lakeshore to Senga Bay, Chintheche and Nkhata Bay. Head up to Nyika NP for horseback safaris, then explore Vwaza Marsh WR.

LAKE MALAWI
The calendar lake

Wildlife highlights

Diving and snorkelling to see cichlids (99% of which are endemic) is the top attraction. Good fish-watching sites include 'The Aquarium' at Thumbi (where there are also Cornish jacks), Namanje Island, Meliere's Islands and Nkhata Bay (also catfish, dolphin-fish). Mumbo Island has otters, Nile monitors and a cormorant colony. Namanje Island also has monitors and cormorant colonies.

PRE-METRIC Lake Malawi was described as 365 miles long by 52 miles wide – hence the nickname. The third largest lake in Africa and third deepest in the world, it fills a trench formed by the eastern Great Rift Valley. For tourists, Lake Malawi is synonymous with sun, snorkelling and diving; and it's the lifeblood of most Malawians. But for nature buffs it means **cichlids**. These brilliant freshwater fish occur in their thousands and some dives here are like swimming in an overstocked aquarium. Conservatively there are at least 1000 different species of cichlids in the lake, perhaps 1500 – only around 400 species have been scientifically described. The main diving areas are Cape Maclear (which contains Lake Malawi NP), Nkhata Bay and Senga Bay.

Lake Malawi NP, a World Heritage Site, is comprised of 13 islands, part of the lake and the Nankumba Peninsula. Over 300 birds are recorded in the region, and a hike to Mt Nkunguni may yield a few. Near the park HQ and visitor centre (at the Golden Sands Holiday Resort) is Otter Point, which has a popular snorkelling trail. From Cape Maclear you have access to two islands: Thumbi (2km offshore) and Domwe (4km). 'The Aquarium' in front of Thumbi is a busy snorkelling site with a

Cichlids by the mouthful

The huge array of cichlids that inhabit the Rift Valley lakes evolved from a few river-dwelling species to fill every feeding niche and form the largest freshwater family in Africa. To attract mates, males build sandy courtship sites or establish rocky territories; rival suitors are grappled, tossed and chased away. Females are attracted by the males' brilliant coloration and shepherded in. Females lay their eggs one at a time (up to 200), grasping each in their mouth and nuzzling the genitalia and anal fin (which look uncannily like fish eggs) of several males. Sperm is released, which she sucks into her mouth where the eggs are fertilised and develop. When hatchlings leave the mouth they stay close to their mother, darting back into the mouth of the nearest female if danger arises – fingerlings of several broods and even different species can end up in the same mouth. But one predatory species has overcome even this defence by knocking eggs out of the mouth of other cichlids.

variety of **cichlids** – night dives here reveal schools of **Cornish jacks**, eel-like predatory fish.

Among Domwe Island's granite rocks are **agama lizards**, **skinks** and **snakes**. **Vervet monkeys** and **yellow baboons** are common. There are two walks here – a short one to a lookout point, or a two hour climb to the summit. Alternatively, bound along the boulders on the shore. You'll see **Nile monitors**, **dassies**, maybe **Cape clawless otters**, lots of **pied kingfishers**, **white-breasted cormorants** and loads of **lizards**. **Scarlet-chested sunbirds** hang around camp and **trumpeter hornbills** regularly fly over in the early evening.

Access is restricted to use by clients of Kayak Africa, but the waters near Mumbo Island (10km from shore) offer the best visibility in the area. The island itself has plenty of **monitors** and harmless **snakes**, and ever-watchful **African fish eagles**.

This is easier to walk around than Domwe and birds recorded include **paradise flycatchers**, **little bee-eaters**, **red bishops** and **red-billed firefinches**. **White-breasted cormorants** nest on the northern side between March and October. Rather relaxed **otters** sometimes swim alongside snorkellers. Over 10km from shore are the rarely dived Zimbabwe Rocks (Lighthouse Rock). Deep dives here feature lots of big **catfish** and **kampango**.

Diving for dolphin-fish

North of Cape Maclear is Senga Bay – those who do their scuba training here will usually be taken to Namanje Island (Bird or Lizard Island) which lies just offshore. This island has large **monitors**, and breeding colonies of **white-breasted** and **reed cormorants**. **African fish eagles** are fed here to provide tourists with photo opportunities (although this activity may foster dependence). Other regular dive sites include an area 15km offshore near Nankanlenga Island, one of the three Meliere's Islands – this area reputedly has more **cichlids** than 'The Aquarium' at Cape Maclear. Around 30km north of Senga Bay is Mbenjii Island which is a target for hard-core divers. Diving here is best between August and September; from February to March silt reduces visibility.

Far north on the lake is Nkhata Bay. The bay here has a stepped shoreline that rapidly drops off to 150m just 500m from the shore, so dives here are shore-hugging. In addition to **cichlids** are **catfish**, **crabs** and night dives reveal schools of **dolphin-fish** and occasionally **eels**. Best visibility here (average 12 to 15m) is from September to December. South of Nkhata, the Chintheche Strip has superb birding – **green coucals**, **Gunning's robins**, **narina trogons** and **palmnut vultures** are all seen at camps here. ∎

Location Cape Maclear 250km southeast of Lilongwe, Senga Bay 123km east of Lilongwe, Nkata Bay 430km north of Lilongwe.

Facilities Scuba schools, diving equipment, boats and guides for hire at all three areas. Visitor centre, aquarium and museum at the Lake Malawi NP HQ.

Accommodation Camping, simple to upmarket accommodation available at all areas.

Wildlife rhythms Best diving is between August and September; poor visibility in wet season; June and July are windy months.

Contact Department of Parks & Wildlife (☎ 771 295, fax 770 650). Parks & Wildlife Officer, Lake Malawi NP (☎ 587 456).

The shores of Lake Malawi promise some excellent birding. Make sure you leave the beaches to look for species such as paradise flycatchers, green coucals and narina trogons.

Watching tips

Whether snorkelling or diving, avoid sudden surges. Not only does this minimise your impact on the aquatic environment, it will improve your viewing. Best of all is to stay still for a while – the cichlids come to you.

LIWONDE NATIONAL PARK

Waterbirds and wallowers

Wildlife highlights

Malawi's premier park with 407 bird species including Lilian's lovebirds, brown-breasted barbets, Böhm's bee-eaters and Pel's fishing owls. Boat safaris skim past waterbirds, hippos, Nile crocodiles and elephants in dry season. Malawi's largest sable population, and a black rhino sanctuary. Excellent guides at Liwonde are a boon to bird-watchers, even if you're just day-tripping.

Location Entrance 6km from Liwonde town, Mvuu 33km from town and accessible by boat. Rhino sanctuary 1km east of Mvuu.
Facilities Mvuu offers game drives (day and night), boating and walks. Hiking in hills is the main activity at Chiunguni.
Accommodation Camping, self-catering chalets, camps and tented lodge.
Wildlife rhythms Best birding and wildlife between September and December.
Contact Central African Wilderness Safaris (☎ 771 153, fax 771 397, **e** info@ wilderness.malawi.net).

HUGGING the banks of the Shire River, the waterway that drains Lake Malawi and courses down to the Zambezi River, Malawi's premier park has terrific birdlife. Boat trips along the Shire get very close to large numbers of **waterbirds** and in dry season (June to December) **elephants** are common along the water's edge. The elephants disperse with the rains but the river remains thick with **hippos** and **Nile crocodiles** all year. Only one company operates on the river so the boating is tranquil. Self-drive visitors can explore the roads during the day or join guided game drives, walks and night drives.

Best chance for black rhinos

Yellow baboons and **vervet monkeys** are common throughout the park and with a little effort you should be able to find **sable antelopes**. Some 200 are resident and in dry season they often mill on the floodplain north of Mvuu. A herd of about 120 occurs near the Likuzu River and a small herd frequents the southern Chiunguni area. Down here near the Likwenu River – the park's southern boundary – is the best place to see **greater kudus** and **waterbucks**. Greater kudus can also be found in and near Liwonde's rhino sanctuary. Liwonde is the only park in Malawi where there is a chance to see **black rhinos** and six are kept in the safety of the sanctuary's fences. Guided drives are available and there is a proposal to begin walks within the sanctuary. Thick vegetation and high grass reduce the chance of

First there were two

In an ocean of dusty mango tree savanna, Liwonde is a defiant island of wilderness. Years of hunting, 'pest control' and poaching decimated its wildlife and nine species of large mammal disappeared. Yet Liwonde is recovering, mainly thanks to Frankfurt Zoological Society and the J&B 'Care for the Rare' program. It began with a breeding pair of black rhinos in 1993 then another pair in 1998, which have produced offspring. In 1999 buffaloes, Burchell's zebras, elands, hartebeests and roans were reintroduced, and all have bred successfully. Improved relations with villagers bordering the park and increased vigilance against poaching appears to be paying off. A further two rhinos were added in 2000, Cookson's wildebeests were introduced in 2001, and there are plans for lions in 2002 – a nasty surprise for Liwonde's herbivores.

seeing rhinos, but concentrations of some animals are higher inside the sanctuary than outside, and **impalas**, **warthogs** and **sables** are often spotted.

Looking for lovebirds

Liwonde's bird variety reflects the diversity of vegetation in the park. There are grasslands, thickets, mopane woodlands thick with python vine, open areas dotted with baobabs, riverine forest fringed by fever trees and palms, and the Shire River itself. Boat trips drift past an array of **kingfishers**, **herons**, **egrets**, **ducks** and **storks**, while **African fish eagles** are ever present. Hyphaene palms on the river's edge are white-washed with the guano of vast numbers of **white-breasted cormorants**. The main breeding colony is located at the boat launch for Mvuu Camp – it's risky to be hatless in this area. On the river's sand bars **African skimmers** are present from September to January and **Pel's fishing owls** roost in shady trees close to the river – the best time to see them is between October and December. **Swallow-tailed bee-eaters** appear in September and breed in the river banks, and **white-backed night herons** roost in thickets overhanging the water.

On dry land a guided walk will usually find **Böhm's bee-eaters** (this is the best place in Malawi to see this species). Keep a lookout for **mosque swallows** and **mottled spinetails** around the baobabs in which they nest. Around the open area of towering cathedral mopane north of Mvuu, watch out for **racket-tailed rollers** and **Arnot's chats**. The special of this habitat type is **Lilian's lovebirds** and Liwonde is the only place in Malawi where they are regularly seen. They are particularly fond of the flowers and fruits of the enormous candelabra-like euphorbias so look around these when they are in flower (August to September). At Mvuu Camp **collared palm thrushes** flit through the dining room while normally retiring **green coucals** scamper outside.

Night drives routinely reveal the eyeshine of **genets**, **white-tailed mongooses**, **four-toed elephant shrews**, **bushpigs**, **bushbucks** and **bushbabies**. The artificial waterhole 300m from Mvuu Camp is a favourite dusk spot for **scrub hares** and **impalas**. **Dikkops**, **coursers** and **nightjars** are commonly seen at night, and **African barred owlets** and **white-faced owls** might be seen in mopane areas. One of Liwonde's guides is renowned for spotting chameleons at night so you may even see **flap-necked chameleons**. ■

Watching tips

Chiunguni Hill is good for klipspringers and oribis, and the caves on its side house porcupines and civets. For Pel's fishing owls, ask staff whether these are roosting at the end of the lagoon at Mvuu Lodge. A pair of brown-breasted barbets nests near there and also in the fever tree between tents 2 and 3 of this lodge.

NYIKA NATIONAL PARK

Grasslands in the sky

MALAWI'S largest park is located some 2600m high on a plateau of rolling montane grasslands interspersed with granite hills, streams and soggy dambos. Small remnant patches of montane forest are tucked down near the heads of valleys. In the north the escarpment drops sharply, and below 2000m grasslands change into woodland. Nyika is home to several mammal species but birds, a wealth of orchids and walking trails are the highlights.

Wildlife highlights

A must for serious bird-watchers: montane forms star among 435 species. Roan antelopes, Crawshay's zebras, reedbucks, elands, bushbucks, spotted hyenas and jackals are common, and horseback safaris get you very close to roans and elands. One of the richest orchid areas in south-central Africa, with 200 species identified – twelve endemic to Nyika. Two frogs and two skinks are also endemic.

Malawi high

Chelinda Camp is the centre of activity in the park and the greatest concentration of animals is within about a 10km radius of here. The Chosi Loop area is a good place to begin exploring as it contains two dams which attract wildlife, especially herds of **roan antelopes**. In the grasslands roans are readily seen and often associate with **Crawshay's zebras** – this subspecies has thin, tight stripes and lacks shadow-stripes. There are old salt licks around Chelinda in which the zebras like to roll – perhaps to remove parasites. **Southern reedbucks** muster in small groups on the grasslands and if you think you've spotted a **puku** among them you are not mistaken – this is not puku country but one seems to have taken up residence here. **Elands** graze and browse the plateau but they, zebras and roans move off the grasslands in dry season. Meander around the forested areas near Chelinda to look

Unique montane flora

Isolated by steep escarpments and populated by East, West and Southern African montane flora, many of Nyika's plants (like this aloe, inset) have evolved into separate subspecies and even new species. Below 1800m, proteas abut bracken and msuku woodland. In the zone above are relatively poor grasses in soil that has been leached of its nutrients by rains – this is why some antelopes leave the plateau in dry season in search of fertile sward. Lobelias sprout in bogs, as do yellow lilies, irises and insectivorous sundews. In grasslands and evergreen forests are epiphytic and ground-dwelling orchids. Highland woodlands are stocked with rosewoods and Nyika is Malawi's southernmost point for junipers. After grassland fires, Nyika's legume (pea family) species come into flower then produce pods. Legumes convert nitrogen in the air into plant proteins stored in the pods, which are consumed by antelopes, particularly reedbucks. With the plateau's poor graze, legumes play a vital role in the ecosystem.

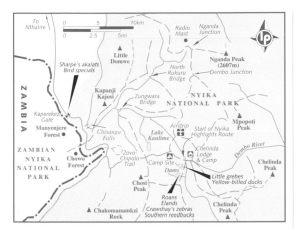

Location Chelinda 189km north of Mzuzu, 507km north of Lilongwe.
Facilities Maps and books at Chelinda, horse riding, day and night drives, walking trails, guided walks.
Accommodation Camping, self-catering chalets, luxury log cabins at lodge.
Wildlife rhythms October best for wildflowers and mammals. Best for birds October to April, orchids January to March.
Contact The Nyika Safari Company (☎ 752 379, ☎/fax 757 316, **e** reservations@nyika.com).

for **bushbucks** – normally shy, here they are more approachable. Predators on the plateau include **side-striped jackals,** which can be seen during the day and on night drives – which may also yield **bushpigs**. **Spotted hyenas** are also common – in the absence of carcasses left by other predators (although in some years **leopards** appear abundant) they rely on their hunting skills and regularly dispatch reedbucks at the dams.

The best way to get close to Nyika's wildlife is on horseback – you can often get within 50m of **roans** or **reedbucks**. There are morning or afternoon rides from Chelinda or escorted multi-day horseback safaris into the wilderness. Within walking distance of Chelinda, Lake Kaulime is a good bird and mammal spot. For keen hikers (come self-sufficient), hire a scout and head for the wilderness trails within the park, the Nyika Highlands, or the popular trail to Livingstonia.

Some 50 species of birds recorded at Nyika don't appear in South African bird books. In addition, four subspecies are entirely restricted to Nyika and four species have their only Malawi presence here. Nyika is also the Malawi stronghold of two threatened species – **wattled crane** and **Denham's bustard**. Although only eight pairs of wattled cranes occur here, they are readily visible and often feed around the dambos. Giant lobelias in the dambos attract **scarlet-tufted malachite sunbirds** (one of Nyika's 14 sunbirds). Large **Denham's bustards** strut through the grasslands – usually seen singly or in pairs, up to 50 have been recorded following a burn (burning is a common management practice in the grasslands). **Red-winged francolins** (a subspecies endemic to Nyika) are typically spotted darting along the road. Of the more common species, **red-breasted sparrowhawks** hunt with their wingtips almost touching the ground, often skimming along the road in front of vehicles. **Cisticolas** and **larks** are commonly flushed from the grasses beside the road, while **white-necked ravens** fly above. From October to April the dambos and grasslands are great for seeing **pallid, Montagu's** and other **harriers**. **Yellow-billed ducks** and **little grebes** frequent the dams, and **black-headed herons** might be spotted at the dam below Chelinda Camp. ■

Despite the hilly terrain, the reedbuck species at Nyika is not the mountain reedbuck (which does not occur in Malawi): this is a southern reedbuck.

Watching tips

For birds, try neighbouring Chowo and Manyenjere forests in Zambia (access is no problem); around 30 pairs of Sharpe's akalats occur in Manyenjere. Zovo-Chipolo Forest (Malawi side) has trails through forest, bogs and grasslands – look here for bar-tailed trogons and moustached green tinker barbets.

LENGWE NATIONAL PARK

Bushveld, browsers and birdlife

> ### Wildlife highlights
> Africa's most northerly location for nyalas and one of the best places to see shy sunis, which occur in a high density; samango monkeys and a large buffalo population are also present. This is the only place in Malawi to see crested guineafowl – among 334 bird species – and one of two locations for Woodward's batises.

Location 83km southwest of Blantyre; closed in wet season.
Facilities Waterholes, hides, 2.5km self-guided walking trail. Facilities generally poor.
Accommodation Camping, caravan site, chalets at Lengwe Visitors Camp.
Wildlife rhythms Dry season good (July to November), best birding December to January.
Contact Department of Parks & Wildlife (☎ 771 295, fax 770 650, e tourism@malawi.net).

UNLIKE other areas in Malawi, Lengwe is choked with thickets, which makes animal-spotting difficult when driving around the park's road network. But there are no permanent waterways here and in dry season animals congregate at Lengwe's four artificial waterholes. Waiting at waterholes, such as Main Hide, and watching what comes in is a far more productive way of seeing animals here. Thickets are ideal **suni** habitat and in a morning you may see a few hundred **nyalas** drinking at the waterholes. Around 1200 formerly occurred in the park and although poaching has severely reduced their number, you should see nyala herds along the tracks. Early morning is the best time to wait for sunis (they are usually found in pairs); Lengwe's southeast has a high density of sunis – around 15 per sq km. **Impalas**, **bushbucks** (inset),

greater kudus, **warthogs**, **vervet monkeys** and **yellow baboons** are fairly common. Lengwe boasts Malawi's largest herd of **buffaloes** (although they are generally hard to see) and the 1000 in the park make up a third of Malawi's buffalo population. **Bushpigs**, normally nocturnal, are sometimes seen drinking during the day and there are always big **Nile monitors** at the waterholes. This is one of the few places where you can find **samango monkeys** in lowland forest – these are usually seen around camp in the mornings.

For birders the park's thickets (especially around Main and North hides) are good for skulking species, flycatchers and warblers. Lengwe is an excellent place in which to see **raptors, bush shrikes, Böhm's bee-eaters, Livingstone's flycatchers, crested guineafowl, eastern bearded robins** and **grey sunbirds** (try North Thicket Drive). Greenish **yellow-spotted nicators** move slowly through bushes, flashing their yellow-tipped tail in flight. Open patches in the park's south are good for **black-bellied korhaans**. ■

> ### Watching tips
> Southeast of Lengwe, Elephant Marsh is renowned for its waterbirds including colourful malachite kingfishers, goliath herons, pygmy geese, and African and lesser jacanas. Boat trips can be organised at Mchaba James village, at the southern end of the wetlands.

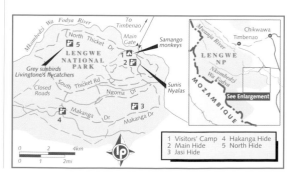

1 Visitors' Camp
2 Main Hide
3 Jasi Hide
4 Hakanga Hide
5 North Hide

VWAZA MARSH WILDLIFE RESERVE

Tranquil waterways, babbling woodlands

THE reserve's southeastern corner is easy to get to and most visitors confine activities to the area around Lake Kazuni (Vwaza Marsh, to the north, is inaccessible). On and around Lake Kazuni are some of Vwaza's many bird species – **wattled** and **blacksmith plovers**, **storks** (**open-billed**, **yellow-billed** and **saddle-billed**), **ibises** (**hadeda**, **sacred** and **glossy**), **herons**, **teals**, **ducks**, **sandpipers** and **geese**. On an early morning walk around the lake (you must take a guide) **yellow baboons** may be seen digging for grass bulbs, and **open-billed storks** probe the clay for aquatic snails. Approximately 150 **hippos** inhabit the lake area, **buffaloes** are present and you'll often see **impalas**, **reedbucks** and **greater kudus**. Solitary **slender mongooses** and groups of **banded mongooses** are both common residents. Around the camp on the lake's edge, **arrow-marked babblers**, 'bubbling' **tropical boubous** and **collared palm thrushes** fossick among the bushes. During the night **elephants** may forage through camp, littering the paths with broken branches – they are typically present between January and September, before moving west into Zambia's Luangwa Valley.

If you have wheels Zaro Pools is worth a visit. In addition to **waterbirds** this is the best place in Malawi to see **southern crowned cranes**, which are almost guaranteed. Much of Vwaza is dominated by miombo woodland, which provides camouflage for **greater kudus**, **bushbucks** and **duikers**, and has many woodland birds – **doves**, **drongos**, **lilac-breasted** and **racket-tailed rollers**, **blue-eared starlings** and **widows**. Patience is needed for birdwatching here because birds often amass in 'bird waves' – you'll see nothing for ages, then spot a large, mixed-species flock feeding together. Some specials to look out for are **white-winged starlings** (restricted to the north), **chestnut-mantled sparrow-weavers** and **miombo pied barbets**. If entering or exiting the reserve via Kawiya, the woodland at the gate is one of the world's best places to find **white-winged starlings**. Other specials here include **spotted creepers**, **Böhm's flycatchers** and **streaky-headed canaries**. ∎

Wildlife highlights
A quiet but accessible reserve that is home to elephants, hippos, kudus and plentiful waterbirds among 300 recorded species. Woodlands house numerous specials, including white-winged starlings. The best site in Malawi for southern crowned cranes.

Location Approximately 100km northwest of Mzuzu.
Facilities Bird list, guides for hire on walks, and day and night drives.
Accommodation Camping, basic bush huts and a luxury camp.
Wildlife rhythms Mammals concentrate from June to November. Birdlife good year-round.
Contact The Nyika Safari Company (☎ 752 379, ☎/fax 757 316).

Watching tips
If wild about elephants and here during wet season, stay in Bush Hut 4 – it is beneath a marula tree and elephants adore marula fruit, so they'll keep you company all night.

ZAMBIA

Highlights

- Watching a solitary shoe-bill's whale-like head rise above the reeds at Lake Bangweulu
- Stalking elands, tracking lions and watching huge colonies of yellow-billed storks on a hike through Nsefu, South Luangwa NP
- Sitting in a tree-hide in Kasanka's swamp forest, waiting for sitatungas and Ross' louries
- Waiting by the Luangwa River at dusk as elephants drink, then setting off on a night drive to spotlight leopards
- Canoeing the Zambezi past pods of hippos, bathing elephants and noisy heronries
- The sound of lechwes' hooves as they crash through the water at any of Zambia's wetlands
- Scouring Kafue's vast Busanga Plains for cheetahs, sables and lions, then at night spotlighting leopards
- Massive 'fishing parties' of herons, pelicans, marabou and saddle-billed storks gathering around near-dry lagoons in the Luangwa Valley

Diversity at the crossroads

ZAMBIA is wedged like a jigsaw puzzle piece between Central, East and Southern Africa, and its flora and fauna have affinities with all three regions. Most of the country undulates across a plateau between 1000 and 1600m which is fissured by several rift valleys, dipping at the Bangweulu Basin and at Lakes Kariba, Mweru and Tanganyika. In Zambia's west are the Mafinga Hills, while to the east rise the Muchinga Mountains, which divide the Luangwa and Congo watersheds. Miombo woodlands cover 70% of the country, while river valleys are characterised by mopane and acacia woodlands, riverine forests, grasslands and wetlands – habitats typical of most of its 19 national parks. The southwest is dominated by Kalahari sands while the tropical north has higher rainfall (over 1500mm) and moist evergreen forests.

With a moderate climate, Zambia's top game-viewing period is during winter (May to August) and the dry, hot months from September to November. During wet season (December to April) floodplains such as Busanga and Bangweulu often become inaccessible. Floodwaters wash alluvium across the plains and shallow waters attract countless waterbirds. As waters recede grassland is exposed, attracting congregations of plains game.

Zambia's geography has created isolated pockets of wildlife and this has resulted in several unique subspecies of mammals. The Luangwa Valley shelters Cookson's wildebeests and Thornicroft's giraffes, while the Kafue region has endemic subspecies of lechwes and waterbucks. Black lechwes aside endemic and are best seen at the Bangweulu Swamps. Aside from endemics, Zambia has two of Africa's prime leopard spots – South Luangwa and Kafue NPs. An astonishing 733 bird species occur in Zambia but only one is endemic: Chaplin's barbet of southern Kafue. Zambia's 'big tick' is the shoebill, which breeds at Lake Bangweulu. Its many migrants start arriving in September and October, most departing by April.

Management of national parks is in transition, with the National Parks and Wildlife Service being replaced by the Zambian Wildlife Service (ZWS). Zambia still has vast tracts of wilderness untouched by pastoralism, but poaching is widespread and animals remain difficult to approach in some areas. In recent years Kafue and Lower Zambezi NPs have staged impressive recoveries, while community-based ecotourism initiatives are showing promise at South Luangwa and Kasanka NPs.

Surrounding many parks are Zambia's 31 Game Management Areas, effectively buffer zones where hunting is permitted. Hunting by Zambian citizens is poorly monitored, but hunting safaris bring in revenue for communities and the government. However, possibly the biggest hurdle to tourism is Zambia's poor roads. Many lesser-known parks are difficult to visit, while most parks are inaccessible in the wet season. In contrast, Zambia's premier park, South Luangwa NP, is accessible year-round. ∎

Opposite: Sunset over the Luangwa River, South Luangwa NP. The river provides a focus for wildlife-viewing in this magnificent park.

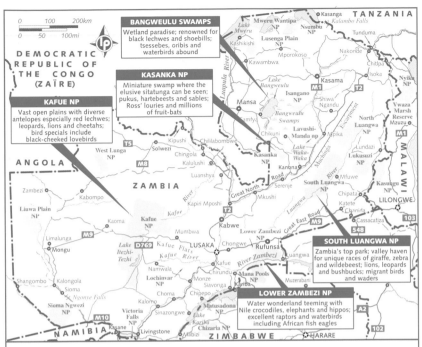

BANGWEULU SWAMPS
Wetland paradise; renowned for black lechwes and shoebills; tsessebes, oribis and waterbirds abound

KASANKA NP
Miniature swamp where the elusive sitatunga can be seen; pukus, hartebeests and sables; Ross' louries and millions of fruit-bats

KAFUE NP
Vast open plains with diverse antelopes especially red lechwes; leopards, lions and cheetahs; bird specials include black-cheeked lovebirds

SOUTH LUANGWA NP
Zambia's top park; valley haven for unique races of giraffe, zebra and wildebeest; lions, leopards and bushbucks; migrant birds and waders

LOWER ZAMBEZI NP
Water wonderland teeming with Nile crocodiles, elephants and hippos; excellent raptors and waterbirds including African fish eagles

Suggested itineraries

One week Starting from Lilongwe (Malawi), drive across to South Luangwa NP. Spend 3 days at the Mfuwe or Nsefu region (including night-driving and leopard-spotting) then take a walking trail through the Luangwa Valley (3 days). Drive or fly back to Lilongwe.

Two weeks Via an organised safari, trek up to Kasanka NP for sitatungas, then across to the Bangweulu Swamps to see shoebills. Swing across to North Luangwa NP, via Kapishya Hot Springs, then meander down the Luangwa Valley to South Luangwa NP.

One month Combine the two-week trip (taking in Kasanka NP, Bangweulu Swamps, and North and South Luangwa NPs) with a visit to Kafue NP. Explore the north and south sections of the park before ending your trip with a canoeing safari through Lower Zambezi NP.

SOUTH LUANGWA NATIONAL PARK

Isolated haven for unique creatures

Wildlife highlights
Zambia's premier park and one of the only parks accessible in the Wet. Thornicroft's giraffes and Cookson's wildebeests are endemic and a limited-range subspecies of zebra lives in the park. Lions, leopards, elephants, crocs, hippos, pukus, waterbucks, impalas, bushbucks and kudus are plentiful and used to vehicles. Night drives and walking safaris a speciality with high quality guides. Lagoons attract spectacular bird 'fishing parties' in the dry season.

SPANNING about 700km long and 100km wide, the Luangwa Valley is the western part of the Great Rift Valley and an isolated haven for unique races of **giraffe** and **wildebeest**. A mosaic of mopane, miombo woodlands, acacia and grasslands carpets the valley, through which the Luangwa River carves a tortuous and ever-changing course south to the Zambezi River. Each wet season the river floods and slices new shortcuts, leaving behind bends that eventually form oxbow lakes. Most of the park's roads lead to these oxbows, around lagoons and along the shore of the river. Only a small section of South Luangwa is accessible: Mfuwe sector is much visited and use of the Nsefu sector is largely restricted to specific tour operators. Mfuwe's loamy sandy soil and all-weather roads ensure year-round access when other areas are waterlogged.

Unique zebras and dark-necked giraffes

As you approach the park, the 1km stretch before Luangwa Bridge is where **bushbucks** are often seen. Once inside the park, **impalas** and **pukus** are common and the stretch between Mfuwe Lagoon and Luangwa Wafwa is especially good for seeing **waterbucks**. Cryptically striped **greater kudus** meld with woodlands, but most other antelopes are rarely seen; **roans** and

Foot power

Luangwa is the birthplace of African walking safaris. Conceived by Norman Carr, a champion of conservation, today's options range from mobile safaris to casual strolls. All the small things missed from a vehicle become apparent and even poo becomes fascinating – you compare size, shape, spread and texture. A freshly renewed impala dung midden signals the active territory of an impala (leopards roll in these to disguise their smell); dispersed, thinly spread pellets are giraffe dung; elephant dung often contains buffalo-thorn fruit, its red seed coat digested. Baboons, squirrels and birds spread this out in search of insects, especially dung beetles. Then there are the tracks – of porcupines, giraffes, buffaloes and lions. The chance of encountering lions is high so instructions are given beforehand – stand still, stay in single file behind the scout and back off slowly while facing the lions. And no panicking.

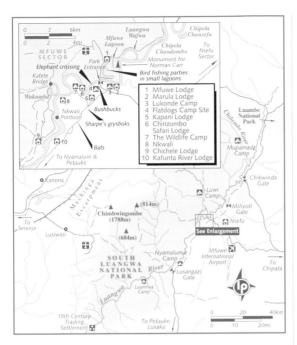

Location Mfuwe 704km northeast of Lusaka.
Facilities Map at park entrance, lodges conduct game drives. Last fuel Chipata. International airport.
Accommodation Camping ground and lodges outside park. Bush camps and two lodges inside park.
Wildlife rhythms Animals concentrate around water from June to October. Migrant birds are present from November to April.
Contact South Luangwa Area Management Unit (**e** deloitte@zamnet.zm) or Zambian Wildlife Authority Private Bag 1, Chilanga.

sables live in the Muchinga Mountains west of the park, **duikers** are nocturnal and shy.

Chacma baboons, **vervet monkeys** and **warthogs** are common everywhere, and this is great **elephant** country. In the late afternoon, elephants wade or 'snorkel' across the river (watch this near Flatdogs Camp). The river is filled with **hippos** and numerous 3m-long **Nile crocodiles** bask on the banks of Luangwa Wafwa. Just north of here, between Wafwa and the main river, is an area where **antelopes, Crawshay's zebras**, **giraffes** and **greater kudus** are regularly seen.

Look carefully at the **zebras** here – their stripes are thin, numerous and extend down to the hooves, under the belly and have no shadow stripe. These zebras are an intermediate form between the extra-stripy subspecies in Mozambique and the subspecies in East Africa. **Thornicroft's giraffes** are restricted to Luangwa Valley and are distinguished from other giraffes by their dark brown neck blotches (most apparent in older males) and lack of blotches below the knees. There are no other giraffes north of the Zambezi as far as Tanzania, and of the approximately 1200 Thornicroft's giraffes in existence, 700 reside in South Luangwa – it was partly their presence that created the impetus for Luangwa to become a national park. On the river's western bank, giraffes range from Manze in the south to Chibembe. Between November and April, when other areas are sodden, they concentrate around Mfuwe.

The defined banks of oxbow lakes house colonies of **sand martins** and migratory **carmine bee-eaters**. One large accessible colony forms between August and September near the

Thornicroft's giraffe. This unique subspecies is the most northerly occurring population of giraffes in Southern Africa.

Crawshay's zebra, a distinct subspecies of Burchell's zebra which lacks the shadow stripes of other populations.

western end of Luangwa Wafwa; this is also an excellent place for **waders** from August onwards. As small lagoons dry out in winter, fish writhe about in isolated mud pools and birds mass together to form 'fishing parties'. **Pelicans** and **yellow-billed storks** stuff themselves to the point that they can't fly. **Herons, spoonbills** and **marabou storks** join the party and up to 40 **saddle-billed storks** have gathered. Often at this time, the grasses and seeds around the lagoon attract a moving carpet of colour as **Lilian's lovebirds** and **queleas** mass in their thousands to feed. Anywhere grassland abuts watercourses **southern crowned cranes** can be found probing. These can congregate in flocks of up to 300 during winter.

Unusual wildebeests and other specials

The Nsefu region is on the eastern side of the Luangwa River and here large, skittish herds of **elands** are often seen. **Cookson's (Nyassa) wildebeests** (a subspecies confined to the valley) and **Lichtenstein's hartebeests** are found in wooded grasslands. Cookson's are smaller and have a browner pelt than other wildebeests; they are most abundant in the northern reaches of the park. The east bank has more **giraffes** than the

North Luangwa National Park

A five-hour drive upstream from South Luangwa, North Luangwa NP is open between May and October and is accessible only through two private operators – Shiwa Safaris/Zambian Safari Company (☎ 01-228682, fax 222906) or Remote Africa Safaris (☎ 062-45018, fax 45059) – which have semi-permanent camps along the Mwaleshi River.

The park's habitats and fauna are similar to South Luangwa, except for a few bird species. Yet North Luangwa's appeal lies in its isolation – with few roads and a trickle of visitors, you practically have the park to yourself. Walking safaris are virtually the only way of exploring the park, and usually follow the perennial Mwaleshi River. Mammal specials include elands, Cookson's wildebeests and Lichtenstein's hartebeests – all scarcer further south. Lions and spotted hyenas are regularly seen, as are large buffalo herds, particularly between August and September when smaller streams dry up (also a good time for birding). Owing to years of poaching, elephants here remain difficult to approach.

west, and these are mainly south of Nsefu. Populations may mix when the river is low, communicating by sight the rest of the year. During winter animals regularly ford the shallow streams and **Nile crocs** lie in wait. Chipela Lagoon, 10km north of Nsefu Camp has the largest colony of **yellow-billed storks** in Africa – it contains over 1000 nests, perched in massive trees.

The Luangwa River supports large numbers of hippos (below) as well as Nile crocodiles. Both may be seen basking on sandbanks.

Nocturnal hunters

Night drives (organised through lodges) are a major drawcard of the park. **Elephant shrews** are plentiful in thickets and dash across the roads; **genets**, **civets**, **scrub hares** and **white-tailed mongooses** are all readily seen. **Lions** are often found and Luangwa is well known for its high density of **leopards**. **Giant eagle-owls** and **nightjars** are common night birds, and **pennant-winged nightjars** arrive in the wet season, their streamerlike flight feathers unmistakable. Animals are not subjected to endless scrutiny and vehicles must leave the park at 8.30 pm.

If staying in a bush camp the activity never stops. Harmless **spotted (variegated) bush snakes** move across rafters and you may share your shower with **square-marked toads** or a **grey tree frog** – the largest arboreal frog in Southern Africa. At night, **geckos** cling to the walls. Dinner may be accompanied by the rumble of **buffalo** hooves (in dry season herds of up to 1000 form) and the cacophony of **hyenas** trashing the kitchen stores. No matter where you stay, expect at sometime to open a tent flap and find an **elephant** munching on greenery outside your abode. Even in upmarket lodges elephants amble through camp and take a drink out of the pool. **Hippos** have been known to take a dip in Mfuwe Lodge's pool!

Although mammals disperse during the rains, this is a fantastic time for birding because of the migrants. Also, **butterflies** come out – **monarchs**, **pansies**, **swallowtails**, **common leopards** and **common jokers** to mention a few. **Scorpions** and **spiders** become active, including palm-sized **baboon spiders** (so named for their coarse hair) and frenetic 'hunting spiders' – these are **solifuges**, not spiders. ■

Watching tips

Although self-drive visitors can't spotlight within the park, you can outside it and there are plenty of animals to see. Sharpe's grysboks are often seen along the southwest road below Chinzomba Lagoon (near Kapani Lodge). On your left 500m before the Nkwali turnoff is a baobab with an obvious hole – wait near this at sunset, as it's inhabited by a colony of tombbats. For birders, there is a resident Pel's fishing owl at Mfuwe Lodge.

KAFUE NATIONAL PARK

Vast wilderness along the Kafue River

> **Wildlife highlights**
> Kafue is renowned for its diversity of antelopes and its plains are home to thousands of red lechwes. One of the best places to see leopards; good numbers of lions and cheetahs. African wild dogs present. Bird specials include black-cheeked lovebirds (southern sector).

A T 22,480 sq km, around the size of Israel, Kafue is the second largest national park in Africa. Vast and wild, the park boasts 482 bird species and a diverse array of antelopes including **red lechwes** in thousand-strong herds. Predators occur in good numbers including packs of endangered **African wild dogs**.

Administratively Kafue is divided into the south and north. In the north is the Kafue River and its main tributaries – the Lufupa and Lunga – are the places to head out on boat safaris to see **hippos** and **Nile crocodiles** and to do a little birding. Riparian forest along the water's edge conceals **Pel's fishing owls, African green pigeons, purple-crested** and **Knysna louries**. **African finfoots** lurk cryptically around tangled root systems while **African fish eagles** are conspicuous atop exposed limbs. **Nile monitors** forage for crocodile eggs and bask on riverbanks.

Away from the rivers is a mixture of miombo woodlands and open grassy areas – **waterbucks, pukus** and **impalas** inhabit the dambos. A variety of **storks, egrets, herons** and **cranes** – which includes **wattled** and **southern crowned cranes** – are regular sights. In wet season (November to April) the floodplains become an impenetrable quagmire.

To the far north is the star attraction of the park – the vast Busanga Plain, which is home to thousands of **red lechwes**. Inaccessible during and following the rains, it can only be reached between July and November. On approaching the plains the first species likely to be encountered are **roan antelopes** and **oribis**, at the drier fringes of the floodplains. Lechwes become visible from Shumba Camp onwards. **Lions** and **spotted hyenas** are plentiful and this is the region to look for **cheetahs**. During

Lochinvar National Park

En route to Kafue's eastern entrance, Lochinvar NP is a stop off birders shouldn't miss. Sitting on the Kafue Flats, the park is dominated by a vast clay-bottomed floodplain where the Kafue River spills into the Chunga Lagoon. Four hundred and twenty-eight birds are on the species list here, including huge flocks of wetland residents, summer Palaearctic migrants (December onwards), and more than 50 different raptors. Lochinvar is low on mammal sightings with the spectacular exception of 40,000 Kafue lechwes (a distinctive subspecies). In summer, males defend tiny territories, called leks, crammed around the lagoon: females visit them for a brief week-long period to mate during December and January. You'll need a 4WD for most of the roads but walking is encouraged (and recommended), and WWF operates a nice camp site near the southern gate.

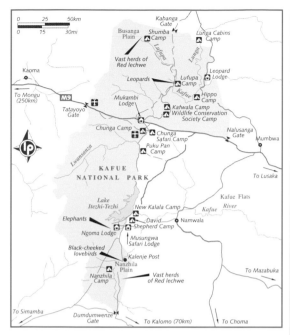

Location Chunga HQ 360km from Lusaka, 4WD only. Flying in recommended.
Facilities Lodges provide day and night drives, walking and boating safaris.
Accommodation Camping, self-catering chalets, fully inclusive lodges.
Wildlife rhythms Animals concentrate about water sources between July and October. Busanga best between August and October.
Contact Zambian Wildlife Authority, Private Bag 1, Chilanga.

the dry season **buffaloes, Burchell's zebras** and **blue wildebeests** move onto the plain from the surrounding areas. **Sitatungas** occur here but are rarely seen as they reside in inaccessible wetlands. **Servals** and **secretary birds** stalk small prey across the grasslands. In July **eastern white pelicans** and **wattled cranes** congregate in large flocks.

Night drives can be undertaken if staying at a lodge. A speciality of the Lufupa Camp is leopard spotting: habituated to spotlights, **leopards** are an almost guaranteed sighting on night drives and this is one of the best places in Africa to see them. Other night drive regulars are **African civets, genets, bushbabies** and **African wild cats. Dikkops** stand in the middle of the road and **white-faced owls** might be seen atop termite mounds. After the first rains keep a look out for snakes – **rock pythons** become a regular sight on night drives.

Like the north, a main feature of south Kafue is the river. This has been dammed to form the Itezhi-Tezhi Dam where you can go out by boat to view **hippos, Nile crocs** and **waterbirds.** The Nanzhila Plains support an abundance of **red lechwes** and among them you can find **oribis, roans, sables, Lichtenstein's hartebeests, blue wildebeests** and **pukus.** Herds of 400 buffaloes occur in the area, and **lions** and **cheetahs** are present. Zambia's only endemic bird, **Chaplin's barbet**, is seldom seen but occurs in woodlands stretching east from the dam.

South Kafue is by far the best area to visit if you want to see **elephants** (found at Ngoma in tracts of Zambezi teak forest). The south is also the stronghold for **black-cheeked lovebirds** – keep a look out for them around Kalenje Post. ■

Watching tips
To be assured of access to Busanga Plains, plan to visit after August; in some years heavy or long rains can keep the area off limits longer than anticipated. Once there, scan the wild date palm clusters that litter the plains – they often shade predators.

LOWER ZAMBEZI NATIONAL PARK

A park for water-lovers

Wildlife highlights
Famous for water-loving animals – masses of crocs, hippos, elephants and buffaloes. Waterbucks, impalas and bushbucks are common and the park has good numbers of lions and leopards. Approximately 400 bird species have been recorded, including palmnut vultures among 50 or so birds of prey, and Angola pittas. Ideal for boat and canoe safaris.

THIS recently developed park has staged an impressive turn around. Although most travel literature claims that this park is poached out, safari operators here have coordinated activities to stamp out poaching, **elephant** numbers have stabilised, **lions** are back and there are plenty of animals to see. Lower Zambezi NP is opposite Zimbabwe's Mana Pools NP, but it is not a mirror image. The Muchinga Escarpment drops dramatically from nearly 1500m down to 600m, forming a backdrop covered in miombo woodlands – the inaccessible northern region of the park. Most visitors explore the Zambezi River and the western section of the valley – sandy flats fringed by acacia and mopane woodland. There are no maps, so many visitors opt to stay at the park's camps and join guided walks, game drives (day and night), boat trips and canoe safaris.

Canoeing with crocodiles

From a canoe or boat you'll see countless **Nile crocodiles** and **hippos** along the park's 120km river frontage. The density of crocodiles is estimated at 100 per kilometre of river; the hippo density stands at 70 per kilometre. Although mostly nocturnal feeders, hippos often graze the grassy flats during the day. If disturbed they trundle back to the safety of the river – both in and out of water they must be given a wide berth. **Buffaloes** and **elephants** feed along the shoreline and in the marshy grasses on exposed shallows, while **waterbucks** crop grassy islands. Elephants casually wander through camps so being escorted to and from tents is a good precaution.

A thorny larder

Exiting the flats and entering acacia woodland, the limbs of winter-thorns arch overhead, almost touching each other's spindly branches and creating a ceiling of thorns, tiny leaves and spiralling pods. Aside from their majesty, winter-thorns are larders during cool dry months. The average *Acacia albida* produces 300kg of pods each year and sprouts leaves during the dry season, which provide shade and protein. Elephants shake their limbs for pods, then pick them up with their trunk as impalas vainly try to snare a few. At other times, bushbucks pick through seedpod litter discarded by baboons. The pods are resilient, and even after passing through an elephant's digestive system they are mostly intact, enabling seed dispersal.

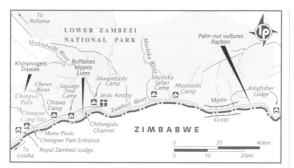

Location Chongwe entrance 216km southeast of Lusaka. Alternatively canoe, powerboat or fly in.
Facilities Lodges provide bird lists, game drives, canoes, boats, walking safaris.
Accommodation Camping and self-catering camps (park edge) or all-inclusive lodges. Kingfisher and Kayila open year-round. Most camps close during wet season.
Wildlife rhythms Good between May and November. Top game-viewing between August and October. Migrant birds present between October and April.
Contact Private operators are the best source of information. Zambian Wildlife Authority Private Bag 1, Chilanga.

The Zambezi's birdlife creates a constant background din – from the alarm calls of **blacksmith** and **white-crowned plovers** to the ringing duets of **African fish eagles. trumpeter hornbills** wail atop ebony trees. **Storks, egrets,** and **herons** probe the shallows, **spur-winged geese** honk and **African jacanas** tiptoe across water shields. Vertical riverbanks are dotted with the holes of bee-eaters with **white-fronted bee-eaters** resident, and **blue-cheeked** and **carmine** appearing in October and August, respectively. **African skimmers** gather on sandbars but their numbers, and those of **white-fronted plovers**, are falling because vegetation is encroaching on the sandbanks they require for breeding sites (Kariba Dam now prevents the annual flooding which used to keep the sandbanks free of growth).

Kingfisher Lodge is close to the steep, forested Mpata Gorge – a fabulous place for seeing **raptors. Palmnut vultures** – also called vulturine fish eagles because they feed on fish and crabs, in addition to palm nuts – are often seen perched here. The hilly area around the lodge is the place to look for **roan antelopes**.

On dry land

Away from the water, the shore is flat and sandy, and it is in this poor soil that winter-thorn acacias grow. Their protein-rich seeds are relished by animals and **elephants** sometimes stand on their hind legs, grasping at the topmost pods with their trunk. Patches of open plains studded with baobabs occur throughout the valley floor and these areas are ideal for searching the horizon for evidence of kills. A swirl of descending **vultures** and **marabou storks** often marks the spot. **Ground hornbills** wander in open areas and if staying at Chiawa Camp you may meet 'Momba', an outrageously behaved, tame ground hornbill (she even has her own Web site).

Vervet monkeys, chacma baboons and **Meyer's parrots** forage through fig and nyala-berry trees and tangled riverine gullies that lead onto floodplains. The baboons here are slighter and more yellow than the chacma baboons south of the Zambezi and appear more like yellow baboons. Search the leaf litter of thickets for brilliant **Angola pittas**, once disturbed they may perch and sit still. These intra-African migrants arrive with the rains and breed here. The **narina trogon** is another colourful migrant that favours thick forest. Listen for its hoarse hoot and look for its bobbing tail among foliage. ∎

Watching tips
The best wildlife is seen in the area that extends between the Chongwe and Mushika rivers. Chifungulu Channel (between Sausage Tree and Mwambashi camps) is nicknamed 'Hippo City' and in addition to hippos, often has lions and large herds of buffaloes in dry season. Chongwe Falls is a pretty spot to spy rock-dwelling species such as klip-springers and dassies.

BANGWEULU SWAMPS

Wetland paradise that nourishes life

Wildlife highlights
The only place to see black lechwes, which mass in their thousands, and possibly Africa's best site for shoebills. Tsessebes and oribis occur in large number. Oodles of waterbirds and floodplain-associated birds.

Location 700km north of Lusaka. In wet season pre-arrange boat transfers.
Facilities Shoebill Camp conducts drives, walks and canoe trips. NP scout for hire at Chikuni.
Accommodation Permanent tents at Shoebill Island, chalets at Nsobe Camp (open May to December).
Wildlife rhythms March to July good for seeing shoebills and lechwes.
Contact Best information from Kasanka Trust (☎ 01-224 457, satellite ☎ 00 873 762 067 957, **e** kasanka@aol.com). Zambian Wildlife Authority Private Bag 1, Chilanga.

Watching tips
To observe shoebills with ease visit between March and July. This is also when 1000-strong herds of tsessebes form in the Mandamata area but access is tricky – seek local advice.

EMERGING out of woodlands onto Bangweulu's expansive floodplain, you are immediately among thousands of **black lechwes**. Bangweulu is the only place where these semi-aquatic antelopes occur and nights at Shoebill Island feature the sound of splashing hooves as lechwes retreat into the reeds. At edge of the plains are herds of **tsessebes**, and tiny **oribis** can be found singly or in pairs in adjacent dry grasslands.

Wildlife-watching at Bangweulu is determined by the seasonal flooding and receding of the wetlands. Seventeen rivers feed the Bangweulu Basin, which supports extensive reedbeds dissected by hundreds of streams. Its plains are dotted with termite mounds from which waterberry and sausage trees grow. These become islands once the floodwaters arrive.

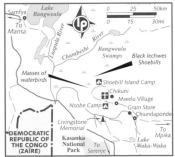

From December to March floodwaters spill across the plains, providing feeding grounds for **migratory birds**. As floodwaters recede exposing fresh graze, herds of **lechwes** and **tsessebes** congregate, and **waterbirds** concentrate around isolated pools. Hundreds of **sacred ibises** probe the grassland, and mix with flocks of **wattled cranes** and **ground hornbills**. **Denham's bustards** are common, and **Abdim's** and **white storks** seasonally drop in. Pools teem with **eastern white pelicans**, and **yellow-billed** and **marabou storks**.

Bangweulu is one of the few places to see the rare **shoebill** (inset). Often called the shoebill stork, its closest relative is in fact thought to be the pelican. Standing up to 1.5m high with a huge cloglike bill, shoebills ambush prey by lunging both beak and feet forward. Typically found deep in wetlands, shoebills sometimes wander around Shoebill Camp during wet season. Even in June several are often spotted not far from camp. Once the floods recede you can walk or take a canoe into the marshy areas – look among floating mats of papyrus. If you're very lucky, you may flush a **sitatunga**. Bangweulu is sometimes referred to as a national park, but it isn't – there is intense fishing throughout. Tourist interest in Bangweulu's wildlife seems imperative to protect it. ■

KASANKA NATIONAL PARK

Miniature swamp that houses an elusive antelope

ANYONE who has searched fruitlessly through mosquito-infested swamps for a glimpse of the elusive **sitatunga** will appreciate Kasanka. From Fibwe Tree Hide sitatungas can be seen most mornings and evenings grazing below in the Kapabi Swamp amid reeds and papyrus. Their long, splayed hooves are adapted to wading through floating vegetation and bogs.

Tiny Kasanka is Zambia's only privately managed park. Lying in a high rainfall area close to the DRC border, many birds found here are more typical of species you would expect in Central Africa. Top of the list is **Ross' lourie** – big, noisy and brightly coloured, it is easy to find around Fibwe Hide and other streams and lakes. This species is not found south of the Zambezi and is one of Kasanka's two dozen 'Zambian specials'; others include **red-and-blue sunbirds**, **Anchieta's** and **black-backed barbets**, and **Böhm's flycatchers**. Also watch out for **Schalow's louries**.

The park's flat terrain accumulates water during the summer rains and maintains a permanent wetland that attracts a diverse array of **waterbirds**. **African marsh harriers**, **spur-winged geese**, **African fish eagles** and **wattled cranes** are common sights around the main camp at Lake Wasa. Guided walks through miombo woodland and patches of evergreen forest are a must for birders.

During November and December, visit Fibwe at dusk – millions of **straw-coloured fruit-bats** flap out of the canopy of this red mahogany swamp forest. Other mammals at Kasanka include **pukus**, which are common near water sources. The airstrip is a favourite place to look for **sable antelopes** and **Lichtenstein's hartebeests**, while an early morning drive out to Mpueulwe Hill may reward you with sightings of **roan antelopes**. Other mammals include **elephants**, **bushbucks**, **grey duikers**, **reedbucks**, **baboons**, **vervet monkeys** and **warthogs**. Night drives regularly reveal **genets**, **African civets**, **bushbabies**, **elephant shrews**, **mongooses** and **side-striped jackals**. ∎

Location Approximately 520km northwest of Lusaka.
Facilities Tree hide, canoes, guided game drives, boat trips and walks. Bird list at Wasa Camp. Child-friendly.
Accommodation Two camps with self-catering or fully inclusive bungalows. Camping by prior arrangement.
Wildlife rhythms Game-viewing best between July and November. Fruit-bats between November and December.
Contact Kasanka Trust (☎ 01-224 457, satellite ☎ 00 873 762067957, e kasanka@aol.com).

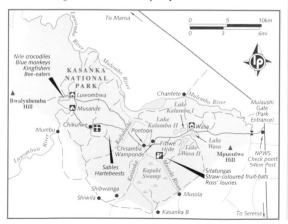

To Mansa

0   5   10km
0   3   6mi

Nile crocodiles
Blue monkeys
Kingfishers
Bee-eaters

KASANKA
NATIONAL
PARK

Bwalyabemba
Hill

Luwombwa

Musande

Chikufwe

Mumbu

Chantete
Mulembo River

Lake
Kalamba I

Lake
Kalamba II

Wasa

Pontoon

Mulaushi
Gate
(Park
Entrance)

Chisamba
Wamponde

Fibwe
Hide

Lake
Wasa

Lake
Wasa II

Mpueulwe
Hill

NPWS
Check point
54km Post

Sables
Hartebeests

Kapabi
Swamp

Sitatungas
Straw-coloured fruit-bats
Ross' louries

Shibwanga

Shiwila

Musola

Kasanka B

To Serenje

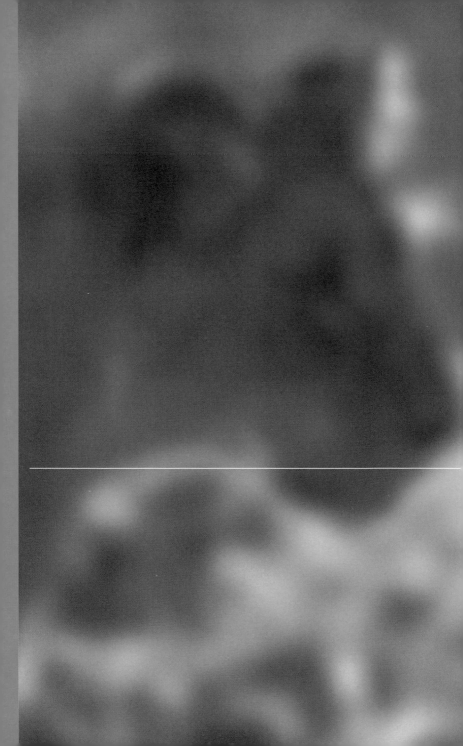

WILDLIFE GALLERY

*Recognising, understanding and
finding Southern Africa's key wildlife*

MAMMALS OF SOUTHERN AFRICA

WITH a complement of more than 350 mammal species, Southern Africa is a must for wildlifers who like their fauna furred. About two-thirds of that total are tiny, nocturnal and secretive so unless you're a rodent or bat specialist, you're not likely to find most of them. But of course, it's the other third that most people come here to see. Southern Africa is, as the ecologists would have it, a haven for charismatic mega-vertebrates (big game). In a few weeks' worth of dedicated viewing, you could easily clock up 50 species including some of the most sought-after creatures on earth. Elephants are abundant, big cats are remarkably tolerant of human observers, and there are more rhinos here than on the rest of the planet combined. At least four of the Big Five are virtually guaranteed and, with a bit of luck, even chances of sighting leopards are high.

It's also a place rich in species found nowhere else. Excluding bats, around 85 species are endemic to the region, most of them concentrated in the South West Arid Zone and the Cape's fynbos (see the Fynbos section in the Habitats chapter). For predator spotters, there are seven carnivores restricted to Southern Africa as well as nine endemic ungulates (and that's not counting the distinctive subspecies, which count as a further 'tick' on your list, such as bonteboks and blesboks and two races of mountain zebras). Along the coasts, Cape fur-seals and Heaviside's dolphins are further highlights that you can't see anywhere else on the globe.

Fair game

And nowhere else on earth will you feel such a sense of what it must have been like for our hominid ancestors. The distant roar of a lion or the frenzied whoops of a hyena clan evoke memories from a past when humankind regularly formed a part of the food web. Even today, there are more mammalian species in Africa known to kill humans than on any other continent. But rest assured, most of them prefer to avoid our kind and it's usually only those people who do the wrong thing that become lion-food. For everyone who sticks to the rules (see the Wildlife-Watching chapter), Southern Africa has the potential to be the most rewarding – and entirely safe – mammal-watching destination they'll ever visit.

The Mammal section of the Wildlife Gallery highlights the species most likely to be seen and aims to provide a little insight into what makes them tick. Some people come on safari hoping simply to notch up a long list of species spotted; Southern Africa certainly won't disappoint there, but take some time to actually observe the mammals. There are few places on earth where so many different species allow us so closely into their world and reveal their behaviour. Whether it's the lone territorial defence of male antelopes, the love-hate relationship among Cape fur-seals or the prodigious reproductive capacity of lions, Southern Africa is an extraordinary arena where every possible facet of mammalian behaviour is on show. ■

CHACMA BABOON

Recognition Chacmas have uniform grey-brown fur, large dog-faced head and distinctive kinked tail. A yellowish subspecies known as the yellow baboon (above) occurs in Malawi and northern Zambia.
Habitat All habitats where refuges (tall trees or cliffs) and water occur.
Behaviour Highly social and strictly diurnal; sleeps in trees or on the sides of cliffs at night. Most active early morning and evening.
Breeding Breeds year-round. Single young born after 140-day gestation approximately every 2 years.
Feeding Mostly fruits, seeds, bulbs and insects, occasionally catches small mammals and birds.
Voice Very vocal, most distinctive call is the two-toned *wa-hoo!* alarm bark.

Hotspots
Hwange NP, Chobe NP, Kruger NP (chacma); **Nyika NP, North Luangwa NP** (yellow)

Dear enemies

The largest primate in the region (aside from humans) and also one of the most common is easily overlooked once you've crossed it off your list. However, their intensely complex social behaviour ensures constant action and spending a little longer with them reveals alliances, cliques, co-operation and deceit. Continual social tension within the troop fuels the drama. Living in a troop helps to avoid predation because many pairs of eyes increase the chances of spotting carnivores. But it also heightens competition for food so individual baboons are torn between the benefits of foraging alone and the need to stay with companions to avoid winding up as a leopard's next meal.

To ensure antagonistic competitors don't steal every morsel, baboons make friends. Grooming strengthens the bonds between potential allies that might assist in a dispute over food, and every baboon spends a large percentage of its day cultivating and maintaining friendships. Such alliances also help during clashes over dominance, particularly for females where allies often assist in clashes with rivals. Interestingly, male baboons elsewhere in Africa also form alliances but not in the southern subregion.

With such complex relationships, the potential for deception is rife and baboons exploit this using their considerable intelligence. Subordinates give false predator alarm calls to distract attacking rivals, and young males may form enduring associations with babies, which are used as a kind of peace-offering to inhibit attacks by dominant males. The deception starts young. Juvenile baboons scream as though being attacked to incite their mother to set upon a troop member which has food the youngster wants.

Although life within the troop may seem like a Machiavellian struggle, group members unite against a common threat. Adult males form the front line of defence and cooperate to drive off rival troops and predators. Males are formidable combatants and alone are easily able to kill dogs; together, they can occasionally kill leopards. ■

VERVET MONKEY

Bushveld linguists

Africa's most common monkey is also one of the most terrestrial and like baboons, vervets spend much of their time foraging on the ground. However, combined with their smaller size, being abundant and ground-dwelling means they attract a greater range of predators than their larger relative and have evolved a complex vocabulary in response. Six different calls are used to indicate different predators and vervets respond accordingly. When a leopard is spotted, a sharp staccato bark tells the troop to race for the treetops where big cats can't follow. If the danger is a raptor, the 'eagle' call sends them into dense thickets or the inner branches of trees, while the 'snake chutter' causes vervets to stand on their hind legs and search the surrounding grass. Other calls indicate minor threats such as small cats or African wild dogs, and where vervets are persecuted by people they have yet another to say 'run for it!'.

Dominant males do most of the sentry duty and troop members are more likely to heed their calls than those of unreliable sentinels such as youngsters. Juvenile vervets have to learn the appropriate calls for different threats and are prone to false alarms. Falling leaves or harmless birds can provoke the 'eagle' cry while distant antelopes may be mistaken for leopards.

In total, at least 36 different calls are used for communication but complex visual signals have an equally important role in vervet language. Raising the eyebrows exposes bright white eyelids to indicate aggression, a gesture stereotyped enough that young vervets will respond to clumsy human imitations. Increasing aggression is shown by displaying canine teeth; subordinate monkeys indicate compliance by looking away and grimacing, or else risk attack. The dominant male signals his status by showing his powder blue scrotum and vivid scarlet penis. ■

Recognition Grizzled grey coat with white underparts, dark feet and hands. Black face is fringed by white.
Habitat All wooded habitats except for dense forest. Common in open savanna but never far from trees.
Behaviour Highly social, occurs in troops of about 20 with a single dominant male and complex dominance relationships within the troop. Strictly diurnal, sleeps in trees or cliffs.
Breeding Mate March to May. Single infant born after 140-day gestation.
Feeding Omnivorous: fruits, seeds, flowers, leaves, sap, grass, invertebrates and occasionally lizards, eggs and nestlings.
Voice At least 36 calls known. Loudest and most obvious are alarm signals.

Hotspots
Kruger NP, Hwange NP, Moremi GR, South Luangwa NP

SAMANGO MONKEY

The gentle monkey

Also known as blue monkeys, samangos are larger and much darker than related vervet monkeys. They're also the sole southern forest-dwelling representative of a family which, in the rich equatorial forests of East and Central Africa, numbers almost 20 species. Southern Africa's relatively poor forest cover doesn't support multiple species, freeing up samango monkeys from intense competition. Combined with a stable social structure centred on a matriline (a group of closely related females), this is thought to contribute to the samango's unusually placid nature. Conflict among troop members is rare and dominance relationships are weak, giving rise to yet another name, the gentle monkey.

Troops are territorial but even among strangers, clashes are low-key and injuries are rare. The troop's females band together and make unified charges at the enemy until one family decides to move off. Unusual among primates, adult males show little interest in defending the family's turf. However, of all troop members, they are the most vigilant and usually the first to spot the opposition, as well as their main predator, crowned eagles.

Drawing the line

Dominant males may be indifferent to turf wars but they defend their harem fiercely from other males, the only extreme aggression usually observed in samangos. Young males are violently evicted from the troop before sexual maturity and live as loners or form small bachelor groups of two to three. During the mating season, these 'floaters' attach themselves to a troop, and attempt to sneak copulations with females out of sight of the alpha male. The dense vegetation of the canopy and the samangos' tendency to spread out while they forage, facilitate matings by these satellite males, which almost certainly father some of the troop's infants. If caught in the act, the ensuing battle can leave them with severe wounds, which the attacking males inflict on the head and shoulders. Such encounters are occasionally fatal and are not always one-sided. Challengers regularly oust the troop's leader and males are replaced every one to three years. ■

Recognition Vervetlike but darker: blue-grey to dark-grey above and creamy-white underparts. Back is grizzled olive to rust.

Habitat Various evergreen forests including montane and coastal. Deciduous sand-forest.

Behaviour Multi-female troops up to 35-strong with a single alpha male. Diurnal, with foraging peaks in the morning and mid-afternoon.

Breeding Mates to time births with the onset of the rainy season. Single young born after 140-day gestation.

Feeding Very herbivorous, concentrating on fruit, leaves and flowers. Occasionally insects.

Voice A relatively quiet monkey with seven known calls. Males give the only loud calls, including a low-frequency 'boom' to keep troop members in touch.

> **Hotspots**
> **Nyanga NP, Nyika NP, Greater St Lucia Wetland Park**

GREATER BUSHBABY

Crybabies

Named after their childlike wailing cry used to demarcate territory and communicate with family members, bushbabies (galagos) are primitive primates related to Madagascar's lemurs. The largest and most social species, the greater (or thick-tailed) bushbaby occupies individual home ranges but tolerates considerable overlap. Although they forage alone, fruit clusters and gum seeps attract up to 10 individuals which feed amicably and indulge in occasional grooming sessions. Such interactions are most common during summer, which is outside the mating season and when food is more abundant.

With the onset of dry season, clashes between adult females increase and dominant males become intolerant of other males as they prepare for the breeding season. Females attempt to stake out productive territories to ensure that they can provide for their offspring while males fight for the right to control up to five females' ranges. Their rewards are considerable. Females in a given population synchronise their oestrous periods to within a two-week period, during which dominant males attempt to inseminate all females in their area. However, competition for females during this period is intense from neighbouring males and transient subordinants; perhaps in an effort to guard receptive females, matings last almost an hour. ∎

Recognition Cat-sized, woolly grey-brown fur, bushy tail, large eyes and rounded ears.
Habitat Woodland and forest.
Behaviour Nocturnal.
Breeding 1–3 young at start of rainy season.
Feeding Insects, fruit and gum.
Voice 18 different calls; most common is 'baby crying' wail.

> **Hotspots**
> **Mana Pools NP, Hluhluwe-Umfolozi GR, South Luangwa NP**

LESSER BUSHBABY

Pocket predator

Heightened night vision, extremely sensitive hearing and unparalleled agility make these tiny primates formidable nocturnal hunters. Insects are their staple, plucked from foliage or in mid-flight with a snake-like strike anchored by the hind feet holding a branch. Even more acrobatically, they sometimes launch themselves into the air at aerial prey. However, their real agility is displayed in 5m-long leaps between trees as they commute between known food sources or flee predators such as genets and owls.

Like the much larger greater (thick-tailed) bushbaby, related females often share home ranges. Along with their young and sometimes the resident male, familiar females occupy daytime nests in a tight, furry cluster of up to seven animals. Dominant males avoid contact with one another and maintain territories with prodigious urine marking and a high-pitched barking call. Proclaiming ownership of turf is only one function of their complex vocal repertoire of at least 25 different calls. All family members use calls to maintain contact and warn of danger. Unlike greater bushbabies, lesser bushbabies can call when inhaling as well as exhaling and the distinctive two-toned result is easily mistaken for a calling pair. ∎

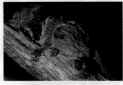

Recognition Tiny, silvery-grey to grey-brown with bushy tail, huge ears and eyes. Grant's bushbaby (a very similar species) brown overall (eastern Zimbabwe).
Habitat Savanna woodlands, mopane forests.
Behaviour Nocturnal.
Breeding Usually twins.
Feeding Insects and gum.
Voice Alarm 'chipping'.

> **Hotspots**
> **Pilanesberg NP, Mana Pools NP, Kafue NP**

CAPE PANGOLIN

Recognition Up to 1m long, covered in brown scales.
Habitat Savanna woodland, grasslands and semidesert.
Behaviour Solitary; largely nocturnal. Adults rest in underground dens during the day.
Breeding Single young born July to August.
Feeding Ants and termites.
Voice Usually silent.

Hotspots
Hwange NP, Kafue NP, Kruger NP, Moremi GR

Armoured ant assassins

Belonging to a unique order comprising seven species world-wide, there are two pangolins in the region and both are rare, special sightings. Diminutive tree pangolins of the Central African rainforest just make it into the extreme northwest of Zambia and their nocturnal, arboreal habits mean they're rarely seen. However the terrestrial and relatively widespread Cape pangolin is a much better prospect, often sighted crossing roads at night in search of their prey. Entirely insectivorous, these large pangolins eat ants and termites which they lap up with a 25cm-long tongue and then, completely lacking teeth, grind up using ingested sand in their muscular stomach.

Even more remarkable is the pangolin's unique defence – modified hair in the form of hard, overlapping plate-like scales. When threatened, pangolins roll into a tight ball, protecting the vulnerable face and belly, and presenting their attacker with layers of impenetrable, sharp-edged scales. Looking like an enormous pinecone, this defensive tactic also protects the vulnerable young: females carry their single offspring on their backs but pull the baby onto the stomach and roll around it when threatened. Ironically, the scales are highly valued for traditional medicine and human collectors are their primary predator. ∎

AARDVARK

Recognition Pinkish-grey colour; 1.4–1.7m long.
Habitat Grasslands, open woodland and farmlands.
Behaviour Primarily nocturnal, spends the day in a burrow.
Breeding Single young born after 7-month gestation.
Feeding Ants, termites and aardvark cucumbers.
Voice Mostly silent.

Hotspots
Gonarezhou NP, Karoo NP, Chobe NP

Bush bulldozer

Resembling pangolins only in diet, aardvarks have no close relatives and are the only living member of a once widespread group of mammals. And even though their Afrikaans name means earth-pig, they're only superficially porcine with an appearance as unique as their ancestry. With a sparse covering of coarse hair over pink-grey skin, an elongated movable snout, tubular ears and a heavy kangaroo-like tail, there is no other mammal like them. Powerful front legs end in massive claws suited to excavating insect prey or digging themselves out of danger. Indeed, aardvarks are the most prolific diggers of all African mammals and many other species, including hyenas, honey badgers, porcupines, warthogs and pangolins, rely on their burrows for shelter.

Widely distributed throughout Southern Africa, aardvarks are rarely seen because they usually emerge from their deep burrows very late at night. When foraging, they walk at a leisurely pace, sniffing the ground for ant and termite nests, which are speedily excavated and then tackled with the long ribbonlike tongue and its coat of sticky saliva. Aardvarks are extremely resistant to their prey's noxious chemical defences and a feeding bout may carry on until their entire body is submerged in the cavity. ∎

HARES & RABBITS

Telling the difference

Often mistakenly classified as rodents, hares and rabbits actually belong in their own order called lagomorphs. There are six of them in Southern Africa (not including the introduced European rabbit), two hares and four rabbits. All of them prefer fresh sprouting grass but readily browse shrubs and also practise coprophagy, the reingestion of soft faecal pellets for a second round of digestion. In the field, the two groups are usually distinguished by their ears: hares have very prominent ones, rabbits less so. It's a useful rule of thumb, but the differences are blurred among Southern African representatives. Both the lanky scrub hare and the smaller Cape hare have elongated ears, but the latter are overall more rabbitlike with a small, 'rabbity' face and body. Riverine rabbits (inset) have extremely prominent ears, enough for them to be once considered hares.

*Small ears and a very bushy tail are the giveaway characteristics of **Jameson's red rock rabbits**.*

Hares and rabbits are very similar in appearance, but they differ in one fundamental way. Hares give birth to precocial young – fully furred with open eyes and ears and mobile within 48 hours. In contrast, rabbits have young that are altricial – blind, naked and helpless, with closed eyes and ears. Whereas young hares move about and seek the nearest available cover when the mother leaves to forage, female rabbits construct a nest in which to raise their kittens.

***Scrub hares** are very common and the most likely lagomorph to be encountered during the day.*

Their distribution overlaps but another useful way to distinguish hares and rabbits is by habitat. The two hare species prefer open savanna terrain: semiarid scrublands for Cape hares; but any scrub, grasslands and open woodlands for the ubiquitous scrub hare. Southern Africa's rabbits, however, are either rock or riverine dwellers. Between them, the three rock rabbit species (Natal red, Smith's red and Jameson's red) inhabit the rocky hillsides of the Drakensberg Mountains, the fold mountains of the Cape, Namibia's Naukluft Massif and Zimbabwe's Matobo Hills. In contrast, as its name suggests, the endemic riverine rabbit is confined to the dense scrub alongside rivers. Except for the common and occasionally diurnal scrub hare, all the lagomorphs are nocturnal and fairly difficult to see; night drives usually turn up at least one species. ■

*At around 1.5kg, **Smith's red rock rabbit** is the smallest rock rabbit species in the region.*

Hotspots

Karoo NP One of the few places where riverine rabbits occur, as well as Smith's rock rabbits and both hares. **Makgadikgadi Pans NP** and **Nxai Pan NPs** Excellent for both hare species, often flushed by diurnal hunters on winter mornings. **Pilanesberg NP** Abundant Jameson's rock rabbits and scrub hares.

*Endemic to South Africa, the **riverine rabbit** is now highly endangered.*

SQUIRRELS

Tree squirrels vary greatly, from a pale grey desert form to rusty-yellow coloration in woodlands.

Red squirrels use tail-flicking displays to communicate with each other in their dense habitat.

Cape ground squirrels are constantly vigilant and respond to the alarm calls of birds.

Camp site companions

Most of Southern Africa's 80-plus rodents are tiny, timid and nocturnal, but although they may not always be visible, rodents occupy every available land habitat in the region. Five species of mole-rats live underground, cane rats infest sugar cane fields and the Drakensberg Mountains are home to little ice rats. Most people see few of these but there are a few species that are far more conspicuous.

Heading the list, Cape ground squirrels are restricted to the region's semiarid southwest. Diurnal and highly gregarious, they form groups based around a core of related females while the males roam between colonies looking for mating opportunities. Colonies number up to 30 and sometimes share their burrows with meerkats and yellow mongooses. Although mongooses occasionally eat young squirrels, the two species respond to one another's alarm calls and young of both play with one another. Like all rodents, ground squirrels are mainly herbivorous and forage during the heat of the day for grass leaves, roots and bulbs. Their distinctive bushy tail is held over the body like an umbrella but in midsummer, they invariably head below ground for a noon siesta. Around camp sites they become extremely tame and will beg for food; biscuits are a favourite but sweet hand-outs can result in serious nutritional problems (see 'Feeding wildlife' in the Wildlife-Watching chapter).

Well above ground, there are a further four squirrel species. Resembling the squirrels of the northern hemisphere (but not closely related), they're all tree-dwellers and mostly inhabit dense forest. Northern Namibia's striped tree squirrel and the sun squirrel of northern Mozambique and Zimbabwe's Eastern Highlands are both extremely elusive. Far more common, the vividly coloured red squirrel and the tree squirrel (inset) are closely related to each other and share many similarities. Both are diurnal and form small groups comprising a number of females and their pups, with a single male heading the hierarchy. The red squirrel is restricted to the coastal and montane forests of the eastern seaboard, but the tree squirrel is widespread throughout savannas where it is probably the region's most visible rodent. ∎

*Highly social, **Cape ground squirrels** dig communal burrows with numerous exit holes.*

Hotspots

Kgalagadi TP, **Etosha NP** and **Augrabies Falls NP** Camp sites have extremely tame ground squirrels. **Greater St Lucia Wetland Park** Tree squirrels very tame here and red squirrels can be spotted. **Moremi GR**, **Kruger NP** and **Victoria Falls NP** Tree squirrels are very common.

SPRINGHARE

African kangaroos

Resembling a miniature, rabbit-faced kangaroo, the nocturnal springhare is the only truly bipedal mammal in Southern Africa aside from people. They prefer the nutritious, short grasses growing on dry pan beds and floodplains so they're fairly easy to spot in the open on night drives. But night-time predators have the same idea and everything from owls and mongooses to hyenas and lions prey on them. So springhares always have a bolt-hole close by and rarely forage further than 400m from a burrow; on bright moonlit nights they stick to cover.

Springhares spend the day below ground, generally on their own. Their burrows are usually no deeper than a metre but they can be almost 50m long and have as many as 11 entrances, some of which are plugged with soil to prevent smaller carnivores and snakes making uninvited appearances. Although springhares are not particularly gregarious, their day burrows are often clustered together and small groups of up to a dozen congregate amicably to share feeding patches.

With no close relatives and no evidence of their ancestry (they have been classified in their own family), they're a unique species well worth searching for. The characteristic bobbing motion of their eyeshine – due to their kangaroo-like locomotion – when spotlit is a giveaway. ∎

Recognition Rufous-cinnamon with black-tipped tail. Eyeshine usually blue-green.
Habitat Savanna grasslands.
Behaviour Strictly nocturnal.
Breeding Usually one young.
Feeding Grass, roots, stems, leaves and seeds.
Voice Usually quiet. Bleats and screams in distress.

Hotspots
Central Kalahari GR, Pilanesberg NP, Gonarezhou NP

CAPE PORCUPINE

Hairs to beware

Africa's largest rodent, the Cape porcupine occurs in virtually all habitats, but being largely nocturnal, they're another reason to book a night drive. Small family groups comprising a single adult breeding pair and their young are typical, but they mostly forage alone. Juveniles younger than six months are accompanied by an adult, usually the male, to help deter predators. Although rodents are fair game to a legion of predators, porcupines are one of the very few species with any advanced defence mechanism. Modified hairs in the form of quills discourages many a threat, but contrary to the campfire stories, the quills are not poisonous or barbed and cannot be fired at their foes. And they're not foolproof: lions, leopards and caracals will harry a porcupine until it's too exhausted to defend itself. In the Kalahari Desert, about a quarter of all lion kills are porcupines. Although inexperienced cats sometimes wind up with a face full of quills, debilitating injuries are actually quite rare.

Porcupines are monogamous and remain in close physical contact for much of the time; indeed, females do not come into oestrus unless the male is present. The young of past years often share the territory and families share extended burrow systems where up to a dozen may shelter. ∎

Recognition Covered in glossy black fur and quills.
Habitat All in the region.
Behaviour Sociable in small family groups. Teeth chattering and quill rattling are used to warn predators.
Breeding 1–3 young.
Feeding Bulbs, roots, fruit and bark.
Voice Largely silent.

Hotspots
Hluhluwe-Umfolozi GR (especially Mpila Camp), **Okonjima, Chobe NP**

AARDWOLF

Termite terminator

The smallest of the hyena family (which comprises only four species), the aardwolf is also its least predatory member. Unlike their carnivorous relatives, aardwolves subsist almost entirely on termites. Nocturnal harvester termites give away their position by feeding sounds – the whisper of thousands of tiny jaws cutting grass – and aardwolves home in with their acute hearing. Sound carries best on still, dry nights: the best time for aardwolves to hunt and also the best time to look for them. With their long pink tongue coated in glue-like saliva, aardwolves may spend 10 hours of the night foraging and can lap up 250,000 termites.

Recognition Miniature yellow-grey hyena.
Habitat Grasslands and open woodlands.
Behaviour Monogamous pairs defend a small territory.
Breeding 2–4 cubs born in October. Both sexes care for the cubs.
Feeding Termites; ignores meat.
Voice Largely silent.

While their diet is unique among the family, the aardwolf's hyena ancestry remains apparent. A caustic digestive system enables them to cope with noxious terpenes secreted by defensive termites. Although their cheek teeth are mere stumps, they retain a carnivore's prominent canine teeth, used in territorial clashes and to defend their cubs from their main predator, black-backed jackals. And like all hyenas, they also have well developed scent glands and assiduously scent-mark their turf with a pungent paste-like secretion. Perhaps also because of their predatory heritage, they are widely persecuted in the entirely erroneous belief that they kill livestock. ■

Hotspots
Karoo NP, **Pilanesberg NP**, **Kgalagadi TP**

BROWN HYENA

A true scrounger

With their massive head, sloping back and shaggy dark cape, you could be forgiven for thinking that brown hyenas were the inspiration for the werewolves of European mythology. However, these medium-sized hyenas are not nearly as rapacious as they look, and they live almost entirely off scavenging. The remains of kills left by other predators are their mainstay; in the arid southwest region, they're virtually guaranteed visitors to large carcasses.

Recognition Dark, shaggy hyena. Pale neck and striped legs.
Habitat Arid savanna, woodland and desert.
Behaviour Nocturnal.
Breeding 1–5 cubs.
Feeding Scavenges. Eats insects and small mammals.
Voice Mostly silent. Growls during territorial clashes.

The large cats provide brown hyenas with most of their spoils but it's an uneasy relationship. While brown hyenas may drive cheetahs and occasionally even leopards from their kills, lions kill hyenas when they can; brown hyenas linger at a safe distance, usually more than 50m away, until the lions leave.

Although they're mostly seen alone, brown hyenas live in loose clans numbering up to a dozen. They forage on their own but come together at large kills and all clan members may carry food back to the den to feed the cubs. Interestingly, the clan males are usually not the cubs' fathers. Typically, all clan members are related, so the females avoid inbreeding by seeking out nomadic males who visit them only for a brief mating period and then move on. ■

Hotspots
Central Kalahari GR, **Kgalagadi TP**, **Pilanesberg NP**

SPOTTED HYENA

The sisterhood

Probably the most maligned mammal in Africa, the spotted hyena is also one of the continent's most fascinating. Unusually among mammals, females dominate hyena society. Averaging 10kg heavier than their male counterparts, females have also assumed other, more extreme male attributes. High levels of male hormones (androgens) have led to an extraordinary masculinisation in which females have a fully erectile pseudo-penis and false scrotum. Important during their greeting display, when clan members erect their genitals for mutual inspection, it takes an expert to differentiate the sexes. At a distance, the most reliable way is to look for the female's prominent nipples (only apparent if she's had a litter).

Females are terrifically aggressive on kills, probably the evolutionary drive that led to their 'maleness'. Being able to compete for meat is crucial for mothers with the huge energetic burden of suckling cubs and the fastest step to aggression (as well as increased size and strength) is via elevated androgen levels. This also means that females are the clan's warriors and tend to take the initiative in the sometimes violent clashes against rival groups.

Females are dominant to males and live in a strict hierarchy led by a single matriarch. Female cubs inherit their mother's rank and fight furiously for it from birth. Born with eyes open and fully developed teeth, they emerge from the womb awash with androgens, and siblings (particularly female twins) sometimes kill one another in the resulting fights. Called siblicide, this behaviour is common among birds but spotted hyenas are the only mammal in which it regularly occurs.

Spotted hyena society may seem harsh, but the clan functions to make them one of the most efficient and versatile of all carnivores. Together, they are able to kill buffaloes and may even drive lions from their kills. Long considered a cowardly scavenger, the spotted hyena is, in fact, the most successful large predator in Africa. ■

Recognition Heavily-built and doglike. Off-white to reddish brown with dark spots that fade with age.
Habitat Open woodland, savannas and semidesert.
Behaviour Largely nocturnal. Clans may be as large as 80 but are fluid, with individuals and small groups breaking off constantly and rejoining later.
Breeding Non-seasonal. 1–3 cubs born after a 3-month gestation. Females den communally with up to 20 litters together. Typically, females only suckle their own cubs.
Feeding Scavenges but also very efficient cooperative hunters.
Voice Very vocal; long-distance *whoop*. Also whine, moan, giggle and cackle, especially when they congregate on kills.

> **Hotspots**
> **Kruger NP**, **Etosha NP**, **Kgalagadi TP**, **Chobe NP** (Savute)

LION

Recognition Africa's largest cat; males up to 240kg.
Habitat Wide habitat tolerance including open plains, woodlands, thick bush and semidesert.
Behaviour Prides number up to 50. Related females form the core of the pride. Male coalitions hold tenure for 2–4 years. Young males expelled around 3 years old.
Breeding Non-seasonal. 1–5 cubs. Related lionesses suckle each other's cubs.
Feeding Kills virtually everything except healthy adult rhinos and elephants; usually large herbivores like wildebeests and zebras. Scavenges up to 25% of its diet.
Voice Roar proclaims territory and maintains contact between pride members. Low grunts for close-range contact.

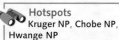

Hotspots
Kruger NP, Chobe NP, Hwange NP

Working on the night shift

Probably the single greatest wildlife drawcard in Africa, lions are actually easy to find (except in Malawi). Abundant in large reserves and with few natural enemies, lions lie in the open and mostly tolerate vehicles. However, the challenge with lions is seeing them in action. It's true they spend most of the day asleep but to a lion, this makes perfect sense. It's too hot to hunt during the day and sunlight foils efforts to sneak up on prey. To see lions at their best, go on a guided night drive; darkness provides cover for over 90% of their hunts.

Lionesses usually lead the hunt but contrary to popular belief males are active and competent hunters. They tend to let the females initiate the work but their presence is crucial for dispatching large prey such as buffaloes and giraffes. Separated from the females, they are successful hunters in their own right. Male coalitions spend much of their time away from the pride on territorial patrols during which they make to up to 85% of their own kills.

If nocturnal viewing is impossible, early morning and late afternoon are worthwhile. Lions snoozing during the day usually stay at the same spot until nightfall so head back there in the afternoon, particularly if there are cubs, which inevitably start playing as the temperature drops. A male and female away from the pride are probably mating, which guarantees constant action. Lions may mate hundreds of times during the female's three to four day oestrous, sometimes as often as every 15 minutes. This prodigious frequency probably stems from the high failure rate of matings: only about one in three copulations results in cubs. But in fact, by being difficult to inseminate, females are probably ensuring that they conceive to a healthy male and to a good father. Males play a critical role in protecting cubs from intruding males so for a female, the more persistent a male is, the greater likelihood he'll be around until her cubs are grown. ∎

LEOPARD

The quintessential cat

Ironically, Africa's most common large cat is also the most difficult to spot. Leopards are more abundant and widespread than both lions and cheetahs but you're far less likely to see one. They are the quintessential cat: stealthy, secretive and adaptable. Tolerant of great environmental extremes, they occur in the desolate riverbeds of the Namib Desert, the swamps of the Okavango and occasionally in the mountains above Cape Town. Whoever said, 'a leopard can't change its spots' wasn't referring to the adaptability of this versatile cat.

A remarkably catholic diet is one reason behind their success. Eating everything from dung beetles to baby elephants, leopards can persist in areas long devoid of other large predators. They prefer medium-sized antelopes like impalas but if those are lacking, they turn to dassies, porcupines and francolins. At waterholes in the Kalahari Desert, leopards may spend hours making repeated catches of doves as they come in to drink. Leopards can drink water from hot thermal springs and survive on domestic dogs near cities.

However, it's in the protection of parks and reserves where leopards really thrive. Where antelope prey is abundant, individual leopards can occupy very small home ranges, allowing them to reach high densities. Furthermore, although leopards are territorial, they tolerate some overlap with neighbours, allowing even greater numbers. Rivals appear to avoid one another in the shared areas in a sort of time-share system: if a resident is active in a particular portion of overlapping turf, his neighbour avoids the area. However, a week or a month later, the situation may be reversed. Neighbours show mutual respect for this arrangement, reducing the likelihood of conflict.

Some of the finest reserves in which to view leopards are found in Southern Africa. Largely free of persecution and poaching, they have enjoyed decades of protection and have grown completely accustomed to vehicles, permitting some unparalleled viewing. ∎

Recognition Muscular, lithe cat up to 2.3m long. Orange-yellow fur with black rosettes.
Habitat Wide habitat tolerance but most easily seen in open woodland-savanna mosaics.
Behaviour Largely solitary. Mostly nocturnal, but often active in early morning and evening. Seeks out large trees in which to sleep and to store kills.
Breeding Non-seasonal. 1–4 cubs born and hidden in dens until about 8 weeks old. Females raise cubs.
Feeding Very catholic with at least 92 prey species on record. Usually small to medium-sized antelopes.
Voice Rasping cough, which sounds like a wood saw, proclaims territory (both sexes) or advertises sexual readiness (females).

Hotspots
South Luangwa NP, Kgalagadi TP, Kruger NP, Moremi GR

CHEETAH

Recognition Tall, slender cat with black coinlike spots on yellow fur. Face has 'tear streaks'.
Habitat Prefers open savanna-woodland mosaics.
Behaviour Most active in the early morning and late afternoon. Mothers may hunt during the heat of the day.
Breeding Non-seasonal. As many as 9 (but usually 3–6) cubs born after a 95-day gestation.
Feeding Mainly small and medium-sized antelopes. Also hares, large birds (including ostriches), and the young of large herbivores. Male coalitions can tackle prey up to the size of near-adult wildebeests.
Voice High yelps used to maintain contact; in cubs, this call sounds like a bird. Growls, barks and 'chutters' during courtship.

Hotspots
Kgalagadi TP, Nxai Pan NP, Phinda Resource Reserve, Moremi GR

Kalahari Ferrari

To see a cheetah at top speed is, for many, the pinnacle of African wildlife-viewing. Reliably timed at 105km/h (but probably able to hit 115 to 120km/h), there is no animal faster on land and cheetahs are probably the fastest land mammals ever to have existed. Nonetheless, nature's arms race has equipped their favourite prey with almost comparable fleetness and some gazelle species can clock almost 100km/h. Antelopes also easily outperform cheetahs in endurance, so like all cats, cheetahs stalk close to their prey before unleashing their phenomenal acceleration. Most sprints begin within 60m of the quarry and if they haven't succeeded after around 500m, the crushing physiological stresses imposed by the chase force them to give up.

Although widely considered solitary, cheetah social life actually falls somewhere between the lone existence of most felids and the extended family structure of lions. Females are loners but males form lifelong alliances known as coalitions. Males defend their turf from interlopers and teamwork makes all the difference in a fight. Usually, coalitions consist of brothers born in the same litter but lone males will often team up with other, unrelated singletons. On their own, male cheetahs have little hope of a carving out a territory but by recruiting a 'friend' they have a chance at securing turf and the females that go with it.

The process is complicated by the females' tendency to wander. Female cheetahs are non-territorial, covering huge ranges that they don't defend. So males have to look for those areas where females are likely to spend much of their time. Prey concentration and the availability of cover in which to hide cubs are the critical factors but both vary with the seasons. So, some males never form territories and adopt an alternative tactic, roaming over vast distances in search of the wide-ranging females. ∎

CARACAL

The African 'lynx'

With its tufted ears and shortened tail, it's little wonder that the caracal is often called the African lynx. However, caracals are only distantly related to the lynxes and in fact, are more closely allied to the African golden cat of Central Africa's rainforests. But unlike that rare and little-known felid, the caracal can exist just about everywhere. Highly adaptable, their range includes most of Africa and Southwest Asia but nowhere are they more abundant than in Southern Africa. Inhabiting every conservation area in the region except for a narrow coastal band of the Namib, caracals tolerate high levels of human activity and are also widespread on farmlands. Much of the caracal's success is due to its explosive hunting prowess. They tackle antelopes three times their weight and execute 4m-high leaps to take birds in flight; indeed ancient Asian nobility hunted birds with tame caracals. Today however, their relationship with people is largely adversarial and farmers persecute caracals relentlessly for occasionally taking young sheep and goats. Fortunately, they are extremely shy and avoid people but this also makes spotting one a rare event. Mountain habitats offer the best chances where klipspringer, dassie and black eagle alarm calls often give them away. ■

Recognition Medium-sized muscular cat. Sandy to rust red. Black ear tufts.
Habitat All habitats except true desert and rainforest.
Behaviour Largely nocturnal and solitary.
Breeding 1–4 cubs.
Feeding Birds, rodents and up to medium-sized antelopes.
Voice Spits, hisses and growls when threatened.

Hotspots
Mountain Zebra NP, Okonjima, Matobo NP

SERVAL

High-rise hunter

Raised on stiltlike legs and with its huge oval ears, the serval is uniquely equipped as a specialist rodent-killer. Preferring wetland grasses and reeds where small mammals are abundant, servals hunt primarily by sound. Extremely keen hearing pinpoints rodent rustles which the cat homes in on until it's close enough to launch a characteristic arching pounce, up to 4m long and 1m high. Sometimes they land directly on the unseen target but if that fails, the attack often flushes the prey and about half of all hunts are successful.

Servals are essentially solitary, occupying home ranges as large as 30 sq km. However, overlap between ranges may be extensive, and unusually among cats, they seem not to defend a territory. Instead they avoid one another by very frequent urine-marking and defecation which indicate areas in use; neighbours avoid areas with fresh marks and conflict is rare. This system of land-sharing means they can be quite common in optimum habitat, but are shy and difficult to spot. Fortunately, they are most active at dawn and dusk, probably to exploit the peak activity periods of certain diurnal rodent species – be out looking at sunrise and late afternoon for a chance to find one. ■

Recognition Tall, medium-sized cat. Fur pale yellow; long blotches and spots.
Habitat Well-watered long grass habitats.
Behaviour Crepuscular. Nocturnal near human activity.
Breeding 1–5 kittens.
Feeding Mostly rodents.
Voice Largely silent.

Hotspots
Moremi GR, Greater St Lucia Wetland Park, The Drakensberg

AFRICAN WILD CAT

Recognition Similar to domestic tabby. Red-backed ears and long, striped legs.
Habitat All including desert watercourses.
Behaviour Primarily nocturnal. Active at dawn and dusk in protected areas.
Breeding 2–5 kittens.
Feeding Primarily rodents.
Voice Similar to domestic cat.

Hotspots
Kgalagadi TP, South Luangwa NP, Central Kalahari GR

Puss' progenitor

At first glance, these little cats barely differ from domestic moggies. Indeed, tamed African wild cats actually gave rise to our pets at least 6000 years ago, probably in the Middle East and Egypt where wild cats were kept to hunt mice in grain stores. Although the similarity is unmistakable, African wild cats have longer, striped legs, a leaner build and, most distinctive of all, russet-red backs to the ears. Ironically, their link to the past is probably their greatest threat. Wild cats freely interbreed with domestic cats (most specialists classify them as the same species) and their genetic purity has been eroded wherever people and their cats have settled. Pure African wild cats now exist in only the most remote places; their red ears distinguish them from hybrids in which the colour is lost.

Despite being Africa's most common and widespread cat, there is surprisingly little known of the species in the wild. They appear to follow the typical felid pattern of being largely solitary and are probably territorial. Unlike feral domestic cats, they are not inclined to form colonies; domestication has almost certainly selected individuals tolerant of one another and has gradually given rise to heightened sociality in pet cats. Wild cats are nearly always spotted alone except for females with kittens. ■

BLACK-FOOTED CAT

Recognition Tiny squat cat. Dark spots, blotches on buff to tawny fur.
Habitat Arid, short-medium grass savanna.
Behaviour Nocturnal, solitary.
Breeding 1–4 kittens.
Feeding Rodents, shrews, birds and reptiles.
Voice Loud *raough* during mating period.

Hotspots
Kgalagadi TP, Central Kalahari GR, Makgadikgadi Pans NP, Nxai Pan NP

The anthill tiger

The only endemic cat in the region, the black-footed cat is also one of the world's smallest. The largest males weigh in at only 2.4kg and stand about 25cm high. But its miniature stature conceals a predatory Goliath. An accelerated metabolism and the low prey density of their arid habitat means that black-footed cats have to hunt continually to satisfy their energetic needs. Covering up to 15 to 20km a night, these little predatory powerhouses average a kill every 50 minutes. Mice, shrews and small birds constitute most of their diet but they are capable of attacking prey much larger than themselves including hares and black korhaans.

Flexible hunting methods contribute to their predatory success and black-footed cats use at least three different strategies. Like all cats, they stalk inexorably closer to prey before the final, explosive rush. But more jackal-like, they also employ a fast zigzagging trot through high grass to flush prey from hiding. Particularly effective with ground-roosting birds, success depends on their ability to take birds on the wing in acrobatic leaps six times their height. Finally, they also use ambush tactics, waiting outside rodent burrows for up to an hour in the hope that the occupant emerges. ■

CIVETS & GENETS

Musk bearers and tree-dwellers

Nocturnal and quick to duck for cover, these distant relatives of the cat family are usually seen as fleeting glimpses in headlights. But except for the rare and little known tree civet of northwest Malawi and eastern Zimbabwe, the viverrids are common and widespread. Largest of all African species, the solitary African civet sports a dark facial mask, vivid white throat-stripes and dark blotches on a light grey coloured body. Equipped with a robust capacity to digest toxins, civets are able to deal with noxious species like millipedes, scorpions, toads and even highly venomous snakes. Ironically, civets produce their own pungent defence, a greasy powerful-smelling paste secreted from perineal glands (a pair of glands situated near the anus of certain mammals). Named after its animal source, musky 'civet' has been collected from captive individuals for centuries as the basis

*The **African civet's** vivid throat markings may function to direct attacks away from the face.*

of perfume manufacture. In some parts of Africa, the practice still continues.

Whereas the civet's squat, doglike build confines it to a terrestrial existence, other members of the family are equally at home in trees or on the ground. The region's two genet species – the large-spotted and small-spotted – have fully retractile claws and long, counter-balancing tails for treetop agility but actually do most of their hunting on ground. It takes experience to tell them apart but the tail tip is usually a giveaway – white in small-spotted genets and black in large-spotteds. Along with appearance, both genets are almost identical in lifestyle. Like all viverrids, they are largely solitary, and adults only pair up to mate. After a gestation of 10 to 11 weeks, between two and four kittens are born, usually during the summer, though a second litter can be produced later in the same year. The male has little to do with raising the young. The female teaches them how to hunt (rodents mostly, their main prey) so that by around the age of six months, they leave her to become independent.

African civets have an excellent sense of smell and sometimes investigate camp barbecues.

*The **small-spotted genet** has an Africa-wide range which extends into Spain, Portugal and France.*

Though secretive and nocturnal, civets and genets (such as the large-spotted genet, inset) are occasional night-time visitors to camp barbecues; to see them in their element, try spotlighting along trails and roads – genets can be called-in close on night drives by kissing the back of your hand. ■

Hotspots
Kruger NP and **Moremi GR** Night drives (Kruger only) and camp site barbeques hold good chances for African civets and both genets. **Chimanimani NP** and **Nyika NP** Tree civets in forested areas, but spotting one is a real challenge.

*Daylight sightings of genets (here, the **large-spotted**) are restricted to very early morning .*

*In their open habitat, **meerkats** are vulnerable to predators and spend considerable time alert.*

*Young **meerkats** are largely independent after 10 weeks and reach adult size at six months.*

MONGOOSES

United we stand

A symphony of birdlike peeps, chirps and twitters announces the presence of some of the most gregarious animals on earth. While most mongooses are solitary, a few African species display a level of cooperation rarely equalled in the animal world. From diminutive dwarf mongooses weighing only 400g to 1.5kg banded mongooses, these little social carnivores are surrounded by potential predators and tightknit family groups have the advantage over loners in spotting danger.

Among desert-dwelling meerkats (suricates), keeping a lookout is refined to a dedicated art. While the troop forages for scorpions, insects and lizards, a lone sentinel occupies a high point and braves temperatures topping 50°C to watch for eagles and jackals. One shrill alarm shriek from the guard and the band rushes for cover. When escape is impossible, mongoose troops show extraordinary tenacity. Faced with predators many times their size, the entire family bunches together to form a bristling, chattering collective to intimidate the enemy. Troops of banded mongooses – inhabitants of more wooded and grassland regions – even mob predators that have taken a family member and adults will climb trees to harass eagles that have snatched an unwary youngster.

Raising the young is also a communal effort. All adults in the band provide for youngsters and relinquish even the most prized prey to their begging cries. They even leave a baby-sitter behind at the den to tend kittens too young to join foraging expeditions. Most adult meerkats and banded mongooses breed and collectively care for each kitten as their own but reproduction in dwarf mongooses is largely restricted to the dominant pair; other troop members act as 'helpers' in raising the young. Even so, these tiny mongooses are highly vulnerable to predation and only 30% of kittens survive to adulthood.

Loners and middlemen

Likely to be spotted as a fleeting blur dashing across the road, there is a legion of less social species. Driving through the

*Conspicuous troops of **banded mongooses** may number as many as 75 individuals.*

*The **white-tailed mongoose** fluffs its prominent tail when alarmed or threatened.*

Snake killers

Famed for their snake-killing prowess, most mongooses actually avoid dangerous snakes. Indeed, African rock pythons are one of their most feared predators, active at night and able to slide into the subterranean mongoose burrows as they sleep. Encountered during the day, pythons are less threatening and mongoose families gang up to drive them away. Lightning reflexes keep the mongooses out of danger and severe nips to the tail force the snake to seek cover. The same tactic is used on highly venomous species including cobras, mambas and puff adders. So how did the reputation for snake-killing arise? African mongooses (such as this yellow mongoose) do kill snakes, usually juveniles or harmless species. However, some Asian mongooses are true snake specialists. All loners, what they lack in numbers they make up for with unique immunity. One species, the common Indian mongoose, can withstand a dose of cobra venom that would kill a child.

*In the daytime, the **slender mongoose** is the most frequently observed mongoose in savannas.*

semiarid southwest, you'll almost certainly spot a yellow mongoose (inset, opposite). Varying from light grey to russet-yellow with a white-tipped tail, this little mongoose lives in colonies usually 3 to 12 strong but forages alone. They probably represent an intermediate stage of sociality, somewhere between the gregarious species and true loners. Similarly, the ubiquitous slender mongoose has a halfway social system, in which males sometimes form coalitions, probably to defend multiple ranges of the solitary females. They carry their tail aloft when running, the flaglike black tip giving rise to their other name, black-tipped mongoose.

Among the true loners, the largest mongoose in the region, the white-tailed mongoose, weighs up to 4.5kg. Spending most of the night foraging for insects, frogs and rodents, it is the most common nocturnal mongoose and readily seen while spotlighting.

Finally, two similar species, the large grey and small grey mongoose, are best distinguished by size; around 3kg in the former and rarely above 1kg in the latter. Both are common around camping grounds of the southwest Cape and while the large grey's distribution heads north around the coast into Mozambique, the small grey's range extends the other way into Namibia. ∎

*Quite common but hard to spot, the **marsh mongoose** feeds on crabs, fish, prawns and frogs.*

Dwarf mongooses are one of the smallest carnivores in the world and use termitaries as refuges.

Hotspots
Kruger NP Excellent for slender, dwarf and, on night drives, white-tailed mongooses. **Kgalagadi TP** Virtually guaranteed meerkats, yellow mongooses and Kalahari slender mongooses (red phase). **Chobe NP** Bandeds, dwarves and (rare) Selous' mongooses in the northwest.

*The **large grey mongoose** is common and mostly diurnal, but very difficult to spot.*

AFRICAN WILD DOG

Africa's painted wolves

Science named the African wild dog *Lycaon pictus*, the painted wolf, accurately capturing its mottled, multi-coloured appearance and lifestyle, if not ancestry. Wild dogs are not closely related to wolves but in behaviour and ecological niche, they are very wolflike. Highly social, their packs may number as many as 50 (but average 12 to 20) and are usually centred around a dominant male and female. Known as the alpha pair, these individuals are responsible for most of the breeding in the group and all other pack members help raise their pups. If a subordinate female breeds, the alpha bitch may kidnap the pups and raise them or, in extreme cases, kill them. Probably dependent on prey availability and functioning to protect the pack from starvation by attempting to raise too many puppies, her tolerance increases in good times. When prey is abundant, as many as three females may breed and share the suckling duties of the combined litters.

Persecuted nomads

Wild dogs are great wanderers and a pack's home range may be as large as 2000 sq km. This probably arose in response to the migratory movements of prey, but even where herbivores are resident, wild dogs move over vast areas. Only when the pups are very young is the pack tied to a small area for about three months until the youngsters can accompany the adults. Their need for huge areas is just one factor that has made them one of Africa's most endangered large mammals. Disease, particularly from domestic dogs, and human persecution have also taken a heavy toll. They kill by eating their prey alive, as quick and probably as 'humane' as any method, but they have been widely condemned as cruel and wasteful and were once shot even in reserves. Now considered a special sighting in parks, they are still killed on farms and rangelands. Even protected areas are an imperfect refuge; lions kill many wild dogs and they avoid otherwise ideal habitat if there are lions about. ■

Recognition Collie-sized dog with mottled yellow, black, brown and white markings and prominent rounded ears.
Habitat Savanna woodlands, plains and semiarid bushland.
Behaviour Diurnally active with hunting peaks at dawn and dusk. Pack members are highly social and rarely apart. Small same-sex groups sporadically emigrate in search of opposite sex groups to form a new pack.
Breeding Up to 21 pups in midwinter. Denning period about 13 weeks.
Feeding Probably the most efficient hunters in Africa. Concentrate on medium-sized herbivores, especially impalas, but can tackle larger prey.
Voice High-pitched twittering when excited, owl-like *hoo* contact call and deep, inquiring growl-bark when alarmed.

Hotspots
Moremi GR, Kruger NP, Hwange NP, Kafue NP, Chobe NP (Linyanti)

BLACK-BACKED JACKAL

Jackal-of-all-trades

Probably the region's most common carnivore, black-backed jackals are ubiquitous around the kills of other hunters. But although they're superbly opportunistic scavengers, they're also much underrated hunters. Usually foraging alone or in pairs, jackals easily take duiker-sized prey and larger groups cooperate to kill impalas and springboks. Individuals take turns to harry large victims to the point of exhaustion and then the group jointly pulls down the prey. Often, a single jackal administers a suffocating throat hold, a typically feline technique rarely used by members of the dog family.

Jackal social life is equally versatile. They form monogamous pairs, probably for life – an unusual social pattern in mammals. Grown pups from the previous season often stay on to help raise new pups before leaving to find mates of their own. Helpers gain valuable knowledge about raising young and also delay leaving the area they know intimately for the dangers of unknown turf. Jackal families are territorial but away from the den, they behave as members of a larger society. Unrelated groups share large carcasses and may function as a cohesive pack to tackle large prey. Widely dismissed as 'lowly', their social and predatory adaptability has led to them being the most successful small carnivore of the region. ■

Recognition Small, foxlike dog. Reddish-buff; silvery-grey saddle. Black-tipped tail.
Habitat All bar dense forest.
Behaviour Nocturnal and diurnal. Highly ritualised behaviour at carcasses.
Breeding 1–6 pups.
Feeding Scavenges. Fruit, insects, reptiles, rodents and medium-sized mammals.
Voice Wailing contact call.

Hotspots
Kgalagadi TP, Etosha NP, Hwange NP

SIDE-STRIPED JACKAL

Omnivore

Least predatory of all jackal species, side-striped jackals are true omnivores, subsisting on wild fruit, rodents, insects, reptiles, birds, nuts, maize and eggs. This enables side-stripeds to persist where there is very little mammalian prey, but where big game and the inevitable carcasses do occur, they – like their black-backed relatives – turn to scavenging. Unlike other jackals however, they rarely hunt prey much larger than mice, though they are capable of taking unguarded antelope fawns. Presumably they have ample opportunity to do so during the birth season as they often follow herbivore herds to clean up afterbirth, but the final word on their predatory abilities is still disputed.

Common to all jackals, side-striped jackals form long-lasting pairs which maintain a small territory. Their offspring of the previous year remain with them to help raise pups and defend their range. But whereas other jackal species often congregate to hunt or share carcasses, side-stripeds of different families rarely interact. They tend to take turns at kill remains and have not been observed hunting cooperatively for large prey. As a result, they do not reach the densities of black-backed jackals in the region and although fairly common, are less likely to be seen. ■

Recognition Lacks the black-backed's grey saddle. White rib stripe. White-tipped tail.
Habitat Woodland savannas.
Behaviour Usually seen alone or in pairs.
Breeding 3–6 pups.
Feeding Highly omnivorous.
Voice Yapping *raou* for contact and when mobbing predators.

Hotspots
Moremi GR, Mana Pools NP, Kafue NP, Phinda Resource Reserve

BAT-EARED FOX

Insect radar

The enormous ears of these little foxes are their livelihood. Concentrating mostly on the rustle of surface feeders like harvester termites, they also listen for subterranean prey when topside pickings are slim. Swivelling like two radar dishes, their ears rotate independently a few inches above the ground to pinpoint beetle larvae, millipedes and other invertebrates below the surface. With a burst of frantic digging, they unearth their prize and pulverise it almost instantaneously using a unique jaw musculature that allows them to chew five times a second.

Similar to jackals (to which they are not closely related), bat-eared foxes usually live as monogamous pairs with attendant helpers. However, unlike jackals, males often take a second mate and the two females communally suckle and care for their combined litters. These groups are not territorial and different families often intermingle when foraging is good (for example, following rains when large patches of insects abound). Although the pair bond may persist for many years, they are not loyal to the same range and they establish dens wherever food is abundant. Highly social, these diminutive foxes will fiercely harass predators such as jackals and caracals to rescue a captured relative. ■

Recognition Dark grey fox. Huge ears and bushy tail.
Habitat Semiarid woodland and open savanna.
Behaviour Forms family groups.
Breeding 2–5 pups.
Feeding Mainly insects, also rodents, reptiles and scorpions.
Voice Alarm bark and soft whining contact call.

Hotspots
Central Kalahari GR, Kgalagadi TP, Etosha NP

CAPE FOX

Cape's only endemic canid

Occurring only in Southern Africa, Cape foxes are restricted to the region's arid southwest. A limited range is no reflection of their abundance however, and they thrive wherever there are insects and rodents. Farmlands offer rich pickings for Cape foxes but although they probably help farmers by keeping pest numbers down, thousands are killed each year in the mistaken belief that they kill lambs. Fortunately, human persecution on farms is probably balanced by the removal of their enemies such as brown hyenas, jackals, leopards, caracals and honey badgers, all of which hunt them. Diminutive and essentially defenseless, they have a remarkably agile zigzagging escape pattern in which the bushy tail apparently acts as a decoy.

Despite being widespread, Cape foxes are poorly studied. They are thought to be less social than other canids and are usually observed alone. However, monogamous pairs are probably the norm, at least during the breeding season if not year-round. Larger groups are known, suggesting that more than one female may den together and, like other small canids, helpers probably assist in raising the pups. Cape foxes are shy, but in protected areas viewing young pups at dens can be enormously rewarding. ■

Recognition Small, slender silvery-grey fox. Bushy tail.
Habitat Arid grassland, dry woodlands and semidesert scrub.
Behaviour Nocturnal.
Breeding 1–5 pups.
Feeding Primarily insects and mice. Occasionally scavenges. Eats wild fruit.
Voice High-pitched *wow* repeated several times.

Hotspots
Kgalagadi TP, Central Kalahari GR, Etosha NP

HONEY BADGER

The bush bull terrier

Armed with potent secretions produced by their perineal glands, a pugnacious nature and astonishing strength, honey badgers (ratels) deserve a wide berth. They attack fearlessly when threatened and, like a bantam bull terrier, have a massively constructed skull in which the jaw can 'lock'; incensed honey badgers will clamp on until their opponent is dead or sometimes until the honey badger itself is killed. Much larger predators usually leave them alone.

But while their reputation for ferocity is well earned, honey badgers are not the indomitable warmongers so often portrayed. Like all animals, they prefer to avoid conflict and only unleash their formidable defences if provoked. And although they're mostly solitary, occasional gatherings of up to eight adults show them to be tolerant and playful with their own kind. Stories of them dispatching large herbivores by mauling the testicles are probably folklore and while they occasionally scavenge from lion kills with the owners still feeding, lions do kill them.

But of all the campfire stories told about honey badgers, the most enduring is the one about honeyguides. Greater honeyguides supposedly direct honey badgers to beehives; honey badgers use their bearlike ability to plunder hives for honey and the bird's reward is access to beeswax, a favourite food. But the honey badger's mostly nocturnal behaviour means that they were probably never a very reliable partner for the diurnal honeyguide. So how did the tale arise? Surprisingly, the bird does form a hive-hunting partnership but not with honey badgers. As abundant, diurnal lovers of honey, human hunter-gatherers were (and in some areas, still are) perfect partners. Honeyguides might show hives to honey badgers, but until irrefutable evidence presents itself, we are their only confirmed accomplices.

While their relationship with honeyguides is dubious, foraging honey badgers are often accompanied by an entourage of pale chanting goshawks, hoping to catch small birds and rodents making their escape. Small clusters of these raptors, particularly on stumps and low bushes are an effective beacon for honey badger-spotting. ■

Recognition Low-slung, robust build, up to 1m long and 15kg. Silvery-grey cape over black underparts.
Habitat Most habitats; common in semiarid areas.
Behaviour Usually nocturnal, active around dawn and dusk, especially in winter. Very little is known about their social system; they seem to be non-territorial and home ranges probably overlap considerably. They may congregate where food is readily available.
Breeding Poorly known. Apparently breeds year-round. 1–4 (typically 2) young.
Feeding Mostly rodents, scorpions and snakes; readily scavenges carrion; honey is probably a rare treat.
Voice Usually quiet. Rattling growl given in threat.

> **Hotspots**
> **Hwange NP** (Sinamatella Camp), **Kgalagadi TP**, **Central Kalahari GR**

WEASELS & ZORILLA

Smells to remember

Like their larger relative the honey badger, both the zorilla (or striped polecat) and African weasel have evolved pungent perineal secretions and aposematism (warning coloration). However, weighing 1kg in the largest zorillas and 350g for African weasels, they lack the honey badger's brute force and rely chiefly on nocturnal, secretive behaviour to elude predators; if they do en counter trouble, they're quick to air their acrid, chemical punch.

Both zorillas and African weasels are rodent killers. The weasel kills little else and, contrary to many field guides, rarely takes insects, snakes or eggs. Zorillas have wider tastes, supplementing their rodent kills with reptiles, scorpions, spiders and insects. Their generalist diet lets them occupy a broad range of habitats and zorillas occur throughout the region. Weasels, however, require prolific rodent populations to sustain them, which makes farmland ideal habitat – at least in theory. Overgrazing reduces rodent numbers and weasels are easy targets for farm dogs. Persecuted by farmers merely for being a predator, weasels are now rare. Zorillas are spotted more often; take a guided night drive. ■

*The three white spots on the **zorilla's** face quickly distinguish it from the African weasel.*

*The **African weasel** is the most endangered small carnivore in the region.*

> **Hotspots**
> **The Drakensberg** (Royal Natal NP), **Nyanga NP** and **Kruger NP** (especially in the south) Both species. **Kgalagadi TP** Good for zorillas.

OTTERS

Water weasels

Amphibious members of the weasel family, both otter species take watery refuge at the slightest disturbance. Size is a useful clue for distinguishing them: with an average top weight around 18kg, Cape clawless otters are the largest of Africa's four otter species; the much smaller spotted-necked otter has a top weight around 6kg. Otter paws provide a further lead. If the tracks lack obvious claws and webbing, the owner is a Cape clawless; claws and webs mean spotted-neckeds. Finally, while their ranges overlap, spotted neckeds are restricted to freshwater.

Cape clawless otters' dexterous 'fingers' allow them to manipulate fish, crabs, reptiles, frogs, birds, insects and small mammals, and they hunt 'by hand'. In contrast, spotted-neckeds make all their catches by mouth and concentrate on fish, crabs or frogs. Both species are mainly solitary, though breeding adults are playful and young male spotted-neckeds sometimes form small groups. ■

*The throat markings of **spotted-necked otters** may be reduced to a few flecks in Southern Africa.*

Cape clawless otters forage along the coast, but rely on freshwater to wash salt from their fur.

> **Hotspots**
> **Lake Malawi** Spotted-necked otters are sometimes seen at Cape Maclear. **The Drakensberg** Rivercourses here have both species. **Tsitsikamma NP** Cape clawless sometimes seen on The Otter Trail.

CAPE FUR-SEAL

Anti-social socialites

There are seven seal species in Southern African waters, but except for very occasional vagrants from the Antarctic and sub-Antarctic islands, the only mainland species is the Cape fur-seal. It's also a Southern African endemic but this limited range is no indication of numbers; there are an estimated two million scattered along the Southern African coastline. Communal to the extreme, this massive population is divided between only about 25 different colonies; a few of them, like Kleinsee on South Africa's west coast, number up to 400,000.

Despite their gregariousness, Cape fur-seals are not especially sociable; colony living makes sense for breeding opportunities and to reduce the chance of predators sneaking up, but individual seals are essentially loners on land and constantly quarrel over their own little patch. Except for pups playing with each other in crèche-like 'playgrounds', virtually every other interaction in the colony is hostile, creating extraordinary opportunities for watching behaviour (see the Cape Cross Seal Reserve account in the Parks and Places chapter).

Seals are far more playful with each other in the water, where staying close together also has survival value. The massive congregations attract their main predator, the great white shark, in droves. Between Cape Town's False Bay and Mossel Bay, the sharks have developed a unique predatory breaching tactic for seals, launching themselves vertically from deep water with astonishing power. The seals' main defence is to cluster together as they enter the water, benefiting from the 'many-eyes effect' in spotting sharks. If they do see one, a frantic scramble for landfall results but if caught in open water, seals occasionally mob the massive fish, speeding along behind it in the shark's slipstream. Being far more agile in the water, it's the safest place for them until they can reach land and the shark hasn't a chance of a kill with the element of surprise lost. Only when sharks are absent do seals disperse to forage – but often the predator is merely lurking in deep water. ■

Recognition Large, grey-brown seal. Pups born black. Adult males are usually dark. Top weight 350kg (males), 80kg (females).
Habitat Rocky or sandy beaches and small rocky islands.
Behaviour Highly communal but generally forages alone, usually during the day. Dives to 400m and can submerge for 10 minutes.
Breeding Highly seasonal, from November to December. Single pup. Female mates within 6 days of giving birth and the embryo goes into 'hibernation' for 4 months.
Feeding Mainly fish, also squid, cuttlefish, lobsters and occasionally smaller crustaceans.
Voice Highly vocal. All growl and bellow over territories. Females *maaaa* for their pups. Pups have a lamb-like bleat.

Hotspots
Cape Cross Seal Reserve, Skeleton Coast NP (Cape Frio), Kleinsee, Seal Island (False Bay)

AFRICAN ELEPHANT

Social giants

The largest mammal on earth is also one of the most social. Leading a core group of closely related females, one of the older females makes most of the decisions about where and when the herd forages, drinks and rests. Younger members of the herd act as nannies to the calves, and all family members are protective of the calves. Males live alone or in small bachelor groups, often comprising an old male accompanied by two or three 'apprentices', known as askaris, and only join herds when females are in heat. The askaris are prevented from coming into musth – the heightened state of a bull's sexual readiness – by the presence of mature bulls, a system which probably prevents young males from attempting to breed until they are fully mature. Elephants live for about 65 years, during which they maintain enduring relationships with the same individuals; the death of a family member provokes grieving behaviour very similar to our own.

Reaching seven tons and 4m high in the largest bulls, an elephant's daily requirements are prodigious. They eat up to 170kg of vegetation each day and drink 60 to 70L of water (though a thirsty elephant can guzzle twice that volume). Massive resource demands translate to unrivaled destructive potential and the damage wrought by feeding elephants can transform entire habitats, converting dense woodlands into plains. The process opens up overgrown habitat, returns nutrients to the ground and promotes soil turnover but it may also drive woodland species toward extinction. A natural factor in the functioning of savanna ecosystems, elephant engineering may be extreme where populations are confined to reserves, true for almost all of Southern Africa's population. Having enjoyed far greater protection than their counterparts elsewhere in Africa, southern elephants are now one of the most intensively managed species on the continent. Capture, culling, contraception, translocation and trading their precious ivory are among the arsenal of controversial strategies employed in the effort to establish a balance. ∎

Recognition Unmistakable. Colour varies from dark slate grey, reddish-brown to light grey. Both sexes carry tusks or may be tuskless.

Habitat Primarily savanna and woodland habitats. Semidesert at very low densities.

Behaviour Small family groups are the basic social unit, congregating into larger herds around water or food. Active around the clock; rest during the heat of the day. Entirely nocturnal where persecuted.

Breeding Non-seasonal. Gestation is 22 months. Single calf suckled for up to 2 years.

Feeding Leaves, bark, wood, bulbs, grass, fruit, flowers, shrubs and roots.

Voice Trumpets, growls, rumbles and snorts. Infrasound for long distance communication, largely inaudible to humans except in upper range (sounds like a rumbling belly).

Hotspots
Chobe NP, Addo Elephant NP, Hwange NP

DASSIES

The elephant's little brother

Known throughout Southern Africa by their Afrikaans name dassie, which means 'little badger' (elsewhere they are called hyraxes), and looking like a portly guinea pig, these unusual creatures are neither badger nor rodent. In fact, as improbable as it may seem, their closest relatives are elephants, dugongs and manatees. Padded hooves and open-rooted tusks are the only outward similarities but DNA and anatomical analyses reveal a far deeper resemblance. Even so, dassies have probably been separate and distinct from the elephant's ancestors for perhaps 75 million years and rather than close relatives, they should be thought of as distant branches of the one evolutionary tree.

*Up close, the **tree dassie** shows distinctive white markings above the eyes and upper lip.*

Southern Africa has three species, of which rock dassies are the most obvious. Widely spread throughout the region except

in dense forest or where rocky outcrops are lacking, these dassies live in colonies that may number in the hundreds. Within the colony, family groups are territorial and adult males acquire a harem of up to a dozen females by fighting other males using their extremely sharp tusks. Despite their aggression, rock dassies are entirely vegetarian and utilise a wide variety of plant matter; they graze when grass is abundant and browse on leaves, buds and twigs when it's not. When foraging, a sentinel (usually an older female) keeps a lookout for danger (inset) and sends the colony racing for a cover with a shrill warning bark.

*A pale chin and eyebrows help distinguish the **yellow-spotted dassie** from other dassies.*

In Zimbabwe, western Botswana and northern South Africa, they share their rock habitat with very similar yellow-spotted dassies. Distinguishable by the yellow pigmented gland on their back and generally lighter colouring, the two species have very similar behaviour and often occur in close association. In fact, they respond to one another's alarm calls, groom one another and even share nurseries.

***Rock dassies** are vulnerable in the open and never stray far from a rocky refuge.*

The rarest dassie in the region occurs along the KwaZulu-Natal and Eastern Cape coast, and in much of Zambia and Malawi. As their name suggests, tree dassies normally eschew rocks and live in forests. Skilful climbers, solitary and nocturnal, the closest most people come is to hear their tremulous, screaming call. ∎

Hotspots
Augrabies Falls NP Very obvious and tame rock dassies. **Nyanga NP** and **Matobo NP** Good chances for seeing mixed colonies of rock and yellow-spotted dassies. **Kasanka NP** and **North Luangwa NP** Tree dassies occur, but are elusive.

*Chilly early mornings are excellent for spotting **rock dassies** sunbaking on koppies.*

WHITE RHINOCEROS

Fermentation factories

Despite their armoured appearance and formidable bulk, white rhinos are actually fairly placid. In fact, although Southern Africa has the best rhino-viewing on the continent, exciting moments are rare because they spend most of their lives doing one thing – eating. Rhinos need to process up to 100kg of food each day and spend about 50% of daylight hours cropping grass with their distinctive broad snout (hence their alternative name, the square-lipped rhino). Their preference for short, young grass means they are easily spotted on plains and in open woodland but early morning is the best time to go looking; as the day warms up, white rhinos do even less than normal and seek shade to rest and ferment their gargantuan breakfast.

Although often seen alone, white rhinos are the most gregarious of the world's five rhino species and social interactions flesh out their behavioural repertoire beyond the basics. Friendly rhinos nuzzle and rub against one another and always rest with close body contact. Waterholes can provide rewarding viewing, especially in the early morning as the small family groups come to drink and wallow. A mud coating provides a cooling layer and helps to rid their hide of parasites like ticks. The ritual is almost always followed by a bout of obviously pleasurable rubbing against trees, termite mounds or rocks. Favourite sites become polished with use and are well worth noting for excellent chances of seeing rhinos at their best.

Water also attracts rivals, in which the interactions may be less amenable. Bulls are territorial but will allow intruding males to commute to water so long as they perform the oddly menacing but actually submissive ritual of roaring and squealing with the tail raised and ears laid back. Failure to do so can lead to titanic jousts that are sometimes fatal. Perhaps even more dangerous, mothers are extremely protective of calves; maintain a healthy distance but spend some time watching the young – baby rhinos can be hysterically playful. ■

Recognition Males weigh up to 2000kg, females 1800kg. Larger size, square-shaped lip and massive neck hump distinguishes them from black rhinos.

Habitat Well-watered savanna and open woodland. Feeds on open grasslands but never far from cover.

Behaviour Mostly diurnal, though often feeds at night. Forms groups up to 10 comprising a few females, their calves and subadults. Adult males maintain exclusive territories and attempt to herd oestrous females into their patch.

Breeding Non-seasonal. Most calves are born March to July after a 16-month gestation.

Feeding Exclusively grazes, favouring short young grass.

Voice Pant, snort and huff when startled. Bellow in threat, calves squeal when alarmed.

Hotspots
Hluhluwe-Umfolozi GR, Phinda Resource Reserve, Pilanesberg NP

BLACK RHINOCEROS

The hedge-clipper

More solitary, less relaxed and far more endangered than their white counterparts (which are, in fact, essentially the same colour), black rhinos present more of a challenge for wildlife-watchers. They mostly avoid open areas and a sighting is usually the result of some time invested looking in the right places. Black rhinos prefer thick vegetation and gravitate towards thorn tree thickets and the denser bush in valleys or lining rivers. As well as providing cover, thick bush reflects their feeding specialisation as a browser of small trees and shrubs. The triangular-shaped upper lip is highly mobile and acts like a giraffe's tongue, grasping branches and pulling them into the mouth. Black rhinos literally prune trees, neatly slicing off the branch tips at a precise 45-degree angle. The clipped tips are extremely distinctive, both on the trees themselves and strewn in middens, large mounds of accumulated dung used as a territorial signpost. The presence of uniformly clipped twigs with 45° edges is a sure way to determine the midden belongs to a black rhino rather than to its grass-eating cousin. However, don't be surprised if you find one containing both grass and twigs; occasionally, both species use the same mound.

If you do see black rhinos, chances are they won't hang around for long. Despite their size and weaponry, they're nervous animals and inclined to flee when disturbed. However, if they feel threatened, they are far more likely than white rhinos to confront the danger or, at least, investigate it. For this adrenalin-pumping honour, South Africa's KwaZulu-Natal province is the black rhino-viewing capital of the world. Guided Black Rhino Trails allow you to track rhinos on foot, inspect their hedge-clipping action up close and tease out the evidence from their middens. With everyone safely installed in trees, the trackers might even call in a rhino with flawless imitations of a baby rhino's incongruous mewing noise. An adult black rhino huffing curiously a few metres below is a wildlife experience without parallel. ■

Recognition Smaller than white rhinos, males reach a maximum of 1200kg females 800kg. Lip is triangular rather than square. Lacks the neck hump of white rhino.
Habitat From semidesert to dense woodland. Avoids open spaces (except at night).
Behaviour Largely solitary. Bulls set up exclusive territories and may kill intruding young males. Females non-territorial but remain in the same home range accompanied by successive calves.
Breeding Non-seasonal. Single calf is born after a 15-month gestation.
Feeding Trees, bushes and leaves. They occasionally eat grass if nutritionally stressed.
Voice Repeated explosive snorts when charging and loud grunts, growls and screams when fighting. Calves mew as a contact call.

Hotspots
Etosha NP (especially at Okaukuejo waterhole), **Mkuzi GR**, **Pilanesberg NP**

MOUNTAIN ZEBRA

Recognition Small, stocky Cape subspecies is around 1.2m tall at the shoulder and weighs up to 260kg. Hartmann's is about 1.5m tall and weighs 320–350kg.
Habitat Mountain grasslands.
Behaviour Non-territorial and shares home ranges but at much lower densities than Burchell's. Mostly diurnal.
Breeding Year-round with a peak over summer. Gestation is 12 months and a single foal is born.
Feeding Largely a grazer, using both high and low quality grasses. Browses only when nutritionally stressed. Requires water daily.
Voice Quieter than Burchell's. Stallions utter an alarm snort and high-pitched alarm call. Subordinate males use a prolonged squeal to signal submission.

Hotspots
Namib-Naukluft Park, **Daan Viljoen Game Park** (Hartmann's subspecies); **Karoo NP**, **Mountain Zebra NP** (Cape subspecies)

Equine barcode
Found only in Southern Africa, mountain zebras are a distinct species from the savanna-dwelling Burchell's zebras. Their natural distributions probably never overlapped but Burchell's zebras have been so widely introduced across South Africa that there are a few reserves (such as Karoo NP) where you could see both species in a day's viewing. They're very similar but a minute's careful observation reveals a suite of distinctive characteristics unique to mountain zebras: a dewlap under the throat, a gridlike pattern of close-set stripes over the rump and a lack of shadow stripes. Their legs are richly striped all the way to the hooves (Burchell's usually aren't) and the stripes on the face fade into a rich rusty colour. Finally, whereas Burchell's stripes extend all the way across their belly, mountain zebras' underparts are unstriped white.

Once you've mastered these differences, the challenge is in identifying different mountain zebra races – there are actually two distinct subspecies. Fortunately though, their ranges don't overlap, so discrimination by geography is easy. Anywhere along Namibia's central rocky escarpment, they're Hartmann's mountain zebras while Cape mountain zebras only occur in South Africa's Cape region.

Earning their stripes
Mountain zebra society is based on the same building blocks that make up the large herds of Burchell's: small family groups and bachelor herds. But their arid habitat generally prohibits large congregations and small discrete units are the norm. Interactions between families are less frequent but within the small groups, it's easier to discern the subtle dominance behaviour common to all zebra species. The stallion heads the hierarchy, herding his harem with head held low and ears laid back. A strict pecking order also exists among his mares, who use the same signals to display dominance; a submissive mare lowers her head and makes open-mouthed chewing movements exposing the teeth. Very frequent friendly contact among family members balances out the little power plays and all zebras in the group groom and nuzzle one another regularly. ∎

BURCHELL'S ZEBRA

Harem-masters and bachelor boys

Probably the most recognisably African herbivore after the elephant, zebras are a guaranteed sighting. In fact in certain parts of the region, they form the largest herds of any ungulate in Southern Africa. At first glance a haphazard horde without order, zebra congregations actually comprise many small groups with very defined relationships. Adult stallions each command a harem of between four and ten mares, which they defend vigorously from other males. Rivals will attempt to abduct one another's females so stallions maintain strenuous control over their charges, herding wanderers back to the fold and racing ahead to engage challengers. Established herd males largely leave one another alone but small clusters of young bachelors constantly attempt to acquire individual females to kick-start their own harem. The bachelors form the main target of the herd stallions' aggression so in large herds, bachelor males keep a low profile by sticking to the fringes. This makes them more vulnerable to predation, so as well as irate stallions and unattended females, bachelors must keep a constant watch for lions.

Life and death at the water

Zebras are dependent on water and rarely occur more than 15km from a source – an easy day's walk for them. Family groups and bachelors intermingle at waterholes, an excellent spot to observe skirmishing stallions. Like a fingerprint, every zebra's stripes are unique, a useful way to identify individuals, though it takes terrific powers of observation to keep track in the melee. Zebras' main enemy, lions, also converge on waterholes to lay ambushes. Even single lions are able to take down a zebra but it's a dangerous task; zebras defend themselves with lethal kicks that easily break a jaw or leg. Except for lions and large hyena groups, adult zebras are beyond the grasp of most predators but hyenas, African wild dogs, leopards and cheetahs do take foals. However, stallions are formidable guardians and, so long as the attacker isn't a lion (in which case it's every zebra for itself), they have been known to kick a predator to death. ■

Recognition Large horse covered in black-and-white stripes, often with brown 'shadow stripes' on the rump.
Habitat Grasslands and savanna woodlands. Avoid dense vegetation and require water daily.
Behaviour Non-territorial. Fairly stable home ranges, which are shared with other family groups and bachelors. In some areas, they migrate between separate summer and winter ranges.
Breeding Single foal born after gestation of 360–390 days. Foals born year-round, with a peak over summer.
Feeding Primarily a grazer, attracted to short fresh growth.
Voice Very vocal; the alarm, contact and territorial calls are variations of a braying *kwa-ha*. Snorts when uncertain of danger.

Hotspots
Nxai Pan NP (summer); Linyanti region, **Chobe NP** (winter); **Etosha NP**

BUSHPIG

Night sounders

Far less conspicuous than warthogs, bushpigs are nocturnal residents of dense forest or riverine thickets. Resembling the European boar, they're covered in a shaggy coat of coarse reddish-brown hair with a white mane of bristles fringing the face and along the spine. Like warthogs, bushpigs live in 'sounders', small family groups numbering about six to eight animals. But unlike the warthog's matrilineal clans, bushpig groups are usually headed by an alpha pair dominant to their family of younger sows and piglets. The boar actually assumes the protection of the piglets and is the frontline of defence against predators. Lions occasionally take bushpigs but their main predator is the arboreal leopard; snatching a bush-piglet from the family, leopards retreat tree-wards to escape the wrath of the group. Adult bushpigs use their elongated lower incisors to fight back and inexperienced big cats risk serious injury.

Bushpigs remember favourite feeding areas and habitually return to them from their daytime rest sites in dense cover. This habit creates narrow well-worn trails, a good sign of bushpig activity, particularly where they lead to waterholes – bushpigs require water daily and a night's foraging is usually prefaced with a drink and a mud bath. ■

Recognition Reddish-brown pig with white facial blazes. Averages 60kg.
Habitat Forests and riverine vegetation.
Behaviour Largely nocturnal.
Breeding 3–4 piglets.
Feeding Roots and fruits.
Voice Grunts.

Hotspots
Phinda Resource Reserve, Hluhluwe-Umfolozi GR, Liwonde NP, Kruger NP (Pafuri region in the far north)

WARTHOG

Warts 'n all

The ubiquitous warthog is a diurnal, savanna-woodland dweller and the butt of endless ridicule about its appearance. But in fact, each of its homely features has important survival value. Protruding high-set eyes and large flaplike ears maintain constant vigilance for predators while warthogs feed head-down. The massive, over-sized head acts as a powerful lever for shoveling up bulbs and roots, as well as during clashes when the 'warts' also come into play. Composed of densely packed connective tissue, they protect the skull during head-hammering contests between males. Males' warts are much larger than the females' and they have two pairs rather than the females' single set. Even their spindly, stringy tail has a function; raised like a flag when alarmed, it probably helps fleeing warthogs stay together in long grass.

Warthog society revolves around matriarchal groups of related females and their offspring. Lone males or bachelor groups visit them only to mate. Indeed, despite the male's more formidable arsenal (both sexes have tusks but the males' are generally much larger), it's the females who defend youngsters from predators. A mother warthog will bravely engage cheetahs, African wild dogs and even leopards or lone hyenas, but they're essentially helpless against lions. ■

Recognition Stocky grey, sparsely haired pig. Males up to 70cm high and 80kg.
Habitat Mostly savannas and grasslands.
Behaviour Diurnal.
Breeding 1–8 piglets.
Feeding Mainly grass, also bulbs, roots, fruit, occasionally carrion.
Voice Grunts when feeding, screams in distress.

Hotspots
Hwange NP, Chobe NP, Pilanesberg NP

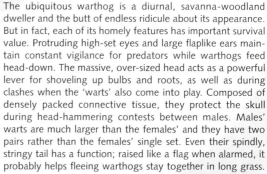

HIPPOPOTAMUS

River pigs

Distantly related to pigs, hippos are the only large amphibious mammal in the region. They spend the day resting in water or close to it and at first glance, their small social groups are easily mistaken for clusters of water-polished boulders. Family groups numbering around 15 are the norm, lorded over by a dominant bull that controls a small stretch of the river or lake shore. Bulls are extremely aggressive to challengers but subordinate males are tolerated so long as they avoid sexual behaviour. Sociable by day in water, they emerge at sunset to graze alone on nearby grasslands. Except for calves, who remain near their mothers, hippos have few predators on land and can afford to forage on their own. Floodplain grasses near the water are preferred but they may commute up to 10km a night in search of good grazing; regardless, they always return to the water before dawn.

Recognition Unmistakable. Adults average around 1500kg. Males are usually larger and covered in scars from territorial battles.
Habitat Deep freshwater bodies with nearby grasslands.
Behaviour Remains close to water during the day and can submerge for up to 6 minutes. Grazes on land and always by night.
Breeding Non-seasonal. Single calf is usually born in shallow water. Females are extremely protective of their young. They hide the calf in reeds for up to a week before rejoining the pod.
Feeding Crops grasses with the broad lips. Very occasionally eats carrion.
Voice Very vocal. Grunts, squeals and growls used in social interactions. Prolonged honking grunt used to proclaim territory.

Myths and falsehoods

For such a recognisable and widely distributed mammal, hippos are difficult to study. Their nocturnal habits, huge mass and aquatic behaviour makes them difficult to capture for marking or radiocollaring, without which individual hippos are very difficult to tell apart. This may be why such a rich mythology surrounds the species. One of the most dramatic falsehoods is that heat-stressed hippos sweat blood. In fact, hippos lack sweat glands entirely and mucous glands in the skin exude a gluey, bright red fluid that hardens into a lacquered, natural sunscreen. Another tall story claims that hippo mothers transport their calves on their backs. You may witness this for yourself but calves are good swimmers and don't actually hitch a ride to get around; they climb onto adults' backs merely to sunbathe and snooze. And finally, among mammals, hippos are universally held to be the number one people-killers in Africa. Though undeniably dangerous (extremely so, in some circumstances), accurate figures have never been compiled. Simply by virtue of their greater abundance and habit of raiding villages and crops, the title probably belongs to the elephants. ∎

Hotspots
Vwaza Marsh WR, Greater St Lucia Wetland Park, Chobe NP

GIRAFFE

Recognition Unmistakable. Males grow to 5.5m tall and weigh 900–1800kg. Females 4–4.4m and 600–1000kg.

Habitat Mainly open *Acacia* savannas, also woodlands and scrub.

Behaviour Active day and night. They sleep standing or resting on their haunches. Non-territorial and move over large home ranges, intermixing with other giraffes they encounter.

Breeding Non-seasonal. Single calf suckled for up to a year.

Feeding Leaves, flowers and pods, primarily of *Acacia* trees. Very occasionally grazes and chews bones (osteophagia) for trace elements.

Voice Most communication is by infrasound, which is too low for human hearing. Grunt and bellow under stress, prolonged huff in alarm.

Stilt-browsing

As the world's tallest mammal, giraffes are able to exploit a feeding niche that is shared only with elephants. And even among giraffes, 'niche differentiation' occurs. Males can reach a metre higher than females and browse the tops of trees up to 6m high, whereas females tend to bend down and feed from smaller trees: at a distance, this is one way to distinguish the sexes. Apart from their elongated neck (which, contrary to most sources, has eight vertebrae, one more than most mammals) and a 45cm-long tongue, other adaptations assist feeding. An extremely convoluted stomach gives giraffes the most efficient digestive system of any ruminant and they can survive on less than half the browse that would be otherwise predicted by their massive size. This means giraffes can afford to be terrifically selective and they use their horny lips and tongue to choose the most nutritious leaves. Even so, thorns slow the process down and they can spend as many as 20 hours a day feeding to fulfil their 25 to 35kg daily quota of browse.

Beyond modifications for feeding, their unique form carries further adaptations. When giraffes move or lower their heads, sudden changes in blood pressure are buffered by muscular valves in the blood vessels of the neck, an intricate filigree of vessels (called a rete) at the base of the brain, and a 7cm-thick heart. Being so large also requires prodigious heat dissipation and the giraffe's markings function to channel heat build-up out through the skin. Markings are unique to individuals and although one theory suggests they may also be important for individual recognition, their very loose social system hardly requires it. Giraffes are gregarious but float among groups without any enduring bonds except for those between mother and calf. Group composition changes constantly and at any one time, there can be any combination of age-sex categories in a herd. A day later, it could be entirely different. ■

Hotspots
Etosha NP, Hwange NP, South Luangwa NP

BLUE & BLACK WILDEBEESTS

Blue ■ Black □
Blue & Black ▧

Brindled blues and white-tailed blacks

Often described as looking like a cross between a horse and a goat, wildebeests actually belong to the same family as all African antelopes, the Bovidae. Southern Africa is home to two species, the widespread blue wildebeest (below) and a South African endemic, the black wildebeest (right). Having similar coloration, their common names can be confusing; their alternate names make better sense (though are not widely used). The brindled gnu (blue wildebeest) arises from the characteristic dark bands on its neck and shoulders while the black wildebeest's other appellation, the white-tailed gnu, highlights its most distinctive feature, one which cannot be confused with its dark-tailed cousin.

Minor cosmetic differences aside, the two species share much in common. Wildebeests are gregarious, with small groups of females and their calves forming the most common unit. The female herds wander widely so in order to maximise their reproductive chances, lone males carve out small territories where the females are likely to congregate. In the case of blue wildebeests, good sites are those with the best grazing, such as river beds in the Kalahari Desert, which are more productive than the surrounding dunes and bound to attract females. For highveld-dwelling black wildebeests, visibility rather than grazing is the key and the best territories are those with an expansive view of their surroundings. For both species, young males or those that fail to defend a territory, form floating bachelor herds.

In productive habitats like the moist bushveld of South Africa's KwaZulu-Natal, localised female herds and territorial bulls can be the norm year-round, but where conditions fluctuate, wildebeests become nomadic or migratory. Female herds aggregate and males abandon turf to move together in huge herds in search of better grazing. A biannual event in East Africa, wildebeest migrations in Southern Africa are now rare due to human-made obstacles. Of the two species, blue wildebeests undertake the only significant movements in the region in Botswana – though even there, veterinary fences have taken a massive toll (see the boxed text 'Veterinary fences' in the Central Kalahari GR account). ■

Recognition Blue: Males stand up to 1.5m at the shoulder and weigh 250kg. Black: Males are 1.2m and 160kg. Both sexes (in both species) have horns.
Habitat Blue: Occurs throughout savanna grasslands. Black: Restricted to the Karoo and highveld grasslands.
Behaviour Diurnal and gregarious. Blue: Form herds between 10 and many thousand. Black: Herds rarely larger than 30.
Breeding Seasonal breeders, mating March to April, calving in summer.
Feeding Primarily short grasses, also some herbs and shrubs.
Voice A metallic-sounding low is made by wildebeests in herds. Territorial males *gnu* (blue) or *oink* (black). Both species snort in alarm and bleat in distress.

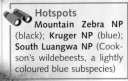

Hotspots
Mountain Zebra NP (black); **Kruger NP** (blue); **South Luangwa NP** (Cookson's wildebeests, a lightly coloured blue subspecies)

RED HARTEBEEST

A hartebeest by any other name

Recognition Large, reddish, heavy bodied antelope, with elongated head, humped shoulders and sloping back. Both sexes have angular, curving Z-shaped horns.

Habitat Open grassland, sparsely treed woodlands and the ecotone between them.

Behaviour Mostly active early morning and late afternoon, moving to water later in the morning. Territorial males mark with dung piles and stand prominently on mounds.

Breeding Rut occurs March to April. Peak birth period is October to November. Single calf born.

Feeding Medium-length grasses and new grass growth. Occasionally browses to increase water intake.

Voice Horse-like, sneezing alarm snort.

Hartebeests once had a distribution that encompassed virtually all of Africa except the equatorial forests and the Sahara. Now extinct in northern Africa and much reduced over the rest of their range, they still occur fairly widely in grassland-savanna habitats across the continent, but in mostly disjunct populations. The differences between them can be considerable and at least 50 different forms have been described, but today most authorities distinguish between eight and twelve subspecies. There are two forms in Southern Africa, although this is still a source of disagreement between experts. The widespread red hartebeests are universally recognised as the most southern subspecies of the Africa-wide hartebeest group, making them the same species as Coke's hartebeest (kongoni) of Kenya and Tanzania. But whereas Lichtenstein's hartebeests are occasionally included as yet another race in this huge species-complex, they probably should be treated as a separate species entirely. Taxonomy aside, Lichtenstein's are one of the rarest antelopes in the region but red hartebeests are easily seen.

Red hartebeests are dwellers of open, arid country where resources are thinly spread. They need to cover large distances for water and grazing so herds roam in home ranges of around 1000 sq km. However, solitary adult bulls seek out higher-quality patches as territories, defending an area that may be only one-eighth the size. The payoff for them comes when female herds, numbering up to 30, seek out the productive patches. Territorial males are particularly aggressive defending their harem, and fatal fights are not uncommon.

Territory maintenance becomes untenable, particularly during dry seasons, and (like many arid-adapted antelopes) males abandon their turf and join the female herds. The resulting congregations can number in the thousands as they amass in the search for grazing and water. Most dramatic in Botswana, veterinary fences there now largely curtail the migrations and many thousands of hartebeests die against the barriers. ∎

Hotspots
Mountain Zebra NP, Hwange NP, Kgalagadi TP, Central Kalahari GR

BONTEBOKS, BLESBOKS & TSESSEBES

Like blesboks and tsessebes, both sexes of **bonteboks** *have ringed, lyre-shaped horns.*

Two endemics and a marathon mammal

These three antelopes are closely related and all occupy a very similar ecological niche – that of a medium-bodied grazer preferring short grasses. Competition for the same resources is probably why they have clearly distinct distributions, meaning you have to travel around a little to see all three.

Generally accepted as two races of the one species, bonteboks and blesboks (inset) are both South African endemics and very similar in appearance but easily separated by geography. Bonteboks only occur on fynbos grasslands in the southwest Cape whereas blesboks have a wide distribution throughout central South Africa (and elsewhere from artificial introductions). The bontebok was driven to near extinction in the 1830s but today, both are fairly easily found.

Like many gregarious antelopes, their social system is driven by clusters of females, which solitary, territorial bulls attempt to 'acquire'. Bontebok males compete for herds of two to eight females but in blesboks, the harems can be as large as 25. In both subspecies, young bulls and subordinate males form bachelor herds and are excluded from the territorial patches but will attempt to mate unguarded females. The rut is the most exciting time to watch as males chase the bachelors and engage in highly ritualised stand-offs with neighbours.

The **bontebok's** *glossy purplish tinge sets it apart from the overall duller blesbok.*

Like their relatives, hartebeests and wildebeests, tsessebes have elongated forelegs and high shoulders, producing a characteristic sloping back. The resulting appearance is ungainly but it enables tsessebes to adopt an energetically economical canter. Tsessebe social structure is similar to that of its relatives, with female herds, territorial males and bachelor groups. But across their considerable range (including East and Central Africa, where they're a distinct race called topis) they show more social flexibility than virtually any other antelope. In poor habitat, they become nomadic and males only occupy territories in good seasons, but in better areas, some males remain territorial year-round. And most extreme, they also form leks, huge breeding arenas where males compete for central positions, which females seek out only when ready to mate. ∎

The **blesbok** *has a pale-coloured rump but not pure white as in the bontebok.*

 Hotspots
Bontebok NP and **De Hoop NR** Virtually assured bonteboks. **Mountain Zebra NP** and **Golden Gate Highlands NP** Good herds of blesboks. **Chobe NP** (Savute area), **Pilanesberg NP** and **Waterberg Plateau Park** Tsessebes.

The **tsessebe's** *horns sweep backwards and are shorter than those of its relatives.*

SMALL ANTELOPES

Grey duikers are tolerant of human activity and survive even on the fringes of cities.

Cape grysboks occur only in South Africa's Western Cape region and are usually seen alone.

Sharpe's grysboks are very secretive and crouch low in thick cover when danger threatens.

Black spots below their ears and a black tail help distinguish the **oribi** *from the similar steenbok.*

Bush divers

Easily overlooked compared to their larger relatives, there's a legion of miniature antelopes in Southern Africa. Along with their diminutive stature, most are very shy, keep to dense cover and don't form the obvious herds of large species. Nonetheless, while most mammals of their size are strictly nocturnal, small antelopes are active around the clock; dawn and dusk hold reasonable chances of spotting them.

Named with an Afrikaans word describing their habit of diving into thick bush when alarmed, duikers are found in all the forests and woodlands of Africa and four species occur in the southern region. The appropriately named grey (or common) duiker is the most likely to be seen. Unlike the rest of this forest-loving group, they occur throughout open savanna and grasslands, providing there are thickets in which to take cover. They're also the only duiker in the region in which the female lacks horns, but be sure to check closely; like all duikers, a conspicuous tuft of hair can obscure the horns.

The goliaths of the group, yellow-backed duikers grow to the size of a small calf and weigh up to 80kg, but despite their size, are difficult to spot. Characteristic of Central Africa's forests, they're at the southern limit of their range here and are restricted to the very dense forests of northern Zambia.

The other two species, red duikers (inset) and blue duikers inhabit the indigenous forests along the eastern seaboard. Watch for troops of vervet and samango monkeys; they're often accompanied by a duiker retinue mopping up fallen leaves, fruits and flowers (the mainstay of their diet). Whether grey, blue, yellow-backed or red, duikers spend most of their time alone, but deeper bonds exist just under the surface. In the case of tiny blue duikers, this extends to lifelong pairs but the arrangement is looser for other species, in which pairs jointly occupy a territory but only come together intermittently. Regardless, breeding takes place throughout the year.

Why monogamy?

Very unusual among mammals, the monogamous behaviour of small antelopes (like these Damara dik-diks) is driven by numerous factors, but size is the key. Africa's highly variable rainfall drives large-bodied antelopes to wander in huge home ranges, or else migrate to satisfy their food and water needs. However, antelopes weighing less than 20kg can subsist in far smaller areas, even during the dry season. Occupying the same range means little antelopes grow extremely familiar with the best places to find food and flee predators. By teaming up with a long-term partner, they also eliminate the risk of leaving home to find a mate and double their chances of spotting danger, all without the conspicuousness of large herds.

The downward-pointing hooves of *klipspringers* provide them with excellent grip on rocks.

The seven dwarves

Known collectively as the dwarf antelopes, a further seven species make up a seperate tribe, but being the stem group which gave rise to duikers, they share many similarities. Permanent pair bonds are the basis of their social system, most apparent in klipspringers, dik-diks and oribis, which are almost always together. Pairs jointly hold a territory and while both scent-mark with conspicuous facial glands and dung piles, males readily over-mark their mates to conceal the female's presence from rivals. Steenboks and sunis are usually spotted alone but, like most duikers, pairs share a territory and come together to groom, share a food patch or to breed. Most solitary of them all, the grysboks (two species, Sharpe's and Cape) seem to have the loosest bonds. Males are territorial and may associate with the same female in consecutive years but only if she remains in the area.

The *blue duiker* is the smallest antelope in the region and relishes fruit when it is available.

Except for oribis, which feed mostly on grass, dwarf antelopes have a duikerlike diet of leaves, flowers, fruits and herbs. Steenboks and grysboks are also fond of crops and adopt nocturnal behaviour to raid farmlands. This leads to inevitable conflict with people but while their secrecy baffles reliable population estimates, most dwarf antelopes seem secure. In common with duikers, the spread of agriculture and plantations is their greatest threat, not only due to habitat destruction but also because of the inevitable influx of domestic dogs. ■

Steenboks are widely distributed and the most common small antelope in arid habitats.

Hotspots
Greater St Lucia Wetland Park Three duikers as well as sunis and steenboks. **Etosha NP** The best place for dik-diks. **Karoo NP** and **Augrabies Falls NP** Excellent for klipspringers. **Kruger NP** Six species including Sharpe's grysbok. **Cape Peninsula NP** and **University of Port Elizabeth** (Grysbok Trail) Both areas good for Cape grysboks. **North Luangwa NP** and **Kafue NP** Yellow-backed duikers. **Lengwe NP** Good for oribis.

The elusive *suni* sometimes gives itself away by its constantly flicking tail.

SPRINGBOK

Recognition Medium-sized antelope with distinctive tan, white and brown coat. Both sexes have ringed lyre-shaped horns.
Habitat Dry short-grass plains and semidesert.
Behaviour Diurnal and gregarious, forms mixed-sexed herds (up to 50), sometimes much larger herds in high quality grazing. Males form territories but may accompany the herds. Females with young form separate nursery herds.
Breeding Year-round but mostly during the rut, which may be associated with rainfall.
Feeding Primarily grazes, but browses when grass availability is limited. Eats roots and tubers for moisture.
Voice Sharp nasal alarm-whistle, short recognition bleat and males make a loud *urrrr* during the rut.

The southern gazelle

Across the open plains of Africa (and Eurasia's steppes), small-bodied antelopes which could afford to select the freshest grass and had the narrow muzzles to do so proliferated in the niches unavailable to larger herbivores. These are the gazelles and their relatives. Reaching their greatest diversity in East and North Africa where they number 10 species, Southern Africa's woodland-dominated habitat held fewer opportunities for them and there is only a single species here, the springbok.

Restricted to the South West Arid zone, this southern endemic is well adapted to dry and unpredictable conditions. They're very selective feeders, always choosing the best quality food available. Following rainfall, they concentrate on young grass shoots and flowers but as conditions deteriorate, springboks switch to the leaves and buds of bushes – less nutritious than new grass but the best food in dry season. Like other gazelles, they're highly mobile and undertake large migrations to track flushes of new growth. In the past, these 'treks' numbered in the tens of thousands and although springboks are still common, fences and habitat fragmentation means such massive migrations are a thing of the past.

Wanderers and stayers

Obstacles notwithstanding, springboks become nomadic where possible and herds move widely to exploit better feeding patches. In the dry season, herds are usually small and dispersed as they track fleeting cloudbursts and the temporary flush of growth that follows. For mature males, however, holding a territory that will eventually attract many females is more important and they tend to stay put. In their arid habitat, that often means securing a stretch of riverbed, which is why lone males can be seen evenly spaced along the Nossob and Auob in the Kgalagadi year-round. When the rains arrive, the influx of females makes the wait worthwhile. But having to endure poor feeding during the dry season and remaining alone makes them particularly vulnerable to predators. Clocked at 88km/h, they rely on their speed and hyper-vigilance to escape danger. ◼

Hotspots
Etosha NP, Kgalagadi TP, Nxai Pan NP

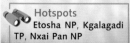

IMPALA

Bushveld sheep

With more than 100,000 in Kruger NP alone, impalas are often the first African mammal to be checked off the list and locals understandably dismiss them as 'bushveld sheep' or 'Zambezi goats'. But their success is due to a suite of adaptations that warrant a second, closer look. Foremost is dietary flexibility. Impalas are mixed feeders, able to alternate between grass and browse as the need arises. Combined with a prodigious capacity to reproduce quickly, this has enabled them to invade the transition zone between open plains and dense woodlands, a habitat which has spread with increased human agriculture. Unlike most species, where people have spread, so too have impalas. And they're not fussy about sticking with family. Impalas have very loose inter-relationships and, except for the bond between mother and lamb, they have no enduring social ties. Although they're highly gregarious and generally remain in the same home range, overlap with other groups means that inter-mixing and exchange of herd members is routine. It further enhances impalas' ability to colonise; lacking strong social ties, they're uninhibited in their exploitation of new areas.

The rut

Despite their social promiscuity, there are distinct rules for the breeding season. As the rut approaches, adult males abandon their bachelor herds and seek out female herds. They furiously set about carving out a territory, frantically herding the harem, chasing challengers and mating with oestrous females. It's an exhausting routine and males usually hold their patch for only a few weeks then yield to a challenger. Regardless, by the end of the rut, all adult females will be pregnant and will synchronise their births to within a couple of weeks of each other. Known as 'predator swamping' it's a reproductive strategy that relies on there simply being too many lambs for carnivores to catch them all. Even so, up to 50% will be killed in the first few weeks but enough will survive to ensure as much as a staggering 35% increase in the population each year. ∎

Recognition Medium-sized antelope with red-brown, fawn and white coat. Only males have horns. Black-faced impalas (above) are slightly darker with a black facial blaze.

Habitat Woodland savannas, ecotone between open plains and bush. Water-dependent.

Behaviour Females and young form herds of 30–150, which occasionally amass into larger clans. Males form separate bachelor herds (less than 30), which break down during the rut.

Breeding The rut takes place March to April. Single lambs are dropped mid-November to January.

Feeding Grass, leaves, *Acacia* pods, fruit.

Voice Males roar during the rut. A sharp nasal snort is given in alarm and a soft murmuring grunt is given between herd members.

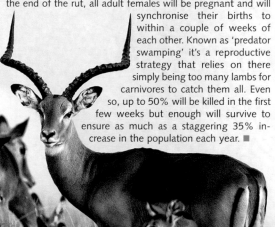

 Hotspots
Kruger NP, Hwange NP; Etosha NP (black-faced impalas)

ROAN ANTELOPE

Fussy, retiring and rare

Recognition Third-largest bovid; weighs up to 300kg. Strawberry-roan colour. Black-and-white facial mask. Both sexes carry horns.
Habitat Open savanna and tall grasslands.
Behaviour Small breeding groups and bachelor herds.
Breeding Single calf.
Feeding Grass.
Voice Alarm snort.

Hotspots
Nyika NP, Marakele NP, Waterberg Plateau Park

With a horse-like bulk that defies most predators and a distribution that encompasses virtually all woodlands south of the Sahara, roan antelopes seem a highly successful species. Yet they're actually a surprisingly specialised antelope, one with such a strict criteria of requirements that they are common nowhere.

Firstly, they're very selective grazers, preferring to crop the tips of medium-length grasses, a diet that makes them vulnerable to drought as well as to competition from less fussy eaters like zebras and wildebeests. And despite their size, roans also actively seek out areas where predators are few. Wherever there are many other herbivores and the predators which follow them, roans are rare or absent.

This means that roans tend to be pushed into marginal areas where other wildlife is thin on the ground, but they are extremely loyal to their home ranges. Breeding herds, numbering up to 15 with a single adult bull, sometimes stick to a few square kilometres for months, especially in the wet season when grazing is good. Their dry season wanderings inflate the range but if left alone, a herd will stay in the same area for years. A little local knowledge is invaluable for finding them. ■

SABLE ANTELOPE

Colour-coded command

Recognition Large horse-like antelope. Both sexes carry backward-curving horns.
Habitat Open woodlands.
Behaviour Females and juveniles form herds. Adult males territorial.
Breeding Most calves born January to March.
Feeding Mostly grass.
Voice Territorial males bellow and roar.

Hotspots
Hwange NP, Pilanesberg NP, Kafue NP

With its monochrome mask and ringed half-moon horns, the sable's shared ancestry with the roan is obvious. But while the roan's body colour reflects the subdued colours of the bush, sables exhibit one of the most striking of all antelope coats. Physical presence proclaims rank in sables and they advertise it by colour – the blacker, the better. Adult males in command of a harem are a glossy raven black, high ranking females are very dark brown and low ranking females a russet colour. Born pale sepia, sables assume their regalia as they age.

Being obvious helps to intimidate rivals and males assume very erect poses in prominent places to declare ownership of a herd. Even so, their custody is fleeting. Female herds wander widely and territorial males can only hope to mate when a group enters their patch. And females are only worth fighting for when they enter oestrous, usually around April to June, so males spend the bulk of their time alone. Nonetheless, they hold their patch year-round and assume the territorial posturing at any time. It makes them extremely photogenic but, more importantly, very conspicuous to predators. Fortunately for them, sables are alert and able combatants; males defend themselves against all comers except lions. ■

GEMBSOK

A design for desert-dwelling

Sometimes called the southern oryx, gemsboks are endemic icons of the South West Arid zone. Much admired by hunters for their rapierlike horns and by wildlife photographers for their conspicuous, contrasting beauty, gemsboks are desert specialists without equal. A lowered metabolism is the nucleus of their adaptive repertoire. It enables them to survive on far less than equally sized wildebeests, which means they evade the obligatory nomadism that forces other desert inhabitants to wander over huge ranges. It also frees them of the need to regularly trek to water and, in fact, they can survive indefinitely without drinking; gemsboks extract all the moisture they need from water-rich tsama melons and subterranean taproots. A slower metabolism also lowers their body temperature to minimise the risk of overheating, further enhanced by their short, reflective coat. Even so, gemsboks can tolerate body temperatures that would kill other mammals. Allowing the body to heat up to 45°C conserves valuable water that would be lost by panting or sweating. All the while, a remarkable network of blood vessels inside the nose called the carotid rete is cooled by inhaled air so that blood going to the brain maintains a comfortable 36°C.

Gemsboks maintain far smaller ranges than species less suited to arid conditions but resources are thinly spread for all desert species and gemsboks nonetheless cover large distances. Herds of females and their young average a range of about 1000 sq km but like most large antelopes, dominant males are faithful to a much smaller territory. Females moving onto a territory are checked by the resident male for sexual readiness and any in heat are subsequently mated. In prolonged droughts, even males are forced to abandon their home turf and they accompany the female herds. Clashes between males are common and they fight one another viciously with a well-honed stabbing technique but injuries are actually rare. Both sexes also use their horns against predators: there are a few reliable accounts of gemsboks impaling even lions. ∎

Recognition Heavily built antelope; males weigh up to 240kg, females 200kg. Both sexes carry horns, longer and more slender in the females.
Habitat Arid grasslands, rocky deserts and dune fields.
Behaviour Gregarious; females, young and subordinate males form herds up to 30. Larger herds assemble during the rains. Dominant males are usually territorial. Restricts activity to morning and evening to avoid overheating and may be active at night.
Breeding Non-seasonal but births tend to correspond with rains. Single calf is cinnamon-coloured for camouflage.
Feeding Mostly grazes, resorting to leaves and flowers in dry season.
Voice Largely silent except for a deep alarm snort.

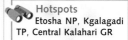
Hotspots
Etosha NP, Kgalagadi TP, Central Kalahari GR

*The **bushbuck** varies greatly; the darkest, least spotted ones occur in coastal KwaZulu-Natal.*

*Female **bushbucks** lack horns and are solitary except when accompanied by a lamb.*

*The male **nyala's** shaggy belly fringe and mane distinguish it from the bushbuck.*

SPIRAL-HORNED ANTELOPES

Antelopes with a twist

Ranging in size from 45kg bushbucks to 940kg elands (inset), this small tribe of antelopes (called the Tragelaphini) are instantly recognisable by their horns. Like all antelopes, each horn is a single unbranched structure but in tragelaphines, it undergoes a gentle corkscrew twist as it grows. There are nine species Africa-wide, five of which occur in the subregion; for all of them, if your antelope comes with a twist, it's one of the tragelaphines.

The tragelaphines are exceptional among antelopes not only for their spiral horns but also their social organization: males never establish territories. Rather than defend a patch and command those females that come onto it, they go directly to the reason for territory – the females themselves. Males wander between female groups and compete constantly with one another for the right to mate. It's a system that has given rise to elaborate displays by which males establish dominance. In the 'lateral presentation' contest, two rivals walk stiffly opposite each other with manes and crests raised, showing off their potency. A flattened body profile and striking white markings enhance the show and although the differences between competing males are typically too subtle for human onlookers to pick, males usually resolve their differences without combat. The most spectacular lateral displays are performed by nyalas (waterholes in KwaZulu-Natal parks are excellent places to witness this) and they're least obvious in bushbucks and sitatungas, in which the females are solitary or form small groups. As opposed to the clustered resource that female greater kudu and nyala herds represent, scattered lone females provoke less male interest and contests between male sitatungas and bushbucks are rare.

Home is where the food is

Spiral-horned antelopes are predominantly browsers but they also have a penchant for fresh grass, a combination which

*In contrast to the dark grey male, female **nyalas** are coloured russet-red.*

Female impersonators

Sexual dimorphism among the tragelaphines (like these sitatungas) is very marked. Apart from the females lacking horns (except elands) and being considerably  smaller, they lack the accoutrements that males use to judge one another's status – dewlaps, manes, crests, beards and dark pigmentation. So too, of course, do the young. In fact, all tragelaphines at birth look exactly like a miniature female. Young males start out looking like their sisters and only begin developing their male adornments at about a year old. By mimicking the females, they avoid the aggressive attention of the constantly competing males until they're old enough to fend for themselves. Ultimately, their maturing maleness will give them away and they'll be evicted from the herd to form small bachelor groups. It usually happens between 12 and 18 months but adolescent elands stay for an extra year or two; perhaps because females have horns, their gender remains inconspicuous for longer.

Elands are the only spiral-horned antelope in which the female also has horns.

Male **greater kudus** have the longest horns of any antelope, reaching 1.8m.

means they inhabit all types of woodlands, from the very open to the very closed. Nyalas and bushbucks rarely venture out of thick bush but greater kudus and elands inhabit open woodlands and tolerate the dry bush of northern Namibia and Botswana.

The exception among them are sitatungas. They're restricted to permanently inundated swamps and marshes, feeding off fresh reed tips. Capable swimmers, they take refuge by submerging and make their way through reedbeds with extremely elongated hooves that spread their weight like snowshoes. Largely solitary and extremely shy, they are very difficult to spot. Like all the tragelaphines, they have a deep, gruff bark given in alarm. It's a giveaway to their position but mostly heard at night; nocturnal boat trips make the calls well worth following but sitatungas disappear beneath the surface when spotlit directly.

Greater kudus browse a wide range of plants, especially Acacia trees.

The spiral-horns breed year-round but most of them have a distinct birth peak; winter for sitatungas, early winter and spring for nyalas and bushbucks, early summer for elands and late summer for greater kudus. All give birth to a single calf (very rarely twins) which in all species, bar elands, lies up for one to two months during which the female visits it for suckling. Perhaps because elands are the most nomadic of the group, their calves accompany the female within a few hours of birth. ∎

Hotspots

Etosha NP Excellent for photogenic greater kudus and elands. **Mkuzi GR** Abundant nyalas, greater kudus and bushbucks, as well as a few elands. **Moremi GR** and **Kasanka NP** Best areas for sitatungas.

Sitatungas are mainly solitary, but females sometimes form small groups.

AFRICAN BUFFALO

Recognition Massive dark brown to black cattle-like bovid weighing up to 800kg. Both sexes have heavy curving horns meeting in a central 'boss', which is massive in the male.
Habitat Open and wooded savanna with suitable grass cover.
Behaviour Mostly diurnal. Breeding herds, comprising all age-sex categories (except old males), occupy home ranges but are non-territorial and tolerate overlap with other herds.
Breeding Single calf born year-round, but birthing peak is during February.
Feeding Mainly fresh grass but also the leaves of shrubs and trees during drought.
Voice A variety of cattle-like lows and bellows.

Killer cows

Buffaloes belong to the same tribe as domestic cattle and indeed, they're Africa's only wild cows. However, despite a basic bovine appearance, the similarity to their docile domestic counterparts is slight and early trophy hunters included buffaloes as the one of the Big Five, the five most dangerous species to hunt. Even so, not all buffaloes are killers. Large herds are fairly relaxed and unlikely to attack except when confronted by a known threat, particularly their main enemy, lions. However, older males usually live away from the herd, alone or in small groups, and are more easily provoked into a charge, perhaps because they lack the safety of numbers. Known as dagha boys, their 'attack is the best defence' tactic makes them extremely dangerous. Take note of the warnings posted at lodges, especially at night; lone males readily stake out a patch of cultivated lawn at sunset and sleep there.

Dagha boys inhabit the fringes of buffalo society but only during the dry season. Following the summer rains, they seek out females for breeding and rejoin the small family groups, which are the basic buffalo social unit. Normally, a number of these units congregate to form huge 'breeding herds' creating a concentration of females worth fighting for. The arriving bulls establish a pecking order with head-tossing, soil-gouging, 'tall-walking' and other ritualised threats. Occasionally, colossal duels are required but a single bone-crunching charge is usually enough to resolve the hierarchy. Best seen during the summer (winter in Moremi GR) when grazing is rich, breeding herds may be a few thousand strong. The massing persists all year when conditions are good but splits into individual family groups during particularly dry winters.

Buffalo herds have fairly predictable movements, seeking out good grazing and water during the early morning and again towards dusk – the best times to view them. As the day warms up, they disappear into thick cover to rest and ruminate. ■

Hotspots
South Luangwa NP, Chobe NP, Gonarezhou NP, Moremi GR (winter)

SOUTHERN & MOUNTAIN REEDBUCKS

Southern ■
Mountain ▬

Reeds versus rocks

The two reedbuck species in Southern Africa look similar but are easily distinguished by habitat. Southern or common reedbucks (below) are found in reeds, floodplains and moist grasslands. In contrast, mountain reedbucks (right) favour grassy mountain slopes and are quite at home on scree-covered hillsides where southern reedbucks rarely venture. Further aiding identification, they're much smaller; the average weight for a mountain ram is about 32kg, less than half the average for southern reedbuck males, which can top 75kg. If you're still unsure, geography is often the decider. Southern reedbucks occur throughout Southern Africa, whereas mountain reedbucks are only found in South Africa and just over the border on Botswana's Manyelanong Hills and Mozambique's Lebombo Mountains. Even so, there is one final obstacle to a positive identification: mountain reedbucks look very similar to grey rhebucks, another mountain dweller. The easiest way to differentiate them is by their horns – curved and forward-facing in mountain reedbucks, pencil-slim and straight in rhebucks.

Differences aside, the two reedbuck species demonstrate their shared pedigree in numerous ways. Both are primarily grazers, appropriate for the large bodied southern reedbucks with their productive habitat rich in new grass, but surprising for mountain reedbucks. Smaller antelopes usually target high-quality browse because their small rumens could never accommodate enough grass to satisfy their energetic needs. Mountain reedbucks overcome this by selecting the freshest, youngest grass growth but during the dry season where there is none, they rely on an over-sized, compartmentalised rumen to extract the most from dry, coarse feed. Both reedbucks also employ a common 'language'. They're mostly silent but their shrill *tzeee* alarm-whistle is very distinctive. Accompanying the call, they raise their tail as they flee, exposing fluffy white underparts like a flag and adopting a stiff-legged 'rocking horse' gait. Both displays signal danger to other reedbucks and might also act to inform a predator that it has been spotted. ■

Recognition Both medium-sized, tawny-grey antelopes. Only males have horns. Southern: Up to 95cm at the shoulder. Mountain: Up to 75cm.

Habitat Southern: Moist, usually low-lying, grasslands. Mountain: Grassy mountain slopes.

Behaviour Territorial males defend small family groups, often pairs in southern reedbucks but up to 8 females in mountain reedbucks.

Breeding Throughout the year, births peaking in summer. Single calf.

Feeding Primarily grasses, small quantities of herbs.

Voice Largely silent except for shrill alarm whistle.

> **Hotspots**
> **Greater St Lucia Wetland Park, Karoo NP, The Drakensberg** (southern); **Pilanesberg NP** (both species)

WATERBUCK

Too apparent for their own good

Although not nearly as aquatic as sitatungas, red lechwes and pukus, waterbucks are never far from permanent water sources. These large antelopes drink daily and prefer the high quality grass that grows along river edges and on floodplains. Their diet brings them out into the open but waterbucks are always close to dense vegetation. Despite their size, they are vulnerable in the open and they are often preyed upon at great levels, considering their numbers. The trend may arise from being overly conspicuous. Waterbucks have a very strong musky smell and a characteristic white ring or patch around the rump, both probably to maintain contact between herd members. But this also means they're easily found by predators (even humans can smell them at a distance) so the beleaguered waterbuck's solution is to take refuge in woodlands.

Small herds and small home ranges are the norm for waterbucks. Females and calves form loosely aggregated groups which overlap in range with other small herds. They are tolerant of familiar animals in the overlapping areas and herd composition can change daily. Lording over the female groups, males are territorial but they tolerate males they know, so long as the trespasser is suitably submissive. ■

Recognition Robust, grey-brown. White rump ring or patch.
Habitat Woodlands, floodplains and riverine forest.
Behaviour Herds of 6–12, occasionally larger.
Breeding Non-seasonal. Birth peak in mid-summer.
Feeding Good quality grasses and browse.
Voice Snorts in alarm.

Hotspots
Moremi GR, Mamili NP, Kafue NP

LECHWE

Life-giving water

The most aquatic antelope after the sitatunga, lechwes are tied to their watery habitat by a number of adaptations. They eat the grasses and sedges that grow in shallow water, which entails lechwes following the seasonally fluctuating water's edge. Tracking good quality graze can lead to extremely high densities and they are the most abundant antelope of permanent wetlands like Botswana's Okavango Delta and Zambia's Bangweulu Swamps.

As well as diet, they rely on water to escape predators. Their dramatically shortened forelegs create a characteristic sloping build – rather slow and awkward on dry land, but swift and powerful in shallow water. Elongated, pliant hooves enhance the advantage (restricting them to soft, water-sodden soils).

There are three races of lechwes, the extremes of which look like entirely different species; the black 'shin-guard' stripes are the key. Red lechwes of the Okavango (pictured), western Zambia and northern Kafue have the least pigment, with black restricted to the legs. In the Kafue lechwe of the Kafue Flats, the black creeps up onto the body in a distinctive shoulder blaze. And most extreme of all, black lechwes of northern Zambia have black on most of their body, fading to russet along the spine and hindquarters. ■

Recognition Medium-large reddish antelope. Males have backward-curving, lyre-shaped horns.
Habitat Floodplains and grasslands near swamps.
Behaviour High variation in herd sizes and composition.
Breeding Single lamb.
Feeding Wetland grasses.
Voice Bleats and snorts.

Hotspots
Moremi GR, Kafue NP (red), Lochinvar NP (Kafue), Bangweulu Swamps (black)

PUKU

Sun worshippers

Water-loving pukus share with lechwes a preference for grasses and sedges that grow in permanently soaked soils. But they're also able to utilise various other foods and unlike lechwes, they venture into woodlands to browse young leaves, flowers and even seeds. Pukus usually spend the early morning and late evening grazing in the open and retreat into nearby woodlands as the day warms up, but they are not averse to spending the entire day in the open. Indeed, the Bemba people of eastern Zambia believe the puku's tough, stringy meat is a result of all the time it spends in the sun.

Common to many African antelopes, the basic structure of puku society is small female herds roaming widely over the territories of lone males. When a herd wanders onto a male's patch, he divides his attention between attending oestrous females and chasing young males. Once their horns begin appearing after their first year, young males are viewed as competition by adult males and are driven out to form non-breeding bachelor herds. Ironically, if they survive, all territorial males will also end up in the bachelor herds as the maturing younger males in turn drive them from their patch. ■

Recognition Impala-sized but stockier and lacks three-coloured coat.
Habitat Floodplains, riverine woodland.
Behaviour Crepuscular.
Breeding Single calf.
Feeding Wetland grasses, forbs, herbs and some browse.
Voice Whistles.

Hotspots
Chobe NP (along the river), **South Luangwa NP**, **Kafue NP**

GREY RHEBUCK

The antelope and the running shoe

With no close relatives, grey rhebucks (or rheboks) are classified in their own unique tribe. Their relationship to other antelopes is hazy but their appearance and morphology suggests distant affinities to both the kob tribe (reedbucks, lechwes and pukus) as well as to sheep and goats. In appearance, they most resemble mountain reedbucks with straight horns and a moderately woolly coat. Ancestry aside, grey rhebucks are endemic to South Africa and Lesotho. They're also an extremely graceful species, running in a reedbucklike, rocking horse motion and leaping fluidly over rocky obstacles. No doubt, this is the reason the South African founders of the Reebok sports company considered them suitably athletic inspiration.

Rhebucks live in small family groups of a few females and their young, usually accompanied by a male harem-master. The males are territorial and aggressive to intruders; their fights are sometimes fatal and they also have a reputation for attacking mountain reedbucks, though this is probably very rare. Their belligerent behaviour extends to protecting the family group and males occasionally even attack baboon troops, presumably because they sometimes prey on lambs. Even so, rhebucks prefer to flee when danger looms, making most sightings distant and fleeting. ■

Recognition Slender medium-sized antelope. Males have narrow, spikelike horns.
Habitat Mountain slopes, plateau grasslands and fynbos grasslands.
Behaviour Diurnal. Forms small herds.
Breeding Single lamb.
Feeding Mostly browses.
Voice Snorts in alarm.

Hotspots
Karoo NP, **The Drakensberg**

BIRDS

EVEN if you're not a birder, it's impossible to ignore the conspicuousness, diversity and sheer abundance of Southern Africa's birdlife. There are around 1075 species here, 938 of which can be spotted if you don't go any further north than the Zambezi River. Zambia, Malawi and the top of Mozambique collectively hold an additional 140-odd species; most are East African inhabitants at the southern limits of their ranges, as well as a few Central and West African specials that just make it into northern Zambia. Regardless of where you go, even without trying, you'll see far more species of bird than mammal.

The key to their ecological success is feathers, a unique adaptation shared by all birds but not by any other creature. Birds evolved from reptiles and feathers from scales; like reptilian scales, feathers overlap to serve as waterproof insulation, but they have further diversified to provide insulation against extreme heat or cold (keeping birds warm enough to maintain a high level of activity), and showy courtship plumes. But as organs of flight, feathers are unsurpassed: they adjust subtly to the lightest breeze and compensate instantly for wind strength, direction and lift. Each group of birds has differently shaped wings to exploit their preferred habitat, and the independence afforded by aerial manouevrability has allowed the evolution of diverse hind legs, with feet adapted, for example, to swimming, grasping or running.

Favourites revisited and endemics galore

Among the bird families with dozens of Southern African members are herons and egrets, thrushes and robins, larks, fly-catchers, warblers and birds of prey. There's also 10 uniquely African families on show: sugarbirds, louries, mousebirds, woodhoopoes, guineafowl, whydahs, oxpeckers, helmet shrikes, and two families each with a single member: the secretary bird and hamerkop. Despite their endemism, most are easy to spot. And groups whose familiar urban representatives usually provoke indifference take on new life here: starlings come in astonishing iridescent and wattled finery; and the sparrow family includes architecturally gifted weavers, flocks of queleas numbering hundreds of thousands and widows with flamboyant tails almost 10 times their body length.

The other undeniable appeal of birds is that the vast bulk of them are diurnal. Except for owls, nightjars and a few others, every species on the list can be relied upon to make daylight appearances. And although dawn and dusk are as fruitful for spotting birds as other wildlife, birds are less troubled than mammals by high midday temperatures. The small size of most birds translates to efficient heat dissipation so many species brave the hottest part of the day when mammals are seeking shady asylum. When you do likewise at lunchtime, rest assured that finches, starlings and hornbills will still be looking for hand-outs around camp, tinker barbets and emerald-spotted doves will be calling endlessly, and vultures will still be riding thermals in their quest for carrion.

If you're a confirmed bird lover, Southern Africa holds obvious attractions. But even if you've never really taken the time to watch birds, you'll probably surprise yourself here. Whether you're sitting in camp trying to identify feathered scroungers at your feet or just filling in time at a waterhole between mammal appearances, birdwatching in Southern Africa holds rewards for everyone. ■

OSTRICH

Recognition Huge bird with long, featherless neck and muscular legs. Loose plumage is black and white in male, grey-brown in female.
Habitat Dry, open savanna, desert and semidesert; not dependent on water.
Behaviour Alone or in groups. Runs from danger; males aggressive to people and predators. Young follow parents for 12 months. Sexually mature at 3–4 years; may live 30–40 years.
Breeding Nest a shallow scrape; about 20 eggs incubated 6 weeks. Chicks run immediately after hatching and form crèches.
Feeding Seeds, fruits, leaves, insects and small reptiles. Sand, stones and even coins and nails are swallowed to help digestion.
Voice Usually silent. Snaps bill and hisses. Breeding males utter a deep, descending boom.

Winning the ratite race

Ostriches don't bury their head in the sand, although they sometimes sit on their nests with neck outstretched along the ground to protect their eggs or chicks. The ostrich is a ratite, part of an ancient group of flightless birds distributed across the southern hemisphere. Being the world's tallest living bird (up to 2.75m) with the largest eyes of any land animal (50mm in diameter), they normally detect danger from afar. That includes you, but these huge birds become fairly used to vehicles in protected areas. Except during breeding, when pairs are the rule, they generally seek safety in small flocks. Watch for chicks trotting at the heels of adults; and look among herds of antelopes or zebras, with which they often mingle to lessen the chance of being surprised by predators. If threatened they're off, clocking up sprints of 70km/h in 3.5m-long strides, and outlasting any predator with sustained runs of 50km/h for up to 30 minutes. In a tight spot, an ostrich can kill a hyena by kicking with its massive feet – the inner claw is modified into a 10cm-long spike.

During his mesmerising courtship display, the male crouches while rotating outstretched wings and swaying his neck from side to side, his neck and legs glowing bright pink. Several females – normally two to five, but up to 18 – lay eggs (the world's biggest, weighing 1.5kg) in the same nest, although only the male and major hen (she who lays first) incubate them, he by night and she by day.

An incredible total of 78 eggs was recorded in one nest, but since only 20 can be incubated at a time, the major hen rolls away those that aren't hers – perhaps recognising her own eggs by the size, structure and shape of pores in the shell. The abandoned eggs become a feast for other animals: hyenas and jackals are partial to ostrich eggs. Hatchlings leave the nest within three days and follow the parents; when two families meet a dispute usually ensues and the winning pair adopts the other crèche – groups of 100 to 300 young occasionally result. ∎

Hotspots
Makgadikgadi Pans NP, Nxai Pan NP, Etosha NP, Hwange NP

JACKASS PENGUIN

Ecstatic brayers

One of four penguin species that occur in African waters, the jackass or African penguin is the only one restricted to the continental shore (the rest are Antarctic and sub-Antarctic species). It's also a Southern African endemic and breeds only on approximately 18 offshore islands and a handful of mainland locations. It occurs from the Mozambique/South African border, all the way around to northern Namibia, but most birds (and the most visible ones) live on the western coast.

Their common name arises from the male's donkeylike bray, which can be heard continually in the colonies when the penguins are breeding. It forms part of the male's 'ecstatic' courting display, in which he points his bill skywards and holds his flippers out horizontally like a plane's wings. Building to a crescendo, he heaves his breast at an attentive female and then lets fly with a raucous braying chorus. It's obviously an infectious display as nearby birds readily take up the call, setting off a chain of braying with each bird calling for up to a minute. Jackass penguins breed year-round but for the best chance of seeing the ritual en masse, try dawn and dusk during early summer (November to December).

Jackass penguins forage close to shore, setting out in small groups to hunt for small fish, like anchovies, crustaceans and squid. They cruise along on the surface, each bird performing constant head-dipping checks for prey, until, with target spotted, the group dives as one. They are superb swimmers and underwater chases sometimes top 20km/h.

Like many small penguin species, jackasses nest in colonies and lay their eggs (usually two but sometimes one) in burrows or between rocks; where humans have built near colonies, the penguins often nest under buildings or jetties. Egg and guano harvesting (which disturbs the nests; now banned), as well as oil spills and depletion of fish stocks have reduced their numbers, but they are still locally common and a few of the colonies are extremely tame. At The Boulders near Cape Town, penguins have the right of way and swim unconcerned among human bathers. ∎

Recognition Black upperparts, white underparts with black ring in between. Stout grey-black bill, black face and bare pink skin over eye. Length 60cm.

Habitat Offshore islands and a few mainland beaches.

Behaviour Forages mostly by day, usually in groups. Roosts and breeds in large colonies. Elaborate 'ecstatic display' performed by courting male.

Breeding Mainly in summer. Lays 1–2 eggs, usually in a burrow.

Feeding Fish, small crustaceans and squid.

Voice Donkeylike braying, honks and growls. Chicks hiss when threatened.

Hotspots
The Boulders, Bird Island (Lambert's Bay), **Dassen Island, Robben Island**

PELICANS, CORMORANTS & DARTER

*Only a few **white pelican** colonies exist in the region, but each may number thousands of birds.*

*The **crowned cormorant** is found only along the west coast from Cape Town to Swakopmund.*

Darters dry themselves in the sun, but also sunbathe before swimming on cold mornings.

Fishing armadas

At first glance, the varied members of this order of birds don't appear to have much in common with one another. But apart from their water-loving habits, all of them share throat pouches, webbed feet, and non-functional nostrils sealed off by bone. Most conspicuous of the group, pelicans have very prominent pouches; checking the pouch colour is the easiest way of distinguishing the two species: bright yellow in the eastern white pelican, flesh coloured in the pink-backed (inset). In the breeding season, the pouch becomes particularly colourful. In summer, pelicans are often seen pulsating their pouch to cool off.

Cooperative feeding in pelicans is a fascinating sight: up to 40 pelicans form a horseshoe and simultaneously dip their bills in the water to drive fish into the shallows; in a river they form parallel rows and move towards each other with a similar effect. With their prey effectively 'corralled', each pelican scoops fish and up to 13.5L of water into the pouch; the water is then forced out through the closed bill and the fish are swallowed.

Southern Africa's five cormorant species also hunt fish, as well as frogs, crustaceans and octopuses. But unlike pelicans, they mostly feed alone, chasing their prey on prolonged dives, which may last for a minute. The exception to the rule is the Cape cormorant, which targets pelagic baitfish schools and feeds in flocks that may number in the thousands. The Cape's gregarious behaviour is often an effective method for telling it apart from the endemic bank cormorant, also found along the coasts but a loner; if in doubt, check for naked, yellow skin around the Cape's bill. Another endemic species, the crowned cormorant has a small crest, which it typically holds erect.

Restricted to freshwater, the darter is an underwater swimmer extraordinaire. But rather than pursue their prey, darters use their powerful webbed feet to cruise slowly beneath the surface. They hold their wings partly outstretched, inviting fish to take shelter beneath them, then spear them with a dagger-shaped bill. ∎

Hotspots

Greater St Lucia Wetland Park and **Moremi GR** Breeding colonies of both pelicans, plus darters and white-breasted and reed cormorants. **Bird Island** (Lambert's Bay) Cape, crowned, white-breasted and bank cormorants. **Namib-Naukluft Park** (Sandwich Lagoon) Both pelicans and four cormorant species (Cape, crowned, white-breasted and bank).

*The **white-breasted cormorant** is the only species found in both marine and freshwater habitats.*

CAPE GANNET

Depth chargers

Related to pelicans and their kin, Cape gannets breed in just six colonies scattered around the Cape and Namibian coasts. But they disperse widely from these population hubs to forage and may be seen in huge flocks anywhere around the Southern African coastline; indeed, young birds leave the colonies after fledging and may stay at sea for up to three years, dispersing as far as Kenya in the east and the Gulf of Guinea on the west coast.

For really extraordinary viewing, the colonies during the breeding peak are hard to beat. A few adults remain year-round, but from about July huge numbers return to find their mates. Cape gannets are monogamous and renew their ties with long-term partners by elaborate fencing, bowing and mutual preening displays, and continue them throughout the breeding season. Locating partners is no doubt helped by fidelity to the nest site: Cape gannets return to the same colony each year and nest in the same small space. Both sexes help build a hollow-topped mound on their little patch, reinforcing guano with seaweed and sticks. One egg is laid (rarely two) from about September through to December and both adults share incubation, feeding and guarding of the chick. Their gentle 'devotion' to one another and the chick does not extend to neighbours and they constantly threaten and jab nearby birds.

As spectacular as the mayhem of the colonies, Cape gannets feed in flocks that may number in the thousands. Large shoals of baitfish, such as pilchards, anchovies and juvenile mackerel, are attacked by high-speed plunge-dives from as high as 30m. In fact, they are so good at locating the shoals that fishing fleets have used the gannets as a beacon for good fishing: commercial exploitation of the gannet's fish-finding abilities actually resulted in a crash of pilchard numbers in the 1960s. Various gannet colonies were affected by the decline; some of those off Namibia are still decreasing but most other colonies are stable. ■

Recognition Large white seabird with yellow-orange head and neck, black tail and primary feathers. Sexes are alike but males are larger. Length 85cm.

Habitat Offshore islands; fishes in coastal and open waters.

Behaviour Gregarious and monogamous. Many elaborate displays occur in colonies, most to do with breeding, territorial disputes, or as appeasement to hostile neighbours. Usually feed by day.

Breeding Mainly in summer. One egg laid in guano mound. Both parents care for the chick.

Feeding Small shoal fish; also offal from fishing boats.

Voice Rasping *hara-hara-hara* the most common call.

Hotspots
Bird Island (Lambert's Bay), **Bird Island** (Algoa Bay), **Malgas Island** (western Cape)

HAMERKOP

Supernatural shape-changer

Related to the herons and storks, and commonly seen in their company, the hamerkop's distinctive profile earned it an Afrikaans name meaning 'hammerhead'. During courtship, and often at other times, hamerkops engage in a unique 'false-coupling' behaviour where one bird sits on the back of another (male or female) – mating doesn't always occur and birds may even face in opposite directions. Feeding is more conventional: prey is snatched from shallow water; and fish are skimmed from the water's surface while the bird flies into a headwind. For unknown reasons the hamerkop makes a massive nest of twigs, sticks and even bones, usually in the fork of a tree, in which is secreted a brood chamber accessible only through a narrow tunnel. These huge constructions can weigh 40kg and be 1.5m deep; not content with one, some pairs have been known to build and abandon several nests in close proximity – giant eagle owls and barn owls readily take over their vacant nests. But perhaps the hamerkop has got it all sorted out: with so many nests to choose from, a would-be predator probably stands more chance of facing a genet, spitting cobra, monitor lizard or bee swarm (all of which use abandoned nests) than the bird itself. With such tenants in their nests it's no wonder that Africans imbued hamerkops with supernatural powers. ■

Recognition Bronze-brown. Crest offset by heavy bill. Length 50–56cm.
Habitat Lakes and rivers.
Behaviour Usually solitary, roosting in groups. Associates with large mammals.
Breeding Lays 3–6 white eggs year-round.
Feeding Frogs and fish.
Voice Strident yelping *yip-pur, yip-yip-pur-pur-yip*.

Hotspots
Moremi GR, **Victoria Falls NP**, **Lengwe NP**

SHOEBILL

Plunging headfirst

Also known as the whale-headed stork, the shoebill's most striking feature – its bulbous, cloglike bill – measures some 19cm in length and is almost as wide. This unique bird occupies a taxonomic family all of its own. However, it shares with herons the habit of flying with neck retracted; has a small crest at the back of its head like a pelican; and shows storklike behaviour, such as emptying bills full of water on the nest to cool its young. Although it looks like a large, silver-grey stork, it turns out that pelicans may be its closest relatives. This solitary and stately bird is avidly sought by birdwatchers, even though most of the time it stands waiting for prey stock-still and stiff-legged on floating vegetation or at the water's edge. Lungfish are its favourite meal and it's worth watching its technique, for when a likely victim surfaces all hell breaks loose: the massive bill is jerked forward, causing the bird to overbalance, collapse and submerge its entire head. Using its wings and bill it then levers itself upright, manipulates vegetation out of its mouth and swallows the victim – usually decapitated by the bill's sharp edges. Accuracy is everything, for its bill cannot usually be manoeuvred for a second strike. Incredibly, this unconventional and all-or-nothing fishing method is also practiced in flight on occasion – the bird collapsing bodily into the water. ■

Recognition Large (1.2m high), storklike, blue-grey bird with massive bill.
Habitat Papyrus swamps and marshy lakes.
Behaviour Solitary. Walks on floating vegetation.
Breeding Lays 1–3 blue-white eggs during main rains.
Feeding Mainly fish.
Voice Bill-clapping at nest.

Hotspots
Bangweulu Swamps, **Kasanka NP**, **Vwaza Marsh WR**

HERONS, EGRETS & BITTERNS

All niches great and small

Most of the 19 species of heron, egret and bittern in Southern Africa are common and easily recognised, but different enough to make watching them worthwhile. All have long legs, toes and necks, and dagger-shaped bills; differences are chiefly in coloration and size, although the all-white egrets can be difficult to tell apart: bill and leg colour are useful clues. At times the picture of still grace, at others angular and seemingly brittle, all are deadly hunters of fish, frogs, rodents and other small animals. The long neck can be folded in a tight S-shape (and is invariably held thus in flight) and the piercing bill strikes with speed and accuracy to harpoon prey.

Most species feed at water margins and at least one is usually present at every waterway, including mudflats and mangroves;

several species can feed side by side without competing directly and their techniques are interesting to watch. All hunt by posing stock-still for long periods before striking, some even from a perch; other techniques include running, stirring mud with their feet or flapping their wings to startle prey. The 1.5m-tall goliath heron (inset), the world's largest member of the group, spears fish farthest from shore; the 30cm-long green-backed heron snaps up tadpoles and insects. The black egret has an amazing 'cloak-and-dagger' technique of spreading its wings in a canopy over the water then spearing fish that shelter beneath it. Night herons are nocturnal; bitterns are solitary, well-camouflaged inhabitants of dense reed beds. Several species of heron and egret attend locust plagues to feed on the insects, and cattle egrets snap up insects disturbed by buffaloes and elephants.

During courtship, several species of heron, egret and bittern grow long, fine plumes, and patches of bare facial skin change to intense colour. Watch for preening behaviour: herons comb their plumage with a special serrated claw on the middle toe. Usually silent, herons often make harsh territorial calls at the nest; most species also nest communally and heronries can be noisy places. Most species also roost communally, flying sometimes great distances in V-shaped flocks at dusk. ∎

Hotspots

Moremi GR Excellent for multispecies heronries. **Lochinvar NP, Bangweulu Swamps, Vwaza Marsh WR** and **Nylsvlei NR** Good for seeing a wide variety of species. **Chobe NP, Victoria Falls NP** and **Phinda Resource Reserve** River cruises are recommended for great views of several species.

Watch for the amazing 'canopy' fishing technique of the **black egret**.

Green-backed herons are most often seen under overhanging vegetation at the water's edge.

The widespread **great white egret** is the largest of Southern Africa's six egret species.

Black-headed herons are often seen away from water on grasslands and cultivated areas.

Abdim's storks arrive in the region between October and April, often in huge flocks.

Male saddle-billed storks have brown eyes; females have bright yellow eyes.

Like the vultures they compete with, marabou storks have bare faces for scavenging carrion.

Most yellow-billed storks are nonbreeding visitors, but some are resident in the Okavango.

STORKS

Stately sentinels

Stately and often colourfully marked, storks are generally found near wetlands, although some species are far less dependent on water for food resources than other waterbirds. Superficially similar to herons, they share with them long legs, toes and neck, although storks generally have thicker necks and an overall bulkier body shape. All storks fly strongly with necks outstretched; they can often be seen soaring high in thermals, where their distinctive bill shapes make identification fairly easy. Marabou and saddle-billed storks are among the largest of flying birds, the latter with a 2.7m wingspan.

All eight species found in Southern Africa are predominantly white, black or black-and-white, and all have large bills adapted to a carnivorous diet consisting of small animals such as frogs, fish and rodents. The more generalised feeders, including white and Abdim's storks, use dagger-shaped bills to snatch insects, small rodents and reptiles; saddle-billed storks jab at fish in the shallows; and yellow-billed storks find aquatic prey in muddy water by the touch of their long, sensitive bill. Marabou storks, the most predatory, have a massive 35cm-long bill used to pick over carrion and slay other

animals, including birds as large as flamingos. Most specialised of all is the open-billed stork, an all-black species with a distinctive tweezer-shaped bill, which it uses to remove snails from their shells.

White storks (inset) are famous in Europe for arriving en masse in spring and nesting on rooftops; large flocks return to Southern Africa between November and March. The arrival of another migrant, Abdim's stork, is usually associated with rains. Of the resident species, only woolly-necked and saddle-billed storks are solitary nesters; all others nest in colonies, sometimes in association with herons or cormorants. All species construct large, untidy platforms of sticks in trees, often near or over water, in which they lay their eggs. After the chicks have hatched, adults empty bills full of water over them to keep them cool. Marabous have an unusual habit of defecating on their legs to cool off – a habit they share with vultures. ∎

Hotspots

Etosha NP and **Moremi GR** Flocks of open-billed, white and Abdim's storks arrive between October and April. **Moremi GR, Victoria Falls NP** and **Lochinvar NP** Yellow-billed, saddle-billed, woolly-necked and marabou storks are widespread and resident.

IBISES & SPOONBILLS

Sacred waterbirds

Essentially waterbirds, the ibises and spoonbills are biologically akin to herons and storks by dint of their long legs, toes and necks; the differences lie mainly in the shape of their sensitive bills. The most obvious feature of spoonbills – a flattened, spoonlike bill – is swept from side to side as they feed on microscopic water creatures, filtered through fine sieve-like lamellae. The bills of ibises are not flattened and curve strongly downwards – adapted for probing the mud for prey. Despite their different bills (and the fact that spoonbills are more tied to wetlands), the two groups are close relatives: occasionally ibises are seen sweeping their bills from side to side and spoonbills poking in soft mud.

The African spoonbill is commonly seen in shallow, slow-moving waterways, often in the company of other waterbirds.

*In Afrikaans, the **sacred ibis'** name means 'chimney sweep bird' due to its black head.*

Spoonbills and most ibises nest colonially in trees (often in association with herons, storks and cormorants), where they build untidy stick nests.

Ibises use their long, bowed bills to probe for crustaceans, snails and tadpoles. The most widespread species of ibis commonly forages on lawns and grasslands, and adapts readily to agriculture: on occasion it has averted devastation to crops by consuming large numbers of plague locusts. In fact, this common, black-and-white bird was worshipped by ancient Egyptians, who associated its migration with the arrival of the fertile floodwaters of the Nile River every year: it is accurately depicted on wall friezes and mummified specimens have been found in ancient tombs, and to this day it is known as the sacred ibis. While sacred ibises are gregarious waterbirds, nesting in colonies and flying to communal roosts in V-shaped flocks at dusk, pairs of hadeda ibises nest alone and often feed well away from water. The hadeda's (inset) brash *ha-haha* call is one of the most distinctive sounds of the savanna, especially at dusk and dawn, and can be heard even in the parks and suburbs of large cities. At the other extreme, the southern bald ibis is the rarest species in the region, restricted to highveld grasslands and mountains. The glossy ibis is similar to both, with predominantly iridescent green plumage, but is rarely seen away from water. ■

*The endemic **southern bald ibis** is the region's rarest ibis, numbering an estimated 3000 birds.*

***Glossy ibises** are rarely far from water and specialise on frogs, crustaceans, leeches and worms.*

***African spoonbills** are nomadic and nest sites change from year to year.*

Hotspots
Moremi GR, Kafue NP, Kruger NP and **Mamili NP** Home to all species bar the southern bald ibis. **Itala NP** and **The Drakensberg** High slopes and cliffs here are the best places to seek southern bald ibises.

■ Greater only
■ Greater & Lesser

GREATER & LESSER FLAMINGOS

Flocking pink

Masses of pink birds shimmering through the heat haze – audible but inaccessible across fields of treacherous mud – make a tantalising sight, and early Christians considered the flamingo to be the Phoenix, the legendary red bird that rises from the ashes of its own funeral pyre. Flamingos are instantly recognisable by their combination of pink coloration, and long, slender neck and legs. Where the two are found together, the pale pink greater flamingos (below) tower above the deep rose-pink lessers (left).

Few large birds are as gregarious as flamingos: great numbers concentrate in shallow lakes too alkaline or saline to support fishes (which otherwise compete for the tiny water animals or algae sought by flamingos); and food resources occur in such quantities that competition between individual birds is limited. Flamingos may spend hours standing or floating motionless, but their distinctive and characteristic feeding method makes them unique among birds: typically, flamingos walk through shallow water with head upside-down and submerged, sweeping their angular bill from side to side. Food is caught in lamellae (bony filters) and excess water and mud are forced out by the tongue acting as a piston. Enormous quantities are consumed in this way – 100,000 flamingos account for 18 tons per day – and it is from the algae that flamingos receive their pink coloration.

Recognition Greater: Tall (1.5m) white or pale pink with long pale pink legs and S-shaped neck. Lesser: Shorter (90cm); deeper pink with darker bill and red legs.
Habitat Salt lakes, estuaries and coastal lagoons.
Behaviour Highly nomadic and gregarious. Flock-synchronised courtship. Flies with neck and legs fully extended.
Breeding Irregular, usually June to July for lesser. Single egg, normally laid on a semiconical nest of mud surrounded by water on inaccessible mudflats.
Feeding Greater: Aquatic insects, crustaceans and molluscs; some algae. Lesser: Mostly algae. Both filter food by sweeping the beak from side to side underwater.
Voice Gooselike honking; constant low murmuring while feeding in flocks.

Courtship rituals are conducted en masse: hundreds or thousands of birds elongate their necks and twist their heads in unison, stretch their wings and legs, and strut through shallow water before abruptly changing direction. These displays synchronise hormone production and ensure a colony takes simultaneous advantage of optimum conditions to raise their young. Breeding colonies can be densely packed and are mostly protected from predators by their location on muddy islands, but breeding sometimes fails catastrophically: rising water levels can wipe out an entire season's efforts, or conversely the lake may dry up leaving young without food or protection. ■

Hotspots
Etosha NP, Namib-Naukluft Park (Sandwich Lagoon), **Makgadikgadi Pans NP** (Nata Sanctuary), **Greater St Lucia Wetland Park**

DUCKS & GEESE

Dabbling and diving, grazers and dippers

Thanks to their long history of domestication, few birds are as universally recognisable as ducks and geese (collectively known as waterfowl); indeed, few groups are so uniform, with a broad, flattened bill at one end and strongly webbed feet at the other. Several of the 16 resident (including the endemic South African shelduck, inset) or nomadic species grace nearly all lakes, swamps and rivers, and three migrant species from northern Europe – familiar to many birdwatchers – swell local numbers from November to March. The most common species are easily identified by their bill colour. All ducks and geese are adapted to an aquatic life, with insulating down beneath waterproof feathers; and most are strong flyers, taking off explosively, and quickly attaining fast, level flight (among the fastest of flying birds) with neck outstretched. Food is typically vegetation and small invertebrates. Each species of waterfowl occupies slightly different feeding and breeding niches, and thus coexists without direct competition.

The differences in feeding behaviour make fascinating viewing. The so-called dabbling ducks (including red-billed teals and yellow-billed ducks) up-end in shallow water, paddling like mad to stay under and grazing weed from the bottom. In deeper water, Maccoa and white-backed ducks dive for a living, propelled by legs set well back, and swim with bodies low in the water. Geese are primarily grazers, pulling grass sometimes far from water. The African black duck inhabits forest streams and rivers, and even alpine tarns, where it dips its head to take prey from under submerged stones. Southern Africa's smallest duck, the pygmy goose, measures only 30cm long and is at home diving among floating lilies.

Many ducks and geese are nomadic, often covering vast distances to reach new waterholes as old ones dry out. When conditions are favourable, breeding is usually prolific and numbers can build up quickly. Most are solitary breeders, laying in nests the female often lines with down. Young hatch covered in cryptically marked, waterproof down, and can walk and swim almost immediately, following their parents around and catching their own food. ∎

The male **knob-billed duck's** 'comb' is most developed in the breeding season.

The **white-faced duck's** high-pitched whistles are usually given in flight.

The most common goose in the region, the **Egyptian goose** is belligerently territorial.

African pygmy geese are found on quiet waterways with floating vegetation.

Hotspots

Lochinvar NP, Bangweulu Swamps, Greater St Lucia Wetland Park, Nylsvlei NR and **Moremi GR** All common species and occasional northern migrants can be seen here. **Karoo NP** and **Daan Viljoen Game Park** Good for Southern Africa's only endemic species, the South African shelduck.

*The **black-shouldered kite's** hovering hunting method is a giveaway.*

***Tawny eagles** vary from uniform chocolate brown to a pale golden colour with dark wingtips and tail.*

*The rocking flight of the **bateleur** evokes a tightrope walker's balancing act.*

BIRDS OF PREY

Raptor round up

Southern Africa has around 70 species of birds of prey (or raptor) from three distinct families: the falcons; the eagles, hawks, harriers and vultures; and the secretary bird. In open savanna, at least, it is not unusual to see several species in the sky at once, or perched on the same tree. They reach their greatest diversity in the region in semiarid lands, although several species are found in every habitat. Most are fairly plainly coloured in earth tones, although some are adorned with showy crests and contrasting belly plumage.

Raptor-watchers should look for huddled, dark shapes on topmost boughs (larger species take longer to get going, and finish hunting earlier in the day, because they depend on thermals for gaining altitude and soaring). Note large, bulky nests in which an incubating bird may be sitting low with its mate perched nearby; listen for small birds (such as drongos) mobbing; and watch for large hawks drying their outstretched wings on exposed perches after a storm. Other giveaways include antelope legs wedged into branches (eagles' handiwork), piles of feathers where a bird has been plucked, and 'whitewash' below nests on cliffs. Rubbing a piece of styrene foam on glass to imitate a distressed rodent can have spectacular results; and watch for grass fires, from which hawks seize fleeing animals.

Let us prey

Varying in size from pigeon-sized sparrowhawks to mighty eagles with a 2.5m wingspan, nearly all raptors are exclusively carnivorous, with talons to grasp or snatch prey, and a hooked beak for tearing flesh. Raptors have incredible eyesight, spotting a grasshopper at 100m and a hare at 1000m. Woodland hawks are usually on the move with the dawn and insect-eating raptors start out once the sun makes their prey more active. Sparrowhawks and goshawks feed primarily on birds caught in mad dashes through foliage. Snake eagles sit and wait for hours on a perch then drop onto snakes, which they kill and then swallow whole. The gymnogene or African

*The **Gabar goshawk** preys mainly on small woodland birds but also takes francolins.*

Masters of the air

Falcons are voracious predators that mainly kill birds on the wing, although there are exceptions: kestrels hover and pounce on small

animals, and pygmy falcons subsist on insects. Like other raptors, falcons have powerful talons superbly adapted for seizing prey, and a strongly hooked bill. But in flight they show their true mastery, their long, narrow wings scything through the air in quick beats, picking up speed as prey is approached and building to a deadly crescendo in dives known as stoops. Falcons are among the swiftest of birds (although such statistics are rarely measured accurately and doubtless have been exaggerated). The 16 species certainly have few enemies, save larger falcons (such as the lanner falcon pictured), and none normally builds a nest, using instead cliff ledges and the abandoned nests of other birds – the 20cm-long pygmy falcon is smaller than the buffalo weavers whose old nests it uses!

Dark chanting goshawks typically scan for lizards and snakes from a prominent perch.

The *augur buzzard's* all-white underparts are very distinctive for the species in Southern Africa.

harrier hawk (inset opposite) has long legs with which it reaches into nests, cavities and under bark for prey, even hanging upside down from weavers' nests to extract chicks and eggs. Harriers methodically quarter grasslands, gliding on long, slender wings and dropping onto mammals and birds – their facial feathers, like those of some owls, are arranged in a disc, which heightens their hearing. And there are many other hunting strategies: bat hawks swallow bats whole in midair; black eagles haunt cliffs and koppies for dassies; crowned eagles snatch monkeys from the forest canopy; and the martial eagle can bring down a small antelope and carry it back to a perch.

Each species has a different proportion of wing length to breadth, which in turn determines aerobatic manoeuvrability and speed. Thus, the broad wings of forest hawks help them manoeuvre through branches and foliage; and the great eagles have long, broad wings on which they can glide to great heights and distances. Instead of elaborate plumage, raptors rely on dramatic aerial displays during courtship – such as free falling while grappling talons, and passing prey to one another while one bird flies upside down. Most aerobatic is the bateleur (from the French for 'acrobat'), a consummate glider that in courtship displays performs fast rocking motions on the wing. Hawks often display late in the morning – watching for this behaviour is a good way to detect forest hawks. ∎

Unusually, *long-crested eagles* have no defined breeding season and lay when food is abundant.

Hotspots

Etosha NP, **Kruger NP**, **Hwange NP**, **Moremi GR** (especially Khwai region) and **Kgalagadi TP** All excellent for raptor-watching; dozens of species from sparrowhawks to eagles, as well as pygmy falcons in arid parks. **The Drakensberg**, **Augrabies Falls NP** and **Karoo NP** Cliffs are home to black eagles and several species of falcon.

The mighty *martial eagle* is powerful enough to take storks and small antelopes.

SECRETARY BIRD

A voracious pedestrian

Stalking across grasslands with jerky precision and standing 1.2m high – tall enough to be seen from hundreds of metres away – this high-stepping bird of prey is unique to Africa. Its body, head and hooked bill resemble those of a large eagle, but it differs from other raptors in a number of ways. For example, its legs are three times as long as those of a 'conventional' raptor, jacking it up to an ideal vantage point from which to look for a meal.

The secretary bird is known to stride up to 20km a day in search of prey, which it kills with a rain of swift kicks from its thick, powerful feet. When a snake is encountered – and dangerous vipers and cobras are attacked with relish – it is stamped to death in a lethal 'flamenco' audible from some distance away. Speed and agility are the keys to handling venomous prey – their legs are heavily scaled and secretary birds angle their body away from danger until their victim is subdued. Small prey is swallowed whole – that includes snakes, but also eggs, chicks, entire wasps' nests and golf balls (by mistake); larger items are torn apart or cached under a bush for future reference.

The secretary bird's long, black crest flaps in the breeze and is said to resemble the quill pens worn behind the ears of 19th century scribes; another theory attributes the name to 'saqur-et-air', French-Arabic for 'hunting bird'. Despite the secretary bird's obvious eaglelike features, aspects of its behaviour point to other possible origins. Its long legs suggest a common ancestry with storks, and other storklike traits include extending its neck in flight, and head-bowing and bill-clapping displays between pairs at the nest. But their courtship flights are very raptorlike, and include 'pendulum displays' where one bird drops in a graceful swoop from a great height with wings folded then pulls out of the dive to climb slowly and repeat the show. Pairs also tumble in midair with feet outstretched towards each other. ■

Recognition Uniform grey with black 'thighs', flight feathers and loose crest. Bare orange facial patch and deep pink legs and feet. Long central tail feathers and outstretched legs obvious in flight.
Habitat Short grasslands with scattered thorn trees; common in agricultural land. Avoids hilly or rocky country.
Behaviour Usually solitary or in pairs, but groups may gather at locust plagues or bushfires. Nests and roosts on flat-topped acacias. Soars high on thermals. Kicks at tufts of grass or dung for prey. Regurgitates large pellets near roosts and nests.
Breeding Lays 1–3 eggs, usually in wet season; only one chick survives and fledges after 2–3 months.
Feeding Mainly large insects and spiders, but also reptiles, birds up to small hornbill size, small mammals (such as rodents, hares, mongooses and small cats) and carrion.
Voice Generally silent; a deep guttural croaking in displays, fights, at nest and in flight.

Hotspots
Central Kalahari GR, South Luangwa NP, Matusadona NP, Pilanesberg NP

AFRICAN FISH EAGLE

The voice of Africa

Whether perched at the top of a *Euphorbia*, head and breast glowing white, or sweeping low on a dive, few birds beg superlatives like this magnificent wetland predator. African fish eagles are common and in places live in comparatively high densities: along the Chobe River, pairs can occur every kilometer. At some sites, such as Lake Kariba, fish eagles have learned to take fish thrown into the air by boatmen. At first light their loud, ringing calls echo across lakes and river valleys – a sound so distinctive and recognisable that the fish eagle is known as 'the voice of Africa'. Pairs sometimes duet from perches, throwing their heads back until they are bent almost double.

Recognition Pure white head, breast, back and tail contrast with rich chestnut belly and 'trousers', and black wings. Bill black with yellow base. Length 75cm.

Turbot-charged pirate

Closely related to the bald eagle of North America, fish eagles look regal wherever they perch, but these voracious raptors are so effective at fishing they can (and often do) spend as much as 90% of the day resting or preening. A hungry fish eagle stares intently at the water and, when a likely fish is spotted, makes a fast, sweeping dive, at the last second throwing its legs and huge talons forward to seize its slippery catch. Most prey consists of surface-feeding fish taken within 15cm of the top of the water, although if necessary it will plunge in bodily to a depth of 50cm. The largest catch recorded is 3.7kg, but anything over 2.5kg can't be lifted and must be dragged or 'rowed' with one foot through the water to shore. Any fish it can carry are consumed at leisure at a favourite perch.

Habitat Widespread near lakes, rivers and estuaries (occasionally forest); immature birds may wander far from water.

Behaviour Adults pairs sedentary and intensely territorial when breeding; may reuse the same nest for 10 years. Groups gather at fish strandings. Immatures may form loose non-breeding populations. Will cross large arid areas to reach isolated waterways.

Breeding Usually lays 2 eggs in large nest of sticks and papyrus near water. Chicks

Fish eagles also rob other birds (and each other) of their catch: victims of their piracy can be as large as pelicans, herons and storks, or as small as pied kingfishers. Occasionally, they also prey on waterbirds, killing birds as large as flamingos; more rarely, they take terrestrial prey like monkeys, dassies and monitors. ∎

fledge at 65–75 days.

Feeding A large variety of fish and waterbirds (especially young birds); also scavenges dead fish and carrion (immatures may be seen at predators' kills).

Voice A loud yelping *weeah*, *kyo-kyo-kyo-kyo* from a perch or in flight.

> **Hotspots**
> Chobe NP, Moremi GR, Bangweulu Swamps, Mana Pools NP, Kruger NP

VULTURES

The **Egyptian vulture** is locally very rare and has bred only once in the region.

Scavenging angels

Think of the great grasslands and the nightly carnage left by lions and hyenas, and you'll also probably get an image of squabbling flocks of gore-encrusted vultures eating the stuff few animals will touch. And fair enough, because with few exceptions that's basically what they do. Should they need any introduction, vultures are birds of prey adapted to eat carrion, their chief difference to other raptors being a usually bald head and neck (it's easier to feed and keep clean that way), and feet better suited to walking than grasping. It may not be an appealing way of life to us, but it's an extremely profitable niche to exploit.

Look for these great, bulky birds sitting at the top of acacia trees and on large, exposed branches – larger species are usually solitary. Although ungainly on the ground, all have long, broad wings superbly adapted for long spells of soaring, and by midmorning these large birds are usually circling high on thermals. Vultures have a poor sense of smell, instead using their keen eyesight to follow other vultures and eagles, or scavenging mammals on the ground, that might lead them to a kill. If vultures are circling in the air over a carcass it's usually a sign that predators are still chewing away at it; if you're on foot, beware.

Hooded vultures feed on insects, droppings and carrion, and are rare outside main reserves.

Carrion carry-on

Early morning is not usually a vulture's best time. After a cold night on the plains they take a while to get airborne owing to a lack of thermals, especially on an overcast day. Hunched up, most of the eight species are difficult to identify as anything other than vultures, but in flight their various features are more apparent. Larger species usually take precedence at a carcass

The diagnostic feature of **whitebacked vultures** can be difficult to see.

Cape vultures can consume a kilogram of meat in three minutes.

Bone-crusher

Despite its name, which means 'lamb vulture', and great size (having a 2.5m wingspan), the lammergeier (pictured) probably doesn't kill lambs. In fact, it rarely kills anything in the rugged gorges and alpine areas it frequents. Like all vultures, it is a scavenger, but rather than tearing at flesh (something it could easily do with its hooked bill and curved talons), it eats whole bones and scoops out the marrow with its tongue. It particularly favours large leg bones, and any too large to be swallowed are dropped from a height of about 20 to 80m onto a well-used, flattish area of rock (called an ossuary) until they smash or splinter. Ravens in alpine areas have also been seen trying this trick, although they can't seem to manage it as well as their mentor. Also known as the bearded vulture, because of its black, bristly 'beard' of feathers around the beak, the lammergeier is Africa's rarest vulture.

White-headed vultures usually locate a carcass, but are often displaced by later arrivals.

although smaller vultures may gang up and chase them away; and each species is specialised to feed differently and thus has different headgear. White-headed vultures and the largest species, the lappet-faced (inset, opposite), tear open a carcass, eating the skin, as well as bones and sinews. They pave the way for vultures with a long, bare neck (Cape and white-backed) to reach right into the guts to eat soft parts without getting their feathers caked in blood; they will even climb inside a rib cage. The comparatively small hooded and Egyptian vultures can't compete with larger species, instead grabbing scraps from the frenzy; crows and marabou storks also loiter for morsels.

Vultures may fast a week between kills, but it's not all gore and blood lust. Hooded vultures pick over human refuse; Egyptian vultures steal birds' eggs and smash them on the ground, and have learned to break open ostrich eggs with a rock. The boldly marked palmnut vulture is superficially similar to the African fish eagle (and may in fact be closely related), and like it eats fish and crabs. But, despite its hooked bill, this extraordinary vulture feeds mainly on the protein-rich nuts of *Raphia* palms, a food source sought after by many birds and mammals. All vultures are attentive parents, commuting up to 160km in a day in the search for carcasses before returning to the nest with food. ■

The white-headed vulture is solitary and nests on tree-tops in thornveld and savanna.

The palmnut vulture's ancestry is disputed and it may be more closely related to eagles.

Hotspots

Kruger NP, Hwange NP and **Moremi GR** Top spots for vultures because of high concentrations of predators and prey. **Ndumo GR, Moremi GR** and **Kosi Bay NR** Best chances for palmnut vultures. **Manyelanong GR** and **Waterberg Plateau Park** Colonies of Cape vultures. **The Drakensberg** Only place in the region for bearded vultures (lammergeiers).

The white-backed vulture is easily the most common vulture in Southern Africa.

*The yellow eye-ring of the **red-billed francolin** distinguishes it from other species.*

***Shelley's francolins** occur on grassland, open woodland and adjacent agricultural areas.*

*The **crested francolin** is most commonly seen along park roads throughout the region.*

*The **red-necked francolin** prefers dense habitat, but often feeds on clearings and farmland.*

FRANCOLINS

Chickens crossing the road

Francolins belong to the great taxonomic grouping of birds loosely known as 'game birds' – the pheasants, quails, partridges and jungle fowl (precursors of the domestic chicken), which have been the butt of hunters' activities for centuries. And it's not just humans – small cats and other predators readily stalk francolins. But these ground-dwelling birds are great survivors: they are abundant and come in many varieties. Francolins nest on the ground (although the retiring habits of some species mean that their nests are as yet unknown), and the downy, precocial chicks are well camouflaged and can run within hours. Walking (and running) are strong francolin traits – all species have stout legs and feet, and run fast to evade predators – only when push comes to shove will they take to the wing, flying low for a short distance before dropping to the ground again.

The basic francolin design is like a large, upright quail, with heavily streaked upperparts in greys, browns and black for camouflage. Some, eg, red-necked and Swainson's (inset) francolins, sport naked flesh on the face and neck, which enhances their territorial displays. All have a strong, hooked bill useful for snatching small animals, picking up seeds and fruit, and digging for bulbs. Like domestic hens, many rake the soil and leaf litter with their strong feet, and cocks of most species sport spurs on their legs.

Although a few species occur across Asia, Africa is the centre of diversity for francolins, and the 15 species found in Southern Africa range in size from 28 to 42cm. Many are common and a day's birding in any reserve is bound to encounter at least one species. Francolins often feed along roadsides in the early morning and late afternoon, or dart across the road in single file. Two of the most abundant – Swainson's and crested – are decidedly chickenlike, and are commonly seen standing atop termite mounds or roadside banks. Savannas and grasslands with thornbush in particular are their stronghold, although a few (such as grey-wing and red-wing francolins) inhabit the alpine meadows of The Drakensberg; and other species (eg, Hartlaub's francolin) are specialised to life in rocky deserts. ∎

> **Hotspots**
> **Moremi GR, Kruger NP, Hwange NP** and **Kafue NP** All the common species. **Waterberg Plateau Park** and **Etosha NP** Good for the endemic Hartlaub's francolin. **Cape Peninsula NP** Cape francolin (endemic). **The Drakensberg** Red-wing, grey-wing, Natal and red-necked francolins.

GUINEAFOWL

Quintessential ground birds

Both Southern African guineafowl species are immediately recognisable by their boxlike shape and black plumage punctuated by tiny white spots. Their bizarre headgear distinguishes them: the crested guineafowl sporting a dishevelled mop of black feathers, and the helmeted guineafowl a bony casque like a top hat.

Guineafowl are opportunistic feeders, consuming a wide variety of small animals such as insects and small vertebrates; and plant matter such as seeds, fruit, berries and bulbs – and they're not averse to raiding crops. They also swallow grit to aid digestion. Helmeted guineafowl gather in flocks to drink, and they associate with mammals, ranging from rhinos to mongooses, whose presence presumably flushes potential prey. Their relationship with baboons is less benevolent, for each tries to steal food from the other, but watch for the forest-dwelling crested guineafowl picking up scraps dropped by troops of monkeys moving through the canopy. ∎

Crested guineafowl pair up when breeding, but otherwise form flocks numbering up to 30.

Helmeted guineafowl can fly strongly when danger threatens, but rarely stay aloft for long.

> **Hotspots**
> **Chobe NP, Addo Elephant NP** and **Hwange NP** Helmeted guineafowl occur throughout the region but try these reserves for good views. **Mkuzi GR, Mamili NP** and **Matusadona NP** Good for crested guineafowl.

BLACK CRAKE

Waterside opportunist

Crakes and rails almost exclusively exploit the cover and feeding opportunities provided by dense stands of reeds or rushes fringing slow waterways. The downside is that they have a reputation for being difficult to see among the forest of stems (often remaining invisible while calling near an observer). However, the black crake is an exception and this common bird is readily seen on virtually any Southern African wetland.

Black crakes have a similar shape and size to most other crakes and rails, with a rather slender body (hence the expression 'thin as a rail'), strong legs and feet, and a short bill. Using reeds as cover, crakes typically feed on mud exposed at the water's edge, darting back to cover should danger threaten (the best way to see most species is to wait patiently for one to make its nervous feeding forays onto the mud). In contrast, black crakes often feed in the open for extended periods, and readily use hippos' backs as stepping stones (although they can fly and swim well). Like most of the family they feed on a variety of small animals, ranging from worms and snails to insects, tadpoles and frogs. But black crakes also scavenge from carcasses; perch on warthogs' backs to pick off parasites; and climb waterside trees to steal birds' eggs and chicks. ∎

Recognition Slatey black. Pale green bill. Red legs, feet and eyes. Length 20cm.
Habitat Vegetation beside freshwater lakes and swamps.
Behaviour Walks on floating vegetation.
Breeding Lays 3 eggs.
Feeding A variety of small animals; some seeds.
Voice Harsh *krrok-krraaa*.

> **Hotspots**
> **Moremi GR, Vwaza Marsh WR, Lower Zambezi NP, Nylsvlei NR**

*Rarest of Southern Africa's cranes, the **wattled crane** is endangered in the region.*

***Blue crane** life has two distinct phases: summer resident pairs and winter nomadic flocks.*

*Diagnostic features of the **blue crane** include a large head and long, slender neck.*

CRANES

Regal trumpeters

The three Southern African cranes hardly need superlatives – suffice to say, they are among the most elegant birds in Africa, and the national birds of numerous African countries for good reason. In the region, South Africa has claimed the blue crane as its own. Like all cranes, this Southern African endemic forms flocks during the nonbreeding season but pairs off with a long-term partner to mate. In fact, careful observation of nonbreeding flocks usually reveals they are made up of many couples, the members of each pair staying close together.

It's no wonder that cultures around the world associate cranes with longevity and fidelity. Pairs of southern crowned cranes stay together until one dies: they preen each other's golden crest (inset), perform loud duets and dance in spontaneous displays of head-bobbing, bowing, stick-tossing and high leaps with wings outstretched.

One pair's exuberance will stimulate others in a flock to leap into the air, and up to 60 birds have been seen dancing together for a few minutes before settling down again to feed.

The rarest crane in the region, the wattled crane, rarely forms flocks larger than 40 in Southern Africa and most observations are of pairs. Common to the crane family, both parents care for the offspring, but wattled cranes only have one chick (other species have two or three) and breed every 14 months, rather than annually; their slow reproductive output is one reason they are declining.

All cranes favour moist grasslands and wetlands, where they forage for rodents, frogs, small reptiles, insects, grass seeds and rhizomes (underground stems). Of all the species, blue cranes are the most tolerant of habitat modification and are able to occupy farmlands. In fact, they are often more common on the agricultural lands surrounding parks than in the parks themselves, something to bear in mind when crane-spotting. Blue cranes often nest on open grassland or in fields but the other species have their chicks in wetlands and marshes. However, they often commute to nearby plains to feed, sometimes grazing en route or stamping the ground to scare up insects. ■

Hotspots

Austin Roberts Bird Sanctuary Very visible blue cranes. **The Drakensberg** One of the few areas where all three species may be seen together. **Bangweulu Swamps** and **Lochinvar NP** Very good for crowned and wattled cranes. **Moremi GR** Wattled cranes are relatively common.

*Unlike the mottled eggs of other cranes, **southern crowned cranes'** eggs are a pale unmarked blue.*

BUSTARDS & KORHAANS

Strutting their stuff

Although all bustards and korhaans (an Afrikaans name for the seven smaller members of this family) can fly strongly should the need arise, they are consummate walkers – some would say strutters, because their habit of pointing their bill upwards as they walk away from an intruder gives them a dignified, even aloof, air. Southern Africa is a bustard-watcher's haven with 10 species on show, half of them endemic to the region. Two or three species are common in suitable habitat, but they can be hard to see as, despite their conspicuous size, they are typically decked out in greys and browns that camouflage them among the muted tones of the grasslands, and they don't allow close approaches. Binoculars are a must, especially to tell apart the females of different species, which are similarly marked. The chicks and eggs are also superbly camouflaged –

*The male **red-crested korhaan** mates with many females and has no part in raising the chicks.*

all species nest on bare open ground or in grass tufts where cryptic colouration is the main defence against predators.

The kori bustard is the biggest species (closely followed by Stanley's, inset) and Africa's heaviest flying bird, weighing up to 18kg and with a wingspan of 2.8m. Despite having long legs, its rather small feet render it incapable of perching in trees; look for it peering over the top of the grass. It's probably also the least shy species though it certainly cannot be called confiding – no matter how slow and sensitive your approach, koris will always keep a minimum distance of 30 to 40m. Like many bustards, they are especially fond of toasted insects and small animals, and are readily seen gathered at grassfires where pickings are good. Freshly mown wheat fields and other cultivated areas are also rewarding places to look.

***Rüppell's korhaan** occurs only on the gravel plains of the Namib Desert and into southern Angola.*

The best time to watch bustards is during courtship: the male kori puffs out his white throat feathers in a huge bulging ruff, flips up his startling white undertail feathers and booms loudly. Ludwig's bustard performs a similar routine, the white feathers of his display obvious from great distances. The male black-bellied korhaan stands atop a termite mound and launches himself into the air, falling back to earth as if dead, with wings held high and neck arched back, his black belly standing out. ■

*The **black-bellied korhaan** hides when alarmed and slinks off in high grass to avoid danger.*

Hotspots
Nxai Pan NP Red-crested and black korhaans and obvious kori bustards. **Karoo NP** Kori, Stanley's and Ludwig's bustards and Karoo korhaans. **Mountain Zebra NP** White-bellied, blue and black korhaans. **Namib-Naukluft Park** Try here for very elusive Rüppell's korhaans, also kori and Ludwig's bustards.

*Often alone or in pairs, the **kori bustard** may form small groups outside the breeding season.*

AFRICAN JACANA

Recognition Chestnut body, white face and breast. Blue bill and 'shield'. Length 30cm.
Habitat Swamps and lakes.
Behaviour Gregarious outside breeding season.
Breeding Lays 2–5 eggs on floating vegetation.
Feeding Insects and small water animals.
Voice A harsh rattle.

Hotspots
Bangweulu Swamps, Moremi GR, Lake Malawi

Walking on water

Competition for resources is keen at the water's edge, but few birds have adapted to life 'on top' of the water, and none as successfully as the jacanas. Jacanas live virtually their entire life afloat: hugely elongated toes spread their weight so they can run across water lilies, Nile cabbage and other floating masses, as well as soft mud, when walking on submerged vegetation, jacanas can appear to be walking on water. Alternatively, the back of a hippo makes a good vantage point. At a pinch they can dive and fly (clumsily) with legs dangling.

Most bodies of still water with lily pads or other floating vegetation will have a few jacanas (although they can be hard to see if a dropping water level has caused the shadows of drooping lilies to break up the view); watch for the blue headgear, wing stretches and jacanas in flight (they often give their harsh call in flight). The sexes look alike, but jacanas reverse their traditional roles: any aggression is likely to be from a female defending her territory; and all parental care is by the male. The chicks can walk soon after hatching, but the male carries them under his wings for protection and even moves the eggs in this manner should rising water cause the destruction of the nest. ■

SPOTTED DIKKOP

Recognition Fawn upperparts spotted with brown. Long yellow legs. Length 45cm.
Habitat Grasslands, woodland and rocky semiarid country.
Behaviour Hesitant gait.
Breeding Lays 2 eggs.
Feeding Insects, crustaceans and amphibians
Voice Musical *pe-pe-pe-peou-PEOU-PEOU-pee-pi.*

Hotspots
Kruger NP, Phinda Resource Reserve, Hwange NP

Wader that walks by night

Among the many offshoots from the large shorebirds group is a small family of mainly nocturnal waders known as dikkops (Afrikaans for thick-head, which, given that they do have a large head, makes more sense than their alternative name, 'thick-knees' – their 'knees' are barely thicker than those of other birds). Large for waders, long-legged and equipped with very large eyes, dikkops hunt insects and other small animals at dusk and after dark with rather ploverlike 'walk-pause-peck' behaviour. Spotted dikkops are commonly encountered on tracks at night, but during the day rest in dry areas under bushes; when accidentally flushed from cover their large size and sudden appearance can be startling. Normally when danger approaches they crouch down, lying flat on the ground with neck extended; another tactic is simply to walk away and blend in with the countryside. Males and females are thought to mate for life and both care for the young; their nest is a shallow scrape on the ground sometimes lined with vegetation, stones or animal droppings. As with most waders, spotted dikkop chicks can walk soon after hatching, their down blending superbly with rocky soil when they lie flat to avoid detection (the water dikkop is reputed to lay its eggs near basking crocodiles as a deterrent to predators). ■

SHOREBIRDS

Migrants and homebodies

Every spring and summer, thousands of small- to medium-sized shorebirds (commonly known as waders) arrive in Southern Africa to spend the northern winter on coastal mudflats and freshwater swamps. Among them are some long-distance champions – stints, sandpipers, curlew, redshanks and the greenshank – which breed as far away as the Arctic Circle and make a trip of several thousand kilometres twice annually. All but one (the Ethiopian snipe is resident in Southern African marshes) take advantage of the mild climate to regain condition after the rigours of breeding and migration.

The loose term 'shorebirds' also covers several closely related families, not all of whom make these exhausting round trips and many of which are attractively marked. For example, the black-winged stilt and avocet are black-and-white, and both species are common on shallow inland waterways. The stilt's coral-pink legs are matched only by those of flamingos for length in proportion to body size; while the avocet's distinct upturned bill is used to scythe through shallow water for aquatic insects and crustaceans.

Plovers also commonly fall under the 'wader' umbrella although many species are found far from water and most are year-round residents. Several large species are often seen on savanna game drives and act as sentinels of the grasslands, protesting loudly at the approach of any intruder – animal or human. All plovers (eg, the three-banded plover, inset) have a compact body, large head and short, blunt bill. With comparatively long legs, the larger savanna-dwelling species tower above most others, while the smaller species – which tend to stay near the muddy edges of waterways – look decidedly 'dumpy' but run quickly. Savanna specialists eat mainly large insects, but the long-toed plover forages on floating vegetation. Several smaller plovers feed on shorelines and mudflats among other waders; they include some long-distance migrants from the northern hemisphere such as golden and grey plovers, which 'winter' in Southern Africa from October to April. ∎

One of the most common plovers, the **blacksmith plover** is easily spotted near freshwater.

The **avocet's** pied plumage and upturned, black bill make it unmistakable.

The nocturnal **bronze-winged courser** feeds late into the night on termites, crickets and beetles.

Hotspots

Namib-Naukluft Park (Sandwich Lagoon) Huge summer influxes of waders, especially curlew sandpipers, sanderlings and little stints; as well as Arctic, Sandwich and common terns. **Skeleton Coast NP** Some 20,000 to 30,000 Palaearctic waders arrive here in summer, joining resident species such as the white-fronted plover. **Wadrif Saltpan** (Lambert's Bay) Summer visitors include American and Pacific golden plovers, and pectoral sandpipers.

The **black-winged stilt's** highly elongated pink legs distinguish it from all similar species.

AFRICAN SKIMMER

Cuts like a knife

Of the three species of skimmer found worldwide, only one is found in Africa. They are usually seen sitting on sand bars, their heads pointing into the wind in the company of gulls and terns (their close relatives). On close inspection, skimmers reveal an extraordinary feature: the lower half of their bill extends 1 to 3cm beyond the tip of the upper one. While it may look deformed, it is actually a superb design for a unique fishing technique: flying in a straight line some 5cm above the surface, the skimmer's lower mandible slices through the water at a 45-degree angle while the mouth is held open, snapping shut the instant it comes in contact with a fish (an action that whips the head round under the body).

In cross section the skimmer's bill is extremely narrow and so streamlined – to reduce drag in the water – that it can skim while gliding. The lower jaw grows faster than the upper one, and is worn away by abrasion with sand and objects underwater – young birds learning to skim sometimes practice on sand by mistake. Because this is a tactile and not a visual technique, skimmers can fish at dusk and even on the darkest nights (they're best seen heading out to feed around dusk). To compensate for bright reflections a skimmer's pupils narrow to a slit like cats' eyes, unlike those of any other birds. ■

Recognition Black upperparts, pure white below. Large scarlet bill tipped yellow. Length 40cm.
Habitat Broad waterways.
Behaviour Breeds in colonies. Some populations migrate.
Breeding Lays 2–3 spotted eggs in sand scrape.
Feeding Skims for fish.
Voice A repeated, sharp *kip*.

Hotspots
Lower Zambezi NP, **Chobe NP**, **Lake Malawi**

*Male **Namaqua sandgrouse** have a double chest-band and uniformly coloured face.*

SANDGROUSE

Painted water carriers

Unrelated to grouse, although they do look superficially like stocky, painted pigeons (if you ignore the long, pointed tail of some), sandgrouse are primarily birds of semiarid country. The four species are essentially ground birds, eating mainly seeds picked up while walking in pairs or small flocks. Subtle patterns of buff, tan and black disrupt their outline, and the well-camouflaged eggs are also laid on the ground. Strong, pointed wings enable them to fly away from danger and to survive in even the most arid country (if food is available) by transporting them long distances – they will travel up to 20km daily to reach water. Although common enough in suitable habitat, the best way to see sandgrouse is to wait by a waterhole at dawn or dusk, when flocks drift in to drink. Wave after noisy wave lines up at the water's edge, each bird dipping its bill for a few seconds before taking off again. Watch for males bathing – what they're actually doing is using modified belly feathers to soak up water; they then return to the nest and allow the chicks to suck the moisture from the feathers. ■

Burchell's sandgrouse is the least sexually dimorphic species; males (pictured) have a grey face.

Hotspots
Moremi GR, **Central Kalahari GR**, **Etosha NP** and **Kaudom GR** All species at waterholes. **Chobe NP** (especially Savute region) Large flocks of double-banded and Burchell's.

PIGEONS & DOVES

Secrets of success

It would be hard to credit the lives of such ostensibly gentle creatures with any sort of drama, but when it comes to feeding, courting and mating (all of which most pigeons and doves do a lot of) they are as competitive as any other birds. This successful family is represented by 16 species in Southern Africa, although many of the ubiquitous doves and turtle doves look very similar and pose some tricky identification problems for birders. Several of these mainly ground-feeding birds, including Cape turtle (inset), red-eyed and laughing doves, will commonly be seen walking along tracks at the edge of grasslands. More colourful species, such as the African green and Rameron pigeons, are also common but feed on fruit in trees.

All pigeons and doves fly well – the doves and turtle doves often breaking from just under your front wheels. Explosive

take-offs are one of the secrets of their survival, along with good camouflage and loose-fitting feathers, which often leave a would-be predator empty-handed.

They also have a rapid reproductive turnover: most species are prolific breeders (in fact it's all some of them seem to do, and you'll probably see a few bowing and cooing as a preliminary to mating). Their nests are usually just a formality – a loose, untidy platform of twigs, although some nest on rock ledges – but the parents have a legendary propensity to sit tight on the nest, deserting a clutch to a predator only at the last second. And the young grow faster than just about any other birds, developing for the first few days of life on a highly nutritious solution ('pigeon's milk') of digested seeds from the crop of the parent – a trait pigeons and doves share with parrots.

Like those of waterfowl and a few other domesticated birds, the calls of pigeons and doves are famous, and many are variations on the familiar cooing. Although similar, once recognised the calls are a useful aid to identification. Forest-dwelling species can be much harder to pin down among dense foliage, but look for them at dawn winging across the canopy or sitting high on exposed snags, something they may do for long spells. ■

The **Namaqua dove's** long tail makes it unique among African pigeons and doves.

The **African green pigeon** is especially common among riverine fig forests.

Probably Africa's commonest native pigeon, **rock pigeons** are common in built-up areas.

Like all pigeons, **laughing doves** feed their young by regurgitating 'pigeon's milk'.

Hotspots

Nyanga NP A dozen species including blue-spotted wood doves, Delegorgue's and Rameron pigeons. **Hluhluwe-Umfolozi GR** and **Mkuzi GR** Good for cinnamon doves and 10 other species. **Nyika NP** Eleven species and the only site in the region with records of dusky turtle doves.

Rosy-faced lovebirds are restricted to most of Namibia and South Africa's northern Cape.

Meyer's parrot is the most common parrot in the region and easily seen in woodlands.

PARROTS & LOVEBIRDS

Loud colours of the forest

The popular conception of parrots screeching across the African sky is a bit misleading: they certainly screech and all are brightly coloured, but only seven species are found in Southern Africa. Virtually every aspect of parrot biology is related to life in the trees. Strong feet and claws – arranged with two toes pointing back and two forward – grasp food and clamber through foliage. Their distinctive, hooked bills crush nuts and tear bark apart, and act as a 'third leg' when climbing; food is manipulated with the strong, thick tongue while being held in the feet. Their bright colours, so obvious in flight, provide camouflage by disrupting their outline among greenery and blossom. And nests are usually in tree hollows where the eggs are safe from all but monkeys, snakes and a few tree-living mammals. Parrots often alight on exposed perches to take the early sun and are often noisy when feeding – when a threat appears, the birds fall silent only to explode from the foliage in a burst of colour. ■

Hotspots
Etosha NP Two semiarid zone endemics – Rüppell's parrots and rosy-faced lovebirds – as well as Meyer's parrots. **Victoria Falls NP** and **Mamili NP** Black-cheeked lovebirds. **Lower Zambezi NP** Has Lilian's lovebirds and Cape parrots. **Ndumo GR** Good for brown-headed parrots.

CUCKOOS & COUCALS

Parasitic parents

Although the trait of laying eggs in another bird's nest is not unique to cuckoos, few other birds are as adept at shirking the burden of parenthood. And with around 15 species in Southern Africa alone, their diversity reflects the success of 'nest parasitism'. Although most are common, some aspects of their behaviour are still a mystery. During courtship, males typically call for hours on end and even at night. Females lay their eggs in the nests (usually one per nest) of the 'host' species. Upon hatching, the cuckoo chick evicts the rightful eggs or chicks and is raised by the unsuspecting parents. Cuckoos typically choose a species much smaller than themselves for this role, but such are the joys of parenting that the adult hosts (often tiny songbirds, such as warblers) don't seem to realise that their pride and joy is many times their own size. Exceptions to the parasitic rule are the six species of coucal, large, mainly ground-dwelling cuckoos that build their own nests and incubate their own eggs. ■

The diederik cuckoo is widely distributed and the only cuckoo found in very arid regions.

Hotspots
Kafue NP Fifteen species including white-browed and coppery-tailed coucals. **Liwonde NP** Holds chances for 18 species including barred and Madagascar lesser cuckoos. **Mkuzi GR** and **Kruger NP** Good views of all common species and green coucals in Mkuzi.

The white-browed coucal is readily distinguished by its white eyebrow.

LOURIES

Tree turkeys

Unique to Africa, louries reach their greatest diversity in the equatorial rainforests further north (where they're known as turacos), but five species occur in Southern Africa. Two of them, the purple-crested and grey, are widespread and easy to see, but the other three species are restricted to dense forest (Knysna and Ross' louries) or can only been seen in a few sites in far northern Zambia (bare-faced go-away bird).

*The **grey lourie** repeatedly raises and lowers its crest when alarmed.*

The grey lourie is a guaranteed sighting on safari, and unlike most of the group inhabits dry woodlands and semiarid habitat. But like its forest-dwelling relatives, it moves about branches and foliage with agility, running speedily along branches and hopping nimbly from perch to perch. It's also the most drably marked of all the louries: uniformly smoky grey with olive tinges visible up close. At first glance, the purple-crested lourie (inset)

may appear similarly drab, if darker, but through binoculars its colourful, metallic violet and green plumage comes to life. In flight, flashes of deep scarlet under the wings are a further surprise and an ID giveaway. Most impressive of all, the Knysna or green lourie is decked out in iridescent green with red primary feathers and a helmetlike crest with white tips. In South Africa, the

*Difficult to see in its dense habitat, listen for the **Knysna lourie's** loud kok kok kok call.*

crest is a modest affair but the further north you go, the longer it becomes. The Knysna louries of Zambia and Malawi (locally called Schalow's louries) have crests rivaling those of cockatoos.

All louries are almost exclusively vegetarian, eating fruits (especially figs), leaves, flowers and buds. Grey and Knysna louries are also on record as taking insects, many eaten inadvertently on fruit as well as the occasional intentional catch. Most species leave the trees to drink or bathe and large parties of grey louries can be seen drinking at pools; despite their tolerance for aridity, they have to drink regularly. Louries are highly vocal birds, and the raucous calls of the forest species may set off a chain of responses throughout the canopy. The grey lourie's nasal *g'way, g'way* is impossible to miss in dry savannas and gives rise to its other name, the go-away bird. Calls are one of the tricks to locating louries, particularly the forest species, and once recognised, they will be found to be quite common. ∎

__Purple-crested louries__ often perch conspicuously, permitting excellent views.

Hotspots

North Luangwa NP Four species, including occasional sightings of bare-faced go-away birds. **Nyanga NP**, **Ndumo GR** and **Mkuzi GR** Grey, Knysna and very visible purple-crested louries. **Kruger NP** Grey louries and many camp sites excellent for purple-cresteds. **Moremi NP** Abundant grey louries and occasional sightings of Ross's louries.

__Livingstone's lourie__ is the most common lourie in Malawi's denser forests.

OWLS

*The **African scops owl** occurs in two colour varieties; the grey form (left) is more common.*

***Giant eagle owls** can often be spotted on relatively open perches during the day.*

*The **barred owl** is probably the least common owl species in the region.*

*The **spotted eagle owl** is the most commonly observed owl, particularly at dusk.*

Creatures of the night

Most owls are primarily nocturnal and no group of birds is more successful at hunting at night. They're armed with grasping talons, hooked bill, and soft plumage for silent flight. But their greatest weapon is a disclike arrangement of facial feathers that funnels sounds to their hypersensitive ears. In some species, like the barn owl, the ears are asymmetrically positioned with one slightly lower and further back on the head than the other: this enhances the ability to pinpoint the source of the softest noises and owls are able to hunt in absolute darkness.

All owls are carnivorous. Rodents are the preferred prey for most species but the giants of the group, the eagle owls, take mammals up to the size of a vervet monkey. The largest African owl, the giant eagle owl, has even been observed killing its close relative, the spotted eagle owl. Small owls, like the pearl-spotted and wood owls, concentrate on insects. Specialist feeders include the African scops owl, which takes a high percentage of scorpions in its diet; and Pel's fishing owl, which hunts fish along rivers – even wading to do so.

Admirable though their nocturnal lifestyle is, it usually makes seeing owls considerably more difficult than hearing them. Fortunately, several of Southern Africa's 12 species are comparatively common. During the day, savanna-dwelling eagle owls, such as the pink-lidded giant eagle owl, can sometimes be located during the day by the mobbing behaviour of smaller birds. Not surprisingly, most owls are best seen by spotlighting: blundering about at night with a torch won't produce much, but by driving slowly the eyeshine of one or two species can usually be picked out. Spotted eagle owls are often on the move at dusk, their bulky silhouettes standing out against the sky; and wood owls sometime hawk for insects around lodges. Clusters of pellets at the base of trees or cliffs are usually a sign of owls: four species (barn, grass, African scops and white-faced, latter inset) regularly regurgitate the undigested remains of prey. Take note of any accumulations and, if possible, return there at dusk or night for a chance to view the owners. ■

> **Hotspots**
> **Kruger NP** Night drives hold excellent chances for up to 10 species including barred owls. **Moremi GR** Abundant Pel's fishing owls, often seen at dusk, and eight other species. **Pilanesberg NP** Night drives see grass, white-faced, and marsh owls as well as all three eagle owls (Cape, spotted and giant). **Kgalagadi TP** Seven species including abundant white-faced owls, which roost in the rest camps.

NIGHTJARS

Masters of daytime camouflage

On a night drive you're virtually guaranteed to see a few nightjars taking off from the track before you. These nocturnal hunters share with owls soft plumage for silent flight, but unlike owls all are essentially aerial hunters that locate insects with their large eyes and snap them up in flight with their wide gape. Nightjars have weak feet and a small body but long, usually slender wings; most roost and all nest on the ground, a trait for which the birds are superbly camouflaged. Nightjars cannot hunt effectively in dense forest: watch for them hawking in clearings and over fields or grasslands. The problem with nightjars is getting one of the seven species to sit still long enough to look at, although if you're very lucky you may spot one on the ground during the day. Even if you do, identification is extremely difficult for all but a few and is more reliably made by their distinctive calls. The exception is the pennant-winged nightjar, in which the breeding males have extraordinary 50cm feathers trailing from their wings. ■

The **fiery-necked nightjar** inhabits wooded areas and gardens, and calls while perched in a tree.

Hotspots
Kruger NP Six species; far north good for pennant-winged and rufous-cheeked. **Mamili NP** and **Ndumo GR** Try these reserves for the Natal nightjar. **Augrabies Falls NP** Freckled, rufous-cheeked and European nightjars. **Pilanesberg NP** Night drives excellent for five species.

The small **Mozambique nightjar** is commonly seen sitting on roads at night.

LITTLE SWIFT

Aerial sprinters

Swifts share a similar body plan to swallows (having streamlined bodies and long, narrow wings) owing to their similar lifestyles – although the wings of swifts are more scythe-like and they are faster fliers. Despite being close lookalikes, the two groups are not closely related. Like swallows, swifts feed in groups, scooping up insects (their sole food) on the wing – look out for them in vast, swirling 'towers' containing thousands of birds moving ahead of storm fronts to hawk insects that hatch with changes in humidity.

There are 13 species of swift in Southern Africa, but one you're sure to see is the widespread little swift. Ironically, it owes its success to humans: it normally nests on cliffside overhangs or caves but our buildings and bridges provide it with ideal and abundant crannies. From being a fairly uncommon species prior to European colonisation, it is now probably the most common swift in Africa.

Like all the family, little swifts are among the fastest of birds, mobbing their only rivals, falcons, with an insouciance that highlights their supreme skills of flight. They are highly gregarious, foraging in large flocks, often with other species of swift. Their colonies may number over 100 nests, but in rafters and eaves, nests are usually solitary. ■

Recognition Dark plumage with white rump patch. Length 14cm.
Habitat Anywhere with cliffs, gorges, hillsides. Also built-up areas.
Behaviour Gregarious.
Breeding Lays 1–3 eggs.
Feeding Aerial insects.
Voice Very vocal, high-pitched chitter.

Hotspots
Kruger NP, Victoria Falls NP, Etosha NP, Lower Zambezi NP

Speckled mousebirds are great fruit-lovers and often seen in orchards and fruit plantations.

Hanging from convenient perches in the early morning helps speckled mousebirds to warm up.

The bare red patch around the red-faced mousebird's eyes sets it apart from other species.

MOUSEBIRDS

Hanging garden birds

Mousebirds are endemic to the African continent, and have an engaging and comical habit of hanging from branches and wires. A mechanism on their toes locks the feet in position and the articulation of their legs means the feet are held at 'shoulder' height when hanging. Mousebirds are largely vegetarian, and it is thought that hanging in the sun warms their belly and helps them digest food. But during sleep (something they do for up to 12 hours) their metabolic rate can fall by 90% and so they also like to warm up in the early morning – pairs even warm each other by hanging breast to breast.

There are three mousebirds species in Southern Africa and all are highly sociable, living in family groups numbering around eight to ten. They fly with apparent discipline in single file from one bush, only to crash-land in the next. Their flight – whirring wing beats alternating with direct glides – looks fast but actually isn't. Strongly hooked claws help them to clamber about in trees. Large groups may visit a single fruiting tree, a trait that doesn't endear them to gardeners. Garden pests or not, their resemblance to mice is owed to the texture of their soft, hairlike feathers; and to their habit of running fast along branches, up tree trunks and along the ground, long tail trailing behind. When threatened, mousebirds hang in dense vegetation, dropping to the ground to hide if necessary, then climbing back up when danger passes.

Group members cluster together at various times during the day and even nesting is a social affair: chicks are fed by the parents and by young birds from previous broods, which act as helpers. And adding to so many unique features is the extraordinary behaviour of the chicks: when about 10 days old they start toying with nest material; once they leave the nest they play games with other young birds (such as running, wrestling and chasing), and also engage in head-shaking, sudden leaps, mutual feeding, building nests and manipulating leaves or twigs.

All three Southern African mousebirds overlap in distribution but the speckled lives mainly in the well-watered east; the white-backed mousebird replaces it in the arid west; and the red-faced mousebird (inset) is distributed over the entire region. ■

The white-backed mousebird is the most likely species to be spotted in arid country.

> **Hotspots**
> **Karoo NP** All three species, sometimes in association. **Etosha NP**, **Namaqua NP** and **Augrabies Falls NP** Visible white-backed and red-faced mousebirds. **Hluhluwe-Umfolozi GR**, **Kruger NP** and **Gonarezhou NP** Abundant speckled and red-faced mousebirds.

KINGFISHERS

The hole story

Common in most habitats, Southern Africa's 12 species of kingfisher include the world's largest and smallest species, but the basic form doesn't vary: all have a large head with long, pointed bill, compact body and very short legs. During the breeding season, pairs make vocal displays to each other and to defend their nest – woodland kingfishers are particularly aggressive, chasing away other hole-nesting birds, small hawks and even people. But at other times, and despite their bright coloration, most savanna and forest species are easily overlooked because of their habit of perching motionless for long spells – until a large insect or small lizard walks by, in which case it will be suddenly dived upon, taken back to the perch and bashed repeatedly to remove its legs, wings or pincers before being swallowed whole.

*The **grey-hooded kingfisher** is a common summer arrival in the region from September to April.*

Kingfishers also use the diving approach when bathing and hunting by crash-landing in water. Pied, malachite, giant and a few other kingfishers are usually easier to see because they usually dive from exposed perches near water, such as overhanging branches, jetties and boats. The abundant pied kingfisher (inset) can also be seen hovering over water up to 3km from land. To catch fish, amphibians and crustaceans, kingfishers have eyes that adjust instantly from daylight to underwater vision, but they must also learn to judge depth, refraction and the likely escape route of their quarry: watch for kingfishers bobbing their head to take aim before diving.

*The **woodland kingfisher's** constant trilling helps to locate this fairly elusive species.*

The pied kingfisher is the only species that roosts and nests communally – sometimes alongside colonies of bee-eaters – and one in three pairs has helpers that assist with feeding young and defending the nest. All kingfishers nest in holes and their short legs are ideal for scuttling along narrow tunnels. Usually they dig a tunnel in a sand bank (a record 8.5m-long tunnel was dug by a pair of giant kingfishers), but smaller species may nest in the sides of aardvark burrows; tree-nesting species always enlarge an existing hole; and woodland-dwelling kingfishers excavate arboreal termite mounds. After the chicks fledge, adults may be seen feeding them outside the nest for a few days. ■

*The **malachite kingfisher** targets tiny fish and aquatic insects while perched on waterside vegetation.*

Hotspots
Greater St Lucia Wetland Park Ten species including pied, giant and mangrove kingfishers. **Moremi GR** Mokoro rides excellent for close-up views of malachite and pygmy species. **Kafue NP** Eleven species including occasional sightings of shining blue and blue-breasted kingfishers in the north.

*The **giant kingfisher** is twice the length and five times the weight of any other African kingfisher.*

BEE-EATERS & ROLLERS

A visual feast with aerobatic feats

As colourful as kingfishers – and closely related to them – bee-eaters and rollers are bird highlights of any safari. Their glowing range of colours are a delight to the eye and a relief from the greens and browns of the savanna, especially for travellers from higher northern latitudes, where bright colours among birds are comparatively rare.

African bees have a fearsome reputation, but being such an abundant food resource it was inevitable that at least one group of birds should tackle them. Bee-eaters appear to do so with relish, and have reached their greatest diversity in Africa; 10 species occur in the southern region. All are very similar in size (mostly 20 to 25cm in length) and shape: streamlined with pointed, down-curved bills and long, swallowlike wings. But their habit of perching on exposed branches to watch for likely prey makes them easily seen and identified, and their antics and bright colours make them a pleasure to watch.

Many species hunt from perches (such as Böhm's bee-eater, inset), chasing the bees that make up a substantial percentage of their diet, but also tackling dragonflies, cicadas, and potentially dangerous wasps and hornets. After a sometimes animated chase, which can include corkscrew turns, they return to their perch and bash the insect against a branch – taking care to rub off the stings of bees and wasps – before swallowing it whole. These thrashings can often be heard from several metres away.

Larger species, such as the European and carmine bee-eaters, spend much time hawking insects on the wing, although the latter follow tractors and bushfires, and readily perch on mobile sites, such as ostriches, bustards, zebras and antelopes – sometimes subduing prey against the bird's back or antelope's horns! Bee-eaters are so specialised at catching insects on the wing that they ignore insects crawling along the ground.

*Flocks of **European bee-eaters** visit Southern Africa between August and March.*

*The **carmine bee-eater's** vivid plumage renders it unmistakable among other bee-eater species.*

*Summer visitors to the region, **blue-cheeked bee-eaters** are associated with water.*

__White-fronted bee-eater__ pairs have helpers which assist in feeding the chicks.

Rocking rollers

The five species of roller are also colourful, and several, such as the lilac-breasted (pictured) and racket-tailed, sport long tail feathers. The lilac-breasted roller is in places very common, easily seen and photographed, and probably elicits more admiration from visitors than any other bird in Southern Africa. Like most of their relatives, rollers are not known for their song – typical calls are cackling or croaks – but a male displays by 'rolling' (an aeronautical term): flying slowly upwards with languorous flaps, he coasts down again, rocking from side to side to show off his prominent pale wing patches, and usually cackling as he goes. Rollers also catch prey from a conspicuous perch: savanna species pouncing on ground-dwelling invertebrates; forest species hawking flying insects in the canopy. Lilac-breasted rollers also sometimes follow and catch prey disturbed by dwarf mongooses. You might also be the target of attention from one of these flashy birds – male rollers defend a territory and become pugnacious towards other birds, mammals and even people.

Adultery, robbery and other nesting habits

Like their kingfisher cousins, all bee-eaters nest in holes: forest species in trees, others in tunnels excavated in riverbanks or road cuttings. Larger, more aerial feeders often live colonially in cooperative (and competitive) units of related birds. Helpers, usually blood relatives such as the previous year's offspring, assist with incubation and feeding, and in turn gain an apprenticeship in parenthood. But helpers sometimes also lay an egg or two in the nest at which they are helping. In fact, studies of colonies have revealed complicated and shifting alliances: adultery is rife among mated pairs, females lay in the nests of other females (a practice known as 'egg dumping'), and some birds habitually attempt to rob others of food. Pairs will also nest separately, which is the usual practice among smaller species, such as the little and swallow-tailed bee-eaters.

Although hardly musical, bee-eaters have pleasant calls (at least when compared to the kingfishers), described as a liquid, trilling *krreep-krreep*. All species sound more or less the same, and once the basic pattern is learnt, calls are easily recognised and a good way to detect bee-eaters in the canopy or flying overhead. ■

Hotspots

Hwange NP Has all the rollers and six species of bee-eater (some seasonal). **Kasanka NP** As for Hwange but also holds chances for two additional bee-eaters, Böhm's and olive. **Kafue NP** Try for blue-breasted and Böhm's bee-eaters. **Moremi GR** Good for blue-cheeked bee-eaters (November to April), carmine bee-eaters (January to March) and numerous rollers including racket-tailed, purple and broad-billed.

*Usually seen in pairs, the **little bee-eater** is the smallest bee-eater in the region.*

*The **swallow-tailed bee-eater** is the only bee-eater in Southern Africa with a forked tail.*

***European rollers** overwinter in Southern Africa, arriving in October and leaving around April.*

*Most common of the rollers, the **lilac-breasted roller** is a regular sight on safari.*

HORNBILLS

Southern yellow-billed hornbills are gregarious and birds cluck constantly together in chorus.

*The **grey hornbill** is less sociable than other species and is often seen alone or in pairs.*

*The **red-billed hornbill** is the smallest species in the region and feeds on the ground.*

Bradfield's hornbills are largely restricted to mopane and teak woodlands.

Self-sealing prisoners

Omnivorous and voracious, Southern Africa's 10 hornbill species spend much of their day searching for lizards, insects and fruit; and larger species eat virtually any animal they can swallow, including eggs, birds, rodents and snakes. Whatever their preferences, hornbills are among the most conspicuous, noisy and engaging of large birds to be seen in savanna and forest. It's not something you might expect, but hornbills have surprisingly long eyelashes – those of ground hornbills are so long and thick they can be seen easily. And all have a large, sometimes colourful bill, which in some species is adorned with a casque (eg, the trumpeter hornbill, inset) – a hollow protuberance thought to resonate when the birds call. Noise plays a big role in a hornbill's life: they call for many reasons (for example, to contact each other or to establish territories) and their nasal honkings are a good way of locating them.

Several species live side by side in most areas and up to eight may coexist in savanna or forest communities, where different species may even nest in the same tree. Early morning is the time to watch for their complex interactions: calls signal communal roosts waking up and flocks fly across the canopy to fruiting trees with a loud whoosh of wings. They're also often seen in association with other animals, particularly dwarf mongooses. The mongooses' diet of lizards and invertebrates is exactly the same as that of three species of hornbill (grey, southern yellow-billed and red-billed) and a remarkable and possibly unique feeding strategy has evolved: the hornbills walk along with foraging mongooses, snapping up food disturbed or flushed by their companions.

All hornbills nest in cavities, usually in a tree, and pairs spend much time inspecting holes. After mating, females of most species seal themselves into a suitable nest by plastering up the entrance with mud, sticky fruit and droppings, until only a slit remains – an effective barricade against predators. There she raises the chicks, cramped with long tail bent vertically over her back, while the male passes food through the entrance. ■

Hotspots

Kruger NP Six species including abundant ground-feeders like grey, southern yellow-billed and red-billed on the roads, often with dwarf mongooses. **Waterberg Plateau Park** Endemic Monteiro's hornbills, plus grey, southern yellow-billed and red-billed. **Hwange NP** Numerous species and especially good for Bradfield's hornbills at the end of the dry season (especially September to October). **Nyika NP** Silvery-cheeked and crowned hornbills.

GROUND HORNBILL

Ground crew

The largest of Africa's hornbills, the ground hornbill is almost entirely terrestrial and is also the only Southern African bird that walks on the tips of its toes. Like a large turkey (and the ground hornbill is sometimes mistakenly called the turkey buzzard), small groups patrol grasslands and open woodland looking for prey.

The most carnivorous of the hornbills, ground hornbills take insects, snails, frogs, reptiles (including tortoises and snakes) and even mammals up to the size of scrub hares. Sometimes they can be spotted among herds of ungulates, snapping up rodents and insects flushed by the grazers. Their massive black beak is a powerful weapon and prey is speared to death with a single swift stab before being swallowed whole. In the case of snakes and large prey, the group co-operates: each bird takes turns to make fleeting, violent pecks until the victim is dead, but usually only one bird gets the prize.

The small parties of ground hornbills are usually made up of two to four adults and a few immature birds. Groups are territorial and conflict sometimes occurs over borders, with neighbouring groups chasing one another in noisy, aerial clashes. It's the only time they make any sort of prolonged flight, though they are powerful flyers, with strong regular wingbeats and – unlike other hornbills – hardly any gliding. They also fly when threatened by predators, usually taking to large trees for refuge; they roost in trees at night.

Like other hornbills, they nest in hollows, usually in trees but also in cliff-faces and riverbeds. But whereas the females of other species are sealed in, ground hornbill females are not and occasionally leave the nest; it's possible the dominant male of the group contributes to incubation duties but this is still unclear. Of the females in the group, only the dominant female lays and she may be fed by all the males and some of the younger birds. Despite the group effort, usually only a single chick is raised. ∎

Recognition Very large turkeylike bird, weighing up to 4kg. Mostly black with white primaries visible in flight. Very obvious red wattles around face, with blue throat patch in females. Length 90cm.
Habitat Open woodlands and grasslands; also agricultural lands.
Behaviour Gregarious, living in pairs or small related groups. Terrestrial and diurnal. Spends the night in trees, clustered in family groups at the ends of branches.
Breeding October to November. Lays 1–2 eggs in a hole in a tree, rock or riverbank.
Feeding Invertebrates, frogs, tortoises, snakes, rodents and hares.
Voice Booming territorial call, likened to a distant lion's grunting; performed in group chorus. Harsh squawk in alarm.

Hotspots
Chobe NP (Savute region), **Kruger NP** (especially northern section), **Mana Pools NP**

NARINA TROGON

Colourful but cryptic

Trogons are a group of colourful – sometimes spectacular – birds vaguely related to kingfishers. But although they are not uncommon and quite large (about 30cm), narina trogons can be difficult to spot. Almost entirely arboreal, they often perch for long periods with their back to the observer, their intense green coloration blending in with the foliage. This is their kingfisher-like, sit-and-wait hunting strategy, and if you can pin one down it's worth watching: sitting hunched and motionless, long tail hanging vertical, the trogon slowly turns its large head as its large eyes watch for movement among the foliage. Seen side on, its stout, wide bill gives the bird a 'smiling' appearance, but a bristled fringe makes the bill an effective insect scoop. Short, rounded wings allow great manouevrability among the foliage, and when prey is spotted trogons become galvanised – darting after insects with acrobatic twists and turns before returning to their perch.

The best way to locate a trogon is by its call (something males often do just before or after rain). Although they can be ventriloqual, males usually call from a conspicuous branch up to 20m above the ground. 'Narina' is a Hottentot word meaning flower. ■

Recognition Metallic green back and breast, red belly (male); female duller.
Habitat Forest and woodland.
Behaviour Defends territory against cuckoos, turacos and squirrels.
Breeding Lays 2–3 eggs.
Feeding Insects and small animals.
Voice Series of double-hoots.

Hotspots
Phinda Resource Reserve, Ndumo GR, Lower Zambezi NP

HOOPOE

Outsized pied butterfly

The hoopoe is so unlike any other bird that its image is unmistakable on ancient Egyptian tombs. Its name comes from its call – even its scientific name *Upupa epops* evokes the soft *hoo-poo-poo*, which can be heard from several hundred metres away and is sometimes repeated for hours on end. Their most unusual feature – a large, floppy crest that is usually held flat along the crown – is held erect, like an untidy fan, when the bird is alarmed. But normally they are unobtrusive ground feeders and are often first noticed in flight – a butterfly-like, undulating flap-and-glide that shows off the boldly contrasting black-and-white pattern of their broad wings and banded rump. When feeding, hoopoes walk jerkily on rather short legs (one feature that betrays an ancestry shared with kingfishers), jabbing at loose soil with their bill, or digging vigorously enough to make sods fly. Large prey items may be snatched and beaten against a hard surface (another kingfisher trait). When a predator passes overhead, the hoopoe flattens itself against the ground with wings spread, tips almost touching, tail fanned and bill pointing straight up – the effect of the disruptive pattern on its wings and back makes it almost invisible, especially against rocky ground. Groups of hoopoes sometimes roost one to a tree in copses, using the same perches for weeks on end. ■

Recognition Cinnamon with black-and-white wing bars and black tail.
Habitat Wooded savanna and cultivation.
Behaviour Pairs territorial.
Breeding Lays 4–6 eggs.
Feeding Invertebrates and small reptiles.
Voice Soft *hoo-poo-poo*.

Hotspots
Waterberg Plateau Park, Gonarezhou NP, Greater St Lucia Wetland Park, Liwonde NP

RED-BILLED WOODHOOPOE

Iridescent chatterboxes

Noisy and gregarious, these agile insect hunters typically announce themselves by loud chattering before they break cover and fly between trees in single file. Woodhoopoes are unique to Africa and are related both to true hoopoes and hornbills. All woodhoopoes are characterised by long, slender bodies with a long tail and a long, down-curved bill. Adult plumage in all species is dark but iridescent: appearing black in some lights, close-to it becomes shimmering green to blue or violet. Red-billed woodhoopoes, the most conspicuous species, feed on a wide variety of insects and their larvae and pupae. Small, animated parties of these engaging birds scamper along branches and up trunks, probe crevices and lever up bark as they search for prey, or hang upside down, using their tail as a brace, to peer into holes.

Red-billed woodhoopoes display noisily to each other while foraging – chuckling, bowing and rocking with tail spread and wings partly open. And listen for them hammering like woodpeckers, bashing prey against bark or pecking at beetles wedged in a crevice. Woodhoopoes lay their eggs in hollows and breed cooperatively: up to 10 nonbreeding helpers, usually young from previous broods, assist with feeding young for several weeks after fledging. ■

Recognition Dark iridescent plumage with white wing and tail spots. Bright red bill.
Habitat Grassland, woodland, riverine forest and gardens.
Behaviour Gregarious.
Breeding Year-round.
Feeding Invertebrates, small lizards and nectar.
Voice A cackling chorus.

> **Hotspots**
> **Moremi GR, Mkuzi GR, Mamili NP, Victoria Falls NP**

BARBETS & TINKER BARBETS

Tonks and tinks

Like their woodpecker relatives, the barbets and tinker barbets are usually found in trees (although a few species of barbet spend much time on the ground) and have a similar arrangement of toes – two pointing forward and two back – for clinging to tree trunks. But unlike woodpeckers, the stocky, generally short-tailed barbets and tinker barbets come in many colours and patterns, ranging from bold black-and-white to bright shades of black, orange, red and yellow among the larger species. All barbets and tinker barbets nest in holes, which they excavate in branches or tree trunks with their strong, pointed bill (which in many is surrounded with prominent bristles). Most eat mainly fruit – fruiting fig trees are ideal places to stake out – although all (especially the ground-nesting species) include some insects in their diet. Tinker barbets are the most arboreal and join flocks of other foraging birds in the canopy. ■

Found widely in bushveld, crested barbets are also common garden birds.

> **Hotspots**
> **Mkuzi GR** Six species are common here including red-fronted and golden-rumped tinker barbets. **Kruger NP** Camps good for crested and black-collared barbets. **Nyanga NP** Six species, including Whyte's barbets and white-eared barbets. **Kafue NP** Miombo pied and Chaplin's barbets.

Black-collared barbets are found wherever there are fruits and berries, especially figs.

Golden-tailed woodpeckers are widespread but not particularly common.

*The endemic **ground woodpecker** is the region's only terrestrial woodpecker.*

WOODPECKERS

Woodland drummers

The resonant drumming of woodpeckers is a familiar sound throughout most of the world. Wood is the key to woodpecker ecology – they even drink from small puddles in tree forks – but although some species hammer vigorously to dig out grubs (and all 'drum' to advertise their territories), others pry off flaking bark, glean insects from foliage or extract ants from crevices with a long, barbed tongue. The 10 woodpecker species in Southern Africa exploit many woodland niches (several species can often be found in close proximity) but only one, the olive woodpecker, inhabits evergreen forests in the region. Wherever they occur, woodpeckers play a pivotal role in wooded ecosystems: not only do other small animals pick over the bark they have removed, woodpeckers are among the only animals that actually create cavities in living wood, and their hole construction benefits many species of bird, mammal, reptile and even insect. ■

Hotspots
Liwonde NP Five species including rare Stierling's and speckle-throated woodpeckers. **Tsitsikamma NP** Knysna (a South African endemic), ground, olive and cardinal woodpeckers. **Moremi GR** Golden-tailed, Bennett's, cardinal and bearded woodpeckers.

GREATER HONEYGUIDE

Prince of thieves

It's not much to look at (and this is the gem among the 14 species), but the greater honeyguide is an amazing bird. Firstly, although its standard fare is insects, particularly bees and wasps, it also eats beeswax, which it digests with special stomach bacteria. Secondly, it lays its eggs in other birds' nests – typically those of woodpeckers and barbets. When laying, the female greater honeyguide sometimes punctures or removes the eggs of the host; if she doesn't, her chick has a hooked bill with which it kills its foster siblings (or pushes them out of the nest) so it is raised alone. And finally, and perhaps most astonishingly, greater honeyguides lead people (and possibly also honey badgers) to beehives so they'll break them open.

Conspicuous when 'guiding', it moves from tree to tree with a fluttering flight and a loud, continuous chattering, flicking its white outer tail feathers and stopping to watch the progress of its follower. After the hive is opened and the honey removed, it feeds on the wax, larvae and eggs – any bee stings are resisted by its thick skin. Greater honeyguides also obtain beeswax without a helper at abandoned hives – if the hive has already been broken – where they become pugnaciously territorial. ■

Recognition Grey-brown with white ear patch, whitish underparts and black throat. Stubby pink bill. 19cm.
Habitat Open woodlands.
Behaviour Solitary. Perches for hours. Harasses drongos.
Breeding Lays 1 white egg.
Feeding Insects, beeswax, bee larvae and eggs.
Voice Continuous *bur-witt*.

Hotspots
Nxai Pan NP, Kruger NP, Moremi GR

LARKS

Cryptic songsters

Like many other grassland birds, most of Southern Africa's 23 species of lark are cryptically coloured, their muted upperparts in shades of brown, tawny and buff often echoing the dominant soil colour wherever they dwell. Superficially, many species resemble pipits, although they are now thought not to be closely related.

Larks are essentially ground dwellers: they feed in open savannas and grasslands, where they are often encountered along vehicle tracks; and their nests are always well hidden in grass tussocks. Larks have also successfully invaded the rocky deserts of the South West Arid Zone and many of these are Southern African endemics.

Larks have strong legs and feet – some species with a long hind claw that facilitates walking over grass tussocks – and their strong, hard bill is adapted to a diet containing a high percentage of seeds. Larks advertise their territories with long display flights that often involve complicated – and beautiful – song sequences. ■

*Calling with crest raised, **rufous-naped larks** may incorporate other birds' calls into their songs.*

*Named for its incessant jeep call, look for the **monotonous lark** singing after downpours.*

Hotspots

Namib-Naukluft Park Eight species including three endemics (dune, Sclater's and Gray's). **Kgalagadi TP** Nine species including Stark's lark. **Karoo NP** Seven species, three endemics (thick-billed, Karoo and clapper). **Tswalu Private Desert Reserve** Eleven species, many easily seen.

SWALLOWS & MARTINS

Living the high life

Swallows and martins are small, active birds. Their supremely aerial lifestyle has led to a streamlined body with long, narrow wings for powerful, sustained flight. A short tail adds manoeuvrability and is taken to extremes by the most agile species, whose distinctive forked tails with long streamers have lent their names to entirely unrelated butterflies. All feed exclusively on the wing, and tend to be gregarious in flight. Many flash with iridescence and have contrasting pale underparts or reddish markings on their head and throat. The familiar and cosmopolitan European swallow is just one of 24 resident and migratory species, including various martins and saw-wings, that occur in Southern Africa. Swallows and martins sometimes nest in colonies, most building a cup-shaped nest of mud pellets gathered waterside or at drying puddles. Their readiness to attach nests to eaves is well known; a few nest in holes or cavities. ■

*In the region, **red-rumped swallows** occur regularly only in Zambia and Malawi.*

Lesser striped swallows readily build their nests in the eaves of lodges and verandahs.

Hotspots

Nyika NP Seventeen species, including blue, white-headed saw-wing and eastern saw-wing swallows. **Karoo NP** Gorges provide excellent views of up to seven species. **The Drakensberg** Eleven species including the rare blue swallow (September to March). **Moremi GR** Fourteen species, some nest in camp site buildings.

FORK-TAILED DRONGO

Feisty opportunist

Another contender for ubiquity is an all-black, slightly iridescent bird that can also be quite fearless of people – the fork-tailed drongo (a similar species, the square-tailed drongo is restricted to Southern Africa's eastern seaboard). Although they may sit still for long spells, fork-tailed drongos are usually conspicuous on a horizontal branch or exposed limb. They fearlessly pursue flying predators, such as hawks and crows, sometimes in pairs, and press home their attacks with pecks or buffeting. But for all their jauntiness, drongos (the name predates the pejorative definition familiar to Australians) are rather voracious predators themselves. They take mainly insects, but sometimes rob other birds of their catch and are not averse to taking nestlings. Nonetheless other small birds readily nest in the same tree as drongos, perhaps comforted by their pugnaciousness towards other predators. Typically both drongo species chase likely prey from their perch, snatching it in flight or pursuing it to the ground, where it is dispatched or dismembered. Fork-tailed drongos also follow bands of dwarf mongooses and seize prey disturbed by the mongooses' progress (as do some species of hornbill). Rather tuneless but at times enthusiastic singers, their loud, metallic notes can continue through the day and into the night. ∎

Recognition Black with metallic blue sheen. Forked 'fish tail'. Red eye.
Habitat Drier open, grassy areas, and forest edges.
Behaviour Catches small animals fleeing grassfires.
Breeding 3 eggs.
Feeding Chiefly insects.
Voice Metallic 'twanging'.

Hotspots
South Luagwa NP, Hwange NP, Pilanesberg NP, Ndumo GR

BLACK-HEADED ORIOLE

Golden songbirds

Usually heard before they are seen, orioles are medium-sized, rather starlinglike birds that live virtually their whole lives in the canopies of woodlands and forests. Unlike most starlings they have no iridescence, but all of the four species seen in Southern Africa are mainly golden yellow, suffused with olive or with contrasting black on their wings and tail. If you can locate the source of their liquid, fluting calls – they sound a bit like their common name – you'll also see a strongly pointed, bright red bill and bold, red eyes.

The most common species in the region, the black-headed oriole lives in woodland and wooded savanna; they're also tolerant of human activity and readily colonise parks, gardens and plantations of exotic trees such as gums. Orioles rarely descend to the ground, and fly with deep undulations, sweeping up to a perch like a woodpecker. Watch for them plunge-bathing by dropping from a perch into a puddle or pool and, during showers, tipping forward on a branch with wings outspread.

Generally solitary outside the breeding season, orioles sometimes join mixed feeding flocks and congregate at fruiting trees. They feed mainly in the canopy, targeting fruit and venturing onto aloes for the nectar and pollen. They also take insects, either in the treetops or by sweeping close to the ground. ∎

Recognition Mostly yellow with distinctive black head. Length 25cm.
Habitat Woodlands and forest.
Behaviour Usually alone or in pairs; often seen flying between thickets.
Breeding Lays 2–3 eggs.
Feeding Fruit, insects, nectar and pollen.
Voice Loud bubbling whistle.

Hotspots
Kruger NP, Hwange NP, Moremi GR, Itala GR

BABBLERS & ILLADOPSES

A family affair

Throughout their range in Africa and Asia, the large and varied group of birds that includes babblers, illadopses and chatterers are renowned skulkers of forest undergrowth. Fortunately, in Southern Africa a few species are quite easy to see. Most are thrush-sized birds (20 to 23cm in length) with strong legs and feet, and typically forage on the ground, scuffling among the leaf litter for insects and other small animals. The bush black-cap (a South African endemic), once grouped with the bulbuls, is the only non-insectivorous member of the family – it feeds on fruit and berries.

Southern African babblers are mostly not brightly coloured, although some are boldly marked; most are conspicuous by their highly gregarious nature and most are very vocal. The four species of illadopses in the region are real forest skulkers that can pose a challenge to the most ardent birdwatcher. ■

*Parties of **arrow-marked babblers** forage for insects and other small animals in bushy savanna.*

 Hotspots
Etosha NP Good for arid-zone babblers including black-faced, southern pied and bare-cheeked. **Nyika NP** Try here for the elusive African hill babbler and mountain illadopsis. **Kaudom GR** Four species (Hartlaub's, southern pied, arrow-marked and black-faced). **The Drakensberg** Gully forests have the bush blackcap.

*The **southern pied babbler** is the only babbler in the region with an all-white head and back.*

BULBULS

Tuneful early risers

This group of birds is divided among those that are easily discriminated and impossible to miss, and a suite of very similar species that are very difficult to see. Wherever you go in Southern Africa, you'll encounter the three dark-headed bulbul species but, with largely exclusive distributions, you're only likely to see a single species at any one site. All have smoky grey plumage with black heads and bright yellow vents; you can tell them apart from the eye wattle: white in the Cape bulbul, red in red-eyed and missing in the black-eyed.

The rest of this family (also called greenbuls or brownbuls for their mostly muted colouration) are mostly forest and woodland dwellers. And although their calls are hard to miss, they are particularly elusive. All of them remain under the cover of dense foliage, foraging for fruit, berries, insects and sometimes snails. The exception to the rule, the large yellow-bellied bulbul, often ventures into more open country, foraging in groups. ■

*The **black-eyed bulbul** uses spider's silk to bind together its nest of dry grass and leaves.*

Hotspots
Nyika NP Excellent for hard-to-see species, including yellow-streaked, slender and stripe-cheeked bulbuls. **Chobe NP** Terrestrial and yellow-bellied bulbuls, and very tame black-eyed bulbuls. **Greater St Lucia Wetland Park** Sombre, yellow-bellied and yellow-streaked bulbuls. **Cape Peninsula NP** Tame Cape bulbuls.

*Groups of **yellow-bellied bulbuls** maintain a constant contact call of pao pao-pao.*

THRUSHES, CHATS & RELATIVES

Bush choristers

Apart from the thrushes – famous as songbirds around the world – this large and varied family includes the boldly marked wheatears, which in Africa include both resident and migratory species; a few specialists of cliffs and rocky country (such as the friendly familiar chat and the short-toed rock thrush); and the forest-dwelling alethes, akalats and ground thrushes, which forage among leaf litter for insects, sometimes flushed by columns of driver ants. If the diversity weren't enough, confusion can arise because widely distributed species can go by different names in different countries, for example, Heuglin's robin is also known as the white-browed robin-chat north of the Zambezi River. At least one species is found in nearly every habitat and several may live in close proximity. It's hard to generalise about the 56 Southern African members of this enormous family, but all are usually solitary, small- to medium-sized birds with comparatively long legs and a shortish bill; other features, such as body shape, tail length and coloration vary considerably. But among the many variables one feature stands out in a few species at least: their vocal ability. Tuneful examples include Heuglin's robin – a common garden bird with a fine repertoire of musical whistling and a tendency to mimic other birds and frogs – and the widespread ground scraper thrush (inset), more social than many species and inclined to early morning group choruses.

The southern olive thrush will probably be the first member of the family you encounter: it has adapted well to human habitation and forages while hopping across lawns. Desert lovers will almost certainly encounter the tractrac chat – a confiding bird at picnic areas throughout the Namib Desert – and possibly also the Karoo chat, another arid-zone species. The drably coloured southern ant-eating chat is a conspicuous species of open country, where it digs nest tunnels in termite mounds (on which it frequently perches) and abandoned aardvark burrows. Wheatears also inhabit open country and migrant species can be abundant en route to their northern breeding grounds. ∎

The **short-toed rock thrush** is often seen perched on a prominent rock scanning for prey.

Collared palm thrushes usually occur in river valleys lined with palm trees.

Kurrichane thrushes are shy in the wild, but can become very tame in suburban gardens.

Tractrac chats can live without standing water, relying on their insect prey for moisture.

Hotspots
Namib-Naukluft Park Many arid-zone endemics including tractrac, Karoo and Herero chats and short-toed rock thrushes. **Bangweulu Swamps** Many species including northern wheatears, miombo bearded scrub robins, ground scraper thrushes and Bocage's akalat. **Pilanesberg NP** A mix of arid and bush species, including Kalahari and African white-throated robins, Cape rock thrushes and buff-streaked chats.

WAGTAILS, PIPITS & LONGCLAWS

Tail-pumpers of garden and grassland

Whether running along safari lodge rooftops, flitting along streams, or snapping up flies from under the hooves of large animals, Southern Africa's six wagtail species are distinctive and common. The African pied wagtail is one of the most easily recognised and is readily seen foraging in flower beds and on lawns, snatching insects off the ground or after a chase (inset). All wagtails pump their tail up and down when standing still (something they don't do very often) and walk, rather than hop, with an exaggerated back and forth head movement.

At first sight, pipits bear little resemblance to wagtails, but they are closely related: they too forage on the ground and snap up insects, and typically pump their tail when they stand still. But while many wagtails are boldly marked, most pipits are grassland

dwellers and coloured accordingly in subdued shades of brown and buff. The widespread grassveld pipit is commonly seen running down tracks ahead of a vehicle, pausing often before scooting off again. Several pipits are migratory and sometimes associate with wagtails outside the breeding season at communal roosts, gathering at dusk in tall trees and reed beds. Many pipits and larks look superficially similar, but they belong to different families and are generally not regarded as close relatives.

The five species of longclaw (which at 19 to 21cm in length are the 'giants' of the wagtail, pipit and longclaw family) share the typical pipits' streaky upperparts, but most have colourful underparts with a black 'necklace'. Longclaws – so-called because their hind claw is extremely long, enabling them to walk over grass tussocks – tend to stand more upright than pipits, have longer legs and don't pump their tails. Both pipits and longclaws avoid long grass; longclaws are usually not difficult to spot, and often indulge in melodious territorial songs in flight or from an exposed tussock. Both groups build a grass nest on the ground during and after the rains, when growing grass affords more concealment for nests and young. ■

Hotspots

Ndumo GR Three longclaw species (orange-throated, yellow-throated and pink-throated) plus numerous pipits and wagtails. **Liwonde NP** Five wagtail species (including grey), yellow-throated longclaws and five pipit species. **The Drakensberg** Many pipits including rock, mountain and yellow-breasted; long-tailed wagtails and orange-throated longclaws. **Kafue NP** Fuelleborn's and pink-throated longclaws plus short-tailed, tree and bushveld pipits.

African pied wagtails are highly adaptable, and can live in cities, cultivation or forest edges.

The *grassveld pipit's* song and display flight differ from all other pipits except the mountain pipit.

Yellow-throated longclaws inhabit moist grasslands and the edges of vleis and swamps.

Orange-throated longclaws tolerate more arid conditions than other longclaw species.

Marico flycatchers are endemic to the region and best seen in the drier areas.

Fiscal flycatchers mimic the larger, aggressive fiscal shrike, possibly to deter predators.

*Although its colour can vary, the **paradise flycatcher's** tail makes it unmistakable.*

FLYCATCHERS

Restless wing and bill snappers

Three families of birds (the 'true' flycatchers, monarch flycatchers, and a family of 'African flycatchers' that includes the batises and wattle-eyes) are broadly lumped as flycatchers, largely as a result of similarities in their foraging behaviour. All are small, sometimes hyperactive birds that catch insects in a variety of ways. Gleaning insects from foliage is a feeding technique common to most, but aerial pursuits launched from a perch are more characteristic of some groups. These insect-catching sallies are also used by other birds, such as drongos and some kingfishers, and are known as 'flycatching' (appropriately enough) regardless of the species. Flycatching is entertaining to watch, and can involve sudden turns and corkscrew movements during which the bill is sometimes heard snapping shut.

One or more flycatchers can be seen in most habitats, and they can be quite tolerant of people. Wattle-eyes are small flycatchers of forest undergrowth, reaching their greatest diversity in equatorial forests and represented in Southern Africa by a single species, the wattle-eyed flycatcher (or black-throated wattle-eye). Wattle-eyes are replaced in drier habitat by batises – small, shrike-like birds boldly marked in grey, black and white – which hunt in pairs or small family groups. Wattle-eyes and batises both 'snap'

their wings in flight but are readily distinguished: only wattle-eyes have a coloured fleshy wattle surrounding the eye.

The so-called monarch flycatchers are larger and pugnacious, and some are colourful. They are renowned for their crests and long tails, but without a doubt the most spectacular species is the common, easily recognisable paradise flycatcher. The male's long tail streamers can measure more than twice his body length and are shown off to perfection in flight. Like many flycatchers, monarchs build a neat, cup-shaped nest (inset) decorated with lichen and moss, and bound with spiders' webs. These may be built quite low to the ground, frequently in lodge verandahs.

The 'true' flycatchers are rather nondescript grey and brown birds of forest edges, some of which are Eurasian migrants, and an identification challenge to the dedicated birder. ■

Hotspots

Nyika NP Many species including white-tailed, paradise, blue-mantled and wattle-eyed flycatchers. **Mamili NP** Paradise flycatchers (September to March); fan-tailed and Marico flycatchers year-round. **Lower Zambezi NP** Good for Livingstone's and collared. **Liwonde NP** Numerous species including Cape batises, and Vanga and wattle-eyed flycatchers.

SHRIKES, BUSH SHRIKES & HELMET SHRIKES

Living larders

With such an abundance of thorns across the savanna, it's not surprising that something has put them to use. Thus lizards, beetles, crickets, small birds and rodents may sometimes be seen impaled on acacia spines (and, since European occupation, barbed wire). This is the work of shrikes, predatory birds boldly marked in black, white, greys and browns.

True shrikes are birds of open country that hunt by waiting on a perch and dropping onto their victim. Slender and upright, they have short legs, strong feet and hooked claws; at the business end, their large head supports a heavy, thick bill with an obvious hook at the tip. Several species are resident and common; others are migrants, and when passing through can be abundant one week and gone the next.

*Small, active groups of **white helmet shrikes** are common in savanna and semiarid country.*

Glamorous it ain't, but their hunting is effective: small vertebrates are pinned down and killed by repeated strikes to the back of the head before impaling, while insects are usually pinned alive. Spikes steady prey for eating but, immediate needs catered for, shrikes also store food for later – useful on a cool day when insects are few. It's also believed that these larders attract females, who presumably are impressed by the male's hunting skills.

*Both sexes of the **crimson-breasted shrike** have brilliantly coloured underparts.*

In complete contrast, the many species of bush shrike run the gamut of colours from subdued browns and greys, to radiant gold and scarlet contrasting with black (eg, the bokmakierie, inset). Most are skulking inhabitants of dense foliage and are difficult to see. Rather than sitting and waiting, they are active hunters and don't impale their prey on spikes. Helmet shrikes are yet another family of shrikes that takes advantage of the abundant insect prey (although some ornithologists don't regard 'true' shrikes, bush shrikes and helmet shrikes to be closely related). Helmet shrikes travel in parties of up to 20 birds (often containing mixed species) searching trunks, branches and leaves for prey. ■

*The **long-tailed shrike** is the only member of the family with such an elongated tail.*

 Hotspots
Chobe NP Good for lesser grey and red-backed shrikes (both October to April), Souza's shrikes and swamp boubous. **Ndumo GR** Chestnut-fronted helmet shrikes, four-coloured and olive bush shrikes. **Addo Elephant NP** Southern boubous, southern tchagras, puffbacks and bokmakieries. **South Luangwa NP** Füelleborn's black and tropical boubous, black-fronted bush shrikes (three colour phases), marsh tchagras and Souza's shrikes.

__Fiscal shrikes__ are aggressive predators of lizards, frogs, insects and small birds.

STARLINGS

Look no further than city streets for *red-winged starlings*, which nest on cliffs and buildings.

The **long-tailed (or Meve's) starling** is a common resident of mopane and baobab forests.

The **plum-coloured starling** is the smallest species in the region; only breeding males are purple.

Africa's birds of paradise

The oily gloss of the common starling so familiar in Europe (and where it's been introduced in South Africa, North America and Australia) offers only a glimmer of the magnificence that its African cousins attain. Starlings have been described as Africa's birds of paradise and nowhere else on earth can display such a colourful range of this garrulous, sociable family (of which ox-peckers also form a part – see separate section). Many of the 16 species (eg, the pale-winged starling, inset) in the region are brilliantly iridescent, the various glossy starlings flashing blue, violet, indigo and bronze, and others sport wattles and bold patterns.

Starlings reach their greatest diversity in savanna, but at least one species can be seen in most habitats, from high mountain grasslands and forest canopies to semidesert – look for the red-winged starling in cities, where it clings to the vertical faces of tall buildings like artificial cliffs.

Most African starlings are omnivorous opportunists, eating insects and spiders, or vegetable matter such as fruit and grain – the various glossy starling species can even become quite fearless of people and take to raiding picnic tables.

Starlings inhabiting forests generally have shorter legs and a larger proportion of fruit in their diet, whereas longer-legged savanna species spend more time on the ground where they take live food. Starlings readily feed in association with others, eg, savanna starlings with weavers, and forest starlings in bird parties. The harsh alarm calls of each species are similar and can be recognised by different starling species – even monkeys and oxpeckers' hosts (such as buffaloes and antelopes) are known to respond to them. Most starlings nest in loose colonies, or at least in clusters of nests. A nest is usually in some sort of cavity, most commonly a hole in a tree, cliff, river bank or building, but for forest dwelling species it can be a tangle of vines or epiphytes; nest holes of barbets or woodpeckers are readily appropriated. A few never use holes, building instead bulky nests of grass, twigs and leaves with a side entrance. Some glossy starlings place shed snake's skin in a nest, and many species decorate with fresh leaves. ■

Glossy starlings are the most common Southern African starling, and also occur in cities.

> **Hotspots**
> **The Drakensberg** Pied, wattled and red-winged starlings. **Kruger NP** Tame Cape glossy starlings (in the south) and greater blue-eared starlings (especially north of Letaba Camp). **Chobe NP** Burchell's starlings (Savute region) and long-tailed starlings (riverfront). **Waterberg Plateau Park** Plum-coloured, pale-winged, wattled and Burchell's starlings. **Nyika NP** Numerous species including rare Waller's red-winged starlings.

OXPECKERS

Lust for lice

The two species of oxpecker are members of the starling family specialised to eat parasites, such as ticks and lice, clinging to the skin of large animals. Red-billed oxpeckers have yellow eye-wattles and red bills; yellow-billed oxpeckers have no eye-wattles and the base of their bill is yellow with a red tip. Both have stiff tail feathers and particularly sharp claws for clambering up and down their hosts. Flocks of one or both species can usually be seen on or near herds of antelopes and many other herbivores, large and small, including livestock. At first glance the relationship seems rosy – the oxpeckers perform a service by removing parasites – but elephants are particularly intolerant of these birds and pastoralists regard them as a nuisance. Both species certainly eat a significant quantity of parasites (100 adult ticks per day, according to one estimate) but they also keep wounds open to feed on blood, pus and any parasites attracted to the gore – injured animals are particularly susceptible and often lack the strength to chase the birds off. Oxpeckers also rip mouthfuls of hair from mammals to line their nests. ■

*The **yellow-billed oxpecker** is now rare outside reserves; its pale rump stands out in flight.*

 Hotspots
Moremi GR, Kaudom GR, Kafue NP, South Luangwa NP and **Hwange NP** All have both species, often in association, wherever there are herds of ungulates.

*Both oxpecker species (here, the **red-billed**) rapidly sift antelope fur with a scissoring bill action.*

PIED CROW

Murder most fowl

Because of their large size, mainly black coloration and often haunting calls, crows and ravens are well known around the world. Several species commonly associate with humans, and their apparent liking for battlefields has instilled a crow mythology in many cultures. Crows mainly eat small animals, but also carrion when available (a group of crows is called a 'murder') and they often arrive at a carcass even before vultures and kites assemble. Like many members of the family, pied crows are bold and mischievous, and can be enormously entertaining to observe. They strut around carcasses, harassing birds of prey, even tugging at the tail feathers of much larger vultures. The pied crow is a consummate opportunist and readily takes food scraps discarded by people; it is now the common scavenger in many settlements, where flocks of hundreds may gather at rubbish dumps. Indeed, in the region they are now found only where there are people and it is rare to see them in wilderness areas. Many sightings occur along roadsides. They are quick to find roadkills and, with larger scavenging birds such as vultures and eagles mostly eliminated from inhabited areas, the crows usually have the spoils to themselves. In mountainous regions, they give way to the larger white-necked raven, distinguished by its white-tipped bill. ■

Recognition Glossy black; white saddle and belly. 50cm.
Habitat Grassland, cultivation, savanna and towns.
Behaviour In pairs and small flocks; roosts communally.
Breeding Lays 4–5 eggs.
Feeding Carrion, small animals, fruit and grain.
Voice Harsh *aaahnk*; croaks.

Hotspots
Kruger NP, Etosha NP, Cape Peninsula NP, Victoria Falls NP and virtually any town or village.

CAPE SUGARBIRD

Recognition Streaky brown upperparts with rusty breast and white belly. White throat and white stripe below the eye. Very long tail. Bill, legs and feet black. Length up to 44cm.
Habitat Fynbos in the southwest Cape. Also gardens.
Behaviour Very active, flying rapidly between protea bushes and then hovering or scrambling over them to feed. Male have a very distinctive territorial display. Solitary, in pairs or groups.
Breeding April to July. Nest is an untidy cup made with twigs, grass and pine needles, lined with protea 'down.' Lays 2 eggs (rarely 1).
Feeding Nectar, mainly of *Protea* species. Also insects and spiders.
Voice Male has a grating chirp interspersed with metallic notes. Alarm call like a rusty hinge.

> **Hotspots**
> **Kirstenbosch National Botanic Gardens, De Hoop NR, Cape Peninsula NP**

Protea pirates

Once considered relatives of Australian honeyeaters, the sugarbirds are a uniquely African group now thought to be distantly related to starlings. There are only two species – both of them Southern African endemics. Gurney's sugarbird has the wider distribution, existing in a string of mountainous pockets beginning in the southern Drakensberg Range and then running north into Zimbabwe's eastern highlands. The other species, the Cape sugarbird, only exists in the southwest Cape's relict fynbos patches, but despite a more limited range, it's a far more conspicuous bird. In the winter when they breed, the males call incessantly, a jangling *churr* interspersed with various metallic notes. Combined with their long tail feathers and territorial display – hovering above a protea bush, jerking his body, beating his wings and flapping his tail – they are hard to miss.

Cape sugarbirds are usually seen alone or in pairs when breeding, but over summer they can be more sociable and form groups numbering up to 12. Despite this, summer actually presents a greater viewing challenge. They rely mainly on the nectar of Cape protea flowers: these all die by midsummer, forcing sugarbirds to disperse to higher altitudes where they can find alternate foods such as aloe nectar. Gardens are also attractive to them, especially where introduced plants such as eucalypts are flowering, and the calling of sugarbird groups is a common feature of Cape Town summers.

Sugarbirds feed similarly to sunbirds, with whom they are often seen feeding on the same bush – though not always amicably. Sugarbirds constantly chase the much smaller sunbirds off 'their' bush, proprietary behaviour that often extends to other sugarbirds. Like an oversized hummingbird, sugarbirds feed by hovering or perching on flowers and then thrust into the inflorescences with their long beak for nectar. Spiders and insects are also taken this way and they also hawk insects in flight. Sugarbirds are fast flyers and their long tail streaming out behind in flight is a giveaway for identification. ■

SUNBIRDS

Iridescent jewels

If not the biggest, then sunbirds are certainly among the most colourful of Africa's birds (like this miombo double-collared sunbird, inset). They are invariably compared to the hummingbirds (not found in Africa), but the similarity is superficial and they are not closely related. The basic sunbird body plan is small (as small as 8cm, but ranging up to 15cm in some species) with a sharp, down-curved bill. Males of nearly all species have patches of iridescence that can cover most of the body or be restricted to swatches on the throat, rump or head. Unlike 'normal' feathers, in which colour is caused by pigmentation, iridescence is caused by a modified feather structure that creates a reflective surface. But the rainbow-coloured result comes at the cost of a weakened structure so flight feathers are not iridescent and are generally drab. Iridescent feathers change colour according to the angle of the viewer; for the wearer, this may have a role in bluff and territorial display: when a male that appears dull side-on suddenly turns to face a rival the rival is suddenly confronted by an intimidating burst of colour.

The combinations are dazzling, and many species look very similar, providing the type of enticing identification problems so valued by birdwatchers. And it gets harder with females and immature males – these generally have drab plumage with little iridescence. Still, identification isn't everything and sunbirds are worth watching as they flit about restlessly – males pugnaciously defend territories against other sunbirds.

Although all sunbirds eat at least some insects, caught in flight or while perched, the main food source for most is nectar sipped with a specialised tongue while beak-deep in a flower, or after the base of the bloom has been pierced with the sharp bill. They lean into flowers while perched next to them, or feed while hanging upside down. Usually solitary or in pairs, larger groups may congregate during seasonal flowerings of favoured plants, such as aloes and mistletoe. Nesting in all species conforms to a pattern: a domed nest woven of grass and fibres of vegetation, usually suspended by several tendrils or fibres from a branch or twig (variations include a 'porch' over the entrance). Most species lay only one or two eggs; both parents raise the young. ∎

Hotspots

Nyika NP Good for montane and forest species including bronze, miombo double-collared, yellow-bellied and olive sunbirds. **Kasanka NP** Up to 14 species, including green-headed, coppery and Shelley's sunbirds. **Mkuzi GR** Forest/sandforest species such as Neergaard's, purple-banded, olive and grey sunbirds.

Collared sunbirds (female pictured) inhabit dense forest and coastal dune scrub.

Like most sunbirds, the male scarlet-chested sunbird is brilliantly coloured; the female is drab.

The yellow-bellied sunbird inhabits rank vegetation such as misty highland forests.

White-bellied sunbirds may nest alongside wasp nests or even inside social spiders' nests.

SPARROWS, WEAVERS, BISHOPS & WIDOWS

White-browed sparrow weavers *make untidy nests like wind-tossed grass clumps.*

The ***Cape weaver*** *is endemic to South Africa and is a common garden bird.*

The endemic ***sociable weaver's*** *huge nests may last for well over 100 years.*

Masked weavers *are probably the most common weaver species in the region.*

Chirpy sparrows and eager weavers

A few finches native to Southern Africa are recognisable as sparrows, even chirping and habitually living near people like their kin across much of the world. But their close relatives have evolved into an extraordinary variety, such as weavers, brightly coloured bishops and widows with elaborate tail plumes. The diversity of these groups is staggering – 141 species worldwide, 43 of which can be spotted in Southern Africa. One, the red-billed quelea, is one of the most abundant birds on the planet, at times so numerous that flocks number in the millions and break branches with their weight when they land.

True weavers are decked out mainly in yellow with black, rufous, orange or brown highlights. Confusing enough when nesting, their identification is a birdwatcher's nightmare outside of the breeding season, when many of the colourful males moult into a drab, sparrowlike plumage and form mixed flocks with females and other species. Still, they are energetic builders of intricate and distinctive woven nests. The majority nest socially and weaver colonies can become virtual cities of grass apartments smothering entire trees (like this sociable weaver colony, inset) – they can be seen in virtually any town or village, as well as in the wilds, where palms and spreading acacias might be draped with hundreds of nests.

Each weaver species has its own trademark architecture and the owners of many nests can be identified by the nest's shape alone. Some nests hang from intertwined stems like a pendulum; others are onion-shaped or have a long, narrow entrance like an upside-down flask; some are neat balls holding two papyrus stems together; and red-billed buffalo weavers build large, untidy accumulations of grass with multiple entrances in which several pairs live and roost. Weaver colonies are noisy and constantly busy: birds coming and going with nest material; males courting females, and rivals stealing nest material.

Unlike their savanna counterparts, some forest weavers are solitary or feed in pairs, and don't build colonial nests; they

Cuckoos up the spout

For a weaver, success depends on building a nest secure enough to raise a brood and withstand the attentions of predators. And  so successful are many at building such nests that other birds, such as waxbills and pygmy falcons, sometimes find abandoned weavers' nests attractive enough to shelter or nest in themselves. Pygmy falcons are mainly insect hunters and don't bother the weavers, but there's nothing much the weavers can do about a gymnogene (African harrier hawk) robbing a nest. These specialised raptors hang upside down from the nest and insert a long, double-jointed leg to extract an egg or chick. And diederik cuckoos commonly parasitise lesser masked weavers (pictured), but the weavers are fighting back: certain populations build entrance spouts so tight that the cuckoos can't get into the nest and have even been found wedged in so tightly they have died in the spout.

*The endemic **Cape sparrow** readily nests in exotic trees and is common in suburbs and farms.*

frequently associate with 'bird parties', ie, feeding flocks composed of several unrelated species moving through the forest. Another outstanding species is the cuckoo finch, which lays its eggs in the nests of warblers such as cisticolas.

Red bishops and black widows

Outside the breeding season, male bishops and widows are streaked and drab like many other weavers, and sometimes form large, nomadic flocks. But when courting is in full swing they are eye-catching and colourful birds, moulting into black plumage with flashes of orange, yellow or red; male widows also grow elaborate plumes – those of the long-tailed widow can be three times as long as its body.

*Male **red bishops** get their brilliant plumage only in the breeding season.*

Males of most species of bishop and weaver are polygamous, mating with several females if their courtship performances are suitably impressive, and building a nest for each. Male bishops perch conspicuously on stems at regular intervals across swathes of rank grasslands and perform display flights with feathers fluffed out (some becoming almost spherical in the process). Male widows stake out territories where they display, the most spectacular being the long-tailed widows, which fly slowly over their patch, the down-turned tail perhaps signalling to rivals that the area is occupied. ■

Hotspots

Etosha NP Chestnut weavers (January to March) and huge flocks of red-billed queleas at Namutoni and Halali Rest Camps. **Nyika NP** Many species including fire-crowned bishops and forest weavers. **Ndumo GR** Specials include thick-billed, yellow and forest weavers, and red-headed queleas. **Mountain Zebra NP** Red bishops, Cape weavers, and very tame white-browed sparrow weavers. **Kgalagadi TP** Nine species including tame scaly-feathered finches at Twee Rivieren Rest Camp and huge sociable weaver colonies.

*In courtship finery the male **long-tailed widow** grows a tail nearly 50cm long.*

WAXBILLS

Jewels in the undergrowth

'Finch' is a term that covers a multitude of forms, from chirpy sparrows to brilliant seedcrackers, and these mainly seed-eating birds are the most diverse bird group in Southern Africa (other finches include the weavers, whydahs and canaries). There's a lot of grass out on the savanna, and a host of finches has evolved ready to pounce on heads of ripe seeds or slide down stalks to pick them off the ground. Many species have a red, waxy-looking bill, and the term 'waxbill' is commonly used to cover some 33 small, mainly colourful species with names such as twinspots, fire-finches, crimsonwings, cordon-bleus and mannikins. Many are also popular caged birds and known by other names in captivity (the pet trade has seriously depleted several waxbill species).

*Both sexes of **violet-eared waxbills** have the violet facial patch.*

Look for waxbills near water (like these red-headed finches, inset), and on roadsides and the edge of savanna and fields, es-pecially where grass is seeding.

Many are common and some are confiding (such as the red-billed firefinch), often nesting near human habitation, while a number of brilliantly coloured species, including seedcrackers, crimsonwings and firefinches, inhabit undergrowth of the forest edge. Despite their bright colours, waxbills can easily be overlooked: for example, when flushed, quail finches fly a short distance then drop vertically to the ground and run like quail; and all twinspot species invariably take refuge in dense thickets when disturbed. Further confounding a good sighting, waxbill calls are often just high-pitched, sibilant whispers that can be mistaken for those of insects; indeed, the locust finch measures only 9cm in length and looks like a large grasshopper flitting between seed heads. Most waxbills build loose, untidy domed nests of grass. Some simply add material to the gaps under hamerkop or secretary bird nests; others, such as some mannikin species, use old weaver nests; and cordon-bleus and bronze mannikins sometimes build near hornet nests. Chicks have bright spots, usually hard-ened callosities, on their gape and inside their mouth; these invoke an irresistible feeding response in parents in the darkness of the nest chamber – a feature mimicked by whydah chicks that parasitise waxbill nests. ∎

*The male **blue-billed firefinch** (pictured) has a deep red face and underparts.*

*Blue waxbills (or **southern cordon-bleus**) become very tame around human settlements.*

*The **melba finch** has an attrac-tive, trilling call and is common throughout its range.*

Hotspots
Matusadona NP Many species including red-backed man-nikins, red-throated twinspots and golden-backed pytilias. **Matobo NP** Swee, violet-eared and black-cheeked waxbills; and quail and cut-throat finches. **Mkuze GR** Sixteen species, includ-ing green and pink-throated twinspots. **Kafue NP** Many species including fawn-breasted waxbills, black-chinned quail finches and locust finches.

PIN-TAILED WHYDAH

A conspicuous roadside flirt

When travelling between parks you'll often see birds perched along roadsides, and male pin-tailed whydahs quickly become a familiar sight. These gregarious birds normally travel in small flocks numbering 20 to 30 birds. Males are polygamous, and during the breeding season flocks are typically composed of one breeding male for every five or six females and non-breeding males. Outside the breeding season pin-tailed whydahs are conspicuous while feeding: they jump backwards along the ground, scattering soil to expose fallen seeds.

The male's coloration is attained at the start of the long rains; afterwards he moults through motley stages to finally resemble the females and nonbreeding males. While he's in the mood, the male pin-tailed whydah is a sight worth seeing: he sings as he flies with gentle undulations around a perched female, his tail bouncing up and down; she responds by shivering her wings. Once the formalities are over, females parasitise other nests, laying their eggs in the nests of other birds (usually the common waxbill). The female whydah removes one egg of the host for each egg she lays, typically only one or two per nest, but occasionally laying in more than one nest. After laying, the parents abandon their eggs to the unwitting hosts who raise the aliens alongside their own chicks. ∎

Recognition Breeding males black-and-white with long (20cm) tail streamers.
Habitat Forest edge, savanna and cultivation.
Behaviour Males sing while perched conspicuously.
Breeding Lays 2 eggs.
Feeding Mostly seeds.
Voice High-pitched *tseet tseet tsuweet*.

Hotspots
Nyanga NP, Mountain Zebra NP, Pilanesberg NP, Central Kalahari GR

CANARIES & SEEDEATERS

Robust ancestors of caged pets

If you've ever wondered where those caged songsters come from, Southern Africa has 19 species, some of which go under the name of seedeaters and one, the oriole finch, looks like a miniature oriole, complete with black head and red bill. Canaries are yet another part of the great assembly of finches, closely related to goldfinches, and quite common in most bush habitats. The streaky seedeater is common near settlements and a few other species share its reputation as something of a pest. Look at the edge of crops and gardens for canaries and seedeaters associating in small groups with other canary species and with other finches. Wild canaries bear little resemblance to their rather pallid captive relatives, although a few are also prodigious songsters – male yellow-eyed canaries gather to sing in treetops and are also caught for the pet trade. Most canaries build cup-shaped nests of grass in trees and bushes, sometimes in loose colonies. ∎

*The white brow of the **streaky-headed canary** rules out confusion with any other canary.*

*The **yellow-eyed canary's** characteristic song is likened to 'yes, I see you'.*

Hotspots
Nyika NP Numerous species including oriole finches, lemon-breasted canaries and stripe-breasted seedeaters. **Cedarberg Wilderness** Protea, black-headed and white-throated canaries. **The Drakensberg** Drakensberg siskins, forest, bully and streaky-headed canaries. **Kasanka NP** Six species including stripe-breasted seedeaters and occasional sightings of black-faced canaries.

MORE CREATURES GREAT AND SMALL

WITH so many highly visible and world-famous mammals and birds to see, it's hardly surprising that Africa's small, reclusive and cryptic creatures often get overlooked. In fact, the majority of Africa's reptiles, amphibians, fish and invertebrates have never been systematically studied – even though these groups are undoubtedly more diverse than mammals and birds, and some are no less impressive. The showcase includes 6m-long pythons which occasionally swallow people, leaping great white sharks and the world's fastest snake. Less obvious but everywhere you look – if you do it closely – are literally thousands of smaller creatures that offer an alternative and equally unique experience for the keen wildlife watcher.

Let the scales fall from your eyes

Reptiles are abundant and diverse in Southern Africa, from giant carnivores like the bank-basking Nile crocodile, to bold, brightly coloured flat lizards and slow-moving, swivel-eyed chameleons. Snakes are no less varied but, to the relief of thousands, are mostly retiring; a summer visit will probably notch up a sighting or two, but most encounters are brief and far from

dangerous. Land tortoises are more likely to be seen – there are more here than anywhere else in the world; their unhurried, herbivorous habits permit excellent viewing for those with a little patience. Leaving land, Southern Africa's aquatic life alone could fill many books but we've included a few of the more obvious attractions: Lake Malawi's kaleidoscopic cichlids and, more visible here than anywhere else on earth, the great white shark.

Most people would rather not know about some of the smallest animals of the African bush, particularly those that bite. But unpleasant though some are, everything from lions to safari ants plays a role in the ecosystem and the invertebrates, in particular, provide many crucial 'services'. Dung beetles use animal droppings for both food and nurseries, and clean up thousands of tons of the stuff daily. Termites convert cellulose into protein, becoming prey for hundreds of different predators, and their mounds provide dwellings for everything from ant-eating chats to spotted hyenas. Bees, wasps, flies and ants pollinate plants and predatory species reduce the numbers of those insects we'd rather not encounter: spiders snag mosquitoes and velvet ants parasitise flies and bees.

Dangerous hordes?

Of course, invertebrates are, collectively, more dangerous than any other animal group – more so than large and dangerous mammals, with which we have extremely rare but dramatic clashes. Many species are harmless on their own but act as hosts for disease-producing microscopic creatures: *Anopheles* mosquitoes transmit the malaria-causing organism and tsetse flies are carriers of sleeping sickness. Others can kill outright: thick-tailed scorpions carry lethal doses of venom and black-button spiders can immobilise a child. Less lethal but ubiquitous, cattle and bont ticks siphon the blood of mammals and a human makes as good a meal as an impala.

Having said this, Africa's small fry are no more dangerous than those anywhere and with a bit of common sense, the hazardous species can be avoided or even enjoyed. Scorpions on their nocturnal hunts are the lions of the invertebrate world and the varied predatory strategies of spiders are as sophisticated as anything the mammalian arena has to offer. Even the instinctive migrations of ticks to the tips of grass to catch a passing herbivore are awe-inspiring in their own way. Whatever your feeling for the invertebrates, they've been around for 500 million years and will be here long after our kind has departed. ■

NILE CROCODILE

Flat dogs

Recognition Powerful jaws and tail. Olive or dull grey.
Habitat Freshwater.
Behaviour Basks. Hunts by ambush and pursuit.
Breeding Lays 30–40 eggs which hatch after 90 days.
Feeding Strictly carnivorous.
Voice Young yelp when hatching.

Hotspots
North Luangwa NP, South Luangwa NP, Greater St Lucia Wetland Park, Chobe NP

The Nile crocodile is Africa's biggest reptile by far, reaching a length of up to 6m and weighing over 1000kg. Smaller crocs eat mainly frogs and fish or snatch swimming birds from the surface, but for a large one, virtually any animal is fair game, including antelopes, livestock and even adult lions. Adult crocs take many wildebeests and zebras crossing rivers on migration, and are responsible for hundreds of human deaths every year. A crocodile can stay submerged with only its eyes and nostrils above the surface, waiting for as long as six hours to ambush prey – shine a torch over a swamp at night and the reflected eyeshine will show just how abundant 'flat dogs' (which is what South Africans call them) can be. When an animal gets within striking distance, the croc lunges with incredible power and speed, propelled by its massive tail, dragging its victim underwater and drowning it. Several may gather at one floating carcass, clamping teeth on the flesh and spinning to rip off chunks; swallowing takes place at the surface to prevent water entering the lungs. Adults have no predators, although hippos will nudge them off a sandbank and even bite one in two if it threatens a calf, and territorial disputes between crocodiles can cause serious injuries. But for a young croc to reach maturity it must first dodge birds, fish, monitors and larger crocodiles. ∎

NILE MONITOR

The lizard king

Recognition Grey-brown to olive-green with bands of yellowish spots. Up to 2.1m.
Habitat Savanna, waterways.
Behaviour Solitary. Males fight for territory.
Breeding Lays 20–60 eggs.
Feeding Insects, crabs, small vertebrates and carrion.
Voice Hisses if approached.

Hotspots
Lower Zambezi NP, Kruger NP, Hwange NP, Moremi GR

Southern Africa's largest lizard, the Nile monitor (locally known as the water leguaan), is a solitary reptile typically seen ambling through the savanna or lounging on a branch overhanging water. Watch early in the day for Nile monitors catching some rays on an exposed rock, sandbank or tree stump. Basking warms them up for the hunt, but like most reptiles they have low energy requirements and can go for long spells without eating. Normal locomotion is a slow, meandering gait (a large one sometimes drags its belly along the ground), but Nile monitors are proficient swimmers and readily take to water if threatened.

Any nook or crevice is investigated for a morsel, which includes insects, birds and small mammals such as rodents; eggs are a favourite and monitors readily dig up unguarded crocodile eggs and climb trees to rob birds' nests. That long forked tongue constantly flicking in and out is completely harmless; in fact, it helps detect prey by transferring scent to an organ in the roof of the mouth (called the Jacobson's organ). Adult monitors have few predators, although they are sometimes taken by pythons, crocodiles and large raptors such as martial eagles; they inflate themselves impressively and hiss at mammalian predators, which mostly leave them alone. ∎

SNAKES

Stranglers and spitters

Although they universally provoke extreme reactions, it is actually quite a rare event to see even one of Southern Africa's 130 species of snake. Most of them are extremely shy and disappear at the approach of people. Although snakes are generally diurnal to take advantage of solar power, Africa's warm climate allows nocturnal foraging by some of the most impressive species including numerous cobras and Africa's largest snake, the African rock python. Occasionally topping 6m, it crushes prey as large as adult impalas by wrapping it in muscular coils; the lethal embrace prevents circulation and death is actually caused by cardiac arrest rather than suffocation. All snakes are carnivorous and 34 Southern African species use venom to disable their prey; 14 of those are on record for human deaths but normal prey for all includes rodents, lizards, frogs, nestlings, eggs and other snakes. Cobras

Gaboon vipers inhabit the forests of KwaZulu-Natal, eastern Zimbabwe and Zambia.

(such as the Cape cobra, inset), mambas and boomslangs are roaming hunters that actively search for prey and stalk it like a cat before executing a lightning-fast bite. Two species of spitting cobras, the rinkhals and the Mozambique spitting cobra (or m'fezi), can spray venom up to 4m, usually reserved for enemies rather than prey. Spitting cobras aim for the eyes of aggressors but in the case of people, modern fashion sometimes thwarts their aim; they occasionally hit lanyard-suspended sunglasses on walkers' chests. Rather than actively seek out quarry, adders and vipers are generally sit-and-wait predators that ambush their prey. The superbly camouflaged Gaboon viper of evergreen forests is armed with the largest fangs of any snake, up to 5cm, but is extremely docile and rarely bites people. They wait hidden in leaf litter on the forest floor for small mammals to wander into striking range. More commonly encountered and armed with only slightly shorter fangs, puff adders are active at dusk and often found slowly crossing roads on their way to a suitable hiding place or drinking from roadside puddles; although they can survive without standing water, many snakes drink when water is available. In the South West Arid Zone, Peringuey's and horned adders rely on coastal fogs for moisture (as well as the body fluids of prey) and lay their ambush in sand. ■

The horned adder is most frequently found in the South West Arid Zone.

Sluggish and slow-moving, puff adders rarely bite people unless particularly provoked.

The boomslang's short, rear-positioned fangs restrict it to small prey like this rain frog.

Hotspots

Namib-Naukluft Park Excellent for desert endemics including horned and Peringuey's adders. **Kosi Bay NR** Gaboon vipers and many others including green mambas, forest cobras, Mozambique spitting cobras and boomslangs. **North Luangwa NP** Many species including large rock pythons, puff adders, black mambas and numerous cobras.

Ground agamas feed mainly on termites and ants, often raiding nests as the occupants emerge.

The flap-necked chameleon gapes its vivid orange-lined mouth when threatened.

LIZARDS

Koppie hoppers and flying the colours

Southern Africa has over 250 lizard species, but they're usually difficult to see – a few habitats hold the best chances. Koppies (isolated rock outcrops) are probably the best, where brightly coloured agamas and super-abundant flat lizards hunt insect prey or hang around people for hand-outs. Both agamids and flat lizards are highly sexually dimorphic: the males are brilliantly coloured to attract potential mates and intimidate rivals. The champion of camouflage is the chameleon. While remarkable, their colour-changing abilities are often exaggerated, mostly restricted to shades of green, grey and brown, and take a few minutes to perform. However, some males flush swiftly with vivid colours when a female is spied or another male intrudes into his territory. When not engaged in matters of sex, chameleons' resting colours invariably match the environment beautifully; spotlighting sometimes picks out the most widespread species, the flap-necked chameleon. Other nocturnal lizards, the geckos, are more easily seen and often inhabit huts and lodges. ■

> **Hotspots**
> **Augrabies Falls NP** Very common flat lizards, plus numerous geckos. **Phinda Resource Reserve** Flap-necked chameleons, Wahlberg's velvet geckos and tree agamas. **Namib-Naukluft Park** Many arid-zone species.

TORTOISES & TERRAPINS

Land cruisers and marsh ambushers

The easiest way to differentiate between tortoises and terrapins is by where you see them: tortoises live on land and terrapins inhabit fresh water (and turtles are marine dwellers). However, this rule of thumb does not indicate any taxonomic relationship.

Land holds the real attractions for chelonian-watchers in Southern Africa. There are more land tortoise species here than anywhere else on earth, 13 in all; unusually among reptiles, all are largely herbivorous, feeding on flowers, grass, succulents and leaves. Some occasionally take snails, insects or carrion and the ubiquitous leopard (or mountain) tortoise also chews bones and hyenas' calcium-rich droppings for the minerals. Most terrapins are more predatory; the widely distributed marsh terrapin sometimes even ambushes doves and sandgrouse that come to drink. ■

The leopard (or mountain) tortoise is the largest and most common tortoise in the region.

Serrated hinged terrapins are often spotted basking on floating logs.

> **Hotspots**
> **Etosha NP** Marsh terrapins often prey on birds. **Addo Elephant NP** Good for angulate and parrot-beaked tortoises, as well as leopard tortoises. **Mkuzi GR** Leopard and Bell's hinge-backed tortoises, serrated hinged and marsh terrapins. **Moremi GR** Very good for terrapins, including marsh, serrated hinged and Okavango hinged.

INVERTEBRATES

The exterminators

Their lifestyle may provoke revulsion, indifference or even amusement, but dung beetles are the sanitation engineers of the African bush. Dozens of different species relish the droppings of other animals as nourishment and for raising their broods. Armies of them appear within moments of a fresh pile appearing and can demolish an elephant's 10kg deposit in minutes. You'll probably see pairs of them rolling perfectly spherical balls of dung much larger than themselves along paths, destined to subterranean larders where the eggs will develop. Upon hatching, the beetle grubs eat their way through the brood ball before turning into pupae and hatching into adult beetles.

Another group of insects which has an even greater impact on wildlife and ecosystems is termites. Their mounds (inset) are dotted all over the savannas, and other colonies live inside rotten wood or build termitaria high in trees. There's an awful lot of vegetation growing out there, more than the large herbivores can consume, and behind the scenes millions of these in-offensive insects are also chewing away at it, converting cellulose into protein. Watch for irruptions of flying termites after rain – other animals do, and flock for an easy meal. Apart from being a first-class source of protein for a host of predators, from ants to aardvarks, abandoned termite mounds make shelters and nurseries for animals as diverse as mongooses, hyenas, warthogs and reptiles.

Like termites and dung beetles, most of Southern Africa's 80,000 described insect species feed on plant matter in its various forms. But they in turn provide food for a small legion of predatory invertebrates. The best-known are not insects but arachnids, eight-legged hunters which, unlike insects, lack antennae (arachnids occur everywhere, look around camp sites at night with a flashlight). Most of them – scorpions and all spiders, except for a small group called the feather-legged spiders – use venom to disable they prey; in the case of the Transvaal thick-tailed scorpion, they can also spray venom at the eyes of prey or aggressors. Neither spider nor scorpion, solifuges (also called sun-spiders) look like a cross between the two and run down their prey. They lack venom and simply eat their quarry alive. ■

🔭 Hotspots
Addo Elephant NP Unique flightless species of dung beetle. **Namib-Naukluft Park** Endemics including fog-basking beetles, dune crickets and white lady spiders. **Namaqua NP** Endemic bees and scorpions plus monkey beetles and bladder grasshoppers.

*The adult **emperor moth** has no mouthparts and, being unable to feed, lives for only a few days.*

*Most thin-tailed **scorpions** are not dangerous; the thicker the tail, the worse the venom.*

*The large front legs of **dung beetles** are adapted for handling unwieldy balls of dung.*

Stick insects fan their wings and raise the front legs when disturbed.

GREAT WHITE SHARK

Break pointer

People flock to Southern Africa to see its many terrestrial predators but for equally spectacular views of super-predators in action, its coastal waters are unrivalled. Here, the great white shark patrols massive Cape fur-seal colonies and, with a regularity seen nowhere else, launches 'predatory breaches' on its prey. Initiating their attack from deep water where they're difficult to spot, the sharks accelerate vertically towards seals on the surface, hitting – or missing – their target with such explosive force that they erupt from the water several metres into the air. At the premier site for predatory breaching, Seal Island, great whites average a kill in 48% of attempts but some particularly proficient individuals have a success rate of 80%. Young fur-seals make up the bulk of kills; hefty quotas of body-fat, inexperience and helplessness (adult seals, in contrast, can inflict damaging bites) combine to make them a far superior target than adult seals.

Despite the dramatic behaviour, great whites in the region actually prefer fish, and their abundance in an area depends on the movements of species such as yellowtail. During the summer when yellowtails are plentiful, the sharks largely ignore seals and track the migratory fish from east to west along the South African coast. Young sharks have teeth and jaws more suited to a fish diet, and seals probably only form an important part of their diet once the sharks are mature. The dispersal of the fish shoals in winter coincides with the first exploratory swims of young seals (May to June), the best time to view predatory breaching.

Great white sharks typically forage at the surface which explains why our knowledge is restricted largely to their feeding behaviour. They are thought to live between 30 to 40 years and mature at around 12 to 15 years (females) and nine to 10 for males. Mating has never been observed and we still don't know where they go to do it, but like many sharks, the male has prominent twin claspers used to flush sperm into the female; if you're fortunate enough to see a shark breach, it's the easiest way to differentiate the sexes. ∎

Recognition Massive. Swollen torpedo shape. Gunmetal grey upperparts, white below. Top size controversial but at least 6.4m and 2500kg (females larger).
Habitat Tropical and temperate coastal waters worldwide. In the region, most visible off South Africa's Cape coast.
Behaviour Mostly hunts in coastal waters but can be found hundreds of kilometres from shore. Semi-nomadic, tracking movements of fish schools but probably does not make long-distance migrations. Largely solitary, sometimes congregating at rich feeding grounds where interactions seem largely peaceful; they feed amicably together on large carcasses.
Breeding Largely unknown. Females have litters of between 7–9 'pups', born swimming freely and around 1.2–1.5m long.
Feeding Carnivorous; mostly fish, seals and sea lions. Also carrion such as whale carcasses.
Voice None.

Hotspots
Seal Island (especially May to October), **Dyer Island** (Gaansbai), **Struis-baai**, **Mossel Bay**

CICHLIDS

A niche for all fish

With over 2000 species worldwide, the family of perchlike fish called cichlids make up more than 5% of known vertebrate species. The great majority of cichlids occur in the Great Lakes of the African Rift Valley, particularly Lakes Victoria and Tanganyika, but for the largest number of species in one place, Lake Malawi is tops. Here, over 30% of all cichlids – more than 600 species – can be spotted and more than 90% of them are endemic to the lake. Both the astonishing variety and extreme levels of endemicity are a result of a remarkably rapid speciation rate (the speed at which different species arise from a common ancestor). Over 450 species of Lake Malawi's cichlids (inset) have arisen within the last two million years, a blink in evolutionary time.

Mouth-brooders such as this **Labeotropheus** *'incubate' their fertilised eggs in the mouth.*

But why the species explosion? It's thought to arise from the female cichlid's preference for flashy colours. Male cichlids are brilliantly pigmented to attract mates and each species is characterised by its own distinctive pattern. Most females have very definite colour preferences which prevent interbreeding between species; but evidently novelty value works for some females. Slight shifts in the patterns caused by naturally occurring mutations need be chosen by only a few females for the genesis of a new species. Over time, the newly coloured males and their females cease breeding with the original colour form and an entirely new species is born.

Pseudotropheus cichlids use empty shells on the sandy bottom as a shelter.

As a result of the proliferation of species (and probably also helping drive it), competition for food among cichlids is intense and different species have evolved to exploit hundreds of different diets. Many are solitary predators on other fish; one species mimics a dead fish on the bottom, ambushing small scavengers that come to feed from the 'carcass'. Others are scale-eaters and fin-biters; mimicking other cichlids, they cruise alongside beside their victims and bite chunks from their fins or scales. An entirely different suite of species targets microscopic prey, using mouthparts which can be everted like a tube to suck in zooplankton. And most 'benign' of all, some cichlids remove parasitic lice (actually tiny crustaceans) from larger fish; their vivid bumblebee pattern is thought to advertise the cleaning service. ■

At Lake Malawi, **cichlids** *have become used to human handouts and flock around swimmers.*

Hotspots
Lake Malawi Best places are Cape Maclear (especially Otter Point); Senga and Nkhata Bays; Thumbi (The Aquarium), Nankanlenga and Mbenjii Islands

Cichlids have sophisticated colour vision and use colours for recognising their own species.

RESOURCE GUIDE

The following information isn't intended to be comprehensive; we've put together some key references and contacts as a starting point.

RECOMMENDED READING

Field guides

Mammals Probably the best guide for the region is C & T Stuart's *Field Guide to the Mammals of Southern Africa*. Their compact *Southern, Central & East African Mammals – A Photographic Guide* is a concise pocket-guide to 152 species most likely to be seen. The *Kingdon Field Guide to African Mammals* by J Kingdon, covers the whole of continental Africa and is packed with information and colour illustrations.

Birds The original and still one of the best, *Roberts' Birds of Southern Africa* by G Maclean, is a little weighty for the field but is extremely comprehensive and excellent value. K Newman's *Birds of Southern Africa – The Green Edition,* and *Sasol – The Illustrated Guide to the Birds of Southern Africa* by I Sinclair, P Hockey & W Tarboton, are also excellent. *Collins Illustrated Checklist – Birds of Southern Africa* by B van Perlo covers the entire region including Malawi, northern Mozambique and Zambia (which the others don't). For Malawi alone, K Newman's *Birds of Malawi* is excellent and D Aspinwall & C Beel's *Field Guide to Zambian Birds not found in Southern Africa* illustrates over 100 species not found south of the Zambezi.

Reptiles and amphibians B Branch's *Field Guide to the Snakes & Other Reptiles of Southern Africa* is the most comprehensive guide and covers 480 species in detail. *South African Frogs* by N Passmore & V Carruthers is a start for amphibian watchers, but *Amphibians of Central & Southern Africa* by A Channing covers all frogs and caecilians of the region.

Invertebrates Field guides for the smaller denizens of the bush are a little patchy but some useful ones include *Butterflies of Southern Africa – A Field Guide* by M Williams, *The Centipedes & Millipedes of Southern Africa – A Guide* by R Lawrence, and *Southern African Spiders – An Identification Guide* by M Filmer.

Aquatic life *Reef Fishes & Corals – East Coast of Southern Africa* by D King illustrates the common reef fish and coral species along the KwaZulu-Natal and Mozambique coasts, while *A Guide to Whales, Dolphins & Other Marine Mammals of Southern Africa* by V Cockcroft & P Joyce covers marine mammals. *A Guide to the Fishes of Lake Malawi National Park* by D Lewis, P Reinthal & J Trendall, is invaluable for cichlid identification, and *Ad Koning's Book of Cichlids & All the Other Fishes of Lake Malawi* by A Konig is excellent. A Koornhof's *The Dive Sites of South Africa* details more than 160 sites along the coast.

All-in-one *The Wildlife of Southern Africa* by V Carruthers covers everything, from lower invertebrates though all the animals and plants; for identifying virtually every species you're likely to encounter in the one volume, it's hard to beat.

Background reading and references

R Estes' *Behaviour Guide to African Mammals* is comprehensive; his *Safari Companion* is a more compact version designed for the field. *Creatures of Habit – Understanding African Animal Behaviour* by P Apps & R du Toit is more condensed with outstanding photographs. To identify spoor, scats, nests, wallows and even skulls, you can't go past C & T Stuart's *Field Guide to Tracks & Signs of Southern & East African Wildlife*; *The Art of Tracking – The Origin of Science* by L Liebenberg gives fascinating background theory to the subject.

Island Africa by J Kingdon is a readable and well-illustrated book on the evolution of rare species across the continent while *Pyramids of Life* by H Croze & J Reader examines the intertwined ecological relationships in African ecosystems. *The Mammals of the Southern African Subregion* by J Skinner & R Smithers is the standard mammal reference for the region; for a comprehensive and beautifully illustrated coffee table version, get a copy of *The Complete Book of Southern African Mammals* by G Mills & L Hes.

Ornithologists should dip into the companion volume *The Complete Book of Southern African Birds* by P Ginn, G McIlleron & P Milstein; for some really serious reading, consult the multivolume *Birds of Africa* series by L Brown, E Urban & K Newman, or the 12-volume *Handbook of Birds of the World* edited by J del Hoyo, A Elliot & J Sargatal – both profusely illustrated and covering all the birds of Africa in detail.

For a taste of what field work is like in a few of the most remote southern African wilderness areas, have a look at *Horn of Darkness – Rhinos on the Edge* by C Cunningham & J Berger, and M & D Owen's books *Cry of the Kalahari* and *Survivor's Song – Life & Death in an African Wilderness*. *Kakuli* by N Carr is a very personal insight on Africa's conservation challenges.

Periodicals

Africa Geographic (⌨ www.africa-geographic.com) is probably the best magazine covering Africa's wildlife and conservation issues, with detailed articles and beautiful photography. The same group produces the equally excellent *Africa – Birds & Birding*. *Getaway* magazine (⌨ www.getawaytoday.com) is also very worthwhile, especially for up-to-date travelling details for parks and reserves all over Africa. Magazines with more of a local scope include *Zimbabwe Wildlife* produced by Wildlife & Environment Zimbabwe, and *Endangered Wildlife* produced by the Endangered Wildlife Trust, which deals mainly with South Africa. SANP's *Timbila* (e timbila@pentapub.co.za) has excellent coverage of South African parks with the occasional feature from elsewhere in Africa. For the conservation-minded, *Oryx*, published by the Flora & Fauna Preservation Society (c/o Zoological Society of London), has a strong African focus.

International bookshops

Before your trip it's worth checking out the comprehensive range available from mail-order natural history bookshops; several have a web catalogue and online ordering service.

- **American Birding Association** (USA & Canada ☎ 800-634 7736, fax 590 2473; International ☎ 719-578 0607, fax 9705; ⌨ www.americanbirding.org/abasales), PO Box 6599, Colorado Springs, Colorado 80934, USA.
- **Andrew Isles Natural History Books** (☎ 03-9510 5750, fax 9529 1256, e books@AndrewIsles.com, ⌨ www.AndrewIsles.com), 115 Greville St, Prahran, Victoria 3181, Australia.

- **Natural History Book Service** (☎ 1803-865 913, fax 280, **e** nhbs@nhbs.co.uk, 🖳 www.nhbs.com), 2–3 Wills Rd, Totnes, Devon TQ9 5XN, England.
- **Subbuteo** (☎ 870-0109 700, fax 699, **e** info@wildlifebooks.com, 🖳 www.wildlifebooks.com), The Rea, Upton Magna, Shrewsbury SY4 4UR, England.

TOUR OPERATORS

Although safari and tour operators abound throughout Africa, the industry is haphazardly regulated and not all tours are safe, informative or environmentally sound. The following operators we feel know their stuff and will offer safe, informative and interesting wildlife-watching experiences.

International

International wildlife conservation organisations such as the World Wildlife Fund (🖳 www.worldwildlife.org/travel) run natural history tours to Southern Africa. Several specialist wildlife tour companies that only use professional guides also schedule regular trips to the region.

Falcon Tours (☎ 08-9336 3882, fax 3930, **e** falcon@highway1 .com.au), Unit 11, 342 South Terrace, South Fremantle, WA 6162, Australia.

Field Guides Inc (☎ 512-327 4953, fax 9231, **e** fgileader@ aol.com, 🖳 www.fieldguides.com), PO Box 160723, Austin, Texas 78716, USA.

Naturetrek (☎ 1962-733 051, fax 736 426, **e** inquiries@ naturetrek.demon.co.uk), Chautara, Bighton nr. Alresford, Hampshire SO24 9RB, England.

Sunbird (☎ 1767-682 969, fax 692 481, **e** sunbird@demon.co.uk, 🖳 www.osme.org/sunbird/index.html), PO Box 76, Sandy, Bedfordshire SG19 1DF, England.

WCS (Wildlife Conservation Society) (☎ 212-439 6507, **e** travel@ wcs.org, 🖳 www.wcs.org), Central Park Zoo, 830 Fifth Avenue, New York, New York 10021, USA.

Wings (☎ 520-320 9868, fax 9373, **e** wings@wingbirds.com, 🖳 www.widdl.com/wings), 1643 N. Alvernon Way, Suite 105, Tucson, Arizona 85712, USA.

South Africa

Abercrombie & Kent (☎ 011-781 0740), PO Box 782607, Sandton 2146.

Clive Walker Trails (☎ 011-453 7645, fax 7649), PO Box 645, Bedfordview 2008.

Drifters (☎ 011-888 1160, fax 1020, **e** drifters@drifters.co.za, 🖳 www.drifters.co.za), PO Box 48434, Roosevelt Park, Johannesburg 2129.

Gametrackers (☎ 011-481 6052, fax 6065, **e** gtres@iafrica.com), PO Box 786432, Sandton 2146.

Kalahari Adventure Centre (☎ 054-451 0177, fax 0218, **e** info@kalahari.co.za, 🖳 www.kalahari.co.za), PO Box 20, Augrabies, Northern Cape 8874.

Karibu Safaris (☎ 031-563 9774, fax 1957, **e** karibusa@iafrica.com), PO Box 35196, Northway, Durban 4065.

Maputa Safaris (☎ 031-202 9090, fax 8026, **e** maputa@ mweb.co.za, 🖳 www.tembe.co.za), PO Box 6085, Durban 4000.

Spyhopper Eco-Tour Adventures (☎/fax 044-533 6185, e cdswhale@global.co.za), PO Box 1856, Plettenberg Bay 6600.
Wilderness Safaris (☎ 011-833 0747, fax 6255, 💻 www.wilderness -safaris.com), PO Box 78573, Sandton 2146.
Wilderness Leadership School (☎ 031-462 8642/3, fax 8675, 💻 www.wildernessleadership.com), PO Box 53058, Yellowwood Park, Durban 4011.

Namibia
Afro Ventures (☎/fax 061-236 276, e wdh@afroventures.com), PO Box 11480, Klein, Windhoek.
Baobab Tours (☎ 061-232 314, fax 224 017), PO Box 24818, Windhoek.
Crazy Kudu Safaris (☎/fax 061-222 636, e crazykudu@ hotmail.com), PO Box 86124, Windhoek.
Desert Adventure Safaris (☎/fax 064-404 459, fax 072), Namib Centre, Roon Strasse, PO Box 1428, Swakopmund.
Skeleton Coast Fly-In Safaris (☎ 061-224 248, fax 225 713, e sksafari@iwwn.com.na, 💻 www.iwwn.com.na/sksafari/ brochure.html), PO Box 2195, Windhoek.
Wilderness Safaris Namibia (☎ 061-225 178, fax 239 455, e nts@iwwn.com.na), The Namib Travel Shop, PO Box 6850, Windhoek.

Botswana
Afro Ventures (☎ 661 243, fax 791, e mub@afroventures.com), Private Bag 310, Maun.
Gametrackers (☎ 660 351; South Africa ☎ 011-481 6052, fax 6065; e gtres@iafrica.com), PO Box 100, Maun.
Linyanti Explorations (☎ 650 505, fax 342, e chobe@icon.co.za), PO Box 22, Kasane.
Okavango Tours & Safaris (☎ 660 220, fax 589, e okavango@ global.bw), PO Box 39, Maun.
Okavango Wilderness Safaris (☎ 660 086, fax 632), Private Bag 014, Maun.
Phakawe Safaris (☎ 660 567, fax 912, e phakawe@info.bw, 💻 www.phakawe.demon.co.uk), PO Box 20538, Maun.

Zimbabwe
Abercrombie & Kent (South Africa ☎ 011-781 0740), PO Box 782607, Sandton 2146, South Africa.
Afro Ventures (☎ 04-861 479, fax 665, e hre@afroventures.com), PO Box BW1118, Borrowdale, Harare.
Backpackers Africa (☎/fax 113-4510), PO Box 44, Victoria Falls.
Black Rhino Safaris (☎/fax 19-41662), PO Box FM 89, Famona, Bulawayo.
Khangela Safaris (☎ 09-49733, fax 78081, e scott@gatorzw.com), PO Box FM 296, Famona, Bulawayo.
John Stevens Safaris (☎ 04-495 650, fax 496 113, e bushlife@ harare.iafrica.com), PO Box CH 84, Chisipite, Harare.
Leon Varley Walking Safaris (☎ 013-5828, fax 2208, e backpack@ africaonline.co.zw).
Peter Ginn Birding Safaris (☎/fax 179-23411, e pgbs@mango.zw, 💻 www.safari-tours.com/pgbs), PO Box 44, Marondera.
Wilderness Safaris (☎ 013-3371/2/3, fax 4225, e wildzim@ telconet.co.zw), PO Box 288, Victoria Falls.
Wildlife Expeditions (☎ 014-335 716, fax 341, e wildlife_expd@ compuserve.com), 72 King George Rd, Avondale, Harare.

Malawi

Africa Tour Designers (Zambia ☎ 01-273 864, fax 865, **e** atd@zamnet.zm), PO Box 31802, Lusaka, Zambia.

Central African Wilderness Safaris (☎ 771 393/153, fax 397, **e** info@wilderness.malawi.net or wildsaf@eomw.net), PO Box 489, Lilongwe.

Drifters (South Africa ☎ 011-888 1160, fax 1020), PO Box 48434, Roosevelt Park 2129, South Africa.

Heart of Africa Safaris (& Nyika Horse Safaris) (☎/fax 740 848), PO Box 8, Lilongwe.

Land & Lake Safaris (☎/fax 744 408), PO Box 2140, Lilongwe.

Nyika Safari Company (☎/fax 740 848, **e** reservations@nyika.com), PO Box 2338, Lilongwe.

Soche Tours (☎ 620 777, fax 440, **e** sochetours@malawi.net), Box 2245, Blantyre.

Ulendo Safaris (☎ 754 950/717, fax 756 321, **e** info@ulendo.malawi.net, ⌨ www.eclipse.com.zm/ulendosafaris), PO Box 30728, Lilongwe 3.

Wilderness Safaris Malawi (☎ 781 393/153, fax 397, **e** wildsaf@eo.wn.apc.org), PO Box 489, Lilongwe.

Zambia

Africa Tour Designers (☎ 01-273 864, fax 865, **e** atd@zamnet.zm), PO Box 31802, Lusaka.

Chinzombo Safaris (☎ 062-211 644, **e** chinzsaf@zamnet.zm), Box 30106, Lusaka.

Norman Carr Safaris (☎ 062-45015, fax 45025, **e** kapani@super-hub.com, ⌨ www.normancarrsafaris.com/frameset.htm), PO Box 100, Mfuwe.

Robin Pope Safaris (☎ 062-45090, fax 45051), PO Box 320154, Lusaka.

Safari Par Excellence (South Africa ☎ 011-888 3500, fax 4942, **e** safpar@harare.iafrica.com, ⌨ www.itech.co.za/safpar), PO Box 1395, Randburg 2194, South Africa.

Shiwa Safaris/The Zambian Safari Company (☎ 01-228 682, fax 222 906), PO Box 36655, Lusaka.

Steve Blagus Travel (☎ 227 739/40, fax 225 178, **e** sblagus@zamnet.zm), PO Box 31530, Lusaka.

Ulendo Safaris (Malawi ☎ 265-754 950/717, fax 756 321, **e** info@ulendo.malawi.net, ⌨ www.eclipse.com.zm/ulendosafaris), PO Box 30728, Lilongwe 3, Malawi.

PARKS & CONSERVATION AUTHORITIES

South Africa South African National Parks (☎ 012-343 1991, fax 0905, **e** Reservations@parks-sa.co.za, ⌨ www.parks-sa.co.za), PO Box 787, Pretoria 0001, South Africa. KZN Wildlife (covers KwaZulu/Natal; ☎ 033-845 1000, fax 1001, ⌨ www.kznwildlife.com), PO Box 13053, Cascades 3202, South Africa.

Namibia Ministry of Environment & Tourism (☎ 061-36975/33875, fax 229 936, ⌨ www.iwwn.com.na/namtour), Private Bag 13346, Windhoek, Namibia.

Botswana Department of Wildlife & National Parks (☎ 661 265, fax 264, **e** dwnpbots@global.bw), PO Box 131, Gaborone, Botswana.

Zimbabwe Department of National Parks & Wildlife Management (☎ 04-792 786/9, fax 707 624), PO Box CY, 140 Causeway, Harare, Zimbabwe.

Malawi Ministry of Tourism, Parks & Wildlife (☎ 781 073, fax 780 650, e tourism@malawi.net), Private Bag 326, Murray Road, Lilongwe 3, Malawi.

Zambia Zambia Wildlife Authority (☎ 01-278 323, fax 439, e zawares@coppernet.zm, 🖳 www.wildzawa.com/Mainpage.htm), Private Bag 1, Chilanga, Zambia.

NATURALISTS' ASSOCIATIONS

The following local and international organisations run projects and activities in Southern Africa. Inquire about volunteer work.

African Bird Club c/o BirdLife International, Wellbrook Court, Girton Rd, Cambridge CB3 0NA, England.

Chobe Wildlife Trust (☎ 650 516, e cwt@info.bw, 🖳 www.chobewildlifetrust.com), PO Box 55, Kasane, Botswana.

Endangered Wildlife Trust (☎ 011-486 1102, fax 1506, e ewt@ewt.org.za, 🖳 www.ewt.org.za), Private Bag X11, Parkview 2122, South Africa.

Okavango Wildlife Society (☎ 012-365 1625, fax 1622, e owls@global.co.za, 🖳 www.stud.ntnu.no/~skjetnep/owls_memo.html), PO Box 2137, Cresta 2118, South Africa.

Wildlife Conservation Society (☎ 718-220 5111, fax 364 4275, e feedback@wcs.org, 🖳 www.wcs.org), 2300 Southern Blvd, Bronx, NY 10460, USA.

Wildlife & Environment Society of South Africa (☎ 332-303 931, fax 304 576, 🖳 www.stud.ntnu.no/~skjetnep/wlssa.html), PO Box 394, Howick 3290, South Africa.

Worldwide Fund for Nature UK (☎ 1483-426 444), Panda House, Weyside Park, Godalming, Surrey GU7 1XR, UK. USA (World Wildlife Fund; ☎ 202-293 4800, fax 293 9211, 🖳 www.worldwildlife.org), 1250 24th St, NW, Washington DC 20037-1175, USA.

WEB SITES

The following web sites offer useful background information on wildlife, wildlife-watching and wildlife research.

www.african-lion.org Home page of the African Lion Working Group.

www.africat.org Details of the Africat Foundation's efforts to alleviate conflict between farmers and big cats in Namibia.

www.cheetah.org Cheetah Conservation Fund's site, with their excellent newsletter and loads of other information on cheetahs in Namibia.

www.dartsafari.com Darting Safaris' web site with details of their research and darting trips.

www.earthwatch.org Describes research projects coordinated by Earthwatch in which paying customers can participate.

www.mtn.co.za/whaleroute Information on whale watching in South Africa.

www.rhinos-irf.org International Rhino Foundation: rhino conservation around the world including detail of projects in Southern Africa.

www.sabirding.co.za Information on birding in Southern Africa.

www.scuba.co.za Worthwhile technical information on dives sites in Southern Africa.

GLOSSARY

adaptation – physical or behavioural trait that helps an organism survive or exploit an environmental factor.

algae – primitive water plants.

alpha male or female – dominant animal in a hierarchy, eg, primate troop (a sometimes tenuous position).

altricial – helpless at birth, requiring prolonged parental care, eg, primates (*compare with* precocial).

amphibian – animal that lives part of its life cycle in water and part on land, eg, frog.

annulated horns – ridged horns of some antelope species, eg, oryxes, impalas.

aquatic – living in fresh water (*compare with* marine).

arboreal – tree-dwelling.

arthropod – invertebrate characterised by a segmented body and jointed legs, eg, insects, spiders.

asynchronous – not occurring simultaneously, eg, the hatching of eggs.

avian – characteristic of birds, eg, avian behaviour.

bachelor group or herd – aggregation of nonbreeding adult and subadult males, eg, antelopes.

big cat – the three largest cat species, ie, lions, leopards and cheetahs.

Big Five – the five large animals (ie, rhinos, buffaloes, elephants, lions and leopards) regarded as the most dangerous to hunt (and therefore the most prized) by colonial hunters.

binocular vision – vision with overlapping field of view to give a three-dimensional perception of space; best developed in cats and primates.

biodiversity – faunal and floral richness characterising an area.

biomass – total weight of living organisms in an ecosystem.

bipedal – standing or walking on two legs, eg, humans.

bird party – a feeding party of birds, especially in forest, containing various species (*also called* bird wave).

birder – a keen birdwatcher.

blind – *see* hide.

bluff – behaviour to convince a predator or rival that the bluffer is stronger.

boar – male pig.

bolus – ball of food or dung.

boss – head covering that supports horns, eg, on buffaloes.

bovid – a member of the antelope family (Bovidae).

bovine – cattle-like in appearance or behaviour.

brood – group of young animals produced in one litter or clutch.

browse – to eat leaves and other parts of shrubs and trees (*hence* browser).

bull – male buffalo, elephant, giraffe etc.

cache – (*noun*) a hidden store of food; (*verb*) to hide food for future use.

callosity – hardened area of skin, eg, on knees of giraffes (*also called* callus).

camouflage – coloration or patterning that helps an animal blend into its surroundings.

canid – any dog, fox, jackal etc (ie, a member of the family Canidae).

canine – doglike; also relating to or belonging to the family Canidae (dogs, foxes, jackals etc).

canines – the four large front teeth at the front of the jaw; well developed for killing in carnivores and fighting in baboons.

carnivore – a meat-eating animal.

carrion – dead or decaying flesh.

casque – a prominent bony growth surmounting the bill of some hornbills and the head of guineafowl.

cellulose – the component that strengthens the cell walls of plants, supporting them and forming stems.

cetacean – whales and dolphins.

cheek pouch – extension of the cheeks for the temporary storage of food, eg, in monkeys.

class – one of the major divisions in animal classification used for taxonomy, eg, mammals, birds, reptiles etc.

climax forest – mature forest.

colony – aggregation of animals (eg, birds) that live, roost or breed together (*hence* colonial).

commensalism – a relationship between two unrelated animal species in which one species benefits from the interaction and the other is unaffected.

contiguous – adjoining, eg, woodland spanning two adjacent reserves.

convergent evolution – evolution whereby unrelated species develop similar characteristics, usually seen among geographically separate species occupying similar niches, eg, bushbabies and possums or antelopes and kangaroos.

coursing – to run down prey along the ground mainly by sight, eg, African wild dog.

courtship – behaviour (often ritualised) associated with attracting a mate.

crèche – young birds or mammals gathered for safety and play.

crepuscular – active at dawn and dusk.

crustacean – an arthropod with gills, which can breathe underwater or survive in damp conditions on land.

cryptic – behaviour, appearance or lifestyle that helps conceal an organism from predators.

decurved – downward-curving.

dewlap – loose skin (eg, in eland) or feathers hanging under the chin.

digit – finger or toe.

dimorphism – having two forms of colour or size, eg, spotted and black leopard (*see* sexual dimorphism, polymorphism).

dispersal – the movement of animals (eg, after breeding or rains) or plants (eg, seeds) across a geographic area (*compare with* migration).

display – behaviour transmitting information from the sender to another, often associated with threat, defence of territory, courtship etc.

diurnal – active during daylight hours (*opposite of* nocturnal).

diversity – variety of species or forms in an area.

dorsal – upper (top) surface, ie, the back on most animals (*opposite of* ventral).

down – loose, fluffy feathers that cover young birds and insulate plumage of adults.

drey – squirrel nest.

dung – the excrement of animals (*also called* faeces).

dung midden – accumulation of dung as a territory marker, often accompanied by scent-marking (*see* latrine).

ear-tuft – wispy hairs extending beyond ear-tips (eg, caracal) or erectile feathers near ears (eg, some owls).

ecology – scientific study of relationships between organisms, their environment and each other.

ecosystem – community of living organisms and their physical environment.

ecotone – *see* edge.

edge – transition zone between two habitats, eg, savanna and forest – hence edge species (*also called* ecotone).

endangered – in danger of imminent extinction if trends causing its demise continue.

endemic – a plant or animal found only in a certain area, eg, louries are endemic to Africa.

environment – physical factors that influence the development and behaviour of organisms.

epiphyte – plant growing on another for support, eg, orchids on a tree.

equatorial – living on or near the equator.

erectile – can be erected, eg, hair or feathers erected in defence or courtship displays.

estrus – *see* oestrus.

evolve – to change physical and/or behavioural traits over time to exploit or survive changing environmental constraints.

faeces – excrement.

family – scientific grouping of related genera, eg, Felidae (the cat family).

farrow – litter of pigs (*also verb*).

feline – catlike; also related to or belonging to the Felidae (cat family).

feral – running wild, especially escaped domestic stock.

fledgling – young bird able to leave the nest, ie, to fledge.

flight feathers – the large wing feathers of birds (*also called* primary feathers).

flock – group of birds, sheep or other herbivores (*also verb*).

foliage – leafy vegetation, eg, on trees.

folivore – a leaf-eating animal.

fossorial – adapted for digging.

frugivore – a fruit-eating animal.

game – wild animals, especially mammals and birds, hunted by humans for food and sport.

genera – plural of genus.

genus – taxonomic grouping of related species.

geophagy – eating rock or soil.

gestation – period that young mammals develop in the womb before birth.

glaciations – periods during ice ages when glaciers covered large areas of the earth's surface.

gland – *see* scent gland, and inguinal, interdigital and preorbital glands.

gravid – pregnant or bearing eggs.

graze – to eat grass (*hence* grazer).

gregarious – forming or moving in groups, eg, herds or flocks.

guano – phosphate-rich excrement deposited by seabirds and bats, usually accumulated over generations.

habitat – natural living area of an animal; usually characterised by a distinct plant community.

hackles – long, loose feathers or hairs on nape or throat, often erectile.

harem – group of females that mate with one male; the male defends his harem against other males.

hawk – to fly actively in search of prey such as insects, usually caught in the open mouth.

helper – animal, usually from a previous brood, which helps parents raise subsequent brood or broods.

herbivore – a vegetarian animal.

herd – social group of mammals, usually applied to herbivores.

hide – artificial construction, usually of wood, for the observation of animals while keeping the observer hidden (*also called* blind).

hierarchy – order of dominance among social animals, usually with a dominant individual or caste and one or more tiers of power or function, eg, termites, primates.

hive – home of bees or wasps.

holt – otters' den.

home range – the area over which an individual or group ranges over time (*compare with* territory).

host – organism on (or in) which a parasite lives; bird that raises young of parasitic species.

immature – stage in a young bird's development between juvenile and adult.

incisor – front (ie, cutting) teeth.

incubate – to hatch eggs using warmth.

inguinal gland – scent gland in groin area.

insectivore – an insect-eating animal.

interdigital gland – scent gland between toes or hooves, eg, on cats and antelopes.

invertebrate – an animal without a spinal column or backbone, eg, insects, worms.

iridescence – metallic sheen on many insects and birds, eg, sunbirds.

juvenile – an animal between infancy and adulthood (mammals) or with first feathers after natal down (bird).

koppie or kopje – outcrop of rock on savanna plains.

lamellae – comblike plates in the bill of some birds (eg, flamingos) that filter food particles from water.

latrine – site where mammals habitually deposit dung or urine, eg, rhinos (*compare with* dung midden).

lek – a communal arena for mating and territorial sparring (antelopes) or courtship displays and mating (birds).

localised – found only in a small or distinct area.

lying-out – remaining motionless with head flat on the ground to avoid danger (eg, antelopes).

mammal – a 'warm-blooded', usually furred or hairy animal (except cetaceans) that gives birth to and suckles live young.

mandible – lower part of beak or jaw.

mantle – shoulder or upper back area on birds or mammals.

marine – living in the sea.

matriarchal – female dominated.

matrilineal – relating to kinship or descent among related females.

melanism – naturally occurring excess of dark brown pigment that produces black forms of some animals, eg, leopards and servals.

midden – see dung midden.

migration – regular movement, often en masse, from one location to another, eg, wildebeests (hence migrant, migratory).

miombo – fire-resistant deciduous woodland, especially that dominated by Brachystegia.

mob – to harass a predatory animal (eg, small birds mobbing an owl); often in response to a distress call.

monogamy – having one reproductive partner for life or breeding season, eg, bat-eared fox.

montane – living or situated on mountains.

moult – to shed and replace all or selected feathers, skin or fur, usually prompted by seasonal or behavioural changes, eg, courtship.

musth – a frenzied state of sexual readiness in certain large male mammals particularly elephants (also spelt must).

mutualism – interaction between two species where both benefit.

natal – pertaining to birth.

nestling – young bird until it leaves the nest (compare with fledgling).

nest parasitism – laying eggs in the nest of another bird species and taking no further part in rearing the offspring (also called brood parasitism).

niche – specialised ecological role played by an organism.

nocturnal – active at night.

nomadic – wandering in search of resources, eg, food or water.

oestrus – period when female mammal is ovulating and therefore sexually receptive (also spelt estrus).

omnivore – an animal that eats both plant and animal matter.

order – grouping of one or more animal families, eg, cats and dogs into Carnivora/carnivores.

pair bond – social ties that keep mates together, reinforced with grooming, calls etc.

parasite – plant or animal that obtains nourishment during all or part of its life from another life form, usually to the detriment of the host.

pelagic – living at sea, ie, in or above open water.

perissodactyl – an odd-toed ungulate, ie, rhino, horse.

photosynthesis – the process whereby plants convert sunlight, water and carbon dioxide into organic compounds.

piscivorous – fish-eating.

plumage – birds' feathers, often used to describe total appearance, eg, drab plumage.

polyandry – female having access to more than one reproductive male.

polygamy – having access to more than one reproductive mate.

polygyny – male having access to more than one reproductive female.

polymorphism – having more than one adult form, size or colour.

precocial – being able to walk or run (eg, wildebeest), forage (eg, ostrich) or swim shortly after birth or hatching (compare altricial).

predator – animal that kills and eats others.

prehensile – flexible and grasping, eg, tail, fingers.

preorbital gland – scent gland in front of the eyes, especially in antelopes, used to mark territory.

present – to show genital region as appeasement (eg, apes) or to indicate readiness to mate.

prey – an animal which is food for a predator.

pride – collective term for lions.

primary feathers – see flight feathers.

primate – a monkey, prosimian or ape.

primitive – resembling or representing an early stage in the evolution of a particular group of animals.

pronk – see stot.

prosimian – 'primitive' primate, eg, bushbaby.

prusten – loud huffing sound made by female leopard to call cubs.

pug – footprint or other imprint left on the ground by an animal.

quadruped – four-legged animal.

quarter – to systematically range over an area in search of prey, eg, jackals, birds of prey.

race – see subspecies.

raptor – bird of prey, eg, hawk, falcon, vulture.

recurved – upward-curving, eg, bill of avocet.

regurgitate – to bring up partly digested food from crop or stomach, particularly when feeding young.

relict – remnant of formerly widespread species, community or habitat, now surrounded by different communities.

reptile – a scaly, cold-blooded vertebrate, ie, turtles, crocodiles, snakes and lizards.

resident – an animal that remains in an area for its entire life cycle.

rinderpest – disease of cattle that can affect related animals, eg, antelopes.

riparian – see riverine.

riverine – living or occurring near or in rivers or streams (also called riparian).

rodent – any of the many species of rat, mouse, squirrel, porcupine etc.

roost – area where mammals (eg, bats) or birds gather to sleep, sometimes in large numbers (also verb).

ruminant – ungulate with four-chambered stomach (rumen) that chews the cud (hence ruminate).

rump – upper backside of mammal or bird, often distinctively marked, eg, antelopes.

rut – (antelopes) the mating season (*also verb*).

saddle – mid to lower back area on mammals and birds.

sagittal – pertaining to the prominent upper seam of skull, eg, sagittal crest on male lion.

savanna – vegetation zone characterised by contrasting wet and dry seasons where grassy understorey grows with scattered trees and shrubs.

scavenger – animal that feeds on carrion or scraps left by others, eg, hyena.

scent gland – concentration of special skin cells that secrete chemicals conveying information about the owner's status, identity, reproductive state etc.

sedentary – animal remaining in one area for all or part of its life cycle (*see* resident).

selection – process whereby traits that are detrimental to an organism's reproductive success are weeded out by environmental or behavioural pressures.

semidesert – semiarid area with more rainfall, and hence more vegetation and biodiversity than true desert.

sexual dimorphism – differences between males and females of the same species in colour, size or form, eg, the lion's mane and many spectacular examples in birds.

sibling – related offspring with the same parents (*hence* foster sibling in brood parasites).

signal – movement or trait that conveys information from one animal to another, eg, danger.

skein – collective term for geese.

slough – to shed skin when growing, eg, reptiles, amphibians.

sounder – group of pigs.

sow – female pig.

spawn – eggs of fish and amphibians, usually laid in water (*also verb*).

specialised – having particular adaptations to a certain habitat or way of life.

speciation – process whereby species are formed.

species – organisms capable of breeding with each other to produce fertile offspring; distinct and usually recognisable from other species, with which the majority don't interbreed.

spoor – the track or tracks of an animal.

spraint – otter urine, used as territorial marking.

spur – horny growth on some birds, eg, on forewing (lapwings) or 'heel' (francolins).

spy-hop – to jump above vegetation such as grass, or water's surface (whales and great white sharks) to check bearings, threats etc.

stage – level in development of an organism.

stalk – to pursue prey by stealth.

stoop – powerful dive of bird of prey.

stot – stylised high leap while bounding, especially by young antelopes in play and adults when fleeing (*also called* pronk); thought to display fitness to would-be predators.

streamer – long tail feather, eg, of swallows.

subadult – last stage of juvenile development, usually characterised by near-adult coloration, size or plumage.

subordinate – an animal that is ranked beneath another in a social hierarchy, eg, baboons.

subspecies – population of a species isolated from another population (eg, by landforms) that has developed distinct physical traits (*also called* race).

succulent – fleshy, moisture-filled plant, eg, euphorbias, aloes.

sward – grass or a stretch of grass.

symbiosis – *see* mutualism.

talon – hooked claw on bird of prey.

taxonomy – scientific classification of organisms according to their physical relationships (*also called* systematics).

tectonic – pertaining to changes in the earth's crust caused by movement below its surface.

temporal gland – facial glands between the eyes and ears of elephants that secrete temporin.

termitarium – earthen mound constructed by a termite colony (*also called* termitary).

terrestrial – living on the ground.

territory – feeding or breeding area defended against others (usually unrelated) of the same species (*compare with* home range).

thermal – a rising column of air; which is used by large birds to gain height.

troop – group of monkeys or baboons.

tropical – found within the tropics, ie, between Tropics of Cancer and Capricorn.

tsetse fly – a blood-sucking fly.

tusker – large elephant or boar.

tusks – greatly enlarged canine teeth, used as tools, or in defense and ritual combat, eg, in elephants.

ungulate – a hoofed animal.

vent – the urogential opening of cetaceans, birds, reptiles and fish (occasionally applied to female mammals).

ventral – lower (under) side of an animal (*opposite of* dorsal).

vertebrate – an animal having a backbone, ie, bony fish, amphibians, reptiles, birds and mammals.

vestigial – small, nonfunctional remnant of a feature formerly present, eg, vestigial horns.

vocalisation – sound made orally by an animal as a signal.

volplane – steep, controlled dive on outstretched wings, eg, by vultures to a kill.

waders – shorebirds and related families, eg, plovers.

warm-blooded – maintaining a constant body temperature by internal regulation, eg, birds and mammals (*also known as* homoiothermic).

warren – network of holes used as shelter and nursery, eg, by rabbits.

waterfowl – water-dwelling birds with webbed feet, ie, swans, geese and ducks.

wattle – fleshy, sometimes brightly coloured growth often prominent in courtship, eg, on birds.

yearling – a mammal in its second year of growth.

PHOTO CREDITS

Linzee Gordon **44** top, **158** bottom, **275** column 1 Manfred Gottschalk **5** column, **39**, **134** top, **137** top, **140**, **144** bottom, **268** top, **293** column 1 Dave Hamman **74** top, **75** inset, **232** bottom, **235** column 1 & inset, **237** bottom, **264** bottom, **278** column 2, **294** column 1 (right), **307** column 4, **310** inset John Hay **1**, **43** Luke Hunter **5** column 3, **6** column 2, **49**, **59** main, **62** bottom, **65**, **68**, **71** main, **75** main, **78** top, **88** bottom, **91** bottom, **94** top & bottom, **96** top & bottom, **98** bottom, **102** bottom, **104** bottom, **106** top, **108** bottom, **112**, **113**, **116** bottom, **120**, **122**, **132** top, **136** top, **151** bottom, **152** bottom, **160** bottom, **161** bottom, **200**, **215**, **226** top, **228** top & bottom, **233** column 4, **234** column 4, **237** top, **241** top, **242** top, **243** inset, **246** bottom, **250** bottom, **252** top, **253** column 1, 2 & 4, **260** column 3, **261** column 2 & 3, **274** column 2, **287** column 4, **308** column 4, **323** column 4, **324** column 1 & 4 Richard I'Anson **54** bottom, **58** top & bottom, **66** top & bottom, **67** main & inset, **73**, **76**, **78** bottom, **80**, **81**, **86**, **88** top, **92** top, **93**, **97** bottom, **102** top, **125** top, **148** top, **152** top, **167**, **176**, **218** bottom, **231** top, **234** column 3, **247** top, **249** top, **250** top, **253** column 3 & inset, **255** column 1 & 3, **269** top, **278** inset, **301** top, **307** column 2 Dennis Johnson **52**, **63** inset, **64**, **70** bottom, **72**, **188**, **195** Dennis Jones **5** column 2, **27**, **41**, **62** top, **104** top, **130** top, **136** bottom, **138** bottom, **145** top & bottom, **153**, **156**, **162** bottom, **171**, **173** bottom, **175**, **183**, **200** inset, **206** bottom, **210** top, **212** main & inset, **213**, **224** column 3, **225** bottom, **236** bottom, **249** bottom, **251** bottom, **256** bottom, **257** bottom, **261** column 4 & inset, **263** bottom, **278** column 4, **282** column 4, **283** column 4, **285** column 2, **299** column 2 & inset, **295** column 2, **300** column 3, **311** column 3, **325** column 1 Labat-Lanceau/AUSCAPE **327** column 2 & 3, inset Dave Lewis **44** bottom, **46** top, **56**, **77**, **325** column 2 Andrew MacColl **294** inset, **304** column 1, **323** column 2 Richard Mills **274** column 3, **286** column 2, **288** bottom, **297** column 3, **303** column 2, **313** column 3, **317** column 3 & inset, **321** Peter Ptschelinzew **300** column 1, **324** column 3 Mitch Reardon **61**, **95**, **97** top, **123**, **133**, **134** bottom, **196** bottom, **201**, **221** top, **223** column 2, **224** column 1, **230** top, **233** column 1 & inset, **240** column 1, **244** top, **245** top & bottom, **254** column 1, **259** top, **260** inset, **262** bottom, **273** inset, **277** column 1, **280** top, **281** top, **283** column 2, **284** column 2, **286** column 3, **290** column 2, **301** bottom, **303** column 1, **322** top Mike Scott **222** top Deanna Swaney **130** bottom, **143** David Tipling **40** top, **255** inset, **277** column 4, **283** column 1, **289** column 2 Ray Tipper **279** column 4, **281** bottom, **291** column 4, **298** column 1, **299** column 3, **305** column 3, **308** inset, **311** column 4 Adrien Vadrot **144** top Andrew van Smeerdijk **57**, **59** inset, **71** inset, **92** bottom, **110** bottom, **128** top, **149**, **150**, **154** top, **155**, **166**, **194** top, **196** top, **197**, **198** top & bottom, **199**, **227** bottom, **236** top, **238** top, **264** top, **265** top, **271** top, **275** column 3, **276** top, **292** column 4, **297** column 1 Ariadne Van Zandbergen **6** column 1 & 4, **38** top, **55** inset, **98** top, **101**, **103**, **109**, **141**, **142**, **170** top, **172** bottom, **174** top & bottom, **179**, **191**, **203**, **205**, **206** top, **224** column 2, **227** top, **243** column 4, **254** column 4, **260** column 1, 2 & 4, **269** bottom, **270** inset, **273** column 4, **277** column 2, **282** column 2 & 3, inset, **285** column 1, **286** inset, **289** column 3, **293** column 2 & 3, **294** column 4, **295** column 1, **298** column 2, **300** column 4, **303** column 3, **305** column 1 & 4, **308** column 3, **312** column 1, **316** column 1 Andrew & Leanne Walker **172** top David Wall **42** top, **74** bottom, **126**, **135**, **137** bottom, **139**, **157**, **180** top, **182**, **204**, **231** bottom, **241** bottom, **247** bottom, **259** bottom, **272** bottom, **280** bottom, **282** column 1, **283** column 3, **284** column 3, **287** inset Tony Wheeler **184**, **298** column 4

INDEX

MAMMAL CHECKLIST

The following taxonomy is based on *The Mammals of the Southern African Subregion* by Skinner and Smithers, 1990. It includes mammal species and subspecies mentioned in this book, but is by no means comprehensive for Southern Africa.

PRIMATES
- ☐ chacma baboon — *Papio cynocephalus ursinus*
- ☐ yellow baboon — *Papio cynocephalus cynocephalus*
- ☐ vervet monkey — *Cercopithecus aethiops*
- ☐ samango monkey — *Cercopithecus mitis*
- ☐ greater (or thick-tailed) bushbaby — *Otolemur crassicaudatus*
- ☐ lesser (or South African) bushbaby — *Galago moholi*
- ☐ Grant's (or Mozambique) bushbaby — *Galagoides granti*

PANGOLINS
- ☐ Cape (or ground) pangolin — *Manis temmincki*

RABBITS AND HARES
- ☐ Cape hare — *Lepus capensis*
- ☐ scrub hare — *Lepus saxatilis*
- ☐ riverine rabbit — *Bunolagus monticularis*
- ☐ Smith's red rock rabbit — *Pronolagus rupestris*
- ☐ Natal red rock rabbit — *Pronolagus crassicaudatus*
- ☐ Jameson's red rock rabbit — *Pronolagus randensis*

RODENTS
- ☐ Cape ground squirrel — *Xerus inauris*
- ☐ red squirrel — *Paraxerus palliatus*
- ☐ Tonga red squirrel — *Paraxerus palliatus tongensis*
- ☐ tree squirrel — *Paraxerus cepapi*
- ☐ springhare — *Pedetes capensis*
- ☐ Cape (or South African) porcupine — *Hystrix africaeaustralis*

DOGS AND FOXES
- ☐ side-striped jackal — *Canis adustus*
- ☐ black-backed jackal — *Canis mesomelas*
- ☐ Cape fox — *Vulpes chama*
- ☐ bat-eared fox — *Otocyon megalotis*
- ☐ African wild dog — *Lycaon pictus*

WEASELS, POLECATS, BADGERS AND OTTERS
- ☐ zorilla (or striped polecat) — *Ictonyx striatus*
- ☐ African (or striped or white-naped) weasel — *Poecilogale albinucha*
- ☐ honey badger (or ratel) — *Mellivora capensis*
- ☐ Cape (or African) clawless otter — *Aonyx capensis*
- ☐ spotted-necked otter — *Lutra maculicollis*

MONGOOSES
- ☐ large grey (or ichneumon or Egyptian) mongoose — *Herpestes ichneumon*
- ☐ slender mongoose — *Herpestes sanguinea*
- ☐ small grey mongoose — *Gallerella pulverulenta*
- ☐ dwarf mongoose — *Helogale parvula*
- ☐ Selous' mongoose — *Paracynictis selousi*
- ☐ yellow mongoose — *Cynictis pencillata*
- ☐ meerkat (or suricate) — *Suricata suricata*
- ☐ banded mongoose — *Mungos mungo*
- ☐ marsh (or water) mongoose — *Atilax paludinosus*
- ☐ white-tailed mongoose — *Ichneumia albicauda*
- ☐ Meller's mongoose — *Rhynchogale melleri*

CIVETS AND GENETS
- ☐ small-spotted (or common) genet — *Genetta genetta*
- ☐ large-spotted (or rusty-spotted) genet — *Genetta tigrina*
- ☐ African civet — *Civettictis civetta*
- ☐ tree (or African palm) civet — *Nandinia binotata*

HYENAS AND AARDWOLF
- ☐ brown hyena — *Hyaena brunnea*
- ☐ spotted hyena — *Crocuta crocuta*
- ☐ aardwolf — *Proteles cristata*

CATS
- ☐ African wild cat — *Felis sylvestris*
- ☐ black-footed cat — *Felis nigripes*
- ☐ serval — *Felis serval*
- ☐ caracal — *Felis caracal*
- ☐ leopard — *Panthera pardus*
- ☐ lion — *Panthera leo*
- ☐ cheetah — *Acinonyx jubatus*

SEALS
- ☐ Cape fur-seal — *Arctocephalus pusillus*

AARDVARK
- ☐ aardvark — *Orycteropus afer*

DASSIES
- ☐ rock dassie — *Procavia capensis*
- ☐ yellow-spotted rock (or bush) dassie — *Heterohyrax brucei*
- ☐ tree dassie — *Dendrohyrax arboreus*

ELEPHANT
- ☐ African elephant — *Loxodonta africana*

RHINOS
- ☐ black rhino — *Diceros bicornis*
- ☐ southern white rhino — *Ceratotherium simum simum*

ZEBRAS
- ☐ Burchell's (or common or plains) zebra — *Equus quagga burchelli*
- ☐ Crawshay's zebra — *Equus quagga crawshayi*
- ☐ Cape mountain zebra — *Equus zebra zebra*
- ☐ Hartmann's mountain zebra — *Equus zebra hartmanni*

HIPPOS
- ☐ hippopotamus — *Hippopotamus amphibius*

PIGS
- ☐ bushpig — *Potamochoerus larvatus*
- ☐ warthog — *Phacochoerus africanus*

GIRAFFES
- ☐ giraffe — *Giraffa camelopardalis*
- ☐ Thornicroft's giraffe — *Giraffa camelopardalis thornicrofti*

BUFFALO AND ANTELOPES
- ☐ blue wildebeest (or brindled gnu) — *Connochaetes taurinus*
- ☐ Cookson's (or Nyassa) wildebeest — *Connochaetes taurinus cooksoni*
- ☐ black wildebeest (or white-tailed gnu) — *Connochaetes gnou*
- ☐ red hartebeest — *Alcelaphalus buselaphus*
- ☐ Lichtenstein's hartebeest — *Sigmoceros lichtensteinii*
- ☐ bontebok — *Damaliscus dorcas dorcas*
- ☐ blesbok — *Damaliscus dorcas phillipsi*
- ☐ tsessebe — *Damaliscus lunatus lunatus*
- ☐ grey (or common) duiker — *Sylvicapra grimmia*
- ☐ blue duiker — *Philantomba monticola*
- ☐ red (or Natal) duiker — *Cephalophus natalensis*
- ☐ yellow-backed duiker — *Cephalophus silvicultor*
- ☐ Damara (or Kirk's) dik-dik — *Madoqua kirkii damarensis*
- ☐ suni — *Neotragus moschatus*
- ☐ Cape grysbok — *Raphicerus melanotis*
- ☐ Sharpe's grysbok — *Raphicerus sharpei*
- ☐ steenbok (or steinbok) — *Raphicerus campestris*
- ☐ oribi — *Ourebia ourebi*
- ☐ klipspringer — *Oreotragus oreotragus*
- ☐ springbok — *Antidorcas marsupialis*
- ☐ impala — *Aepyceros melampus melampus*
- ☐ black-faced impala — *Aepyceros melampus petersi*
- ☐ grey rhebuck (or grey rhebok) — *Pelea capreolus*
- ☐ roan (or roan antelope) — *Hippotragus equinus*
- ☐ sable (or sable antelope) — *Hippotragus niger*
- ☐ gemsbok (or southern oryx) — *Oryx gazella*
- ☐ African (or Cape) buffalo — *Syncerus caffer caffer*
- ☐ bushbuck — *Tragelaphus scriptus*
- ☐ Chobe bushbuck — *Tragelaphus scriptus ornatus*
- ☐ sitatunga — *Tragelaphus spekei*
- ☐ nyala — *Tragelaphus angasi*
- ☐ greater kudu — *Tragelaphus strepsiceros*
- ☐ eland — *Taurotragus oryx*
- ☐ mountain reedbuck — *Redunca fulvorufula*
- ☐ southern (or common) reedbuck — *Redunca arundinum*
- ☐ waterbuck — *Kobus ellipsiprymnus*
- ☐ puku — *Kobus vardoni*
- ☐ red lechwe — *Kobus leche leche*
- ☐ black lechwe — *Kobus leche smithemani*
- ☐ Kafue lechwe — *Kobus leche kafuensis*

DOLPHINS AND WHALES
- ☐ bottlenose dolphin — *Tursiops truncatus*
- ☐ Heaviside's dolphin — *Cephalorhynchus heavisidii*
- ☐ Bryde's whale — *Balaenoptera edeni*
- ☐ humpback whale — *Megaptera novaeangliae*
- ☐ southern right whale — *Eubalaena australis*

LONELY PLANET

You already know that Lonely Planet produces more than this one guidebook, but you might not be aware of the other products we have on this region. Here is a selection of titles that you may want to check out as well:

Africa on a shoestring
ISBN 0 86442 663 1

Southern Africa
ISBN 0 86442 662 3

Watching Wildlife Australia
ISBN 1 86450 032 8

Watching Wildlife East Africa
ISBN 1 86450 033 6

Cape Town
ISBN 0 86442 485 X

Songs to an African Sunset
ISBN 0 86442 472 8

Read This First: Africa
ISBN 1 86450 066 2

Travel Photography
ISBN 1 86450 207 X

Cape Town City Map
ISBN 1 86450 076 X

Southern Africa Road Atlas
ISBN 1 86450 101 4

Healthy Travel Africa
ISBN 1 86450 050 6

Mozambique
ISBN 1 86450 108 1

Malawi
ISBN 1 86450 095 6

South Africa, Lesotho & Swaziland
ISBN 0 86442 757 3

Zimbabwe, Botswana & Namibia
ISBN 0 86442 545 7

Available wherever books are sold

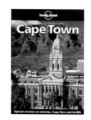

RESEARCH

The authors visited as many of the national parks and other reserves as possible during the research for this book. In cases where access was not possible, material was drawn from sources such as scientific papers and authoritative publications, and corroborated by experts. In their research the authors have drawn on their experience, their contacts and their personal observations. They have not necessarily been able to see everything and have not gone on every available tour. Instead, they have used their expertise to judge what to bring together in as accurate a picture of a place as possible. Common names for many wide-ranging African mammals and birds vary across the continent; and no two references agree completely on names (scientific or common). Mammal names used in this book follow *Mammals of the Southern African Subregion* by Skinner and Smithers. For birds we followed the *Illustrated Guide to the Birds of Southern Africa* by I Sinclair, P Hockey and W Tarboton, and *Collins Illustrated Checklist – Birds of Southern Africa* by B van Perlo.

We welcome feedback to help us improve new editions. All information is passed on to the authors for verification on the road. The best snippets are rewarded with a Lonely Panet guidebook.

Send all correspondence to the Lonely Planet office closest to you:

Australia Locked Bag 1, Footscray, Victoria 3011
USA 150 Linden St, Oakland, CA 94607
UK 10A Spring Place, London NW5 3BH
France 1 rue du Dahomey, 75011 Paris

Map Legend

HYDROGRAPHY

- Reef
- Coastline
- River, Creek
- Lake
- Intermittent Lake
- Salt Pan
- Spring/Waterhole
- Waterfalls
- Swamp

ROUTES & TRANSPORT

- Freeway
- Highway
- Major Road
- Minor Road
- Vehicle Track
- Walking Track
- Fence
- Ferry Route
- Train Route & Station
- Route Number

BOUNDARIES

- International
- Provincial
- Marine Park

MAP SYMBOLS

- ✪ **CAPITAL** National Capital
- ● **CAPITAL** Regional Capital
- ◉ **CITY** City
- ○ **Town** Town
- ○ Village Village

- ● Point of Interest
- ● Geographic Feature
- ● Hydrographic Feature
- ● Reserve/Wildlife Park
- ✈ Airport
- Airfield
- ▲ Camp Site
- ⌂ Cave
- Cliff or Escarpment
- Forest
- ⊢ Gate
- ⊕ Special vegetation
- ● Hotel
- Lodge or Hut
- Lookout/View Platform
- ▲ Mountain or Hill
- Picnic Site
- Ruins
- Shipwreck
- ❶ Tourist Information

AREA FEATURES

- Land
- Park
- Prohibited Area
- Sandforest

ABBREVIATIONS

BR	Botanical Reserve
CA	Conservation Area
CP	Conservation Park
CR	Conservation Reserve
FR	Forest Reserve
GR	Game Reserve
MP	Marine Park
MNP	Marine National Park
MNR	Marine National Reserve
NP	National Park
NR	National Reserve
NrP	Nature Park
PN	Parc National
RR	Regional Reserve
SF	State Forest
SR	State Reserve
WP	Wetland Park
WR	Wildlife Reserve

Note: not all symbols displayed above appear in this book

ABOUT LONELY PLANET GUIDEBOOKS

Lonely Planet published its first book in 1973 in response to the numerous 'How did you do it?' questions Maureen and Tony Wheeler were asked after driving, busing, hitching, sailing and railing their way from England to Australia.

Written at a kitchen table and hand collated, trimmed and stapled, *Across Asia on the Cheap* became an instant local bestseller, inspiring thoughts of another book.

Eighteen months in South-East Asia resulted in their second guide, South-East Asia on a shoestring, which they put together in a backstreet Chinese hotel in Singapore in 1975. The 'yellow bible', as it quickly became known to backpackers around the world, soon became the guide to the region. It has sold well over half a million copies and is now in its 10th edition.

Today an international company with offices in Melbourne (Australia), Oakland (USA), London (UK) and Paris (France), Lonely Planet has an ever-growing list of books and other products, including: travel guides, walking guides, city maps, travel atlases, phrasebooks, diving guides, cycling guides, healthy travel guides, restaurant guides, world food guides, first time travel guides, condensed guides, travel literature, pictorial books and, of course, wildlife guides. Many of these are also published in French and various other languages.

In addition to the books, there are also videos and Lonely Planet's award winning Web site.

Some things haven't changed. The main aim is still to help make it possible for adventurous travellers to get out there – to explore and better understand the world.

At Lonely Planet we believe travellers can make a positive contribution to the countries they visit – if they respect their host communities and spend their money wisely. Since 1986 a percentage of the income from each book has been donated to aid projects and human rights campaigns.

> **Lonely Planet gathers information for everyone who's curious about the planet – and especially for those who explore it first-hand. Through guidebooks, phrasebooks, activity guides, maps, literature, newsletters, image library, TV series and Web site we act as an information exchange for a worldwide community of travellers.**

LONELY PLANET OFFICES

Australia
Locked Bag 1, Footscray, Victoria 3011
☎ 03 8379 8000 fax 03 8379 8111
e talk2us@lonelyplanet.com.au

USA
150 Linden St, Oakland, CA 94607
☎ 510 893 8555 or ☎ 800 275 8555 (toll free)
fax 510 893 8572
e info@lonelyplanet.com

UK
10a Spring Place, London NW5 3BH
☎ 020 7428 4800 fax 020 7428 4828
e go@lonelyplanet.co.uk

France
1 rue du Dahomey, 75011 Paris
☎ 01 55 25 33 00 fax 01 55 25 33 01
e bip@lonelyplanet.fr
🖳 www.lonelyplanet.fr

World Wide Web: 🖳 www.lonelyplanet.com *or* AOL keyword: lp
Lonely Planet Images: 🖳 www.lonelyplanetimages.com